Internet For Teachers, 3rd Edition

Internet Net-Speak Checklist

Get the following information from your service provider so that you have all the information you need to set up your software for Internet access. Examples of the information are shown in parentheses. (If your software comes preconfigured, you can skip all of this.)

- Your Internet provider IP address (it'll look something like this: 123.456.78.90)_____
- Your user name (login name): (flintstone)_____
- Your password (don't write it here!)
- Your domain name: (apple.com)_____
- Your e-mail address: (flintstone@apple.com)_____
- Dial-up phone number(s):_____
- Mailserver name (or POP server or SMTP server): (mail.bedrock.com)_____
- News host server name (or NNTP server): (nntp.bedrock.com)_____
- Primary domain name server: (234.00.123.0)_____
- Secondary domain name server(s): (234.00.123.1)_____
- Subnet mask: (255.255.0.0)_____
- Account type (PPP, DSL, network, shell):_____
- Port settings (modem bps rate, com/serial port #):_____
- Domain suffix: (bedrock.com)_____
- Internet provider troubleshooting phone number:_____
- Software tools available with your account:_____

Doin' It in Your Browser

To Do This	Start with This	Example
View a Web page	http://	http://www.apple.com
Download a file using FTP	ftp://	ftp://ftp.simtel.net/info-mac/_Education
Use telnet to log on to a distant computer (may require helper application)	telnet://	telnet://locis.loc.gov
Search a gopher server	gopher://	gopher://vmsgopher.cua.edu/11gopher_root_eric_ae

...For Dummies®: Bestselling Book Series for Beginners

Internet For Teachers, 3rd Edition

Cheat Sheet

Your Favorite Educational Sites

Site:_____
URL:_____

Site:_____
URL:_____

Site:_____
URL:_____

Site:_____
URL:_____

Site:_____
URL:_____

Site:_____
URL:_____

Site:_____
URL:_____

Site:_____
URL:_____

Site:_____
URL:_____

A+ Net Tools: Which Is Which?

Tool	What It Does
E-Mail	Send and receive electronic mail
Gopher	Locate information on the Internet
Veronica	Search for titles in Gopherspace
FTP	Retrieve files from the Internet
Archie	Locate files to download from the Internet
Sherlock	Browse multiple search engines for Web sites before you launch a browser
IRC	Chat live across the Internet
Usenet	Search and read discussion topics newsgroups on the Internet
Web browser	Search and explore the World Wide Web
Telnet	Act as a terminal on a remote computer

Internet E-Mail

To Send To	Use This Format
America Online	hamlet@aol.com
ATT Worldnet	horatio@worldnet.att.net
CompuServe	98765.4321@compuserve.com
Earthlink	BillS@earthlink.net
Mindspring	brutus@mindspring.net
MSN	Shakespeare@msn.com
Other Internet addresses (see Chapter 11)	henry@<domain name>

Pre-Surf Checklist

- ✔ Instructional goal(s)
- ✔ Estimated time to complete activity
- ✔ Internet resources to be accessed (gopher, Web, and so on)
- ✔ Starting URL
- ✔ Potential trouble spots
- ✔ Expected outcomes

IDG BOOKS WORLDWIDE

...For Dummies®: Bestselling Book Series for Beginners

™

References for the Rest of Us! ®

BESTSELLING BOOK SERIES

Are you intimidated and confused by computers? Do you find that traditional manuals are overloaded with technical details you'll never use? Do your friends and family always call you to fix simple problems on their PCs? Then the ...*For Dummies*® computer book series from IDG Books Worldwide is for you.

...*For Dummies* books are written for those frustrated computer users who know they aren't really dumb but find that PC hardware, software, and indeed the unique vocabulary of computing make them feel helpless. ...*For Dummies* books use a lighthearted approach, a down-to-earth style, and even cartoons and humorous icons to dispel computer novices' fears and build their confidence. Lighthearted but not lightweight, these books are a perfect survival guide for anyone forced to use a computer.

> "I like my copy so much I told friends; now they bought copies."
>
> — Irene C., Orwell, Ohio

> "Quick, concise, nontechnical, and humorous."
>
> — Jay A., Elburn, Illinois

> "Thanks, I needed this book. Now I can sleep at night."
>
> — Robin F., British Columbia, Canada

Already, millions of satisfied readers agree. They have made ...*For Dummies* books the #1 introductory level computer book series and have written asking for more. So, if you're looking for the most fun and easy way to learn about computers, look to ...*For Dummies* books to give you a helping hand.

®

IDG BOOKS WORLDWIDE

THE INTERNET FOR TEACHERS®

3RD EDITION

THE INTERNET FOR TEACHERS®

3RD EDITION

by Bard Williams

IDG BOOKS WORLDWIDE

IDG Books Worldwide, Inc.
An International Data Group Company

Foster City, CA ◆ Chicago, IL ◆ Indianapolis, IN ◆ New York, NY

The Internet For Teachers®, 3rd Edition

Published by
IDG Books Worldwide, Inc.
An International Data Group Company
919 E. Hillsdale Blvd.
Suite 400
Foster City, CA 94404
www.idgbooks.com (IDG Books Worldwide Web site)
www.dummies.com (Dummies Press Web site)

Library of Congress Catalog Card No.: 99-63212

ISBN: 0-7645-0623-4

Printed in the United States of America

10 9 8 7 6 5 4 3 2 1

3O/RU/QX/ZZ/IN

Distributed in the United States by IDG Books Worldwide, Inc.

Distributed by CDG Books Canada Inc. for Canada; by Transworld Publishers Limited in the United Kingdom; by IDG Norge Books for Norway; by IDG Sweden Books for Sweden; by IDG Books Australia Publishing Corporation Pty. Ltd. for Australia and New Zealand; by TransQuest Publishers Pte Ltd. for Singapore, Malaysia, Thailand, Indonesia, and Hong Kong; by Gotop Information Inc. for Taiwan; by ICG Muse, Inc. for Japan; by Norma Comunicaciones S.A. for Colombia; by Intersoft for South Africa; by Eyrolles for France; by International Thomson Publishing for Germany, Austria and Switzerland; by Distribuidora Cuspide for Argentina; by Livraria Cultura for Brazil; by Ediciones ZETA S.C.R. Ltda. for Peru; by WS Computer Publishing Corporation, Inc., for the Philippines; by Contemporanea de Ediciones for Venezuela; by Express Computer Distributors for the Caribbean and West Indies; by Micronesia Media Distributor, Inc. for Micronesia; by Grupo Editorial Norma S.A. for Guatemala; by Chips Computadoras S.A. de C.V. for Mexico; by Editorial Norma de Panama S.A. for Panama; by American Bookshops for Finland. Authorized Sales Agent: Anthony Rudkin Associates for the Middle East and North Africa.

For general information on IDG Books Worldwide's books in the U.S., please call our Consumer Customer Service department at 800-762-2974. For reseller information, including discounts and premium sales, please call our Reseller Customer Service department at 800-434-3422.

For information on where to purchase IDG Books Worldwide's books outside the U.S., please contact our International Sales department at 317-596-5530 or fax 317-596-5692.

For consumer information on foreign language translations, please contact our Customer Service department at 1-800-434-3422, fax 317-596-5692, or e-mail rights@idgbooks.com.

For information on licensing foreign or domestic rights, please phone +1-650-655-3109.

For sales inquiries and special prices for bulk quantities, please contact our Sales department at 650-655-3200 or write to the address above.

For information on using IDG Books Worldwide's books in the classroom or for ordering examination copies, please contact our Educational Sales department at 800-434-2086 or fax 317-596-5499.

For press review copies, author interviews, or other publicity information, please contact our Public Relations department at 650-655-3000 or fax 650-655-3299.

For authorization to photocopy items for corporate, personal, or educational use, please contact Copyright Clearance Center, 222 Rosewood Drive, Danvers, MA 01923, or fax 978-750-4470.

is a registered trademark or trademark under exclusive license to IDG Books Worldwide, Inc. from International Data Group, Inc. in the United States and/or other countries.

About the Author

Bard Williams bought his first computer, an Apple IIgs, just two days after it rolled off the assembly line. He scooped up his first Macintosh two weeks after it was first manufactured (it took the loan sharks a bit longer to give him the money). He still occasionally helps out local schools with their Apple IIs (will they ever break?) and even though his computer habit recently forced him to add a Power Macintosh to his computer collection and turn his old faithful Macintosh 512K into a nifty aquarium. (Anyone know how to feed a live screen saver?)

Bard is an educator, a writer, and a technology visionary who believes, like many educators, that nothing is more exciting than seeing enthusiastic teachers use technology to guide motivated learners toward new ideas and new horizons. He is the author of more than 150 articles and, in his spare time (ha!), he gets his energy from speaking at educational conferences, teaching, and consulting.

After more than 12 years teaching middle school students (the *ultimate* challenge) and a position as Coordinator of Computer Technology and Support for a large suburban school district in Georgia, Bard was recruited by Apple Computer, Inc., to manage strategic education relations in the Northeast U.S. In early 1998, he was coaxed by Apple to move from Boston to the company's Cupertino headquarters where he's now Senior Manager of K-12 Education Marketing where, among other things, he manages Apple's K-12 Education Web site.

Bard received his doctorate in Curriculum & Instruction from the University of Georgia just two weeks before the first edition of this book was published and swears that the journey was worth the reward. After publishing three more titles in the *...For Teachers* series, he's ecstatic that educators everywhere liked the first two editions of *Internet for Teachers* enough to clamor for a third.

ABOUT IDG BOOKS WORLDWIDE

Welcome to the world of IDG Books Worldwide.

IDG Books Worldwide, Inc., is a subsidiary of International Data Group, the world's largest publisher of computer-related information and the leading global provider of information services on information technology. IDG was founded more than 30 years ago by Patrick J. McGovern and now employs more than 9,000 people worldwide. IDG publishes more than 290 computer publications in over 75 countries. More than 90 million people read one or more IDG publications each month.

Launched in 1990, IDG Books Worldwide is today the #1 publisher of best-selling computer books in the United States. We are proud to have received eight awards from the Computer Press Association in recognition of editorial excellence and three from Computer Currents' First Annual Readers' Choice Awards. Our best-selling ...*For Dummies*® series has more than 50 million copies in print with translations in 31 languages. IDG Books Worldwide, through a joint venture with IDG's Hi-Tech Beijing, became the first U.S. publisher to publish a computer book in the People's Republic of China. In record time, IDG Books Worldwide has become the first choice for millions of readers around the world who want to learn how to better manage their businesses.

Our mission is simple: Every one of our books is designed to bring extra value and skill-building instructions to the reader. Our books are written by experts who understand and care about our readers. The knowledge base of our editorial staff comes from years of experience in publishing, education, and journalism — experience we use to produce books to carry us into the new millennium. In short, we care about books, so we attract the best people. We devote special attention to details such as audience, interior design, use of icons, and illustrations. And because we use an efficient process of authoring, editing, and desktop publishing our books electronically, we can spend more time ensuring superior content and less time on the technicalities of making books.

You can count on our commitment to deliver high-quality books at competitive prices on topics you want to read about. At IDG Books Worldwide, we continue in the IDG tradition of delivering quality for more than 30 years. You'll find no better book on a subject than one from IDG Books Worldwide.

John Kilcullen
Chairman and CEO
IDG Books Worldwide, Inc.

Steven Berkowitz
President and Publisher
IDG Books Worldwide, Inc.

IDG is the world's leading IT media, research and exposition company. Founded in 1964, IDG had 1997 revenues of $2.05 billion and has more than 9,000 employees worldwide. IDG offers the widest range of media options that reach IT buyers in 75 countries representing 95% of worldwide IT spending. IDG's diverse product and services portfolio spans six key areas including print publishing, online publishing, expositions and conferences, market research, education and training, and global marketing services. More than 90 million people read one or more of IDG's 290 magazines and newspapers, including IDG's leading global brands — Computerworld, PC World, Network World, Macworld and the Channel World family of publications. IDG Books Worldwide is one of the fastest-growing computer book publishers in the world, with more than 700 titles in 36 languages. The "...For Dummies®" series alone has more than 50 million copies in print. IDG offers online users the largest network of technology-specific Web sites around the world through IDG.net (http://www.idg.net), which comprises more than 225 targeted Web sites in 55 countries worldwide. International Data Corporation (IDC) is the world's largest provider of information technology data, analysis and consulting, with research centers in over 41 countries and more than 400 research analysts worldwide. IDG World Expo is a leading producer of more than 168 globally branded conferences and expositions in 35 countries including E3 (Electronic Entertainment Expo), Macworld Expo, ComNet, Windows World Expo, ICE (Internet Commerce Expo), Agenda, DEMO, and Spotlight. IDG's training subsidiary, ExecuTrain, is the world's largest computer training company, with more than 230 locations worldwide and 785 training courses. IDG Marketing Services helps industry-leading IT companies build international brand recognition by developing global integrated marketing programs via IDG's print, online and exposition products worldwide. Further information about the company can be found at www.idg.com. 1/24/99

Dedication

The third edition of this book is dedicated to four educators from my roller-coaster high school years at M.D. Collins High in College Park, Georgia and two educator friends from my more recent past. From my high school, Mr. Gregg Saunders (HS Chemistry) and Mrs. Sharon Moll (HS Biology), who taught me that teaching was worth the effort just to be able to step back and watch exploration and wonder grow into understanding and curiosity, to Mrs. Ronnie Spilton-Sears (HS English & Drama) who took the time to coax a once-shy student into an outgoing writer and theater producer, and to Ms. Dorothy Espy (Latin) who taught me that language was beautiful. Fast forward some 10 years after high school, when I was recruited by two of most talented and energetic educators I've ever known, Pat Schneider and Jan Jones (and their husbands Steve and Dennis), to weather crazy deadlines and seemingly impossible barriers to turn out huge numbers of teacher activities for CNN, Encyclopedia Brittanica, and more. (When I grow up, I want to be just like them.) After you read this, take the time to jot a note to an educator or friend who's taught you something — anyone who cares enough to share knowledge is truly improving your life and we don't take enough time to thank them.

Author's Acknowledgments

It is not an understatement to say that literally hundreds help with creating this work. Lots of people who read the first and second editions of *The Internet for Teachers* sent e-mail with tips and tricks. Others sent snail-mail with "why don't you update this" ideas that helped me convince the wonderkind at IDG to do another book. I'm especially indebted to a few folks, though, for providing very unique insight, wonderful ideas, or just plain moral support.

Bob Hart, fraternity brother, college instructional technologist and University of Georgia faculty member extraordinaire; Sherah Carr, one of the most creative and energetic educators on the planet; Sandy Ewanowski, brilliant educator and morale coach, for awesome ideas. My friend and co-worker Michael Rex Booth who helped with content for the Web cam chapter is one of those people whose creativity is complimented by the fact that he is more special than he could ever know.

To Michelle Robinette, another original ...*For Teachers* author, who got me into this mess five books ago.

And of course to the amazingly intelligent people who help edit the content and style of my books. Kyle Looper who helped make a second edition into a third edition, filling pages with excellent edits and questions that helped me fill in lots of gaps and whose contagious giggle made touchy situations tolerable. The book's first edition was edited by an amazing editor, Pat Seiler, somewhere in Virginia, who coached me through what it is like to be a "real" writer. I am forever indebted to Pat for making that first experience a joyous one.

For Mom, Tom, Dad, and the rest of my extended family, thank you for visiting bookstores around the planet and moving my books to the front of the shelf and calling me on the phone asking "are you writing?" It worked.

Special thanks go to Julie Sykes, who served as technical editor this edition. She used the 2nd edition of *The Internet for Teachers* in her college courses and was the perfect set of eyes to help reel me in when the words went wacky.

Some of the greatest people on the planet work for IDG Books. Mary Bednarek who had enough faith in my work to stand up in a crowd and yell, "We need *The Internet For Teachers* AGAIN," so that everyone noticed. Joyce Pepple and Sherri Morningstar get gold stars for doing all the hard work to make sure I actually get paid for writing (something I still see as amazing). Special thanks to John Kilcullen, the creator of the IDG Books empire, for vision and knowing — and grabbing the brass ring. If you ever want to experience what it's like to work with a winning team, try working with IDG Books. It's wonderful.

Publisher's Acknowledgments

We're proud of this book; please register your comments through our IDG Books Worldwide Online Registration Form located at http://my2cents.dummies.com.

Some of the people who helped bring this book to market include the following:

Acquisitions, Editorial, and Media Development

Senior Project Editor: Kyle Looper

(Previous Edition: Bill Helling)

Acquisitions Editor: Sherri Morningstar

Copy Editors: James H. Russell, Stephanie Koutek, Donna Love

Technical Editor: Julie Sykes

Media Development Editor: Marita Ellixson

Associate Permissions Editor: Carmen Krikorian

Editorial Manager: Leah P. Cameron

Media Development Manager: Heather Heath Dismore

Editorial Assistant: Beth Parlon

Media Development Coordinator: Megan Roney

Production

Project Coordinator: Tom Missler

Layout and Graphics: Brian Drumm, Thomas R. Emrick, Angela F. Hunckler, Barry Offringa, Brent Savage, Michael A. Sullivan, Brian Torwelle, Mary Jo Weis, Dan Whetstine

Proofreaders: Jennifer Mahern, Marianne Santy, Rebecca Senninger

Indexer: Christine Spina Karpeles

Software Developer: Prime Synergy

General and Administrative

IDG Books Worldwide, Inc.: John Kilcullen, CEO; Steven Berkowitz, President and Publisher

IDG Books Technology Publishing Group: Richard Swadley, Senior Vice President and Publisher; Walter Bruce III, Vice President and Associate Publisher; Steven Sayre, Associate Publisher; Joseph Wikert, Associate Publisher; Mary Bednarek, Branded Product Development Director; Mary Corder, Editorial Director

IDG Books Consumer Publishing Group: Roland Elgey, Senior Vice President and Publisher; Kathleen A. Welton, Vice President and Publisher; Kevin Thornton, Acquisitions Manager; Kristin A. Cocks, Editorial Director

IDG Books Internet Publishing Group: Brenda McLaughlin, Senior Vice President and Publisher; Diane Graves Steele, Vice President and Associate Publisher; Sofia Marchant, Online Marketing Manager

IDG Books Production for Dummies Press: Michael R. Britton, Vice President of Production; Debbie Stailey, Associate Director of Production; Cindy L. Phipps, Manager of Project Coordination, Production Proofreading, and Indexing; Shelley Lea, Supervisor of Graphics and Design; Debbie J. Gates, Production Systems Specialist; Robert Springer, Supervisor of Proofreading; Laura Carpenter, Production Control Manager; Tony Augsburger, Supervisor of Reprints and Bluelines

◆

The publisher would like to give special thanks to Patrick J. McGovern, without whom this book would not have been possible.

◆

Contents at a Glance

Introduction 1

Part I: Knowledge Is Power: The Internet in Education 7
Chapter 1: Roots and Reasons: What Is the Internet, Anyway? 9
Chapter 2: Does the Internet Really Belong in Schools? 21
Chapter 3: I Told You So: Net Responsibility 31

Part II: Ready, Set, Web! 43
Chapter 4: Getting Started 45
Chapter 5: Jumping into the World Wide Web (WWW) 63
Chapter 6: Exploring with Explorer 75
Chapter 7: Navigating with Navigator 91
Chapter 8: The Search Is On 107
Chapter 9: Safe Surfing in the Schoolhouse 117
Chapter 10: Spinning Your Own Web 123

Part III: Communicate, Collaborate, Celebrate 131
Chapter 11: E-Mail: You'll Get Hooked! 133
Chapter 12: Mailing Lists-R-Us 159
Chapter 13: Be a NewsGroupie 167
Chapter 14: Chatting on the Net 183
Chapter 15: I Want My FTP! 197
Chapter 16: Webcams in the Classroom 205
Chapter 17: New Net Tools and Issues 219

The Internet for Teachers Directory D-1

Part IV: Teaching with Terabytes 231
Chapter 18: CyberTeachers, CyberLearners 233
Chapter 19: CyberJourneys: Learning Expeditions into the Net 243
Chapter 20: Rockin' Rubrics and Web Page Evaluation 251

Part V: The Part of Tens: The Net-Ready Educator 257
Chapter 21: Ten (-Plus) Ideas for E-mail Exchanges 259
Chapter 22: Ten Tips for Teaching Others about the Internet 265

Chapter 23: After Recess: Ten Net Trends You Should Know 271
Chapter 24: Ten Cool Sources for Online Projects 277
Chapter 25: Ten Virtual Field Trips 281

Part VI: Appendixes 287

Appendix A: When Things Go Wrong 289
Appendix B: Glossary 297
Appendix C: Getting Connected: You've Got Options.............................307
Appendix D: About the CD 319

Index 331

IDG Books Worldwide End-User License Agreement 354

Installation Instructions 356

Book Registration Information ....Back of Book

Cartoons at a Glance

By Rich Tennant

The 5th Wave — By Rich Tennant

"A BRIEF ANNOUNCEMENT, CLASS – AN OPEN-FACED PEANUT BUTTER SANDWICH IS NOT AN APPROPRIATE REPLACEMENT FOR A MISSING MOUSEPAD."

page 287

The 5th Wave — By Rich Tennant

"Children- it is not necessary to whisper while we're visiting the Vatican Library Web site."

page 231

The 5th Wave — By Rich Tennant

"Our classroom PCs have created a challenging atmosphere where critical analyzing, synthesizing, and problem-solving skills are honed. I think the students have gotten a lot out of them, too."

page 131

The 5th Wave — By Rich Tennant

"I don't care what your e-mail friends in Europe say, you're not having a glass of Chianti with your bologna sandwich."

page 257

The 5th Wave — By Rich Tennant

"You've done a wonderful job using the Internet to improve your math, science, social studies, even your art and music grades. By the way, is there a hair styling site on the Internet?"

page 7

The 5th Wave — By Rich Tennant

"From now on, let's confine our exploration of ancient Egypt to the Internet."

page 43

Fax: 978-546-7747 • **E-mail:** the5wave@tiac.net

Table of Contents

. . . .

Introduction **1**

About This Book..1
How to Read This Book 2
   Conventions 2
   Who am I talking to? (a.k.a. To whom am I speaking?)................3
How This Book Is Organized..4
   Part I: Knowledge Is Power: The Internet in Education...............4
   Part II: Ready, Set, Web! 4
   Part III: Communicate, Collaborate, Celebrate 4
   Part IV: Teaching with Terabytes 4
   Part V: The Part of Tens: The Net-Ready Educator 5
   Part VI: Appendixes..5
Icons Used in This Book...5
   Learning Link 5
   Teacher Approved...5
   Techno Terms..5
   On the CD 5
   Heads Up 6
   Try This 6
   Warning! 6
Just Do It!...6
Feedback! 6

Part I: Knowledge Is Power: The Internet in Education **7**

Chapter 1: Roots and Reasons: What Is the Internet, Anyway? **9**

The Internet: The Textbook of Tomorrow?....................................9
Back to the Roots 10
   Where did it all begin? 10
   The education connection 11
   Log jam — eighties style 12
   The transition continues 12
   History in the making..13
   From roots to rabbit ears? 14
What Can I Do with the Internet? 16
Success on the Net: A Beginner's Journey....................................17

Chapter 2: Does the Internet Really Belong in Schools? 21

The Internet: What Good Is It?..22
Ten Great Reasons to Get Your Class on the Information
   Superhighway...22
     The Internet presents real-world examples of integrated
       knowledge...23
     The Internet facilitates collaborative learning 23
     The Internet offers opportunities for telementoring....................23
     The Internet is all about communicating 24
     The Internet can cater to different learners in different ways 24
     The Internet is a culturally, racially, physically, sexually blind
       medium...24
     The Internet provides an outlet for creativity..............................25
     The Internet allows everyone to become a publisher...................25
     The Internet is a community (maybe)..25
     The Internet provides information not available in your
       media center...26
Talking to Parents and Your Community about the Internet...................27
Nothing but Net?..28
Combating FUD...29

Chapter 3: I Told You So: Net Responsibility .31

The Three Is...32
     Invite your fellow teachers and community members
       to sample the water...32
     Introduce a set of guidelines...33
     Integrate...35
Worth Watching...36
     People..37
     Pictures..37
     Dialogue...37
InternEthics...38
Take Out a Contract on Your Kids...40

Part II: Ready, Set, Web!..*43*

Chapter 4: Getting Started 45

What Do I Need?..45
     All those chips and no place to go...46
     Your gateway to the Net..48
     The Internet on America Online...48
     Get with the program..52
     A modem is a modem is a modem 52
Getting Your Computer Ready for Connection to the Net 55
     CyberMacintosh 55
     Window(s) on the Net...55
     What next?..57

Budgeting for Telecommunications...58
    Going for the bucks...58
Ready to Ride..60
A Word (Okay, a Few!) about NetDay..60

Chapter 5: Jumping into the World Wide Web (WWW) 63

What Is the Web?..64
    Web nuts and bolts...64
    How do I jump on the Web? 65
    Meet URL 66
Surfing with Netscape Communicator and Internet Explorer 68
    Getting around 69
    Back to the future 69
    Getting there quickly...70
    Exiting the Superhighway 71
    Navigating the tangled Web 71
How Not to Get Caught in the Web 72
    Great places for a first visit 73

Chapter 6: Exploring with Explorer 75

Basic Training: Internet Explorer 75
The Internet Explorer Toolbar..78
Browsing Bonanza..81
More Cool IE Functions 82
    Checking out Web pages "off Web" 82
    Printing and saving from the Web..82
    Using Internet mail 83
IE Tips and Tricks...85
    Image off, image on 85
    Saving your favorites 85
    Sharing favorites...87
    Setting a default home page...88
    IE newsreader 89

Chapter 7: Navigating with Navigator 91

Downloading Netscape Communicator...92
Installing Netscape Communicator..93
Rifling through the Various Parts 94
    Sifting through the toolbar buttons 94
    Visiting URLs 96
    Getting at your components and reading your status...................97
Customizing Navigator 98
Dog-Earing Your Pages with Bookmarks 100
Getting Caught in the Web 101
Saving the Cool Stuff..102
Printing Web Pages 103
Smart Browsing 104

Chapter 8: The Search Is On 107

Internet Search 411 108
The Great Search Engine Myth 111
The Basic Search 112
Specialized Searches..112
The Tricks of the Trade...114
    Ifs, ands, and buts 114
    More tricks 116

Chapter 9: Safe Surfing in the Schoolhouse 117

The Filter Fallacy..117
Filtering When You Must 119
Copyright and The Internet 120
    Don't copy that! 121
    What's fair is fair 121
    The bottom line 122

Chapter 10: Spinning Your Own Web 123

Why Web?..124
How Do I Weave a Web Page? 125
    Bodacious ideas...125
    Design and conquer 125
    What tools do I use?...126
    Finding a home for your page 127
    Publishing to the Web 127
Show the World 128

Part III: Communicate, Collaborate, Celebrate 131

Chapter 11: E-Mail: You'll Get Hooked! 133

What Is E-Mail? 134
    What can I do with e-mail? 134
    Okay! I'm convinced! What do I need to do first?..................135
    What's my address? 135
    Can we talk? 137
Sending and Receiving E-Mail 137
    Mail anatomy 137
    Sending and receiving Internet mail via an online service 138
    Sending and receiving Internet mail via a university/UNIX
        network 139
    Internet e-mail 101: Eudora Light 140
Sending and Receiving Attachments via E-Mail 146
Using Netscape Communicator for E-Mail 147
Using Internet Explorer for E-Mail..149
Automating E-Mail Functions..151
Finding Your Friends on the Net 151

Netiquette: Internet Dos and Donts 153
    Do create a custom electronic signature message for
        yourself or your school..153
    Don't send anything through e-mail that you wouldn't
        write on your chalkboard 154
    Don't flame 154
    Do talk to your students about what's appropriate to
        send via e-mail...155
    Don't type in all capital letters 155
Emoticons: Getting That Fuzzy Internet Feeling 155

Chapter 12: Mailing Lists-R-Us **159**
Mailing Lists with Attitude..159
Finding a Mailing List...160
Subscribing to a Mailing List 161
Posting to a Mailing List 163
Weathering the Mail Storm 164
Your First Subscription 165

Chapter 13: Be a NewsGroupie **167**
Newsgroups 101 167
Finding a Newsgroup 168
Read All about It...170
Navigating Newsgroups with Netscape.......................................170
    Accessing newsgroups..171
    Subscribing to newsgroups..171
Newsgroups with Internet Explorer/Outlook Express.................172
    Prepping Outlook Express to read newsgroups 173
    Subscribing to a newsgroup...174
    Reading a newsgroup message 175
Spreadin' the (Deja) News..176
Newsgroup Rules..177
Saving Your Job 179
Extra, Extra! Read These Newsgroups!..181

Chapter 14: Chatting on the Net **183**
Chatting on the Net..183
IRC: Chatter at the Speed of CyberSpace....................................184
Live Chat Via AOL 190
Instant Message Systems and the Classroom..............................193
    ICQ..193
    AOL Instant Messenger...193
A Meeting of the Minds...195

Chapter 15: I Want My FTP! 197

What Can I Do with FTP?..198

FTP: The Basics 199

Finding Files on the Internet: Old and New....................201

Got the File, Now What? 202

Chapter 16: Webcams in the Classroom 205

Turning On to Webcasting and Webcams 205

Getting Started 206

    Computer..206

    Web camera...207

    Webcam software 208

    Modem 209

    Connection to the Internet...............................209

    Web page 210

    Web host 210

Setting Up a Webcam 210

Using HTML for Webcams 212

    Refreshing your Webcam image 212

    Creating remote windows.................................215

Examples and Resources 216

Chapter 17: New Net Tools and Issues 219

What's an Intranet? 220

HTML — Is That All There Is? 220

New Issues, New Challenges 221

Addressing Tough Internet Challenges 222

    Too-tough URLs 222

    Telephonus interruptus 222

    Porno pandemonium 223

    High tech or high touch? 223

    Gender-centric 223

    One-way street 224

    Lost in the mall 225

Warp Ten on the Info Highway 225

    What's Java?...225

    Getting shocked...226

    Audio-R-Us..227

    Motion on the Net 227

    Phone home 228

    Conferencing 228

The Internet For Teachers Directory *D-1*

Part IV: Teaching with Terabytes 231

Chapter 18: CyberTeachers, CyberLearners 233
Planning an Online Experience..233
Managing Time, Materials, and Students 236
Students with Special Needs and the Internet 237
Staff Development and the Internet..239
Keeping Up with Changing Roles 240

Chapter 19: CyberJourneys: Learning Expeditions into the Net 243
A CyberJourney for K–5 244
A CyberJourney for 6–8 244
A CyberJourney for 9–12 245
A CyberJourney for College Students and Educators 247
CyberPlanning for the Teacher 248
A CyberJourney for Your School..249

Chapter 20: Rockin' Rubrics and Web Page Evaluation 251
Believe It or Not...251
I Found It on the Internet 252
Evaluating research resources 252
Evaluating Student-Created Content on the Web....................253

Part V: The Part of Tens: The Net-Ready Educator........257

Chapter 21: Ten (-Plus) Ideas for E-mail Exchanges 259
Survey Says 260
News Hounds..260
Olympic Proportions 260
Play Guess Where...261
Story Starters...261
Gleaming the Cube..261
Newsletter Swap...261
Things That Go Bump..262
Multimedia Mania..263
Send a Letter to the President...263
Interview a Senior Citizen 263
Start a Lesson Plan Chain Letter..263
A Few More Ideas from Other Net-Teachers............................264

Chapter 22: Ten Tips for Teaching Others about the Internet 265
TTOM..266
Resource Roundup...266
Gettin' Tricky with It 266
CyberCamping 267

Surfin' Safari 267
It's the Princip(al) of the Thing 267
Let's Go Shopping 268
It's Elementary 268
Bonzai Bookmarks 268
Wacky Web 269

Chapter 23: After Recess: Ten Net Trends You Should Know 271

One Box, One Connection 272
Wherever/Whenever Technology 272
Finders, Keepers 272
Find It Your (Net) Way 273
The Global Shopping Network 274
SIS Goes Internet 274
Screen Time 275
I Want It Now! 275
Learn 24/7 275
Talking Toasters? 276

Chapter 24: Ten Cool Sources for Online Projects 277

Terra Fermi? 278
Tammy's Tips 278
The Learning Interchange 278
Connected Classrooms 278
The Project Center 278
Globe Trotting 279
The Headbone Zone 279
The Quest, NASA Style 279
Kids Connect 279
Weather, or Not 280
Sister, Sister! 280

Chapter 25: Ten Virtual Field Trips 281

It Takes a Village 282
A Bridge Too Far 282
Interview with a Rock Star 282
Cool Breezes 283
For Your Health 283
Ramblin' Runes 284
Walkabout 284
How'd They Do That? 284
You Were There 285
Web to the Edge 285

Part VI: Appendixes *287*

Appendix A: When Things Go Wrong .... .289
The Internet 289
Is it busy, or is it dead? 289
Picture pains 290
Cold as Ice 290
Troubleshooting Hardware 291
Its dark in here! 291
Crash and burn 292
Troubleshooting Software 292
Undeliverable mail 293
Network nasties 293
The Modem and the Phone Line 294
Custom calling features 294
Can't connect 294
Noisy things 294
Phone extension roulette 295
Moving too slowly 295
No dial tone 295

Appendix B: Glossary 297

Appendix C: Getting Connected: You've Got Options 307
Direct or Not? 308
Go direct 308
Dial it up 310
Decisions, Decisions 313
Locating an ISP 314
Choosing an ISP 314
The Wheeler-Dealer's top ten questions for an ISP 315

Appendix D: About the CD 319
System Requirements 319
How to Use the CD Using the Macintosh OS 320
How to Use the CD Using Microsoft Windows 321
What You'll Find 322
The Internet For Teachers Links Page 322
MindSpring Internet Service 322
Adobe Acrobat Reader 3.02, and 4.0 from Adobe
Systems, Inc. 323
Anarchie 3.0, from Stairways Software 323
BBEdit Lite...324
Convert Machine, by Rod Kennedy 324
Cool Edit 96, by Syntrillium Software 324
CuteFTP, from GlobalSCAPE 324
Dreamweaver 2.0, by Macromedia 325

Enhanced CU-SeeMe 3.1, by White Pine Software 325
Eudora Light 3.1.3, from Qualcomm Inc. 325
Fireworks2, by Macromedia...326
First Aid 2000, from Network Associates, Inc. 326
F-Secure Anti-virus, by Data Fellows, Inc. 326
HotDog Professional 5 Webmaster Suite (Trial), from Sausage
    Software 326
Internet Coach, from APTE..327
Internet Explorer 5, by Microsoft 327
Netscape Communicator 4.5, Netscape Communications 327
QuickTime 3.01, from Apple Computer, Inc. 328
Sherlock Plug-ins, courtesy of Apple-Donuts................................328
Shockwave, from Macromedia...328
SiteCam, by Rearden Technology..328
Sound Machine 2.7.1, Rod Kennedy 329
StuffIt Lite 3.6, from Aladdin Systems 329
Web Painter, Totally Hip Software 329
WinZip 7.0, from Nico Mak Software 329
WS_FTP LE 4.6, from Ipswitch, Inc. 329
If You've Got Problems (Of the CD Kind) 330

Index...*331*

IDG Books Worldwide End-User License Agreement......354

Installation Instructions..356

Book Registration Information ....Back of Book

Introduction

●●●

*W*elcome to *The Internet For Teachers,* 3rd Edition. It's been almost three years since the 2nd edition, and that equates to about a million Internet years. There is much good news and much new information to share. More people than ever are connected (some estimates suggest a quarter of the world's population, a somewhat higher percentage in the US), and using and connecting to the Internet have become virtually effortless. Wait. Only 25 percent? That's right. We still have a long way to go.

Most of your ride through the wealth of resources on the information super-highway will be smooth, but you need to watch out for potholes, too. I've included information on the latest tools to use in exploring the Internet, and I've tried to make your trip easier by giving you tips, techniques, a couple hundred places to visit, and a few anecdotes that you'll especially appreciate as a K-12 or college teacher.

This third edition has provided me an opportunity to update and enhance the content presented in the first and second editions. I appreciate the won-derful support and input from friends and colleagues around the world. Your input shaped the changes in this edition. I've packed in more sites, more ideas and activities, and some cutting-edge stuff like Web cameras to jazz things up a bit.

So, here it is in plain English. All the techno-babble has been stripped away, and here are the basics about how to get started, how to do some cool things after you get online, and how you can harness the power of the Internet in your classroom.

About This Book

This book is designed to be used when you and your students are just begin-ning your trip through the Internet and for times when you get stalled on the info-way and can't find a wrecker. Just jump right into any chapter, get what you need, and jump back to the real world.

You'll find handy information, including the following topics:

- ✔ What is this Internet thing, anyway?
- ✔ Searching Internet roots
- ✔ Getting connected to the Internet
- ✔ Net responsibility
- ✔ Sending e-mail
- ✔ Getting the most out of your Web browser (Netscape Navigator & Internet Explorer)
- ✔ Introducing a Web camera to your classroom
- ✔ Trends in educational technology
- ✔ Creating your first cyberjourney
- ✔ Searching the Internet efficiently

How to Read This Book

Grab this book when you need a quick reference. Glance at the Table of Contents, peruse the Index, and zip right to the page that gives you the answer you need.

The book has been written so that each chapter pretty much stands alone. It's great for those five-minute reading breaks between classes.

Conventions

I love conventions. The freebies in the display area, the pressed chicken at the banquet. My favorite is the National Educational Computing Conference . . . Wait! Sorry, wrong convention.

I've done some things to make your life easier. Watch for them.

When you have to type something, it appears in boldface type: **Type this.** Internet addresses look a bit different:

`socrates@university.edu`

Type it in, just as it appears, capitalization and all, and then press the Return or Enter key on your keyboard.

If you make a boo-boo, just type it again or check Appendix C for troubleshooting tips.

For the purpose of this book, I've tried to present a balanced account (Macintosh and Windows OS) and, whenever possible, I call out differences you encounter. That said, the Internet is pretty "platform independent" and the way browsers work is virtually indistinguishable between types of modern operating systems.

Exciting, huh?

Who am I talking to? (a.k.a. To whom am I speaking?)

In preparing this book for you, I've tried to address all the following needs:

- ✔ You have or would like to have access to the Internet.
- ✔ You intend to get access to the Internet through a direct network connection, an online service, or an Internet service provider.
- ✔ You are an educator who is wondering how you can learn about the Internet and how you can use it in what you do every day.
- ✔ You are responsible for arranging to bring the Internet into your school or your school system or teaching others about using the Internet to enhance and enrich your curriculum.
- ✔ You are a pre-service teacher who can't wait to do your first lunchroom duty and go on a Net-surfing expedition.
- ✔ You are not seeking to be the next Internet swami who, after 1,000 hours of surfing the Net, is more interested in finding out whether Microsoft's Bill Gates really does answer his e-mail than in how the Internet can reduce the time it takes to grade 35 essays.

In order to save you countless hours searching the Net for tools, I've included some of the most often used and most powerful tools for accessing and navigating the Internet on the CD that comes with this book. You'll be delighted to know that it is "cross-platform" (geek-speak for "It works on both Macintosh computers and computers running Windows 95 or 98"). With these tools and others I refer to in the chapters ahead, you'll quickly become King or Queen of the NetSurfers before you can say *telecommunicate!*

How This Book Is Organized

This book has six parts. The parts are designed to be read either in sequence or on their own. You can jump in anywhere you like, but I recommend that you peek at Part I so you know a bit about the Internet before you take the plunge.

Here are the parts of the book and what they contain:

Part I: Knowledge Is Power: The Internet in Education

This part discusses what the Internet is, tells a bit about how it came into existence, and gives you the foundation you need to talk with your students (and your peers) about using the Internet responsibly.

Part II: Ready, Set, Web!

In this part, you learn what hardware and software you need to get started using the Internet. You also explore the features and fun of browsing the Web with today's most common surfing tools. There's even a discussion of "safe surfing" and tips on spinning your own Web page.

Part III: Communicate, Collaborate, Celebrate

There's more to the Internet than just the Web. Find out how to send and receive electronic mail (e-mail), explore online databases, receive files, set up a Web camera, and talk live to others around the world.

Part IV: Teaching with Terabytes

What happens when it comes time to use the Internet with your students? This part gives you a glimpse into how to write lesson plans for instruction that uses the Internet, as well as some tips on your changing role as an "instructor of the 21st century" and on evaluating classroom use of the Internet.

Part V: The Part of Tens: The Net-Ready Educator

Here's the place where you find tips for online projects, net trends, and a few ideas for funding more technology for your school. Even though this part is called "The Part of Tens," I got really carried away and gave you lots more for your money.

Part VI: Appendixes

Find out how to deal with those inevitable hardware and software problems and identify unfamiliar Internet terms. Also find out ways to get connected to the Internet in case you've not jumped on board yet.

Icons Used in This Book

Here are the pretty pictures that can make your life easier:

Learning Link

An opportunity for your students to participate in an Internet-related educational activity.

Teacher Approved

This icon highlights items or activities that I think are a "must use" in your classroom.

Techno Terms

Vocabulary that the teacher (you!) should know to be a true Net surfer.

On the CD

This icon points out programs that are on *The Internet For Teachers,* 3rd Edition CD-ROM at the back of this book.

Heads Up

Handy things you should watch for or things that can make your life easier. They're time savers and frustration savers.

Try This

An activity for you to try so that you can practice using the Internet. Hands-on learning.

Warning!

A danger sign. Hold the mouse!

Just Do It!

Okay. You're ready to go. Learning to use the Internet is not nearly as difficult as others may tell you. You've done much more difficult things, such as learning how to handle fights in the hall and potty patrol after fifth period.

Grab this book and a cup of coffee or a can of soda (essential food groups for educators) and jump right in. You'll be Internetting in no time. Surf's up!

Feedback!

We really, really want to know what you think about *The Internet For Teachers,* 3rd Edition.

Send feedback to:

IDG Books Worldwide, Inc.
7260 Shadeland Station, Suite 100
Indianapolis, IN 46256

Be sure to log on to the official IDG "Dummies" Web site and read about other books in the *...For Teachers* series. You find it at www.dummies.com.

Part I

Knowledge Is Power: The Internet in Education

The 5th Wave — By Rich Tennant

"You've done a wonderful job using the Internet to improve your math, science, social studies, even your art and music grades. By the way, is there a hair styling site on the Internet?"

In this part . . .

Walk over to the shelf and grab a textbook. Open it to any page. You're likely to see:

"Someday, we'll travel to the moon."

"Let's take a look at the Soviet Union."

or

"Modern poets such as William Shakespeare . . ."

Even your most current textbook took more than a year to get from the drawing board to your classroom. Most curriculum adoption cycles are much longer, meaning that three years or more could pass before three-year-old information is put into the hands of you and your students.

Now, don't get me wrong. After 12 years in middle school classrooms, I appreciate the value of a good textbook. They're great for offering skill and drill (or drill and kill) activities, and they do provide a good infrastructure for organizing information, but textbooks, at least in the current form, are always "old news."

Enter the Internet. Right now the Net is a lawless place in cyberspace in which bunches of information are being dumped on a daily basis. That information, however important, trite, or explicit, is, at the least, *current.* It's important for us, as educators, to work together with our students to learn to separate the gems from the junk.

When you and your students log on to the Internet, you're no longer a teacher. Both of you have become *knowledge navigators.* It's up to you to chart a course through cyberspace to find the good stuff. It's up to you to find a way to use the stuff after you find it, too.

In this part, you learn about the structure and history of the Internet, find out the cool things you can do with Internet access, read some compelling reasons for logging on in the first place, enjoy a few success stories, and read some important information about responsible use of the Internet (a must-read). All this should be painless. After all, that's what makes these books great.

If you're really chomping at the bit and already have an Internet connection picked out, go ahead and jump to Part II to find out the particulars for making your first Internet connection or Part III to find out what's beyond the Web.

Chapter 1

Roots and Reasons: What Is the Internet, Anyway?

In This Chapter

▶ Understanding the Internet

▶ Internet roots

▶ Using the Internet in your classroom

▶ Success on the Net: A beginner's Internet journey

A friend once told me that she defined technology as "anything invented after I was born." Just when most teachers are becoming comfortable with using calculators and computers in classrooms and computer labs, this Internet thing comes along.

Never fear, though; this new form of communication and information access is becoming easier to learn as more software developers jump onto the information superhighway. Sure, the highway has some potholes, but my goal is to help you steer clear of them.

Knocking down classroom walls and accessing information and people around the globe is what the Internet *is for*. In this chapter, you get a glimpse of what the Internet *is*.

The Internet: The Textbook of Tomorrow?

The Internet is a large collection of computers in networks that are tied together so that many users can share their vast resources. That's all. Just lots of computers tied together by high-speed communication lines. To get onto the Internet, all you have to do is make arrangements to make your computer one of the millions already online. Easy, huh?

Learning to navigate through the interconnecting networks is as exciting as the information you can retrieve. Not only will your journeys take you around the globe, but you'll also begin to appreciate the rich diversity in humanity and the wide variety of knowledge on Planet Earth.

The Internet holds a wealth of information. In fact, it contains so much information that you and your students could spend your entire lives just browsing. You will quickly find that the key to a successful and efficient session on the Internet is good planning.

As you plan for ways to use the Internet in your classroom, you'll also see that students need a wide variety of skills to be successful on the Net. Well-planned Internet activities tap skills in researching, problem solving, critical thinking, communication, and data management. Thinking about how you want to reinforce those skills before, during, and after your journey into the Net is a good idea.

What's the bottom line? Thanks to the information superhighway system, you and your students can now travel around the world in nanoseconds, collecting more ideas and up-to-the-minute information than you ever imagined. Sounds like something that's right for your classroom, doesn't it? Textbook? What textbook?

Back to the Roots

In the beginning, there was a telephone network, a bunch of wire, and a few big, blinking, data-stuffed mainframe computers. These computers lived in military, research, and educational institutions. One day, someone figured out that tying these electronic giants together would be a good idea. The Internet as we know it today came about largely because of a partnership between the military and educational institutions. Thus, the Internet isn't really in any one place; it's everywhere! As you discover in the following section, the military laid the foundation, and universities and research institutions built the building.

Where did it all begin?

Morse code, cellular phones, and that annoying intercom in your classroom were all developed because someone somewhere wanted to say something to other someones who would listen. Like these arguably vital communication pathways, the Internet began as a result of a need for communication.

Techno-weenie talk about TCP/IP

TCP/IP is an acronym for Transmission Control Protocol/Internet Protocol, the set of rules used to connect servers *(also called hosts)* on networks such as the Internet. TCP and IP were developed through a Department of Defense (DOD) research project to connect a number different networks designed by different vendors into a network of networks (the "Internet"). It was initially successful because it delivered a few basic services that everyone needs (file transfer, e-mail, remote logon) across a very large number of client and server systems.

TCP/IP is even bulletproof . . . sort of. TCP/IP networks were designed to be robust and automatically recover from any node or phone line failure. Nowadays, most modern operating systems, such as UNIX, the Mac OS, and Windows, are all capable of using TCP/IP to communicate across networks. For more insightful cocktail talk about what makes the Web tick, check out TCP/IP For Dummies, 3rd Edition by my colleagues Candace Leiden and Marshall Wilensky (IDG Books Worldwide, Inc.).

In 1969, the Department of Defense (DOD) funded a project to link DOD engineers with civilian research contractors, including a large number of universities that were doing military-funded research. Although the resulting network, called ARPAnet (Advanced Research Projects Administration Network), began with only three computers that were connected via phone lines, it quickly grew to become an essential resource for communication and data exchange for hundreds of military and research contractors.

After the foundations of the network were forged, more and more universities and research institutions jumped onto the superhighway. Eventually, the highway reached gridlock, and ARPAnet was subdivided to provide several different channels for military and research institutions. Today these channels remain linked by a dandy technical scheme called the Internet Protocol (IP). This protocol has made it possible for the Internet to grow and flourish.

The education connection

At the same time that the military and research communities were finding new ways to exchange information over the new information highway, colleges and universities were beginning to change from a centralized host-system data-management architecture to a distributed workstation-based scheme. Huh?

In plain English, the huge, expensive mainframe computers that were connected to "dumb terminals" around campus began to be bogged down with routine traffic from such things as electronic mail, file exchange, and computerized Star Trek games that bored professors and their teaching assistants were playing. Someone had the idea that if more power were moved to the teachers' desktops, the "big iron" would be free for more important work, such as calculating pi to the 10,000th significant digit.

Here's where it gets really crazy. The university workstations needed an operating system, and the bean-counters were going crazy because of the expense of changing the network scheme. Along came UNIX, an operating system that was offered to universities for next to nothing. The cool thing about UNIX is that it was designed to make it easy to connect workstations together. How appropriate, huh? Suddenly, everyone with a workstation had direct access to ARPAnet. Uh-oh — everyone?

Log jam — eighties style

By the late 1980s, ARPAnet was overwhelmed with university traffic. Along came the National Science Foundation (NSF), which decided to unfreeze the jam by going shopping for bigger, faster computers to serve as traffic controllers for the Net. Ten million dollars and five supercomputers later, things weren't much better — mainly, as the NSF folks can tell you, because of politics. The NSF did what any respectable organization that's caught between a rock and a hard place does — it started its own network.

NSFNet was bigger, faster, and easier to access than ARPAnet. Within ten years, in 1990, Grandpa ARPAnet shut down because of lack of use. NSFNet thrived, but because of the expense and complexity of maintaining the finicky supercomputers and the trend toward smaller, increasingly powerful computers, commercial Internet providers began to jump on the bandwagon. People realized that they could provide the on-ramp to the information superhighway, tweaked with dandy front-end graphics software, and make money doing it. Welcome to today's information superhighway — and watch for the billboards as you whiz by them.

The transition continues

Today, there are thousands of commercial Internet providers. Each provider needs only a fast computer and a high-speed, high-quality connection to the Internet to be able to license its services. To show you how far we've come, you can now use a Macintosh or PC running Windows to set up your own Internet service . . . and a Mac is a lot less expensive than a $10 million supercomputer.

An Internet server was once a $15,000 to $50,000 behemoth. Today, any platform that has a powerful CPU and lots of RAM will do. Apple Computer, for example, now offers a desktop Power PC server capable of supporting millions of connections to the Net. A number of other computers can be used as Internet servers as well. In general, you can do up the whole thing for about $5,000.

History in the making

In December 1991, the president signed the House-Senate compromise version of S. 272, the High-Performance Computing Act of 1991. The bill provides for a coordinated federal program to ensure continued U.S. leadership in high-performance computing, and it includes the establishment of a high-capacity and high-speed National Research and Education Network (NREN).

What does all of this mean for education? NREN may seem long in the tooth by technology timeline standards, but it includes some interesting provisions that relate directly to what can happen in the classroom. Some have already begun to come true! The initiatives include

- Training researchers, educators, and students in high-performance computing

- Increasing student and educator access to high-performance computing resources

- Promoting the further development of an information infrastructure of databases, services, access mechanisms, and research facilities that are available for use through the network

- Stimulating research on software technology

- Promoting the more rapid development and wider distribution of computer software tools and applications software

- Accelerating the development of computing systems and subsystems

- Investing in basic research and education and promoting the inclusion of high-performance computing in educational institutions at all levels

- Promoting greater collaboration among the government, federal laboratories, industry, high-performance computing centers, and universities

- Improving the interagency planning and coordination of federal research and development on high-performance computing and maximizing the effectiveness of the federal government's high-performance computing efforts

The NREN will provide users with appropriate access to high-performance computing systems, electronic information resources, other research facilities, and libraries. The Network will provide access, to the extent practicable, to electronic information resources that are maintained by libraries, research facilities, publishers, and affiliated organizations.

What taking advantage of the NREN will cost schools and universities is still in question, but one thing's for sure: The information superhighway is going to get bigger and easier to use. In fact, if the number of people signing on to the Internet continued to grow at its current rate, every person on the planet would be on the Internet by the year 2003. Exponential growth isn't the only challenge, however; the task of taming the zillion-headed monster and steering it toward enhancing and enriching what goes on in the classroom is up to us as educators.

What might the Internet look like in ten years? Ask your students to examine the NREN proposal (visit `www.eff.org/pub/Legislation/nren_congress.report`) and write an editorial describing why the classroom of the future should have access to the Net and what changes they'd like to see to make the Internet more student friendly.

From roots to rabbit ears?

Will the Internet ever replace textbooks as the predominant resource in every classroom? If it does, who'll own the digital pipeline that will bring it to schools? Telephone companies and cable television providers are working furiously to bring the Internet to your home through a variety of channels — for a fee, of course.

Yep, you can now log onto your favorite online service or jump right into the Net through your television. (Like we need yet another reason to spend time in front of the one-eyed entertainment monster!) The real trick is figuring out when using the Net makes more sense than using a more traditional resource, such as your local library. If teachers can find compelling reasons for the Internet to be in every classroom, it'll come. We can be very persuasive at times.

It's inevitable; the Net will come to every classroom. Remember when the first personal computer showed up in your school? I remember huddling around the boxes as the miraculous Apple IIe computer, in all its beigeness, was lifted out and placed on the table. Everyone sort of stared. Plugging the thing in was a cinch. Then we turned it on, heard our first Apple-beep, and saw this:

```
]
```

or, if certain planets were aligned, this:

```
*
```

We've come a long way from the AppleSoft prompt. Now we have computers that look like they came out of the Jetsons TV cartoon and have enough power to launch a space shuttle. What helped make those first less-than-friendly personal computers successful in classrooms? Well, you did.

The fact that you're reading this book means that you want to join the ranks of educators who are willing to explore new ways to use technology in the classroom. Plenty of other educators like you want to know more about harnessing the power of telecommunications for teaching and learning. In 1999, more than 90 percent of schools were connected to the Internet. That's a lot of connections! Unfortunately, less than 45 percent of those connections were in classrooms.

For most teachers, just getting access to a telephone or a network is a hassle, so you may think that the Internet is an impossible goal. Fear not, however, because thousands of creative educators now exchange ideas via e-mail and zip through the World Wide Web (WWW).

If I had to get out the crystal ball, I'd expect the Internet to be in most classrooms by the year 2000 — a likely spin-off of the mother lode of profit: Internet in the home. But then, maybe the classroom of the future will be at home. Or will it? Hmmm . . . makes my brain hurt just to think about it.

Technology flashback!

It's flashback time. Some of you can remember a time years ago when you first attempted to sign onto a local bulletin board service (BBS). You know, back in the dark ages when software wasn't smart and computers were just beginning to be friendly? You sat down at your Apple II or PC AT and realized that plugging in the modem and starting the software program was only the beginning. You had to learn a whole new vocabulary that included intimidating techno-weenie words such as *stop bits, parity, baud rate,* and *error correction.* We thought nothing of waiting 20 minutes (at 300 bps) for a game to download (a game that displayed a single one-pixel box that you could bat around the Pong?).

You'll be very happy to know that, for the most part, life in cyberspace is much easier now.

Most software and hardware communicate well enough to do many tasks that made beginning BBS users crazy. Online services now provide starter kits that are preconfigured to make your first online experience successful. Now you can get turn-key sign-on kits (Mindspring's is conveniently hiding on the CD) for new Internet users. In most cases, you sign on to the service, and all the software you need is there for the taking.

Now if they would just introduce a VCR that sets its own clock. . . .

```
  \  \  |  /  /
—12 : 00 : 00—
  /  /  |  \  \
```

What Can I Do with the Internet?

One day last summer, I was watching an infomercial touting the latest device that could slice, dice, chop, mow the lawn, and grade papers (I wish), and I thought, "They could sell the Internet this way!" It's a great tool for lots of things if you know how to use it.

The Internet can make a real difference in teaching and learning in your school. Not only can using the Internet effectively enhance and enrich the classroom experience, but it also has great value for you as a personal productivity tool.

Here's a sampling of what the Internet has to offer you and your students:

- **Global electronic mail:** Send a note to anyone, anywhere, anytime. Suddenly you have the ability to build links between people everywhere without regard to those things that blind us from the appreciation of knowledge. Things such as race, color, creed, gender, and physical disabilities all disappear when you board the information superhighway. A teacher in my school district used electronic mail to correspond with a teacher in Alaska, who gave a play-by-play description of the Iditarod. Every day she checked to see what condition the dogs were in, who the front-runner was, and what interesting anecdotes were available about the challenges faced by the wind-blown racers. She then passed the information on to her students, who wrote articles for an "Iditarod Update," made maps of the trip, charted weather conditions, and calculated windchill temperatures. Is this project interdisciplinary or what?

- **Knowledge navigation:** Zip around the world via the World Wide Web to locate documents, pictures, sounds, and even digitized movies to keep your knowledge, skills, and curriculum up to date. Glance over at the shelf, tug on the textbook that says "Some day man will go to the moon," and think about how useful it can be to have instantaneous information for use in the classroom. Got a unit on weather coming up? Use Internet resources to pop over to NASA (www.nasa.gov) to access ready-made classroom activities, surf to the Library of Congress (www.loc.gov) (or your local library) and build a bibliography, and then head for the Jet Propulsion Lab (JPL) for digitized satellite photos (www.jpl.nasa.gov). You can even build your own bookmark pages as a resource guide for searching the Internet based on subject area, grade level, or topics of interest and then share them with people in your school and around the globe. Of course, the Net is great for your own professional development, too. You can now take courses online!

- **File exchange:** Send and retrieve files containing documents, pictures, movies, sounds, and programs. Need the latest version of virus protection software? Jump onto the Net, hop to the vendor's file server, and retrieve your file.

✔ **Discussion groups:** Engage in a discussion with other Internet users about any topic you can think of. A media specialist, using a discussion group (also called a *newsgroup*), posted an electronic message asking other educators on the Net about selecting software for a media circulation system. Four weeks later, he went before the board of education with testimonials and facts from 23 school systems around the country about the system he had selected. They bought it lock, stock, and bar code.

✔ **Live conferencing:** Talk live to other Internet users. Get into a debate about outcome-based education or Bloom's Taxonomy or whether to have Coke or Pepsi in the faculty lounge machines. Now you can even tune in to online channels and watch live video!

You're thinking, wowza! Can the Internet get any better than all these features? But wait, there's more! By its very nature, the Internet is a dynamic medium. It changes just about every nanosecond as people add or delete information. The body of knowledge on the Internet is growing exponentially, and the tools we use to access the Net are becoming easier to use and more powerful.

You know the neat activity that teaches kids about compounding interest — the one where you offer to take only one penny per day as an allowance as long as the amount doubles each day? That's the Internet — except that it's growing faster. The emphasis suddenly shifts from how many resources are available to how to find the ones you need and, when you've found them, how to use that information responsibly.

Success on the Net: A Beginner's Journey

Jenny teaches fourth grade at a rural elementary school. She has been in the classroom for more than 12 years, teaching grades one through three. This year is her first year as a fourth grade teacher. She's pretty familiar with using a computer, and her pet peeve is students who get her keyboard dirty because they don't wash their hands.

A few months ago, she got a trial account from a local Internet service provider (ISP). After loading the software into her brand-new iMac computer and connecting her modem, she was on her way to her first Internet cyberjourney.

In three weeks, Jenny's class would begin a study of the government. Because she'd never taught government to fourth graders, she didn't have a lot of resources, so she thought about using the Internet to find some. Was this Internet thing really worth the trouble?

She'd heard all the hullabaloo about the World Wide Web (WWW) and decided to use her Web browser, a tool for navigating the WWW, as a starting point. She double-clicked her Netscape Communicator icon. (Netscape Communicator is the name of a program used to browse the WWW. A copy of the Netscape Communicator and Internet Explorer browsers are included on the CD.) She was then officially on the Internet.

Her first step was to visit a site called Yahoo! (www.yahoo.com), a search engine she'd read about in a magazine. Her browser revealed a Web page containing a blank where she could type the keyword (subject) of her Internet search. A *Web page* is a page of pictures and text with clickable links to other Internet resources.

In the Yahoo! search window, she typed

```
government
```

The screen listed more than 150 places to begin looking for information on the government. Yippee! Success! She clicked Government and Politics, which guided her to a WWW page that looked like Figure 1-1.

She quickly realized that her search would pay off. For the next 20 minutes or so, she browsed selected sites, cutting and pasting information from the screen into her word processor and carefully noting and citing the source of each nugget of information.

Because the Netscape Communicator browser program that she was using also gave her access to newsgroups (electronic bulletin boards), she spent a few minutes reading messages from other educators who were teaching government.

Next, she used an FTP program to *download* (copy to her computer) a program for her computer that allowed students to play a game that explains how a bill becomes a law. (She could have used her Web browser, too!) Next, she visited the White House home page (www.whitehouse.gov), where she clicked on an icon and heard the President speak a personal welcome message. (Yes, the Net talks.) She rounded out her tour by scanning several online magazines for articles.

As she traveled through the Net, she remembered to add electronic bookmarks so she could return to the marked places later with her class. (Chapters 6 and 7 discuss how to create a bookmark.)

After about an hour, she had tons of information to use in preparing her lesson plans, as well as a list of great places on the Internet for her class to visit. As she explained what she'd experienced, the two things she'd learned from her first expedition were

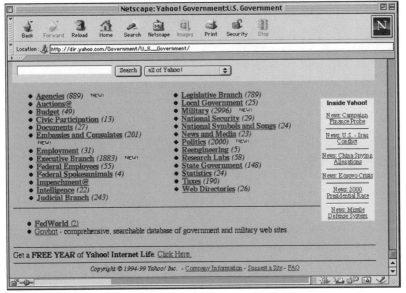

Figure 1-1:
The result of
a Yahoo!
search for
government.

✔ The Internet offers a huge number of resources.

✔ Using the Internet is easier than she thought.

Of course, she still had her work cut out for her. She had to figure out how to use all this information and how to manage and organize the lesson so that her students could experience the same success when they searched for information on the Internet.

It worked. She's hooked. Enough said.

Not every Internet search goes this smoothly. Many Internet searches, especially for topics more narrow than *government,* can take far more time. As you and your students explore, you'll encounter occasional false starts and dead ends. You'll get busy signals from computers and click in the wrong place from time to time. You'll want to throw your computer out the window and rip out the network connection or phone line at times. Never fear, though; chances are, you'll find information about whatever you want, and the time you spend online will probably give you even more ideas for other activities. If you'd like more tips on searching, check out Chapter 8.

Chapter 2

Does the Internet Really Belong in Schools?

In This Chapter

▶ The Internet: What good is it?

▶ Ten great reasons to get your class on the information superhighway

▶ Talking to parents and your community about the Internet

▶ Nothin' but Net

▶ Combating FUD

*I*s the Internet just another passing fad in that huge closet full of plug-in tools that we call educational technology? I don't think so. People said the same thing about calculators and computers not too long ago. Those tools are still around. The real question may be: Will educators (or anyone) be able to understand the implications of instant access to billions of bits of information in the classroom? Will anyone?

Well, we educators are a pretty shrewd bunch. We've managed to squeeze success from a lot of new initiatives and educational innovations — some that survived the test of time and some that didn't. You know the list: open classrooms, outcome-based education, new math, standardized testing, and, yes, ballpoint pens, calculators, and computers.

Get ready to adjust your sails. The winds of the communication age are blowing. It's up to us to grab the video-game generation by the brains and use the Internet to give them something to think about.

The Internet: What Good Is It?

Remember the movie *Shane*? In one scene, Shane takes out his gun and does some fancy shooting, and then when he realizes that his greatest admirer, a young, impressionable lad, is beginning to think that guns are fun, he zaps the kid — with a great lesson. He explains that a gun is just a tool. By itself it's neither bad nor good. The person who uses a gun is the one who determines whether the gun is good or bad. Don't you love those rare nuggets of wisdom in the movies?

The Internet, like many other tools at our disposal, is just a tool. It's a powerful tool, though, which offers students opportunities.

Good Internet tool users have the opportunity to do the following:

- Exchange information via global communication links
- Retrieve information exactly when you need it for use in the classroom (or anywhere else)
- Add to the body of human knowledge (Whoa! Think about the potential of being able to publish instantly to millions of people. Kind of gives you chills, doesn't it?)
- Have a lot of fun browsing the ideas, thoughts, and creations of others

In case you need specific education-related reasons to jump onto the information superhighway, they're in the following section.

Ten Great Reasons to Get Your Class on the Information Superhighway

This tool called the Internet is not the single most important tool that will bring about educational reform . . . or is it? I learned everything I know about the Internet from other people. Whether I'm chatting electronically with other educators in the Education Forums on America Online, reading (shameless self-promotion alert) *Web Publishing For Teachers* (published by IDG Books Worldwide, Inc.), or scanning course outlines for an electronically delivered Introduction to the Internet course, I find new information almost daily. The following ten reasons for logging onto the Net come from many conversations, both electronic and face to face, with people like you who are pondering the Net's possibilities.

The Internet presents real-world examples of integrated knowledge

The Internet provides a great deal of electronic information that's organized in different ways and represents many different topics. As students explore Internet resources, they'll discover how the information they're accessing fits into real life. They'll see that the people working at the Center for Disease Control and Prevention in Atlanta maintain medical databases as well as information about landforms and climate (science meets geography). They'll notice as they scan the files at NASA and note that its libraries are packed with technical writing that describes the design and specifications of the latest shuttle payloads (writing meets mathematics). Later, you may even challenge your students to create their own World Wide Web (WWW) page, giving them an opportunity to link resources that they find useful and important. The Internet is a place where electronic tools can help form the link between learning and life.

The Internet facilitates collaborative learning

You will soon discover that one of the most efficient ways for your students to use and explore the resources available on the Internet is through project-centered activities for small groups. The Internet is so big and offers so many resources that teamwork makes a huge positive difference in the quality of the outcome of any Internet search.

Send four groups of students to separate Internet connections to search for information about any subject; they'll all come back with different information from different sources written with different biases, for different audiences, and with differing levels of credibility. Bring those four groups back together and ask them one question to get the collaboration going: "What is the best (or most useful) information and why?"

Of course, there's that "excited learners are contagious" thing that we educators all understand. Put one student on the Net and watch how many others flock around. Imagine the possibilities!

The Internet offers opportunities for telementoring

Global communication means potentially connecting lots of people, each of whom has lots of ideas. This abundance of ideas translates into lots of opportunities to learn from others. I look back and marvel at those special teachers who have helped me over the rough spots in education, people such as the gifted and caring Mrs. McCue who guided me through student teaching. I think about the fact that there are probably many Mrs. McCues just waiting to teach us all something. You can harness the power of the Internet for teaching, for learning, for chasing away the "teacher isolation" monster, and even for some curbside psychiatry when the going gets rough.

The Internet is all about communicating

Editing a Supreme Court decision and posting it to the Internet takes about eight hours. Finding it takes about eight seconds. The Internet represents a communication opportunity that has a profound impact on everything from politics to potato farming. Posting a message on the Internet and getting replies from Russia is cool. Logging onto the Internet and chatting live with anthropologists who are exploring Mayan ruins is an amazing experience. Students telecommunicating with their peers no matter where in the world they live is about as exciting a prospect as I can imagine.

The Internet can cater to different learners in different ways

Like a good library, the Internet has print, sound, photograph, and video resources. The kind of information that students choose to access and the way they choose to access it is often as revealing about the students' capabilities as the quality of the information they collect. The Internet offers opportunities to browse freely or to target information with excruciating precision. Everyone from the reluctant learner to the bookworm can find something of interest on the Net. It's up to educators, of course, to help them explore their interests and channel their efforts toward furthering their educational goals. With sufficient goals and direction, virtually every student can experience success.

The Internet is a culturally, racially, physically, sexually blind medium

The first time I used electronic mail with my students, I realized that communication through the Internet was blind. After several exchanges of creative writing during a project designed with a teacher friend from Connecticut, my students discovered that they had been writing to other students who were from two to five grade levels ahead of them. Suddenly, they realized that they could communicate effectively with the "big kids." You should have seen the looks on the middle-schoolers' faces when they saw a class picture from the Connecticut high school (and vice versa!).

The Internet is blind to many things. On some online services, the most popular online personalities have physical disabilities. Nobody knows. It doesn't seem to matter. It's pure communication.

The downside is that because much of communication is nonverbal — for example, observing facial features, silly grins and all — you can lose something in the translation. But that makes the challenge even sweeter.

The Internet provides an outlet for creativity

Some people draw, some paint, some sing, some write. You and your students can share all of these things on the Internet. Today's powerful hardware and new advances in software that have made incorporating, viewing, and listening to multimedia easier than ever.

Try challenging your students to think of a theme that best represents their lives and have them author Web pages based upon the theme. Suggest that they push the limit as they learn the process by using multimedia (where appropriate) and other forms of creative communication on their site. You will no doubt find some of your students are "diamonds in the rough" when it comes to expressing themselves in a new digital medium.

The Internet allows everyone to become a publisher

Publishing a book like *The Internet For Teachers,* 3rd Edition takes lots of talented people and around a ton of cold, hard cash. The Internet (the Web in particular) allows anyone with an interest, hobby, passion, idea, business, or, unfortunately, perversion, to slap content into cyberspace where anyone can access it with a few keystrokes — and it costs practically nothing. After you and your students learn to publish Web pages, my guess is that you'll jump on the bandwagon and tell everyone what's in your brain.

The Internet is a community (maybe)

If you ask the experts (you know, anyone travelling more than 100 miles to speak to you), most will tell you the jury is still out as to whether the Internet is a true community. I like Webster's definition of community — (paraphrased) *a unified body of individuals with common interests or characteristics, interacting with various other members of their species.* The Internet is unified (by definition), but are the people? The best answer may be "Well, sort of." Many criticize the Net as a time-eating simulation of life; others note that the population of the Internet is far from diverse. Women, children, and poor and elderly people are under-represented. But wait — the Internet is just an infant. As innovations like video and audio enter the mainstream, perhaps true community will evolve more quickly. What do you think?

The Internet provides information not available in your media center

The good news is that the amount of information available on the Internet is vast. The bad news is that the amount of information available on the Internet is vast. The Internet provides different types of media (audio, video, text) and certainly quite a diverse set of subjects — more than any media center or library could handle (or would probably want to handle). Of course, really big libraries, such as the one represented in Figure 2-1, can now connect directly to other really big libraries, making access to the world's largest library system easier than flipping through what's left of your card catalog. And, just because the information is there doesn't mean it's correct, does it? (See Chapters 3, 8, 9, and 22 for lots more information on the responsible use of the Internet in schools).

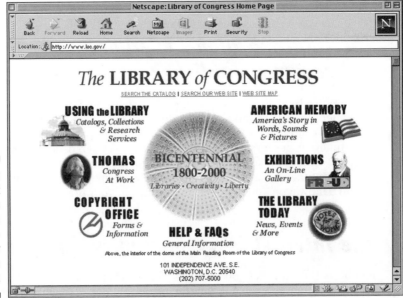

Figure 2-1:
The Internet
provides
information
not avail-
able in your
media
center.

That's the big ten! You can surely come up with more reasons as you think about the role the Internet might play in your classroom.

What's the next step? Get busy and convince the decision-makers and stake-holders in your community that you need this Internet tool in your classroom. Read on!

Talking to Parents and Your Community about the Internet

A science teacher friend of mine decided that setting up a cage and raising white mice in his classroom would be a great idea. He did his homework and figured out the cost, drew up some sample lesson plans, and went to the principal for permission. At first, the principal was less than enthusiastic. After all, mice are hairy and can carry disease. They're messy (the custodians, rulers of the school, would not like that!), and they could escape and terror-ize the faculty. Mr. Science plugged on, driven by the enthusiasm of a possessed mad scientist.

Somehow, Mr. Science convinced the principal that the risk was worth taking, and two weeks later, the classroom had two new residents. Then something happened. Students began, on their own, to ask questions and express a desire to learn more about their classroom neighbors. Some went to the library to find out more about the classroom critters; others drew pictures, asked questions, and smuggled food back from the school cafeteria. Mr. Science's lessons were riveting. Other teachers came to visit. Parents began to call the school and write notes about how glad they were that the principal and teacher had allowed the mice to visit the classroom.

Two years later, the white mouse cage had grown into a condominium, and George and Gracie, the mice, had quite a few roommates. Lots, if you count the iguana, Goliath; the hamsters, Moe, Larry, and Curly; and all the rest of the zoo. Other teachers caught on, too. They looked at the project and made it their own, and the synergy that was created made for better lesson plans that kept the critters (and the students) very busy.

Introducing the Internet to parents, administrators, and the classroom isn't that different from Mr. Science's adventure.

The reason this project was so successful is that the teacher

- ✔ Had an idea that brought surprise and wonder to the classroom
- ✔ Planned well
- ✔ Was enthusiastic
- ✔ Started small
- ✔ Expanded on the original idea
- ✔ Took the time to conduct ongoing evaluation of both project and process

In the beginning, be sure to take the time to look at the technology and see whether it makes sense to you. The Internet has gotten (more than?) its fair share of criticism, much of it by short-sighted people who see it as a diversion instead of an information-rich environment. Just as some activities are best carried out with pencil and paper, perhaps the Net is the best way to accomplish some of the tasks that you and your students attempt.

Next, think about how you and your students can use the Internet. Will it enhance instruction? Can it be a useful reference tool? Will it be a learning center or a full-time classroom resource?

Finally, think about how you want to begin. Will you start with an e-mail exchange or with a search for information on your classroom's latest addition to the critter farm? Armed with a few simple plans and a bit of technical expertise to back it up, you're well on your way.

Nothing but Net?

These days, it's not really difficult to convince your school board, principal, or district technology coordinator that networking is a great idea. The media storm surrounding the Internet has raised the consciousness of even the most Luddite educator. But in our zest to get wired, creating unreasonable expectations about what teaching and learning will be like when all the wiring is finally complete is easy.

Grab a piece of chalk at your next faculty or PTA meeting and run to the chalkboard. In your best D'Nealian, write the words "Wired for what?" and stand back. This question is a fundamental one that will haunt everyone after the fury of wire-pulling gives way to the realities of the classroom. See if anyone can really answer the question.

Here's how several educators and administrators answered the question in a recent discussion I had in conjunction with the incredible National Educational Computing Conference (www.neccsite.org). I asked each of them to state a feature and a benefit to using the Internet in the classroom, and I summarize what they cooked up in Table 2-1.

Table 2-1	Internet Benefits
Feature	**Benefit(s)**
Increased communication	Increased global awareness, more sharing of ideas, better communication with our "customers" (students and their parents)
Richer information sources	Access to more current information, from a greater number of sources; ability to quickly and efficiently collect and compare information from multiple sources
Less isolation in the classroom	Access to people, places, and things that would otherwise be inaccessible
Opportunity to collaborate	Two-way medium that makes collaboration simpler, faster, and more fun
Offers students workplace skills	Builds skills useful in the workplace of today and tomorrow
Changes teaching and learning	Helps educators, students, administrators, and everyone else review their role in light of the other benefits mentioned and offers everyone the opportunity for a high-interest, high-content learning environment (the most powerful reason!)

Working through a "Wired for what?" exercise with your community and peers is a great way to ensure that everyone understands the promises, and limitations, of this amazing medium. Take the time to answer these tough questions now, before the wire-jockeys leave town, and you and your students will reap the rewards well into the future.

Combating FUD

Perhaps the greatest barrier to the introduction of the Internet into most educational situations is FUD. FUD is an acronym for *fear, uncertainty,* and *doubt.* Just as the test drive sells the Ferrari — at least that's what those folks who have megabucks tell me — a proper drive around the Internet can easily allay plenty of FUD.

The best way to set up an Internet test drive for your administration and board members: Take advantage of one or more of the promotions from online services that offer a free hour online, or arrange to use the Internet account of someone who has a connection that enables you to use graphics-based software. (See Appendix A for your options for an Internet connection.) Take the crowd on a little scavenger hunt, showing resources along the way.

One more touch, just so you'll remember. Whip out Print Shop (or your favorite word processor) and print a banner that says "Curriculum drives the use of technology, not vice versa." Focus your presentation on how you can use the Internet's resources in your media center and classroom, not on how to access the resources. Avoid jargon. Smile (especially at your principal, board members, and superintendent!).

Here's a dandy statistic that you can use in your Internet presentation: As of early 1999, more than 3,500 schools regularly published information to the Internet in the form of a home page on the World Wide Web. A *home page* is an electronic Internet document that presents information and gives the user options for jumping to other information resources that the author deems to be interesting or useful. (See Chapter 8 for more information about the Web.)

It's reality time. Textbooks become outdated before they are published. Budgets for educational materials continue to be thin. Libraries and media centers can't keep up with the continued flow of new information. Can your school afford not to investigate the Internet as a source for educational content? Can you afford not to use the Internet as a valuable teaching tool?

Chapter 3

I Told You So: Net Responsibility

In This Chapter

▶ Avoiding potholes on the information superhighway

▶ Introducing the Internet

▶ Maintaining a watchful eye

▶ Thinking ethically

▶ Taking out a contract on your kids

My mother taught me to drive in a bright red Ford Pinto station wagon (with wood-grain sides) in a church parking lot not far from our home. Before she would release me to terrorize the world, she wanted to make sure I was prepared for some of the hazards I might encounter. We parallel parked, we backed in circles, we even made believe there were stop and yield signs. Before long I was the best parking-lot driver you've ever seen.

You know how the story goes. Not long after I got my license, I made an unfortunate decision to take a unfamiliar shortcut on a very rocky dirt road on the way home from the grocery store. I'm not exactly sure what happened, but I know I ran over something that dented the fender (and probably more), and that the "something" was nothing like I had encountered in the church parking lot. That day I learned a lesson — there are some things a Pinto wagon just wasn't designed to do. At the least, I should've driven more slowly, looked ahead, and chosen a better route.

As you and your students navigate the Internet, you need to know where the potholes are and have a strategy for steering around them. As you see in the sections ahead, a little preplanning for your Internet excursions makes the trip much smoother.

Controversy Knocks

Most educators know that sooner or later, controversy follows any innovation or change. The introduction of global resources to the classroom is no exception. As access to databases, electronic mail, computer art, and programs increases, so does the anxiety of your peers and members of your community who don't understand what you're doing.

As in the real world, you and your students will likely stumble on attitudes and opinions that are very different from your own — sometimes even disturbing. The Internet, after all, is a confederacy of single-minded users in a multicultural society. The only thing that governs the content on the Net is the good sense of those who place information there. And, as educators especially understand, not everyone has good sense.

So what's a teacher to do? Do you put all the cards on the table before you introduce the Internet to your school, or do you just stand by and wait until the controversy monster rears its ugly head?

I think the answer is . . . well . . . both. I've developed a plan to help introduce Internet technology to the three *R*s. It's called the three *I*s!

The Three Is

The former CEO of Apple Computer, John Sculley, once said, "The journey is the reward." In some cases, your efforts to introduce the Net to your school in a planned, educational way will both strengthen your resolve and help you appreciate how others think about and learn about the Internet. As you approach the beginning of your journey, check out these three tips:

- Invite
- Introduce
- Integrate

Invite your fellow teachers and community members to sample the water

When I make a presentation at a parent-teacher association meeting or to faculty, I try to focus the group's attention on positive uses of the Internet, not on its pitfalls. Nothing is more dangerous than entering a discussion without all the facts. Most people learn what they know about the Internet from the media or from urban legends that float around and grow into amazing stories of Net use or abuse. You (and your community) need facts.

After your peers and community have firsthand experience of the wealth of resources available on the Internet, they'll have a better idea of its potential uses in the classroom. Only firsthand factual information can facilitate dialogue about the Internet in your school. Chapter 21 has some dandy cyberjourneys that you can try out as you answer questions from the crowd.

Of course, the best way to have people sample the waters is to conduct an after-school class about the Internet. Allow small groups to wander the Net or create cyberjourneys of their own. As you discuss their task, suggest that the focus in using the Internet in the school is both learning about the Internet and learning with the Internet. Find out what their opinions are about the value of each strategy.

Whichever method you use to help folks see what the Net is all about, be sure to shoot straight. Colleges and universities, for the most part, have used educational programs and discussions about responsible use to help purge objectionable graphics from their servers. The Net is, in a way, policing itself. But quite a few things on the Net will give you goose bumps when you read, see, and hear them. Be honest about what you've personally witnessed, if anything, that some people may be uncomfortable with.

After the people who want to dive in and get wet have had their fill, look to your media and technology committee (you do have one, don't you?) to move on to the next step. Be sure that your committee has a broad representation — especially student and parent representatives.

Introduce a set of guidelines

Have you ever driven up to a very busy intersection where the stoplight isn't working? This situation is the quintessential example of how a set of community guidelines — in this case, traffic laws and courtesy — helps things run more smoothly. Sure, the occasional bozo zips through the intersection — and usually pays a dear price, both physically and to the repair shop. But, for the most part, people get through without a scratch. You can, too.

Setting guidelines for the use of the Internet is a great way to ensure that you and your students don't end up as casualties on the information superhighway. The guidelines that you set will help guide administrators, teachers, and students as they find ways to use the technology.

After the decision-makers in your school have taken a test run on the Internet, think about what's important to make the implementation successful. What cost-control issues do you need to consider? Equity issues? Content issues? Training issues? Support issues?

In some cases, schools have to worry about cost considerations. If the call you're placing to log onto the Internet is a toll call, or if you're using a commercial pay-as-you-go service, creating a set of guidelines that relate to your budgetary restrictions is critical. Some online services, such as America Online, enable schools to purchase time in increments of 10, 20, 30, or more hours per month. When the time is up, no more Internet time. Simple, and great for budgeting. But these restrictions make some people very nervous. What if you have a really exciting and innovative project, but you have only 30 minutes left this month? What's a teacher to do? The answer is something teachers are all too familiar with — advance planning.

Equity is also an issue. Are you comfortable with the inevitability that Mr. Jones or Mrs. Smith will be surfing all the time and others will become jealous that they're missing all the great waves of knowledge? Think about

Protecting us from our cyberselves

A number of organizations are thinking about policies and ethics issues that are related to the Net. Among these organizations, the Electronic Frontier Foundation (EFF) is perhaps the one that has the highest profile. Its goal is to "ensure that the principles embodied in the Constitution and the Bill of Rights are protected as new communications technologies emerge." Founded by such high-profile folks as Lotus founder Mitch Kapor, Sun Microsystems founder Bill Joy, and Grateful Dead lyricist John Perry Barlow, the EFF has been very effective in getting the ear of people who matter in Washington. The EFF already has an impressive record in protecting citizens from government interference and helping the computer-using community become aware of issues related to data security, ethics, and free speech. The EFF maintains online support on America Online, CompuServe, and other online services, and it has its own Internet site at www.eff.org.

The EFF isn't alone. Here's a short list of a few other groups that are concerned with issues relating to Internet policy and ethics. As you'll no doubt realize if you request information, each takes a slightly different slant on the issues at hand. All of the groups, however, promote free speech and equal access to electronic communications.

Group   Address

Americans Communicating Electronically (ACE)
www.sba.gov/ACE/

Center for Media Education (CME)
www.cme.org

The Digital Freedom Network (DFN)
www.dfn.org/

Libraries for the Future (LFF)
www.lff.org

finding ways to maximize access to this exciting technology, either through increasing the access to Internet-capable computers or by monitoring time. Think out of the box and try schemes such as issuing time vouchers or rewarding teachers with Internet time for innovative instructional plans.

If your school wants to control the content accessible through the Net, you have some options. Depending on how you access the Net, varying amounts of access control are available. Many universities, for example, lock out access to the much-maligned alt (alternative) newsgroups. The universities aren't concerned about content so much as they are about whether anybody will get their regular schoolwork done because they've turned into Net-addicted cyberjockeys. Some commercial services offer parental control features that may or may not meet your needs. If you're concerned about control issues, contact your Internet provider and find out about your options.

You can also add software and hardware to networks to filter out material that some feel is objectionable. I include lots of details about such options in Chapter 9.

How about training and support? How will teachers learn about the Internet? Should students use valuable time if they haven't been shown the ropes? (The last question is one that only you, as the responsible adult in charge, can answer.) Suffice it to say that this whole Internet business is like a four-legged stool, with a hardware leg, a software leg, a training leg, and a support leg. Leave out a leg and see what happens to the stool. And you thought surfing was hazardous?

Integrate

My friend and school technology coordinator, Dr. Sherah Carr, always says, "The curriculum should drive the use of technology and not the other way around." Nowhere is this statement more true than in using the Internet. The Net, after all, is a huge place. You and your students can spend time wandering aimlessly and get absolutely nothing accomplished. Or you can use the time wisely, enriching and enhancing the curriculum. The choice should be a conscious one.

Now before you jump out of your chair, know that there is something to be said for "playing" on the Net. That's pretty much the way I learned. I got my learner's permit on the information superhighway by getting in and out of places that I'd never heard or thought of. Planning is important, however. Showing your students a valid purpose for the terabytes of information that are floating around out there is essential. However, showing your students the role of the ragged-edged encyclopedia and old magazine articles in research is also important.

Integration means working the wonders of the Net into the parts of the curriculum where they best fit. In some cases, the Internet can be the missing piece in your curriculum puzzle. Integration also means setting curriculum goals and using the Internet as a tool to enhance or enrich instruction. Model this method to others and your journey into the Internet will be richer, as will the journeys of the students you mentor.

Well, there it is. Of course, no plan is perfect. And your school may never be faced with controversy concerning the Net. But if it is, the ayes (and *I*s) have it!

The first K-12 schools connected to the Internet in 1988. If you'd like a list of schools on the Internet, visit Web66 (Figure 3-1) at `web66.coled.umn.edu`. This Web site is a great way to find out how other schools are dealing with integrating the Internet into their curriculum.

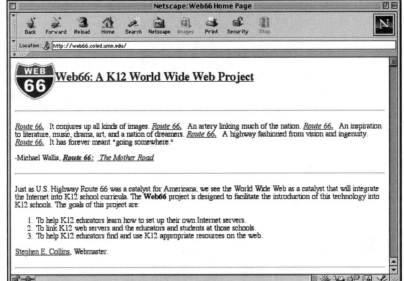

Figure 3-1: Web66 is perhaps the largest collection of school Web sites on the Internet.

Worth Watching

A time will come when someone challenges you or your school about the safety of the Internet. It pays to be informed, especially since most of those broaching the subject aren't. Basically, three aspects of the Internet raise red flags in education (or, similarly, in the home) and are worth monitoring. Here's a look at each of the big three and a way to be proactive in dealing with them before challenges arise.

People

There are many creative people out on the Internet. There are scary people, too. Several teacher friends have recounted instances where students have been stalked or harassed after meeting someone in an electronic chat room (forum) or after posting on a message board. The good news is that by taking some simple precautions, avoiding the weirdoes is pretty easy.

In the event you or your students are being harassed, send a complaint, along with the offending message, to the postmaster of the service provider. In the world of the Internet, *postmaster* refers to the person getting general mail for a site. It's kind of like calling the main number of a large corporation. Usually, the postmaster can be reached by addressing a message to postmaster@ domainname.com (or .edu, .net, and so on).

To avoid the problem before it happens, be sure to coach your students that they should never, *ever* give out their address or phone number (or the school's information) through e-mail, in a newsgroup, on a mailing list, or on online chat without the express permission of a parent, guardian, or teacher.

It also goes without saying (but I'll say it anyway) that at no time should you or your students ever accept an invitation to meet someone in person as a result of an online connection. It's dangerous at best.

Pictures

Just as in many newsstands and on pay cable, photos and video images that are inappropriate for viewing at school abound on the Internet. Some sites use adult age verification systems (age checks based on registration systems, see Figure 3-2) that require passwords to view X-rated material. Others just throw the pictures onto the Net for all to see. As more people learn how to publish to the Web worldwide, more of these pictures may turn up in your students' search sessions.

Aside from turning off your browser's ability to see graphics (which defeats the purpose of the Web's graphical interface), the only thing you can really do to prevent access to objectionable materials is to be vigilant. Watch your students as they surf (software can assist in this monitoring) and let them know in advance that they can expect consequences for breaking the rules.

Dialogue

Places where people post information (pictures and text), like Internet news-groups (see Chapter 14) or online chats (see Chapter 17), are ripe for material you may find objectionable. From inane ramblings to materials preaching hate and destruction, these public forums stretch the boundaries of First Amendment rights. Though the vast majority of chat and newsgroup postings are harmless, there are exceptions.

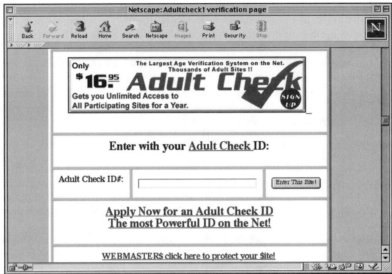

Figure 3-2:
One of several adult verification systems online — a successful example of sites policing themselves.

Most Web servers allow you to filter (restrict) access to newsgroups, picture downloads, and other things that can help these not-always-appropriate resources become more difficult to reach on the Internet. Many colleges and universities, for example, restrict access to alt (alternative) newsgroups. (This restriction is, by the way, still the subject of major controversy at the aforementioned institutions.) For a more complete discussion of this issue, check out Chapter 9.

As I've said before, there's no substitute for a vigilant teacher or parent when students use the Internet at school. Watch 'em, encourage 'em when they follow your policies, and be consistent in enforcement when they break the rules.

InternEthics

Even though the Internet is still the "wild, wild west" of cyberspace — a virtually lawless and totally free environment, people have been talking about Internet ethics and rules since the Net's inception. Groups such as the

Division Advisory Panel of the National Science Foundation's Division of Network Communications Research and Infrastructure (is that a mouthful or what?) have formalized thoughts about unethical and unacceptable activities. They define such activities as those that purposely do any of the following:

- ✔ Seek to gain unauthorized access to the resources of the Internet
- ✔ Disrupt the intended use of the Internet
- ✔ Waste resources (people, capacity, or computer)
- ✔ Destroy the integrity of computer-based information
- ✔ Compromise the privacy of users

Pretty straightforward, no? Scheduling time to read and discuss these statements with your students and talk with your school's technology committee about the issue of ethics on the Internet is a great idea.

After you've taken your students on a tour of the Net and discussed the above list of Internet don'ts, ask them to work in small groups to develop their own Code of Internet Ethics and post each group's work in your classroom. Focus on what effective Internet citizens should know, do, and be like.

You can find more information about Internet ethics through the Software & Information Industry Association (SIIA). The site is also a good repository of information about government and local policy relating to the information industry. Hit the Web and surf to www.siia.net. (For information on entering URLs and using the Web, see Chapters 8, 9, and 10.)

The top ten ways to be a good Internet citizen

1. Never knowingly post or forward information that's not true.

2. Have good manners.

3. Tell people when you like their work.

4. Be creative, not destructive.

5. Always obey copyright laws.

6. Think before you send.

7. Be yourself.

8. Don't use someone else's account or password.

9. Ask for help when you need it.

10. Think before you upload.

(adapted from "Ten Commandments for Computer Ethics," Computer Ethics Institute)

Take Out a Contract on Your Kids

Don't worry, the contract I'm talking about is a simple agreement between you and your students (and their parents) about how, when, and why the Internet is used in the classroom. Having the little piece of paper around (lots of folks call this piece of paper a policy — usually called an acceptable use policy," or AUP) will make you feel better, and it will make what's okay and not okay when surfing the Net very clear to all involved.

Creating a 40-page document that covers all possible angles would probably be pretty easy, but you really don't need that. A brief, well-constructed, well-thought-out document that is collaboratively developed by parents, students, administrators, and fellow teachers is the best bet.

Here are a few questions that you may consider answering as you build your Internet use contract:

- ✔ Is keeping a log of student time and purpose necessary?
- ✔ What are the expectations about adhering to federal, state, and local laws?
- ✔ How about school policies? Should you mention them?
- ✔ What kinds of information (if any) are off-limits?
- ✔ What about copyright laws?
- ✔ What constitutes an "authorized use" and an "authorized access"?
- ✔ What about commercialization and the Internet?
- ✔ How about privacy? Passwords?
- ✔ What are specific expectations for student behavior? What should be done about students who misuse the Net?
- ✔ What are the parent, teacher, and administrative responsibilities related to the contract?
- ✔ Who grants the rights to use the Internet in your school, and who can rescind those rights?
- ✔ Are there time limitations?
- ✔ What happens if someone violates this contract?

I hope that you'll reread my comments about being brief that appear before this too-long listing. You don't, after all, want to scare the students away. They're not buying a house or writing a book. Keep it simple.

After creating your agreement, be sure to develop a plan to inform your students about the contract and decide how it will be signed. Think about enforcement as well. Be as swift with punishment for misuse of the Internet as you are with praise for proper use.

You know your school better than anyone on the outside. Get your media and technology committee together and discuss whether you feel you need policies, guidelines, or contracts for Internet use. Check magazines, online services, and the Internet itself for examples of completed contracts. (I purposely didn't give you a completed contract. Yours will be much better than mine, anyway!) I will share a great site (www.att.com/edresources/ accept.html), shown in Figure 3-3, that seems to be a place where you can find other examples.

Going through the exercise of writing a contract (or AUP) is worth the time and effort. You'll all learn something new, and your journey into the Internet will be much smoother.

Remember, however, that a little forethought and open discussion about responsibility, ethics, and the proper use of the Internet can save you and your students much grief, but no contract can replace close supervision if you're concerned about what students will find.

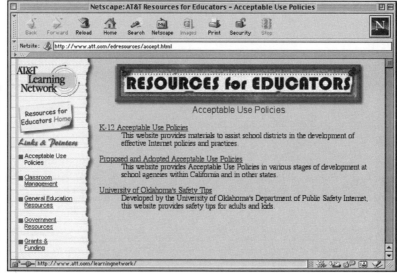

Figure 3-3: AT&T offers some excellent resources to use as you create acceptable use policies for your school.

Part II
Ready, Set, Web!

The 5th Wave   By Rich Tennant

"From now on, let's confine our exploration of ancient Egypt to the Internet."

In this part . . .

*I*n this part, you learn what kind of hardware, software, and connections you need to begin your adventure on the Internet. I'll also introduce you to the most popular Web browsers, some cool tricks for traveling and searching the Internet, and hot new ideas about safe surfing in your classroom. I've topped the chapter off with a short introduction that will give you an idea of what's involved in creating Web pages in your classroom.

If you've already connected to the Internet, jump to Part III, but be sure to check out the chapters in this section entitled "The Search Is On" and "Safe Surfing." You'll be glad you did.

Chapter 4

Getting Started

● ●

In This Chapter

▶ Building an Internet shopping list

▶ Selecting the right hardware

▶ Choosing your gateway to the Net

▶ Getting with the programs!

▶ A modem is a modem is a modem

▶ Searching for a phone line

▶ Getting your Macintosh or Windows PC ready for connection to the Net

▶ Budgeting for Internet access

● ●

*Y*ou can relax. You're about to realize that collecting only five simple things can get you on your way to Internet access. The good news is that between the software that accompanies this book and the hardware that's already in your school, you probably have 90 percent of what you need to connect to the Internet.

In this chapter, you find the "four easy pieces" you need to begin surfing the Internet, a few ideas about budgeting for telecommunications, and the low-down on what you need to do to get your computer ready for logging onto the Net for the first time.

What Do I Need?

This section describes exactly what you need to make an Internet connection. First, look at the basic diagram, Figure 4-1, that shows the "big four" items you need: hardware, software, a physical connection to the Internet (modem and a phone line or a network connection), and an Internet account.

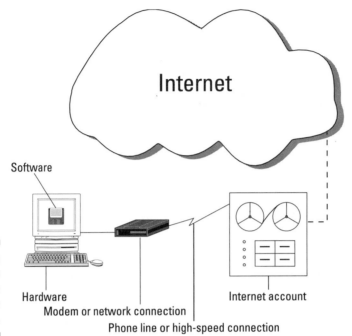

Figure 4-1:
Four things
you need to
connect to
the Internet.

Software

Hardware

Modem or network connection

Phone line or high-speed connection

Internet account

You probably already have a computer and a modem or you use a computer in your school that connects to the Internet through a network. The software that comes with this book should help you well on your way to surfing the Net. You find step-by-step instructions for getting lots of other free tools or tools for other operating systems. Take a look at each section that follows to see how to build the vehicle for your first trip on the information superhighway.

All those chips and no place to go

As of March 1999, nearly 9 million computers were connected to the Internet, ranging from Amigas to Apples, IBMs to Dells, Sun workstations to dumb terminals, and mainframes to minicomputers. Some of these machines, usually big ones (but not always), are the computers that link other computers and networks together (*servers*). Still others are regular desktop computers (*clients*) that extract information from the host computers.

The great news is that you can use just about any computer to connect to the Internet. The only caveat is that you have to have enough memory (*RAM*) to run the software that you use to navigate the Internet and enough hard drive space to handle downloading files or processing and viewing pictures that you download.

If you're using a Macintosh or a PC that's running Windows, I suggest at least 16MB (megabytes) of RAM. _RAM_ is the electronic holding area where your programs and documents live while your computer is on. Having more RAM enables you to work more quickly and efficiently as you process the information that you retrieve from the Net.

About passwords

Whether you're using an online service, a university network, or an Internet service provider, you should never, repeat, never give your password to anyone else. It can be just as valuable (and as potentially dangerous) as your PIN number for your automatic bank teller machine. Here are a few tips for protecting your password:

✔ **Change your password regularly:** The majority of students respect your right to keep your password private. However, some students make it their life's quest to discover your password. Foil them by changing it regularly. And please, don't write it down under the blotter on your desk, tape it to the bottom of your keyboard, or write it on the corner of your grade book. They look there. If you have a really rotten memory, just write it down and stick it in your wallet or purse. But, just to be safe, split the password on two tiny pieces of paper.

✔ **Use a combination of alphabetical and numeric characters:** It's tempting to use the principal's name or the initials of the school as a password — don't. That's the first thing someone trying to gain unauthorized access to your account may try. Make up a password that combines letters and numbers (in upper and lower case) that have some meaning to you but not to others. Try the number of years you've been a teacher and the first and last letters of your two sisters' names, for example (15ScLw). Remember, most passwords are case sensitive!

✔ **Look over your shoulder before typing your password:** Just as teachers have eyes in the back of their heads, students have razor-sharp vision when it comes to getting their teacher's password. Most programs show your password as •••••••• when you enter it so it's protected from prying eyes, but remember, students can see your fingers on the keyboard, too.

✔ **Resist the temptation to use an autologin program:** Autologin settings in your software enable you to access the Internet with a simple mouse click, without having to remember the password. With autologin, you pre-enter your password and save it to disk. This method is very handy when you're in a hurry, but it's also a cinch for others to use when they want unauthorized access to your account. I'd say that you should use autologin only if you, or members of your family, are the only users of your computer and unauthorized users are never anywhere around your computer. (In other words, it's the computer that's in your home or in some other very controlled environment.)

Now, I know this must seem like overkill, but I've seen what can happen when a student breaks into a school account and sends out e-mail messages to the world about the "vicious history teacher." A word to the wise. . . .

The moral of this story? You can never have too much RAM or too large of a hard drive. Many of the popular browser programs I discuss in this book require moderate space on your hard drive to install. Those browser programs eat up lots more space because they often temporarily store, or *cache,* files to make your Internet experience faster. Remember when you thought you could never fill a 5 ¼-inch floppy? Now I'm wrestling with where to put the 3 gigabytes of data that I use on a regular basis.

If you're in the process of making a decision about what computer to use in your classroom and you want an awesome resource, check out *Macs For Teachers,* by my good IDG Books buddy and teacher friend Michelle Robinette. You may also want to check out *PCs For Teachers,* 2nd Edition, by Pam Toliver and Carol Y. Kellogg (both published by IDG Books Worldwide, Inc.). Both are fact-filled, and you'll laugh your way to becoming the computer guru in your school.

Your gateway to the Net

Perhaps the most important choice you make is how to connect to the Internet. If your school already has a connection through your school or district network — you're ready. If not, you have to decide whether to create your own network or use a modem (or even the school's cable TV system) to reach an outside Internet provider such as AOL or Mindspring. The outside provider (or your schoolwide network) supplies your gateway to the Internet and your very own Internet e-mail address. More and more people are putting their e-mail addresses on their business cards. You're a *professional* educator — you should have a business card, too. Get one and put your e-mail address on it.

How you access the Internet determines, in large part, what resources you have access to, as well as whether you operate from a graphical interface or suffer from command-prompt disease (a throw-back to the days when you typed **copy** to copy a file instead of using a single keystroke). You need to ask some essential questions before you select a provider. Asking essential questions is so important that I devote an entire section in Appendix A to them.

The Internet on America Online

America Online, born in 1989, has spread like wildfire. The online service is the largest in the world and currently hosts around 8,000,000 subscribers and more than 4,000,000 sessions a day. It is a virtual circus at AOL headquarters trying to keep up with increasing user demands, but they're managing it well. (Couldn't resist the circus metaphor since AOL's headquarters in Vienna, Virginia, is right next door to Ringling Brothers' headquarters.) Because information providers are flocking to AOL like kids to an ice-cream truck, the quantity and quality of information available continues to grow.

The biggest difference in using AOL as your primary provider is that a visit to AOL is a bit like a visit to a planned community, with neat rows of houses (content *channels*) and lots of kid-safe content. They also have a wonderful "Research and Learn" area online that's chock full of useful resources for classroom and home. Meanwhile, most other ISPs just dump you on the information highway and ask you to find your own way around.

You can access AOL through most school-wide networks through TCP/IP connection options. That is, you can launch AOL and have it work through your current network Internet connection. All you need is an AOL account number and password. (For help, check out the "My AOL" preferences menus on AOL.)

The interface

Like other online services, the folks at AOL ship you a front-end program that provides a *graphical user interface* (GUI). From the very beginning, AOL's clean, friendly interface is the very thing that sets it apart from the other guys. The AOL gurus ensure that what you see is visually pleasing and intuitive. If you're a freebie-watcher like I am, you can even snag a demo disk from AOL that offers 100 hours of online time. That way, you and your students can decide if you like the service before spending money for it.

The opening screen, shown in Figure 4-2, gives you easy access to the myriad of resources that AOL offers. Clickable buttons for AOL *channels* such as shopping, sports, kids, news, the Internet, and entertainment help visitors get where they want to go quickly. As the creative folks at AOL continue to evolve the interface, I suspect that you may see even more bells and whistles. Whether you're a Windows or Macintosh user, you can already click your way through short online movies, vivid graphics, and integrated Internet access. These services are only a hop, skip, and a much faster connection away from full-length video!

Figure 4-2:
AOL offers an easy portal to the Internet and a well-organized online community.

Internet access

AOL currently offers many Internet resources to users. They include

- ✔ A seamless e-mail gateway that enables you to send and receive e-mail from Internet users as easily as you send and receive messages from other AOL junkies.

- ✔ A powerful, integrated Web browser, shown in Figure 4-3, makes mining the Web as easy as jumping around on AOL. You can also run your favorite browser (Netscape Communicator or Internet Explorer) after you sign on to AOL instead of using the browser that AOL integrates.

- ✔ A Gopher/WAIS and telnet interface that's easy to use (and the Gopher icon has cheeks that may make you giggle).

- ✔ FTP (file transfer protocol) via a point-and-click metaphor that's as easy as clearing the hallways at the last bell of the day.

- ✔ Usenet newsgroup access — you pick 'em, you read 'em. (AOL doesn't censor which newsgroups you can subscribe to, so watch for students who stray down forbidden paths.)

- ✔ Access to chats, both on the AOL service, and on the Internet.

- ✔ Mailing lists that give you an easy way to fill your mailbox with lots of tips and ideas from users all over cyberspace.

You reach all these resources through the Internet Connection menu (Keyword: **Internet**). In addition to links to the Internet, you also find other Internet resources, such as online magazines, message boards, and Internet tutorials.

Figure 4-3:
AOL has an integrated Web browser. To launch it, enter a URL and click GO.

Content and organization

AOL offers a virtual cornucopia (did I really say that?) of educational resources. From online conferences to school-to-school projects, you can find lots to browse. The nifty Exam Exchange and Lesson Plan Exchange libraries provide tons of fresh ideas, and the education libraries are brimming with software for you to download.

You find Internet resources ranging from "Zen and the Art of the Internet" (the UNIX lover's guide to the Net) to FAQ (frequently asked questions) files. A very active message board area where AOL answers questions (even from newbies) rounds out AOL's Internet support resources.

The intuitive interface provides a good organizational scheme for educational and Internet resources. Here are a few must-visit locations and the AOL Keywords that you need to remember:

- **Research & Learn:** A collection of education-related resources
- **Education:** The main education area on AOL
- **TIN:** Teacher's Information Network
- **KIDS:** Kids Only Online
- **Internet:** Internet connection (Keywords: **web**, **FTP**, and **newsgroups** also work)
- **Reference** or **Research:** Reference sources, including links to Internet resources

If you're concerned about access to "objectionable" content, nobody beats AOL. Their parental controls (Keyword: **parental controls**) offer control of incoming and outgoing e-mail, instant messaging, access to chat rooms, and lots more. It's fabulous that these folks have thought in advance about such things!

AOL is also doing something I wish the other guys would think about: incorporating Internet resources into its regular online areas. In the Politics area online (Keyword: **Politics**), for example, you find links to Internet sites nestled in between AOL resources. You may even stumble upon applicable multimedia files (audio, video) there, too. That makes sense. Bravo, AOL!

Cost

AOL offers monthly subscriptions and special billing plans for schools. Call 800-227-6364 or 800-344-6219 for more information.

The bleeding edge

Being in the online service business must be tough. Everyone expects you to have the latest and greatest tools available, all wrapped in a clean, easy-to-use interface. Nowadays, all the large online services are close to offering the full suite of Internet services, but not without problems. In early 1994, one service lost more than 4,000 e-mail messages while trying to make things better. Another service experienced a catastrophic 19-hour outage in 1996, wreaking havoc among businesses and personal communication and an all-too-dependent public. These days, of course, networks are more hefty and there are levels of backup that supposedly guard against such things. No network is perfect, though, so beware.

If you stop and think about it, being the first out of the starting block with anything is risky, especially with technology. Being on the leading (or is it bleeding?) edge of telecommunications is fraught with peril. Competitors snapping at your heels. Users screaming that they want it *now!* Not that I feel sorry for the online services, mind you; they're making billions of dollars.

My job enables me to visit lots of schools that also are on the bleeding edge. You know what? Those are the places where I see a staff that's enthusiastic about technology. That's where the excitement seeps from school to community. Sure, you may get nicked now and then, but the ultimate rewards are far greater. Be on the bleeding edge; it's worth it. End of sermon.

Get with the program

The software that you need for Internet access depends on how you decide to connect. If you connect via an online service, all the software you need comes on the disk you get in the mail with your subscription kit. Users of school or university networks are probably already physically connected to the Internet, so all you need are tools like browsers and e-mail programs and a bit of information about how to configure your computer for Internet access.

If you connect via an Internet service provider, most providers send you a disk that's preconfigured with all the necessary software when you subscribe. Simply install the programs on your computer, and you're on your way!

If your Internet service provider doesn't send you any software, you're in luck. Simply use the programs that are on the CD in the back of this book. (See Appendix D for details about the CD.) You find information about how to get other useful software and software updates throughout this book. (See "Getting Your Computer Ready for Connection to the Net," later in this chapter.)

A modem is a modem is a modem

A *modem* is the hardware device that translates the electronic signal from your computer into a form that's transmittable over a telephone line.

(Modem stands for modulator-demodulator, in case anyone asks in the teacher's lounge.)

Modems generally come with two cables, one to connect to the serial or com port on your computer; the other, a standard telephone cable, to connect to your telephone wall jack.

You have only two decisions to make when you purchase a modem:

▶ Do you want an internal or external modem?

▶ How fast do you want to travel the information superhighway?

When you think about internal and external modems, think about the future. Your choice may depend on whether you're a nomad or a settled soul. If you're likely to purchase a new computer within the next year or two or may need to use the modem somewhere other than with your computer, consider an external modem. If you're using a laptop or a computer that's in a place where you have limited desktop space, an internal modem is fine.

One neat thing about external modems is that the only real difference in modems for Macs and PCs is the cable that runs from the computer to the modem, and you can change that. So purchasing an external modem ensures that you can switch platforms should the gotta-buy-a-new-computer bug hit you anytime soon.

There are also network modems. These are modems that work over telephone or cable TV lines and more than one user can share them. Check with your technology coordinator to find out if you have (or need) a network modem.

Because the whole point of owning a modem is to move data back and forth through the telephone lines, the faster you move that data, the better. When shopping for a modem, always get the fastest modem you can afford. Modem speeds are expressed as *Kilobits per second*, with numbers such as 28.8 (28,800), 33.6 (33,600), and 56 (56,000) Kbps. Of course, if you connect through your schoolwide network, you're probably whizzing along at T-1 speeds (more than 1Mbps), so this whole modem discussion is moot. Wait until you get home, though, where you don't have a network. The Net seems to crawl along. Technology is amazing, isn't it?

The industry standard now is 56K (56,000 bps), so if you're buying now (especially for use at home), don't settle for less than a 56Kbps modem that supports the V.90 standard (the most compatible and universal standard for modem protocols). You can also purchase what I refer to as "four-letter-word" services like ISDN and ADSL. ISDN (allegedly "I Still Don't Know" or "Improvements Subscribers Don't Need") uses standard phone wires and plugs into a box that works like a modem in your home or school. ISDN can transmit 128Kbps (much faster than 56K, huh?). One word of warning, the phone companies really make ISDN connectivity difficult. It's pricey because it requires your phone provider to install special connections to some back-end machinery to get you up and running. You inevitably may have to engage in a techno-geeky conversation with someone who knows nothing about communications technology trying to justify why your bill includes per-call charges for things like "multilocation services."

ADSL (Asynchronous Digital Subscriber Line) is yet another alternative to POTS (plain old telephone service). ADSL can run at two, three, or even six *million* bits per second. Wow. ADSL is supposed to offer "video on-demand." Your service provider and the telephone company generally deliver these services. (Are you shaking with fear yet?) It's still experimental and is limited to small service areas. ADSL isn't ubiquitous and still has some technical kinks, so I'd stamp it not-yet-ready-for-prime-time, IMHO. (All these acronyms! *IMHO* is Internet-speak for "In My Humble Opinion".)

If you want to investigate Internet connections at faster than dial-up speeds for your school, you have several options. Your school can pay for the installation of a super fast line, called a T-1 (about $1000/month) or T-3 line (around $20,000/month!), or a not nearly as fast, but quite adequate ISDN connection which will set you back considerably less change, but will likely cause traffic jams on your info highway. (Super fast lines are sometimes known as *leased lines* because you pay a premium to lease the line from the phone company.) You need a T-1 or T-3 line if you want to become your own Internet service provider (that is, have a direct, 24-hour, hard-wired connection to the Net). Note that the figures mentioned above are on the high side and substantial education discounts are often available through partnerships with service providers or telecom companies.

Walls o' Fire

Now that you've been initiated as a true Internet geek, it's time to let you in on a truly geeky concept — firewalls. If you use your school or district network to store student information, such as grades and personal information including address and phone, you don't want that information travelling outside the closed network (a.k.a. LAN) that serves your education needs. A *firewall* is a system placed between your network and the outside world to ensure things don't leak out (or hackers don't chop their way in) to get access to confidential information.

In most cases, the internal network (intranet) doesn't connect directly to the external network that is the Internet. This is the safest, most foolproof method of protecting data. There are other methods, using things like *proxy servers* (somewhat more technical than I want to get in this book) to route traffic through password protected environments. In the case of a proxy server, for example, e-mail can flow in both directions, but folks can't see or access other information (databases, and so on) on your network. At least in theory. Caveat emptor!

Getting Your Computer Ready for Connection to the Net

Before your personal computer can "speak" to the Internet, it needs to have access to the programs that make that connection. On the Macintosh, the operating system already has the Internet connection programs you need, TCP/IP. Some Windows machines already have the programs you need, however you may need a program like WinSock if you have an older operating system. In the following sections, I outline, step-by-step, how to get your computer online. Doing so is not really difficult, only a couple of steps on your Mac and only a few more on your Windows PC. Well, then again, it's easier than redoing your classroom bulletin board — and it takes far fewer steps.

CyberMacintosh

If you're a Macintosh owner with Mac OS 8 or newer, you're in luck. Most of what you need to connect to the Net is already in your computer. If you have an Internet service provider, all you need to do is enter some information into a control panel program called TCP/IP and spend a minute or two entering some information into your browser to allow it to use mail and newsgroups.

Window (s) on the Net

In order to access the Net with a PC running Windows 95 or 98, there's a nifty program called Dial-Up Networking that serves your needs. Windows 3.x users need two pieces of software: PPP software and TCP/IP software. The TCP/IP software helps your computer speak the language of the Internet, while the PPP software manages the pipeline.

Windows 98 comes with an automated sign-up program for several Internet service providers. To sign up or use an existing account (one you establish on another computer), click Start⇨Programs⇨Online Services and then select whatever service you prefer.

If you want to use an account other than the ones with automated sign-up, or you're using a network, there's a nifty Internet Connection wizard. Run the wizard by clicking the Connect to the Internet button on your Windows Desktop, or by clicking Start⇨Programs⇨Internet Explorer⇨Connection Wizard.

When you finish configuring, you should have a Dial-Up Networking icon and a choice on the Programs menu for your Internet provider. To access your account via modem, double-click the Dial-Up Networking icon to run the program and then click Connect.

A word for older Mac users
(uh, users of older Macs)

MacTCP is an extension that enables your Macintosh to speak the language of the Net: TCP/IP. MacPPP is the control panel that enables TCP/IP to work over a serial connection (as with modems).

Here's a screen shot of MacTCP. You get the IP Address from your Internet provider. Clicking the More button reveals more blanks to fill in.

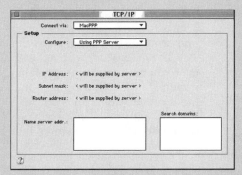

TCP/IP

MacTCP

The control panel (MacPPP or a shareware equivalent) stores specific information about the computer that you're connecting to. The following figure shows the MacPPP control panel configured for an internal modem connected to the Internet service provider, Mindspring.

If you're connecting to the Internet via most information providers or through a local area network, these programs may come to you pre-configured. (Ask your system administrator to give you a hand.) All you have to do is drag them into your Control Panel's folder on your Macintosh hard drive.

You don't need MacTCP or a driver if you're connecting to the Internet through an online service such as America Online — those things are built into the front-end software.

You don't need the aforementioned programs if you're connecting to the Internet through an online service such as America Online, or MSN (Microsoft Network) — these programs are usually built into the front-end software.

To make your life even easier, I included the configuration tools you need for both Macs and Windows in the form of a special Internet sign-on kit from my favorite ISP, Mindspring. Just insert the CD and follow the configuration instructions on the screen!

What about WebTV?

If you don't have a computer, there is an option for accessing the Internet: WebTV. This hardware and service combo is available from Microsoft (www.microsoft.com/webtv) and works kind of like regular dial-up services, but has a customized interface for your TV screen. When you purchase WebTV, you get a box you connect to your TV, a remote control, a remote keyboard (a highly recommended option), and a monthly subscription for Internet access. You need a telephone jack nearby, too, because WebTV doesn't use your cable TV line (unless you're lucky enough to live in a community with specially configured Internet services delivered through your cable).

The WebTV service hasn't caught on yet — mainly because people still associate personal computers with Internet access. (Did you figure out that the "box" you get with WebTV is really a computer?) The other reason people are slow to adopt WebTV is that you have to pay a monthly fee, and because, for some reason, the WebTV folks don't play by the same rules for displaying content as Communicator and Internet Explorer do. This means you simply can't access some sites (especially some with certain kinds of multimedia) and may experience "Internet yuck" when accessing sites tuned for more conventional browsers. Another gotcha of WebTV is that it's generally a *read-only* medium, that is, the ability to print or save files to a floppy isn't built in. (There are optional devices that can help, however.) Only the future knows how much success this connection method may have in homes. Schools should probably opt for less expensive, more standard network access connectivity via computers for their Net connections; although the WebTV wizards are reportedly investigating other network connection options for schools and businesses.

What next?

Okay, you have your software in order. Now here's a checklist of items you need from your service provider so that you can fill in all the blanks in your MacTCP and WinSock/Dial-Up networking software. (I've put some samples in parentheses so you know what to look for.)

If you have preconfigured software, skip all this!

Internet Information Checklist

1. Your Internet provider address: (it'll look something like this: 123.123.78.90)

    (This number is sometimes called a *dotted quad.* Is that geek-speak or what?)

2. Your user name (login name): (fflintstone)

3. Your password: (letters and/or numbers)

4. Your local gateway/IP address: (`123.123.255.255`)

5. Your domain name: (`bedrock.com`)

6. Your e-mail address: (`fredflintstone@bedrock.com`)

7. Dial-up phone number(s)

8. Mailserver name (or POP server or SMTP server): (`bedrock.com`)

9. News host server name (or NNTP server): (`nntp.bedrock.com`)

10. Domain name server: (`234.00.123.0`)

11. Modem port settings: (Com1, Com2, and so on)

12. Internet provider troubleshooting phone number

13. Software tools available with your account

Budgeting for Telecommunications

How much you need to budget for telecommunications depends, obviously, on the deal that you strike with your Internet service provider or if you're on a schoolwide network that's free for the users. There's also the problem of equity of access to the Internet in your school. That is, not enough computers!

If you're connecting to the Internet through an online service such as America Online, you pay a bit more for the all-in-one interface. If you purchase time through an Internet service provider, you have to consider how much time you may use each month or get an unlimited time account. If your school is in a rural area, you may also have to contend with long-distance charges from the school to the nearest service provider. If your school connects through a districtwide network, of course, it's free (for you and your students).

The best way to estimate your budget costs is to find a school that's already connected and ask how much they spend. In my school system, one school that's connected through a PPP account to an Internet provider pays $60.00 per month for a dedicated phone line and $20.00 per month for unlimited access time for one account.

Going for the bucks

How will your school pay for the infrastructure necessary for Internet access (or the computers you use to connect to the Internet)? The first thing to do is check with your district office and state department of education to find out whether they have a source for free access to the Internet. Colleges and universities are also a potential source of free Net time.

Grants are also a great source of funding for telecommunications. Quite a few grant databases are available on the Internet. For information about them, point your Web browser (Netscape Communicator, Internet Explorer, and so on) to one of the following addresses:

The Galaxy Network

```
http://galaxy.einet.net/GJ/grants.html
```

U.S. Dept. of Education: Grants and Contracts

```
http://gcs.ed.gov/
```

National Endowment for the Humanities

```
http://www.neh.fed.us/
```

S.R.A. Grants Web

```
http://web.fie.com/cws/sra/resource.htm
```

Even with grants and free Net time, getting enough computers to connect to the Net costs money. Here are some teacher-tested ideas for raising the money you need to go online:

- ✔ Work with your PTSA to conduct fund-raisers. (Sell bits and bites for chips and bytes.)
- ✔ Seek business partner sponsorships.
- ✔ Sponsor a computer camp.

  A local college makes big bucks each summer with a Tennis and Computer Camp. Students spend half a day with a tennis pro and half in the computer lab. The charge is $100 per student for a week, and the waiting list is a mile long.

- ✔ Offer pay-as-you-learn courses for parents.
- ✔ Sponsor an adopt-a-phone-line campaign.
- ✔ Organize a software fair and invite parents and teachers from other schools. Charge $2.00 at the door.
- ✔ Sell computer services to your community.

  An elementary school once raised $600 making banners for parents. The same school raised another $300 by volunteering to enter data into a database for a local business. The possibilities are endless!

- ✔ Offer to create newsletters (or Web pages!) for community groups, churches, and so on.

The day will come when all schools directly connect to the Internet. The big decisions concern who pays for it and how to maintain the connections. You may be much happier if you keep it simple in the beginning. Get a dial-up account and see how much, and how effectively, your staff and students use the resources available on the Internet before you go to the expense of establishing a direct Internet connection. The data you collect may be invaluable in helping you argue for greater Internet access in your school.

Ready to Ride

You have a configured buggy and you're ready to coerce the horses into their first ride. Now you're ready to surf using Netscape Communicator (see Chapter 6), Internet Explorer (see Chapter 7), or other tools I discuss in this book. Believe me, the configuration of the Internet is getting easier. In the early days of computing and the Internet, you needed many more programs and much more knowledge of the dreaded TCP/IP and other bedazzling acronyms to get logged on.

Computer manufacturers and the makers of operating system software have finally figured out that the Internet is just as important a basic tool as your Program Manager or Finder, so they're beginning to build in Net accessibility. Watch for a whole warehouse-full of easy-to-use, preconfigured tools for your television, backpack, and lawn chair to begin eating up even more of your precious leisure time. Hmmm . . . does that mean I can attend my next class reunion from my lawn chair on the Cancun coastline? (We can all dream, can't we?)

A Word (Okay, a Few!) about NetDay

The latest phenomenon to hit the education world is NetDay. The concept of NetDay was born in California, but like Elvis, NetDay sightings are popping up everywhere! Well-meaning business coalitions have decided that the way to get schools wired is to stage a "high-tech barn-raising" and get local businesses to underwrite the cost and supply the labor to pull wire through the halls of learning. As with any initiative, this kind of barn-raising has good points and not-so-good points.

The good news is that NetDays

✔ Provide the beginnings of the necessary infrastructure for the next level of interactivity in classrooms (the Internet)

✔ Draw attention to the lack of networking and connectivity in today's schools

✔ Create coalitions of school and community that can strengthen interest and involvement for years to come

The not-so-good news is that NetDays typically

✔ Don't include adequate staff development for educators

✔ Don't invest time in helping teachers and administrators answer the question "Wired for What?"

✔ Don't provide the technical and financial support necessary after installation of the wires

✔ Don't (typically) wire an entire school, just a portion of it

✔ Don't prepare schools for the ongoing costs associated with the use of the installed wiring

✔ Don't take into account the fact that our aging schools lack the power resources to support the computers they are attaching to this new "plumbing"

So . . . how can you take advantage of the boost in awareness of the needs in the area of technology and ensure that NetDays now and in the future are successful? Think about these five tips:

✔ Think of NetDay as a catalyst, not a one-shot deal. Make plans for several NetDay-like events throughout the year. Be sure the NetDay effort integrates into, and helps support, your school and/or district's technology plan and your *curriculum.*

✔ Spend some time thinking and planning for the infrastructure necessary to support your new Net connections. Think about staffing, maintenance, facilities (including electrical service), computer hardware, software, and training.

✔ Suggest that your NetDay partners broaden their support to include funding for staff development, awareness seminars, or continued partnerships with your school or district. This is one coalition that could make a huge difference in the quality of teaching and learning in your school!

✔ Set expectations precisely. Will your community think that, after NetDay, your school won't need other funding for technology? Do the educators and technical coordinators in your area really know what the NetDay effort can do for your school — and what it can't do? (Will every classroom have a connection — or just a few? Will Internet access be free — or will the school have to pay for it?)

✔ Find out what other states are doing. Just about every NetDay effort has a Web page explaining the process, the purpose, and the result (after the fact). Take a virtual field trip to California and see what schools there have done; learn from their first year's experience with NetDay to make your life easier.

Here's to a very successful, sustainable, scaleable NetDay! Happy wiring! (For more info, visit `http://www.netday.org`).

Chapter 5

Jumping into the World Wide Web (WWW)

···

In This Chapter

▶ Understanding the Web

▶ Getting down to Web nuts and bolts

▶ Jumping around — Internet style

▶ Meet the URL

▶ Your first visit

▶ Avoiding viruses

···

*L*adies and gentlemen, please return your seat backs and tray tables to their upright position. We're about to take off on a journey you won't forget. The World Wide Web (WWW) is somewhere between a visit to the library and a roller-coaster ride at Disney World.

The World Wide Web, most often referred to as simply the Web, has all the things your students (and you) love — dazzling in-your-face graphics, access to sound and multimedia-rich files, a slick, interactive graphical interface, and thousands of places to visit — many linked to databases, file libraries, and interactive online chats.

The Web is by far the neatest thing on the Internet, and more and more schools and businesses are jumping on the bandwagon. Public schools are creating Web pages that contain information about projects. Universities offer Web tours of their campuses and information about everything from campus organizations to what's on the menu at the cafeteria. Government agencies and nonprofit organizations feature access to huge databases of information and thousands of retrievable files. Companies such as Apple, Microsoft, MTV, IDG Books Worldwide, and Coca-Cola are all sporting fancy new Web pages. And there are plenty more examples of how this new medium is fueling the excitement about the Internet.

So . . . fasten your seat belt and get ready for the ride of your life!

What Is the Web?

Welcome to the World Wide Web. The Web is the place where the emphasis shifts from what information is available to how it is presented. It's the graphical interface of the Internet.

Web browser programs, such as Netscape Communicator and Internet Explorer, are the Swiss Army knives of the Internet world. They slice, dice, and do just about anything. In fact, the Web browser is the primary tool you and your students will use in searching for information on the Internet.

Using the Web and a good browser gives you and your students easy access to

- ✔ Documents available on the Internet
- ✔ Files containing programs, pictures, movies, and sounds from FTP sites (host computers containing files you can copy)
- ✔ Usenet newsgroups (which are like bulletin boards where you can post and read messages on specific topics)
- ✔ WAIS searches (database searches)
- ✔ Computers accessible through telnet (logging into other people's computers)
- ✔ Hypertext (click-and-go) documents
- ✔ Java applets and other multimedia browser enhancements
- ✔ E-mail, interactive chat, and much more!

Web nuts and bolts

The Web was developed and introduced to the world in 1992 at CERN, the European Laboratory for Particle Physics. The object was to build an easy-to-use, distributed, hypermedia system. CERN accomplished its task and more.

The concepts used in designing the Web have even earlier roots — all the way back to 1960 when a guy named Ted Nelson came up with the idea of *hypertext,* a way to link documents that are stored on different computers. The hypertext concept is familiar to people who use HyperCard on a Mac and Roger Wagner's awesome HyperStudio on the Macintosh or PC. (See the sidebar "Getting hyper" in this chapter for more information on hyper-stuff.)

TECHNO TERMS

Getting hyper

The Web offers users an adventure in hypermedia, fueled by hypertext and hyperlinks. It's a truly hyper place that's perfect for hyper students (and teachers).

Hypermedia is a term used to describe the union of hypertext and multimedia. The term *hypertext* describes text that, when you select it with the click of a mouse, zips the user to another source of related information. With hypermedia, highlighted and linked text called *hyperlinks* (or just *links* — they're usually underlined) enable a user to move between data in a nonlinear manner. For example, clicking on the hyperlinked word "projects" in the sentence "NASA offers many online <u>projects</u> to students" might whisk you away to another site (residing on another computer halfway across the globe) that offers a list of specific projects and information about how to participate.

Multimedia refers to the union of different data types, such as text, graphics, sound, and sometimes movies. Hypermedia connects these data types together. You're just as likely to hear a sound when clicking on a hyperlinked word while browsing a hypermedia file, for example, as you are to view a picture.

The language that Web programs use to create hyperlinks is called *HyperText Transfer Protocol*

(HTTP). HTTP, coupled with its scripting cousin Hypertext Markup Language (HTML), enable users to create their own Web pages and post them to the Internet as well as ensure that the file is readable by Web browsers. In the days when browsers were first born, you'd have to type "http://" before each Web address. Modern browsers (like the ones that come with this book) assume http:// unless you type something different. Thus, typing:

```
http://www.idgbooks.com
```

gives you the same result as typing:

```
www.idgbooks.com
```

The "http://" prefix tips off the Internet that the URL (Uniform Resource Locator — an Internet resource address) you're looking for is a Web address and not a Gopher or FTP site. So, in the address, `http://www.aol.com`, the `http://` tells you and the Net that the site you seek is on the Web. (similarly, the `ftp://` in `ftp://whatever.com/bin/whatever.zip`, tells you and your browser it's a downloadable .FTP file.)

So, take the challenge and type your address without the prefix when visiting an http:// site. You and your students will undoubtedly appreciate the savings of effort!

How do I jump on the Web?

You can access the Web through a text-only browser if your connection to the Net won't let you display graphics, or you can use a browser that offers a slick, graphical interface that makes browsing easy.

Whether you're connecting through an online service or through a commercial Internet provider, you've got it made. Or you can use a graphical browser such as Internet Explorer, or Netscape Communicator (both are on the CD that comes with this book).

If you have a Windows PC, you can also try Opera (`www.operasoftware.com`), an up-and-coming contender in the browser wars, for a thirty-day trial period (after that you'll have to pay the registration fee of $35 to continue using it). Mac users can check out iCab (`www.icab.de`), an amazingly small and amazingly powerful browser newcomer from Germany. Browsers read documents, called *Web pages,* that either provide information or are jumping-off points for other information resources. The browser finds Web pages by using an address called a *URL* (pronounced U-R-L).

Meet URL

URL stands for *Uniform Resource Locator.* A URL lists the exact location (address) of virtually any Internet resource. Here are a few sample URLs.

A Web page	`http://www.apple.com/education/`
A picture file	`ftp://fabercollege.edu/graphics/flounder.gif`
A newsgroup	`news://news.lists`
A Gopher site	`gopher://gopher.tc.umn.com`
A telnet session	`telnet://ibm.com`
An e-mail address	`mailto://someone@something.com`

The browser jihad

In the beginning there was Mosaic. Mozilla morphed from Mosaic into the infrastructure for Netscape Navigator (and eventually Communicator). Then along came the 500-pound gorilla, Microsoft, with Internet Explorer, and it's been war ever since. For the purposes of this book, I'm not going to take sides because both major browsers work reasonably well and the differences as both browsers mature are becoming less apparent.

There are some promising newcomers, like Opera (for PCs running Windows) and the new "pre-browser", Sherlock, built into Apple Computer's Mac OS 8.5 (and newer versions). It's clear that nobody is standing still in the war to become the preeminent browser. Watch for more integration between browsers and operating systems (Justice Department willing) and new tools that work with browsers to make your surfing more pleasurable and efficient.

The great .com controversy

Today on the Internet, you can find one of nine different endings (called top-level domains) in an Internet address. These endings give you clues about the source of the address. For example:

✔ **.com:** A commercial service (example: www.socrates.com or ali.apple.com, a corporate address)

✔ **.edu:** An education or education-related organization (example: mailto:yourname @yourschool.edu, perfect for educators who wish to keep a separate address for all those incoming notes from parents)

✔ **.gov:** Government and/or government contractors (example: president@white-house.gov, one of the president's e-mail addresses — the mailbox is always full!)

✔ **.mil:** The military (example: patton@army.mil, one of our nation's finest)

✔ **.org:** Other organizations that don't really fit into another classification (example: franklloydwright@architects.org; a fake address, but my friend Marc is an architect who is probably almost good enough to have this address)

✔ **.net:** Network resources (example: chiphead@mainframe.net, for chip-heads only)

And a few more obscure top-domains:

✔ **.arpa:** associated with ARPANET, the research project that birthed the Internet (example: allknowing@amaging.arpa)

✔ **.nato:** the North Atlantic Treaty Organization (example: general@wherever.nato)

✔ **.int:** international organizations (example: redcross@redcross.int)

You also see endings such as .uk and .fi. These endings are *country codes* (see Chapter 11 for more information on country codes).

Of course the ubiquitous ".com" address is quite broad. It can be a person mailto:your-name@yourname.com or a department store mailto:info@nordstroms.com or small business mailto:info@athensshirtco.com. It's all getting quite confusing.

Inexpensive domain-name registration and companies who have made a business of registering and reselling domain names have unfortunately depleted the name pool (particularly in the .com top-domain). So, leave it to the wizards of the Internet to design some brand new top-domain extensions. These aren't in effect yet, and the issue is very controversial in the Internet community, but my guess is that as people begin to use the Internet more like the yellow pages, we'll see these newbies popping up all over:

✔ **.arts:** Entities conducting cultural and entertainment activities

✔ **.firm:** Businesses (bet the lawyers and CPAs get all of these!)

✔ **.info:** Entities providing information services (online phone books, and so on)

✔ **.nom:** For your own personal Web site and/or internet address. "nom" is short for nomenclature (that is a *nom de plume*)

✔ **.rec:** Recreation and entertainment activities

✔ **.shop:** Online shopping (my guess is you'll have more bookmarks in this category than any other!)

✔ **.web:** Entities emphasizing activities related to the WWW (probably Web authoring or Internet standards)

Right now we don't exactly know when the powers-that-be will make a decision about these new top-domains. If you or your students are interested in tracking the progress of this initiative, however, I'd stay tuned to www.gtld-mou.org.

The first part of the URL, the junk before the colon, tells the browser what method to use to access the file (the Web, e-mail program, and so on). The part of the URL that's after the colon indicates the address of a host computer.

Surfing with Netscape Communicator and Internet Explorer

Whether you use Netscape Communicator or Microsoft's Internet Explorer (IE) to browse the Internet, there are some features and tips helpful in getting you around. After you start Communicator (or the stand alone Navigator browser), you see a screen similar to Figure 5-1. The Internet Explorer window looks like the one shown in 5-2. The page your browser displays depends on how it's set up; many providers have a browser display their home page (like Mindspring); others tend to point to Netscape's and Microsoft's home page. You can change the default home page easily (I show you how in Chapter's 6 and 7).

At the top of the browser window you see a bunch of buttons and the (Communicator) Location or (IE) Address box (Figure 5-2). That's one of the places you see, and are able to enter, a URL (see the "Meet URL" section earlier in this chapter for more info).

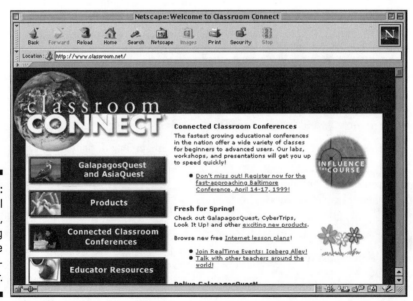

Figure 5-1:
A typical
Web page,
using
Netscape
Communi-
cator.

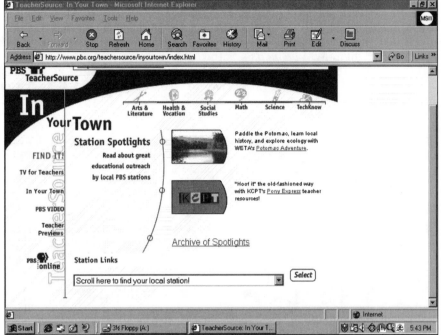

Getting around

You need two basic motor skills to navigate the Web — both involving your computer's mouse: The first is clicking on a link to move from page to page, and the second is typing in or choosing from a list a URL of a page you already know or have visited before and chosen to save.

Both major browsers make moving from page to page very simple. Just click any underlined text item (link) or blue-bordered pictures (also a link). Mouse around most pages and you can tell you're pointing to a link when the default arrow pointer changes to a little hand. If you're not sure something is a link, click it anyway. Go ahead, live on the edge!

Back to the future

Both Internet Explorer and Navigator also remember the last few pages you visit, so if you click a link and end up somewhere you don't want to be, just click the Back button (the icon is an arrow pointing to the left). Just in case you want to go forward again to a page after you go back to one (go back and read this sentence again and it makes sense), click the Forward button (the icon is an arrow pointing to the right) on the browser's menu bar.

Getting there quickly

If you don't have a home page, you have to turn in your computer club pin right away. A *home page* is the main (topmost) Web page in a Web site. It's also the entry point or table of contents for most sites. Figure 5-3 shows the home page for one of my favorite resources, the Apple Learning Interchange (ALI).

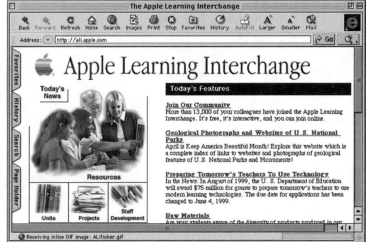

Figure 5-3:
Visit ALI —
an online
community
and
resource
database
for the
education
community.

Follow these steps to get to any URL:

1. **Click in the Location or Address box, near the top of the Communicator or IE window.**

2. **Type in the URL.** Try the URL for ALI: `www.apple.com/education/ali`.

3. **Press the Return key (Enter key on a PC).**

If someone sends you a cool site to visit via e-mail, you can also cut and paste by using standard cut-and-paste techniques to avoid retyping pesky URLs that are ridiculously long. Need a refresher on cutting and pasting?

1. **Highlight the URL in an e-mail message or other text document.**

2. **Press ⌘-C (Ctrl+C on a PC) to copy the information to the Clipboard.**

3. **Click in the Location or Address box to highlight whatever is in it.**

4. **Press ⌘-V (Ctrl+V on a PC) to paste the URL into the box, and then press the Return key.**

Some browsers, and computer operating systems, support *drag-and-drop.* Here's how:

1. **Highlight the URL in your e-mail message or other text document. (Assuming you have an e-mail program or word processing program open as well as your browser.)**

2. **Click and drag the URL from the document into the Location or Address box.**

3. **Press the Return key.**

As word processors and e-mail programs have gotten smarter, many (like Microsoft Word and AppleWorks) have added the ability to jump directly from URLs within the text of a document and automatically launch your browser. All you have to do is highlight the URL within the text and click. (Some programs require a command click.) Zip! Your browser of choice launches and the Web page displays.

Exiting the Superhighway

Sooner or later, you look at the clock and it reads 2:00 a.m., you spin around and note that your significant other and *all* of your pets are asleep (and have been asleep since a more respectable 10 p.m.), and realize that it's time to log off. To leave your browser (and the Internet), just quit the program the same way you quit other programs. Choose File⇨Quit or press ⌘-Q (choose File⇨Exit or press Alt+F4 in Windows). If you dial in through AOL or your service provider, be sure to quit those programs in the same way.

Navigating the tangled Web

Finding things on the Web can be a bit tough. Millions of Web pages are out there, with more being added every day, so it's tough for any one place to have a full listing of what's on the Net.

Having the Internet in your classroom doesn't help if you can't find any content to enhance or enrich your curriculum. You and your students also don't have time to sort through millions of sites each time you sit down to research, communicate, or collaborate. Luckily, there are sites on the Web that offer some organization to the chaos of the Internet, generically known as *search engines.* Some search engines are topic or theme specific (usually known as "portals") and some are more general.

The Web goes 3-D

What's the next level in Web exploration? The Web goes 3-D! A software program called WebSpace is the first commercially available three-dimensional viewer for the World Wide Web. The program, which runs on Power Macintosh, Windows, and UNIX platforms, works along with popular Web browsers. With the WebSpace viewer the possibilities are amazing. The programmers of the viewer, Silicon Graphics, claim that users can

✔ Fly through 3-D worlds, exploring event venues, cities, libraries, museums, tourist resorts, and imaginary places

✔ Inspect 3-D models of products in online catalogs

✔ Visualize information such as stock market trends in 3-D

The new technology also explores a new authoring paradigm called VRML (Virtual Reality Modeling Language), an open, platform-independent file format for 3-D graphics on the Internet. Similar in concept to the core Web text standard HyperText Markup Language (HTML), VRML encodes computer-generated graphics into a compact format for transportation over the network. As with HTML, a user can view the contents of a file — in this case, an interactive 3-D graphics file — as well as navigate to other VRML "worlds" or HTML pages. In addition, VRML is infinitely scalable so that as users navigate through virtual worlds and approach objects, greater levels of detail emerge. Will it catch on? We'll see! (Perhaps in 3-D!)

This new technology has some very exciting possibilities for education. The days of electronic field trips in 3-D are not far away!

For more information on VRML and WebSpace, point your Web browser to `www.sgi.com/Products/WebFORCE/WebSpace`

Finding info on the Internet is so critical to the success of your online experience that I devote a whole chapter to it. Chapter 8 differentiates between the various search engines and shows you various options I bet you may not know you have. Check out Chapter 8 if you already understand the concept of search engines, or else, read on!

How Not to Get Caught in the Web

You'll quickly find that navigating the Web is like any other skill. The more you experiment and practice, the more efficient and enjoyable your experience will be. I've collected a few tips that saved me lots of time in classrooms and during presentations at educational conferences.

Here are some points to ponder that can save you loads of time and a few gray hairs:

✔ If images are coming in too slowly, deselect Auto Load Images from the Options or preferences menus (see Chapters 6 and 7 for info on how to do this in Internet Explorer and Navigator, respectively). This gives you a text-only interface.

✔ Web pages can be very busy. Just click the Stop button on your browser's toolbar and then click Reload (Refresh in Internet Explorer). Sometimes the first time the page loads it just doesn't load everything properly, and reloading it can fill in those gaps.

✔ Remember that you can copy, print, or save the text and graphics that display on any Web page using commands found in the Edit menu or browser toolbar.

✔ Want to write your own Web page? AppleWorks has a neat HTML (Hypertext Markup Language) translator available for download on most online services or from the Apple Web site at `www.apple.com/appleworks`.

Netscape Communicator also enables you to capture the HTML code from any other Web page. That means you can actually see the code example and save it to your disk for analysis. It's a great way to learn, but no cheating, please!

Great places for a first visit

All dressed up and no place to go? Try a few great educational Web links from the Internet Directory that's snuggled in the middle of this book. For your first surfing outing, choose File⇨Open Page in your browser (File⇨Open in Internet Explorer) and type the following URLs exactly as you see them (you can also type the URL into the Location [Address in Internet Explorer] box). Be sure to mind your capital letters!

Here's one place you might begin. Have your students visit the Center for Disease Control and Prevention's Internet sites and find out about the latest nasty diseases. It's easy to reach the CDC. They maintain an excellent Web site at: `www.cdc.gov`

There you have it. A basic introduction to the World Wide Web. You now know just enough to be dangerous. In the next two chapters, I show you how to use and get the most out of your browser of choice. Before you read those chapters, though, go ahead and type in some of those "dot com" addresses you see on billboards, in magazines, on TV, and in the newspaper. Find a page relating to a personal hobby, your pet, family history (genealogy), or favorite travel destination. Do not, repeat, do not surf to anything remotely connected with your classroom duties. This is your time to explore. We get back to the students later.

Electronic Commerce and the Web

When I was about 11, I tried setting up a lemonade stand outside my house. My recipe was flawless, my table attractive, I even wore my Cub Scout uniform to make my proposition irresistible. Unfortunately, I lived in a really, really small town and my lemonade stand was on a back road traveled only by the school bus (on weekdays), the mailman (allergic to citrus) and the occasional neighbor (most of whom were on vacation). I drank a lot of lemonade that day. What I missed was an understanding of the three most important rules of sales: location, location, location.

I guess it was inevitable that someone would figure out how to sell things through the Internet. Now it's a *billion* dollar a year business. Even in its infancy, it makes total sense. Now you can sit down in the comfort of your own home and use your computer to place an order for just about anything you can dream up. It arrives in one or two days at your door.

My great prognostication about online shopping? Banks just began to charge for standing in line and conducting in-person transactions, where electronic banking is sometimes free. I think soon we'll be getting large discounts buying from the Net and paying a premium to browse in person.

Shopping malls may survive as "social gathering spots," but not without adding conveniences (perhaps childcare, adult learning facilities, a wider variety of stores?). Of course something interesting happens if this idea extends to its logical conclusion — thousands of online stores — it's that location thing again. How do you find them? Will you have to copy down their "dot com" (URL) address from a billboard or online ad? Nope, prediction #2 is that there might emerge online shopping malls that will serve as your portal to businesses. For a preview, check out www.amazon.com and see how an online bookseller is expanding to include video, music, auctions, and gifts. What's next — cars, homes, and travel services? Of course, lawmakers might also see the Internet as a source of revenue, so things like information taxes may be in our future. I prefer a more optimistic approach. Of course, I do live in Silicon Valley. We'll see!

Chapter 6

Exploring with Explorer

● ●

In This Chapter

▶ Getting it, installing it, exploring it

▶ IE basic training

▶ Browsing bonanza

▶ Cool IE functions

▶ Taking advantage of IE tips and tricks

● ●

Compared to the software tools available in the early days of the Internet, Microsoft's Internet Explorer (IE) is rocket science. A relatively late entry in the browser market, Microsoft has zipped IE into a neck and neck race with Netscape Communicator by coaxing its way into preinstallation on most modern computers and offering software and upgrades for free. Microsoft's recent upgrades have also introduced new compelling features like "IntelliSense," offline browsing, and even a digital wallet. This powerful browser is packed with features and runs on both Macs and Windows PCs.

All this means that if you have a computer running Windows 95 or Windows 98, for an iMac or recent Macintosh computer, you've probably already got a copy of IE. It might not be the most current version, however, so you might as well grab an updated copy of IE from www.microsoft.com/ie. Remember, it's free!

Basic Training: Internet Explorer

When you first start Internet Explorer on your computer, the main browser window appears. The functionality is similar in the Macintosh and Windows versions, but the interfaces are just different enough to be confusing. If you have a Mac, the browser window will look something like Figure 6-1. Windows users see something like the screen in Figure 6-2. This main browser window is your "dashboard" for the information superhighway, it contains lots of buttons and menu items that will make visiting, navigating, and remembering Web sites easier.

ON THE CD

Getting Internet Explorer

You're in luck, we've included the most recent version of Microsoft Internet Explorer (as of press time) that we could find on your *Internet For Teachers,* 3rd Edition CD. You can also download the most recent version of IE by installing an older version of any browser and surfing to Microsoft's home page (for Internet Explorer): www.microsoft.com/ie.

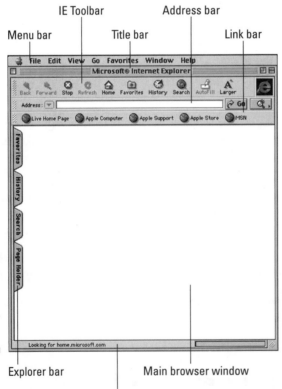

Figure 6-1:
The Macintosh IE browser interface.

Here's a listing of the main areas of the Internet Explorer browser window and what they do:

   ✔ **Title Bar:** This tells you the title of the page you are viewing.

   ✔ **Main Menu Bar:** This contains different submenus that control all the options, functions, and commands for the entire Internet Explorer program. Some navigation controls can also be found in these submenus.

✔ **Internet Explorer Toolbar:** This contains all the most frequently used commands and navigation functions. The following section explains the buttons on this toolbar in detail.

✔ **Address Bar:** This tells you the exact URL location of the page you are currently viewing. You can type a complete Web address directly into this area and then press Return (Enter in Windows) to go to that site.

✔ **Link Bar:** These are buttons that whisk you away to Microsoft's IE home page where you'll find applications and information specifically designed to make using IE easier.

✔ **Main Browser Window:** This window displays Web pages. All text, images, movies, animation, links, or any other application files are displayed in this window. Use the scroll bars located on the right side and on the bottom of this window to navigate within a page if it is too large to fit in the browser window.

✔ **Status Bar:** This gives you a progress update as you access and download the information on Web pages, tells you where links go (when you mouse over a link without clicking), indicates whether or not a document is secure, and displays any other information that the program feels is necessary for you to know. (Smart, isn't it?)

✔ **Explorer Bar:** This feature offers Windows users easy access to Favorites, History, Search Engines, and Page Holder.

Figure 6-2:
The IE
browser —
Windows
style.

The Internet Explorer Toolbar

The main toolbar, shown in Figure 6-3 for Macintosh and 6-4 for Windows, has a most intriguing row of buttons and is where you'll find yourself clicking most often. Each button serves a different purpose, and even veteran users of IE may not have dared to click each and every button for fear the program would reach out and strangle them. Never fear, though, the function of each button is logical and quite useful. Want to see?

Figure 6-3:
The IE
toolbar for
Macintosh.

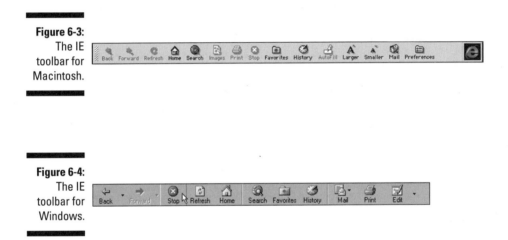

Figure 6-4:
The IE
toolbar for
Windows.

From left to right, here's a quick description of each of the 16 buttons on the IE Toolbar:

- ✔ **Back:** This button takes you back to whatever Web page (document) you were previously viewing. Clicking this button once takes you back one document. If you have browsed many different pages during your current session or are well into a multipage document, clicking it repeatedly continues to back you up one page at a time. After you reach the first page of your surfing session, the back button appears to gray, which means that you can't go back any more.

- ✔ **Forward:** This button takes you forward to the next document if you have previously browsed multiple documents and had then backed-up to the page you are currently viewing. (If you have not backed up at all, the forward button appears grayed-out and disabled.)

- ✔ **Refresh:** This button reloads the current document that you are viewing. Use it to view changes you've made if you're editing and previewing Web pages made by you or your students to see the changes, or to reload a document whose transfer was interrupted.

✔ **Home:** This button zips you to the page you have selected as the default start-up page for Internet Explorer. (Yes, you can change this page! See the "Setting A Default Start-Up (Home) Page" section later in this chapter.)

✔ **Search:** This button takes you to the page you have selected as the default Web search page for Internet Explorer. In IE 5.0 for Windows, you'll see a brand new Search window (Figure 6-5) that allows you to search for Web pages, people's addresses, and more. On a Mac, it takes you to a similar page, or you can use Sherlock, Apple's built-in Internet search tool.

If you have not selected a home page, IE whisks you to Microsoft's default search page.

Figure 6-5:
The IE 5
Search
function lets
you search
for people,
Web pages,
and more in
Windows.

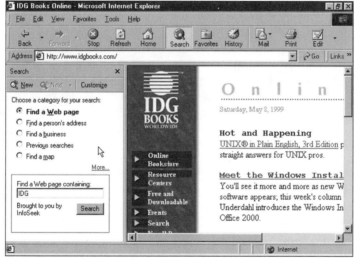

✔ **Images:** This button loads images on the current page (in case they didn't load correctly the first time). This works like Refresh, but it only loads missing images.

✔ **Print:** This button displays the Print dialog box. There you can decide if you would like to print the contents of the page you are viewing, how much of that content you'd like to print, and how many copies you will print. The more graphics that are on a page, the longer that page will take to print. IE does a much better job of printing Web pages than Navigator. It even automatically resizes pages that are too wide for your printer's margins to fit. Nice feature!

✔ **Stop:** This button stops any current operation underway and is very useful in speeding your browsing session! Use it to stop files (pages) from loading (if you hit a page you know is not what you want), to stop animations (moving .GIF images, movies and such), or the operation of any Java programs (like online chat windows) running in your browser window.

If you click Stop before a page has finished loading, the page will display everything it had finished loading before the Stop button was pressed. If a document has already completely loaded and there are no animations, movies, or other files still running, the stop button doesn't do anything.

- ✔ **Favorites:** This button opens the Favorites tab in the Explorer Bar. Favorites (Navigator calls these Bookmarks) allow you to store, organize, and easily revisit your favorite Web pages without retyping the URLs. This option is also available from a pull-down menu in the Menu Bar.

- ✔ **History:** This button opens the History tab in the Explorer Bar (also in the Menu Bar). History remembers all the links you've visited for a time you can set in the Preferences Internet Options menu. This means, by the way, that a crafty teacher can see where a student's been (and they can see where you've been) today, yesterday, or a week ago. The history list can be erased, of course by opening the History tab in the Explorer Bar and dragging the files to the trash.

- ✔ **AutoFill**: This button automatically looks at a form on a Web page and fills in things like name, address, phone, and so on based on criteria you set up by choosing Edit⇨Preferences (or Tools⇨Internet Options in Windows). In the Windows version of IE, AutoFill is called AutoComplete. A real time saver for online shopping, AutoComplete isn't available when you're not filling out a form. You can disable the function in the Forms AutoFill item in the Preferences (or Tools⇨Internet Options under the Content tab in Windows) menu of Internet Explorer.

- ✔ **Larger**: This button increases the font size of text on a Web page. Use this if your bifocals (or contact lenses) aren't working and the text appears too small to read, or too large to fit comfortably in the window.

- ✔ **Smaller:** This button decreases the font size of text on a Web page. Use this if you want to see more of a page on a single screen, or if you distribute magnifying glasses to each of students before a surfing session.

- ✔ **Mail:** This button opens up an options menu that allows you to read or send e-mail using Outlook Express. You can also read newsgroups from this menu.

- ✔ **Preferences (Mac only):** This button provides easy access to set personal preferences for just about everything — IE does a "must-visit" during your first or second surfing session. In Windows, just right-click the Internet Explorer icon on your desktop and select Properties.

- ✔ **Edit:** This button only shows up in your IE toolbar if you have a Microsoft system Web editor such as Microsoft Front Page or Microsoft Word installed on your computer. Clicking this button launches the editor and opens the Web page you're currently viewing in that application.

> ✔ **Internet Explorer logo:** Click this icon to transport yourself to Microsoft's IE Web site. Great for grabbing the latest version and reading lots of tips and techniques.

Wow! That's a lot of features! Of course, the Back button and the Favorites button are the buttons I use most.

Browsing Bonanza

The hard-working programmers at Microsoft have given Internet Explorer some built-in features that make browsing easier. You can use the Search button (see the previous section about the IE Toolbar) to search quickly for content on the Web.

If you're a beginner, an important thing to keep in mind is that if you know the Web address of a site, you don't need use a search engine to find the page. Just hop up to the Address Bar (take a glance at Figure 6-6) and click in the white space. Now type in the Web address (URL) of the site you want and press Return (or click the Go button). Internet Explorer jumps to this site directly from the document you were viewing.

Figure 6-6:
Type a URL
in the
Address Bar
for quick
access.

| Address : ▼ | http://www.idgbooks.com |

In the newest versions of Internet Explorer, Microsoft includes a nifty feature called *IntelliSense*. This feature does things to make your browsing experience more positive. For example, the program has a built-in ability to "guess" at site names as you type them. It also remembers the most frequently visited sites and stores personal information to make filling out forms easier (see AutoFill in your Preferences menu or Tools⇨Internet Options under the Content tab in Windows).

More Cool IE Functions

After you master basic browsing, you're ready for graduate school. Here are a few functions that many people don't even know exist but nonetheless make your life easier in the classroom and at home.

Checking out Web pages "off Web"

Internet Explorer can display HTML documents, images, movies, and sound files located on your hard drive or schoolwide network even if you're not connected to the Internet. Here's how:

1. **Choose File➪Open File (⌘-O).**

   In the Open dialog box, you can type in a Web address to access a page on the Internet, but because you're trying to open a Web page that's not on the Net, you need to make another choice.

2. **Select Desktop (Mac) or Browse (Windows) in the dialog box to look at files on the hard drive.**

   Select the type of file you want to open from the pull-down menu at the bottom of the box.

3. **Click around until you are in the folder that contains the file you want to open and select the file. Then click the Open button.**

   The document, image, movie, or sound file you selected appears in the main Internet Explorer browser window.

You and your students will appreciate this feature if you create an internal Web site (intranet) for your school or if you just want to preview pages your students have created.

Printing and saving from the Web

On occasion, you may want to print what you see, but because the information is digital and readily available online, "printing the Internet" really kills trees needlessly. For this reason, I always encourage students to take notes or copy and paste only what they need instead of needlessly cluttering hard drives and notebooks with page after page of data from the Net.

If your computer is connected to a printer, you can print any Web document whether you are viewing it on the Web, or are viewing it from your hard disk. To print a document:

1. **Choose File⇨Print.**

   The standard Print dialog box will appear. Here you can choose what pages to print and how many of each. Caution, using your printer as a copy machine for documents just as easily viewed online is hazardous to the rain forests. Please don't.

2. **Click the Print button.**

   Wait as the pages print. The more graphics the page contains, the longer printing takes.

You can also save text and images from the Internet to your local hard drive or network.

To save text, just choose File⇨Save and select a destination. Internet Explorer saves the entire *text* content of the Web page. Not the graphics, though, since those are loaded on the fly from elsewhere on the Web server's hard drive. To save only part of the text on a page, just highlight the text and use Edit⇨Copy and then Edit⇨Paste to copy and paste text into your favorite word processor. (Hey! This is a great time to read about copyright and the Internet! Check out Chapter 3.)

Snagging pictures is also pretty easy. In Explorer, just click the picture while holding down the Control key (or right-click your mouse) and choose the Download Image to Disk option. Pictures on the Web are usually displayed in GIF (Graphics Interchange Format) or JPG (JPEG) format. Graphics in these formats are optimized for screen resolution and may not print well. Again, remember that all pictures, drawings, and movies on the Internet fall under the laws of copyright.

Using Internet mail

Another feature of Microsoft Internet Explorer is a full-featured e-mail program, called Outlook Express, that comes free with it. With Outlook Express you can compose, send, and organize e-mail. To activate Outlook Express, click and hold your mouse on the Mail icon on the main Explorer Toolbar. Select Read Mail from the context menu that appears. Doing so displays the main screen for the Outlook Express Internet mail functions.

Before you can use Internet Mail for your particular e-mail account you must set the Mail preferences to your server and account. Here's how:

1. **Click the Preferences icon on the IE Toolbar.**

   This will display the Preferences dialog box like the one in Figure 6-7. (Note that Windows users will see a slightly different content in their Internet Options dialog box, as shown in Figure 6-8).

2. Choose E-mail➪General from the scrolling list on the left.

3. You see all the questions you must answer to enable e-mail.

Ask your school technology coordinator or network administrator for help if you don't have all the info.

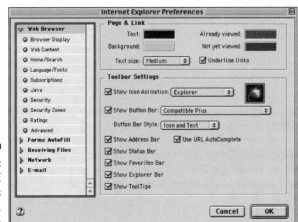

Figure 6-7:
The Mac IE Preferences dialog box.

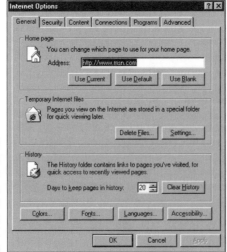

Figure 6-8:
The Windows Internet Options dialog box.

IE Tips and Tricks

You're on the Web and now you want to show off your IE browsing prowess. It turns out that there several ways to make the browsing process much quicker and easier, including turning off the ability of your browser to display images and managing your browsing session through the Favorites menu.

Image off, image on

You can improve the speed of your surfing experience by disabling the display of graphic images in your browser window. You still see text, so you can get an idea of what's on the page. You may, however, miss important navigational information that only the graphic conveys.

To temporarily disable graphic image display:

1. **Click the Preferences icon in the IE Toolbar. (Windows users choose Tools⇨Internet Options.)**

2. **Choose Web Browser⇨Web Content (in the Windows version, click the Advanced tab and deselect the Show Pictures check box under the Multimedia category).**

   Doing this displays a menu that helps you customize the display of graphics, sounds and other "active" content.

3. **Deselect the item that reads "Show pictures."**

   You'll also see other opportunities to optimize you browsing experience in this preferences box.

   Preference changes take effect as soon as you close the Preferences window and remain in effect until you change them back, even if you quit IE.

Another way to speed the process is creating Favorites lists in advance of your classroom research session. In the next section, I walk you through the process.

Saving your favorites

Internet Explorer contains a handy method of marking frequently visited Web sites, they're called Favorites. The settings for your Favorites are located on the main menu bar.

AutoComplete to the rescue

Microsoft came up with a very helpful feature that saves typing and error correction called AutoComplete, which basically reads your mind. When you start typing into a form on a Web page or the Address Bar in IE, the AutoComplete feature automatically suggests a match as you type. If you've consistently visited a page with a URL like this: www.apple.com/education/k12/disability/map.html just typing **www.apple** will likely reveal the rest.

The suggested match is highlighted. When you finish typing, or when AutoComplete finds a match, press Enter. AutoComplete finds a match from a list of Web sites you've visited before, or from words you have added to the AutoComplete word list. Of course, if you're annoyed by the prescient feature, turn it off in the Preferences menu.

1. **Choose Edit⇨Preferences (or Tools⇨ Internet Options in Windows).**

2. **Choose Forms AutoFill, click Forms AutoComplete. (In the Windows version, click the Advanced tab and deselect AutoComplete options under the Browsing category.)**

3. **Select Enabled (or Disabled to cut the feature off).**

If you want to add a word or words to the Word list from which Internet Explorer can match, click the Add button.

A related feature in the Macintosh 4.5 version of IE is AutoFill. After you've entered info in the Preferences mentioned above, try visiting a page where there's a form to fill out (like order-ing more copies of this book from Amazon.com at www.amazon.com). After the form is in your browser window, click the AutoFill icon in the IE Toolbar. IE magically fills in name, address, zip, and so on (where it can) — making it way too easy to spend your hard-earned cash!

1. **Select the "Favorites" icon from the Menu bar or click on the Favorites tab in the Explorer menu to the left of your browser window.**

   The Explorer menu's Favorites tab reveals lots of goodies. Check out Figure 6-9. If the Favorites tab isn't showing, choose Favorites Bar from the View menu (Mac). You can also choose Favorites from the menu bar.

Figure 6-9: The Explorer menu makes adding and editing Favorites a breeze.

Name	Address
Microsoft	http://www.microsoft.com
Apple	http://www.apple.com/
Teaching, Learning & Technology	file:///TLT/html/index.html
▶ Toolbar Favorites	

2. **Click Add Page to Favorites.**

This will add the currently displayed Web page to your Favorites menu. To access this page later, just open the Favorites menu (or tab) and click the item.

 Opening the Favorites tab (Figure 6-10) also reveals the Organize Favorites pull-down menu that allows you to add and remove folders, sort your favorites, open a Favorites window and do anything else needed to manage favorites. You can drag and drop items to move items. Click each name to rename it. You can also delete favorites by dragging them to the trash.

Figure 6-10:
IE's
Favorites
menu
(Windows
version
shown) is
your portal
to sites and
organizing
options.

| Add to Favorites... |
| Organize Favorites... |
| ☐ Channels ▶ |
| ☐ Links ▶ |
| ☒ Software Updates ▶ |
| ⌗ Apple - Hot News |
| ⌗ MSN |
| ⌗ Radio Station Guide |
| ⌗ Web Events |
| ⌗ Welcome to RealMedia ! |

Sharing favorites

Internet Explorer stores Favorites in a separate file that can be copied from computer to computer. This is a perfect remedy for ensuring all the computers in a lab or school have a "basic" search listing.

To share your Favorites file:

1. **Open the directory where your IE Favorites directory is located.**

Using your file management program (Windows Explorer, File Manager, the Mac OS Finder, and so on) locate the file. On a Mac, it's a file called `favorites.html` tucked away inside your System Folder in the Preferences folder in another folder called Explorer. On a PC running Windows use the Find⇨Files and Folders function in your Start menu to search for "favorites" and you'll locate the file.

2. **Make a copy of the favorites.html file.**

On a Mac, select the file and choose File⇨Duplicate (⌘-D) or hold down the Control button while you drag the file onto the disk that you plan to use to transport the file to the destination (target) computer.

On PCs running Windows, hold down the Ctrl key and drag the Favorites file onto your Windows desktop or the disk you plan to use to transport the file to the destination (target) computer or use your Windows Explorer (not to be confused with Internet Explorer) to duplicate the file.

3. **Copy the files onto the hard drive of the "target" computer.**

Either replace the current favorites.html file (found in the same place as the one you duplicated on your machine) or use File⇨Import to add them to the current listing already on that computer. Watch out, though, if you replace the Favorites file you'll wipe out all the old ones!

Setting a default home page

Did you know the vast majority of Web browser users don't even *know* that they can change their default *home* page? Of course the browser-makers love that, but wouldn't your school's home page look better on that prime real estate?

The *Home* page is the Web Site or document that Internet Explorer opens automatically every time that you start the program. These steps show you how you can change this page to whatever location you prefer.

1. **Choose Edit⇨Preferences or click the Preferences icon on the IE toolbar.**

   (Windows users choose Tools⇨Internet Options and click the General tab. Skip to Step 3).

2. **Scroll to find Web Browser and then click the Home/Search button. You'll see lots of options for configuring you Home page and setting the default URL for your Search icon on the IE toolbar.**

3. **In the Address box, type the new home page address.**

4. **Close the window to save your Preferences.**

The next time you launch IE, your new home page is automatically displayed.

✔ To display your home page whenever you open a new window, make sure there's a checkmark in the Automatically Go to This Home Page When Opening a New Window check box.

✔ To quickly set the current page as the home page, open the page in the browser, hold down the mouse button, and select Set Home Page from the shortcut menu.

✔ To use the default home page for IE (http://home.microsoft.com), click the Use Default button.

✔ To have no home page, click the Use None (Use Blank in Windows) button. This causes the Home button on the Button Bar and the Home Page command on the Go menu to be unavailable.

IE newsreader

Access IE's News Services from the IE toolbar's Mail icon by clicking and holding your mouse on the icon and then choosing Read News from the menu. IE uses Outlook Express (the e-mail program) to read newsgroups, as shown in Figure 6-11. If you haven't used Outlook Express before, the Setup Wizard takes you through the setup for your news server's name and a few other items.

Next, Outlook Express downloads a list of all available newsgroups and display them as a list of hyperlinks. This may take some time, as some news servers may have more than 10,000 newsgroups. Click on the Stop icon on the IE Toolbar to halt the download.

Note that in the Address bar, it reads NEWS:* instead of the familiar "http:// where * is the name of the newsgroup you're reading. If you know the name of your newsgroup, you may type it in just as if it were any other URL, inserting the protocol "news:" where "http://" is usually located.

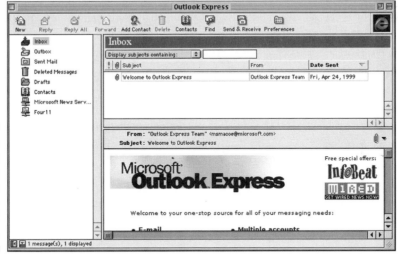

Figure 6-11:
IE uses Outlook Express to view newsgroups and send e-mail.

Clicking on a newsgroup, such as alt.education, brings up a list of articles, again displayed as a list of hyperlinks, within that newsgroup. Each article has a number, subject, and author. By default, IE only displays the last 20 messages within each group. Clicking the Earlier Messages hyperlink brings up the previous set of 20 messages, clicking again brings up the 20 before that, and so on. . . .

Want more information on Newsgroups? Check out Chapter 13.

I've really only scratched the surface of what Internet Explorer can do. Microsoft has provided a "what's new" button in their Help menu (in the IE menu bar) that will give you a rundown of what's changed in IE 5.0. I've used version IE 4.5 (Mac) and 5.0 (Windows) for this chapter.

Happy surfing! Next, visit Chapter 9 to get some tips on making Web surfing more positive for your students or to see how the other half lives in Chapter 7 where I discuss Netscape Communicator.

Another new feature for Macintosh IE: Page Holder

Page Holder is a really cool tool that makes it easier than ever for Mac users to browse the Web. The IE Page Holder pane maintains a Web page so that you can click through the links on the page while viewing the page in the main browser window. Page Holder eliminates the need to have to click the Back button to get back to the targeted page that contains links you want to browse through.

To access Page Holder, click the Page Holder tab in the Explorer bar.

Chapter 7

Navigating with Navigator

- -

In This Chapter

▶ Getting and installing Communicator

▶ Navigator basics

▶ Bookmark bonanza

▶ Saving and printing the cool stuff

▶ Smart Browsing

- -

*T*he Netscape Navigator browser is the granddaughter of *Mosaic*, a free-ware program that was the first browser generally available on the Web. Mosaic itself is the granddaddy of both browser programs currently holding the vast majority of the browser marketplace, including Navigator and Microsoft's browser offering, Internet Explorer. (See Chapter 6 for instructions on using Internet Explorer.)

Netscape Communicator is a suite of programs that includes:

- ✔ **Navigator:** Netscape's browser and the centerpiece of Communicator. Because this book is for the beginning surfer and the intermediate surfer alike, I concentrate primarily on the Navigator Web browser because it's the most important component of the Communicator suite.

- ✔ **Messenger:** Communicator's e-mail program; allows you to send, receive, and organize your e-mail, and do the same for newsgroups. You can also organize your e-mail addresses with Netscape's address book.

- ✔ **Composer:** Communicator's tool for creating and editing Web pages.

- ✔ **Enterprise Calendar:** Keep track of important dates — like the last day of school.

Navigator has a fast, easy-to-use interface that makes zipping around the Web easy. It's feature-rich, too, and combined with Communicator, provides access to e-mail and other goodies.

Note: For a more in-depth look at Communicator, check out *Netscape Communicator 4.5 For Dummies* by my buddy Paul Hoffman (IDG Books Worldwide, Inc.).

Downloading Netscape Communicator

If you don't have a copy of Communicator 4.5 (which contains Netscape Navigator), a copy is provided on the CD that came with this book. No download is necessary here; just pop the CD into your drive and copy the file to your computer's hard drive.

Just in case one of your students used the CD as a drink coaster or you want to update to a version of Communicator or Navigator (also available as a standalone program — if you choose this the instructions in this chapter might be a bit different) that's more current than the one on this disc (they release a new one about once a minute), here are a few instructions about how to get Communicator from the Internet. The following directions are more or less generic, regardless of the computer you're using.

1. **Log on to the Internet and launch your browser.**

   If you're accessing the Net through an online service like AOL, just click Sign On and you're on your way. Otherwise, you can launch Internet Explorer or an older version of Navigator while connected to AOL, your service provider, or your Internet-connected network. (If you wish to take the really easy way out, check out "Navigator for AOL", available at keyword: **Netscape**, which comes preconfigured with all the proxy info for AOL.)

2. **Visit Netscape's Netcenter (**`http://home.netscape.com`**).**

   You are whisked away to the mother ship of Netscape.

3. **Click the Download link on the Netcenter page (the link is in the upper left corner).**

   Choose the Navigator program right for your computer and operating system, click the hyperlink to the file and it automatically downloads (and decompresses) onto your computer's hard drive. If you choose to download with SmartDownload (it's the default choice and takes all of 30 seconds to download), you will download a file that, when started, will download Communicator with SmartDownload, which allows you to pause your download and resume it later (if you need to use the phone, for example). Super cool!

If you don't have a browser and want Communicator, you can also use any FTP (File Transfer Protocol) software (like Fetch or WS_FTP) to visit, `ftp://ftp.netscape.com` click the filename of the version you wish to download, and then unpack the program.

Installing Netscape Communicator

No matter what platform you use, the experience of downloading and installing Navigator is pretty similar. If you've got a Macintosh, locate the copy of Communicator (or Navigator if you downloaded only the browser) you downloaded or received from your ISP and double-click Install Netscape Communicator. Your Mac automatically unpacks and installs all the necessary files.

For Windows users, Netscape sends Communicator in a file that's compressed for faster transmission. Luckily, the expansion procedure is simple and pretty straightforward. Here's what to do:

1. **Run the installer program.**

   Find the folder (directory) icon that copied to your computer and click the installer file icon to begin.

2. **Follow the instructions on the screen.**

   The installer program unpacks your files and then asks you bunches of questions. Usually, choosing Yes or the default option gets you through the installation process painlessly. After the process is complete, you see a brand new icon called Netscape Communicator on your desktop and a new folder on your Macintosh desktop or new shortcut icon (Windows). But wait! Don't click yet; there's one more step!

3. **Connect to the Internet.**

   After you launch Navigator, it looks for the Internet, and your computer scolds you if you're not connected. Depending on how you connect to the Internet, you may be able to just double-click your browser icon and watch as Navigator launches your dial-up programs and does the rest for you. (In Windows, set your Dial-up Connection setting to "Prompt to use dial-up networking"; it's automatic on a Mac).

4. **Fire up Communicator.**

   Double-click the Netscape Communicator icon (or the Navigator icon, if you downloaded the browser stand-alone program). The first time you run Communicator (if you haven't run a browser before on that computer) it will run the Internet Connection Wizard. If it does just follow the on-screen instructions. Note that you may need some information from your Internet service provider, like server info. You can usually check your ISP's home page under Tech Support for this type of information.

Rifling through the Various Parts

Netscape Communicator's browser window is essentially divided into seven main components, which I've labeled in Figure 7-1. Here's a quick overview of what each of the most important components do:

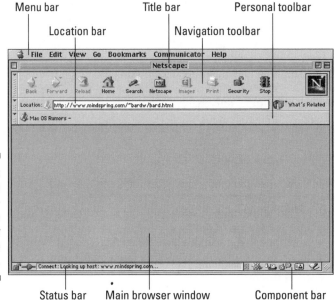

Menu bar · Title bar · Personal toolbar

Location bar · Navigation toolbar

Status bar · Main browser window · Component bar

Figure 7-1:
Netscape
Communi-
cator, the
granddaddy
of Web
browsers.

The following sections explain these components in greater detail.

Sifting through the toolbar buttons

The Navigator toolbar is your control over where and how you browse the Web. The conveniently located buttons can do everything from taking you back from whence you came (don't you love that word "whence"?) to whisk you back to your home page or to a search engine with the click of your mouse. Figure 7-2 shows the Navigation toolbar.

✔ **Back:** Click this button to display the previous page in the history list. Hold down the button (or right-click in Windows) to display a pop-up menu containing the pages you can go back to in the history list, which contains a hierarchy of pages you've already viewed. View a subset of the history list in the Go menu, or the entire list by choosing Communicator➪Tools➪History.

You can also choose Go➪Back or press ⌘-[(Mac users) or Alt+← (Windows users).

Figure 7-2:
The
Navigation
Toolbar —
navigation
central for
Communi-
cator users.

✓ **Forward:** Click this button to display the next page in the history list. Hold down the mouse button (right-click in Windows) to display a pop-up menu containing the history list (the pages you can go forward to). If you've retrieved a page by clicking the Back button or by selecting a page from the history menu, then the Forward button displays the prior page you were visiting. Forward is only available after you use the Back button or a history item.

You can also open the Go menu and choose the Forward command or press ⌘-] (Mac users) or Alt+→ (Windows users).

✓ **Reload:** Click this button to redisplay the current Navigator page, reflecting any changes made since the original loading. To reload, Navigator checks the network server to see if any change to the page has occurred. If no change has taken place, the original page is retrieved from a cache. If a change has occured, the updated page is retrieved from the network server. If you press the Reload button while holding down the Shift key (Option key on the Mac), the cache is ignored, and Navigator retrieves the page from the network server regardless of whether the page has been updated.

✓ **Home:** Click this button to display the homepage designated in the Navigator preferences panel. A home page is the first page you see when you launch your browser. The default page is Netscape's home page: Netcenter. You can change the default home page to any page you wish by choosing Edit⇨Preferences, and then either pushing the Use Current Page button (to make the page Navigator is currently displaying your home page) or just by typing the desired address into the Location box.

✓ **Search:** Click this button to display a page containing a directory of Internet search engine sites and services.

✓ **My Netscape:** Click this button to display a pop-up menu containing links to pages that offer tools and links for personalizing your Internet experience.

✔ **Images:** This button is only available by choosing Edit⇨Preferences⇨ Advanced and deselecting the "Automatically load images" preference item. Icons are substituted for images that would ordinarily load automatically when you visit a page. Click the Images button to remove the substitution icons and display a page's images.

✔ **Print:** Click this button to print the content area of the page currently being displayed in the main browser window. A dialog box lets you select printing characteristics. If you are at a site that uses frames, you first have to click somewhere in the frame you wish to print before clicking the Print button. (Otherwise, Netscape doesn't know which frame to print for you!)

✔ **Security:** Click this button to display the Security Info window, which lets you view and interact with security elements, such as encryption status, personal and site certificates, security-related applications, and passwords.

✔ **Stop:** Click this button to halt any ongoing transfer of page information. *Hint:* If a document is taking too long to load or seems to have stuck, clicking Stop and then Reload can sometimes help. Pressing ⌘-Period (on the Mac) or the Escape key in Windows do the same thing as clicking the Stop button on the toolbar.

The buttons on your toolbar changes if you use features of Communicator other than Navigator. If you launch Messenger, for example, you see the Messenger version of the toolbar (shown in Figure 7-3), which has buttons to send, receive, and print messages.

Figure 7-3:
The
Messenger
toolbar —
e-mail,
news, and
more.

Visiting URLs

If you know the Web address *(URL)* of a site, you don't need to use a search engine to find the page you wish to visit. Just hop up to the Location toolbar (see Figure 7-4) and click in the white space, type in the Web address of the site you want and press Return (Enter key in Windows). Navigator jumps to your desired site directly from whatever page you are viewing.

Figure 7-4:
The
Location
toolbar —
type in a
URL for
quick
access.

Type the address of the site you want to visit into the Location box.

Hint: For addresses that begin with `http://`, instead of typing `http://your.address.goes.here` in the Location box, just type **your.address.goes.here.**

For those of you who want to use anonymous FTP instead of dealing with another FTP program, in the Location toolbar use `ftp://hostname` instead of `http://hostname` — you should automatically be logged into the FTP service. Note that this logs you into an anonymous FTP session. (See Chapter 15 for more info on FTP.)

Getting at your components and reading your status

Two of the most useful elements of Navigator are the component bar and status bar. The component bar, usually found hanging around on the lower right hand corner of your browser window, is really just a navigation tool to let you move around inside the many parts of Communicator. The component bar has icons labeled (from left to right) Navigator, Inbox, Read Newsgroups, Address Book, and Composer. You can *undock* (float) the component bar by dragging it to other locations, or click the close box to *dock* it (send it to the lower-right corner of all Communicator windows).

The status bar shows messages that indicate your progress in downloading Web pages and other content from the Web, and clues you in to the presence of Java applets. In general, the messages that appear when connecting to a Web page appear in the following order:

✔ **Looking up host.** Navigator locates the URL by translating the domain name in your URL to an IP (numeric) address. This process is usually very quick.

✔ **Contacting host.** Navigator is waiting for the host computer to say "hello" and show that it's not busy. Usually, if there's lots of traffic on a site, this is the place you'll get hung up.

✔ **Host contacted.** Waiting for reply. The host computer said "howdy" and is trying to process your request.

✔ **Transferring data.** The data is being transmitted from the host computer to your browser window. Sometimes things just "freeze" at this step because of host traffic or memory issues on your computer. If the transfer freezes, just hit your Return key or click the Reload button on the Navigation toolbar.

✔ **Loading Java applets/Applet <name> running.** Your browser is downloading and running a Java applet (applets are small programs that add functionality to your browsing session).

Customizing Navigator

Navigator offers lots of options for customization. You can choose a different default home page, increase or decrease the size of text displayed on your screen, and more. Choose Edit⇨Preferences to change the settings for the look and operation of your Netscape Navigator browser. The Preferences dialog box, shown in Figure 7-5, is a warehouse of options that you can use to customize your Communicator software. Luckily, most of the default settings work just fine, so you can save your visit to Preferences until later.

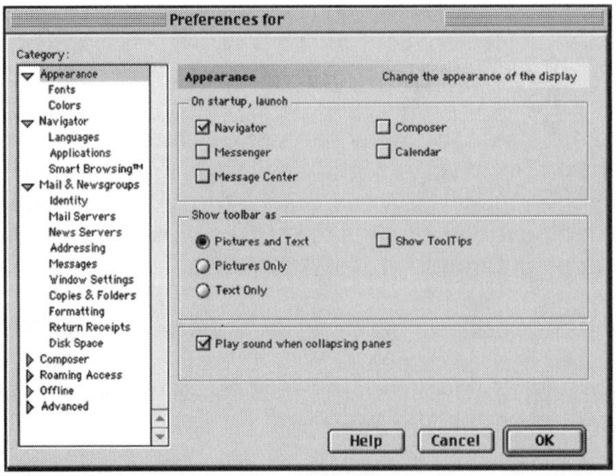

Figure 7-5: Communicator's Preferences window — personalize your browser and more.

The Preferences window allows you to change just about everything about Communicator — from the button styles to how often your browser clears it's cache (temporary memory). The main functions are categorized under seven categories (see Table 7-1).

Table 7-1	Communicator Preferences
This Category	*Allows You To . . .*
Appearance	Change screen fonts and background color
Navigator	Change your default home page, add helper applications, and enable Smart Browsing
Mail & Newsgroups	Customize the format, location, servers, and your identity for sending and receiving e-mail or checking newsgroups
Roaming Access	For network users — retrieve your personal preferences from elsewhere in your school network
Composer	Set options for Communicator's Web page building program
Offline	Set automatic mail functions, and allow offline browsing of newsgroup discussions
Advanced	Enable/disable Java, JavaScript, cookies, SmartUpdate, and set the size of your disk cache

The Web goes 3-D

What's the next level in Web exploration? It might just be 3-D graphic navigation. Enter VRML and QuickTime.

Virtual Reality Modeling Language (VRML) is an open standard development language for displaying 3-D computer graphics, stereo sound, and hyperlinks. With VRML, you'll enter worlds (graphic environments) that allow you to browse for information in a completely different way.

Apple Computer has taken the 3-D space a bit farther by integrating 3-D capabilities into QuickTime, an application that is free for Windows users and built into every Macintosh. With QuickTime, which contains QuickTimeVR, viewers can enter virtual worlds *(panoramas)*, navigate from scene to scene, create *sprites* (animated objects within a QuickTime movie), watch streaming video feeds and read more than 200 different Internet multimedia types (www.apple.com/quicktime).

To view VRML, you need a plug-in or VRML browser. Check out these up-and-coming tools:

✔ **Express VR:** A Netscape plug-in for Mac and Windows users

✔ **Virtus Voyager:** A stand-alone application for Macintosh users

✔ **Live 3D:** Another helper application, available for Macs and PCs running Windows

✔ **RealSpace:** A helper application for Power Macintosh owners

There are others, too, such as Liquid Reality from Dimension X (www.dimensionx.com), Cosmo Player from Silicon Graphics (www.sgi.com), and Community Place from Sony (www.sony.com).

Dog-Earing Your Pages with Bookmarks

You're likely to go bananas your first time on the Web, surfing from page to page and marveling at all the great information and cool graphics you see; forgetting URLs you've visited is easy. Luckily, Netscape Communicator has an easy way to remember where you've been — bookmarks. After saving several bookmarks, however, your menu begins to get crowded so you'll want to bookmark with care!

Setting a Bookmark is easy. Simply surf to the Web page that you want to save and choose Add Bookmark (⌘+D, Alt+D) from the Bookmark pull-down menu. The items are added to the list in the order that you enter them. You can also just drag the bookmark and change its position or drop it into another folder.

Your Bookmark list is now available, and you can "resurf" a Web page, Gopher address, or FTP site by choosing that location directly from Navigator's Bookmark menu. No more messy URLs!

You can add, delete, and reorganize your Bookmarks by choosing Bookmark⇨Edit Bookmarks on the Location toolbar. Don't look now, but you'll have a hundred or so Web sites in your Bookmark before you know it, so a bit of organization goes a long way.

Communicator also allows you to create Internet shortcut icons that let you jump from your desktop, or from folders (directories) on your computer, directly to a Web site. To create a shortcut, do one of the following:

✔ Drag the bookmark icon (it's green and located at the left of your Location toolbar) to the desktop to create a shortcut from a link. You can also drag the icon onto your personal toolbar (a place for your most-used bookmarks) or into any folder on the personal toolbar, as well as into any folder in the bookmarks menu.

✔ Drag the bookmark icon to the desktop (to create a shortcut for the current Web page).

After you get enough bookmarks, you'll come to a moment when you're "URL savvy" enough to want edit your best bookmark lists and exchange them with others (or pre-load them on classroom computers to give all your students the benefit of your awesome browsing skills). To edit or change a bookmark:

1. **Choose Communicator⇨Bookmarks (Mac) or Bookmarks⇨Edit Bookmarks (on the Location toolbar in Windows).**

   The Edit Bookmarks window appears.

2. **Select a bookmark or bookmark folder from the Bookmarks window.**

   Click the plus sign next to a folder (or the triangle on a Mac) to expand and collapse its contents.

3. **Choose Edit⊅Get Info (Mac) or Edit⊅Bookmark Properties (Windows).**

   To make a change in a URL, type the new URL or edit the one that's displayed in the Bookmarks window. Rename a bookmark by selecting its current name and choosing Get-info (Mac) or Properties (Windows), then retyping the name. (That Instant Messenger icon takes up a lot less space on your Personal toolbar if you rename it IM, for example.)

4. **Click OK.**

Saving your bookmarks is very wise every couple of weeks or so, just in case your hard drive should crash or some other similar catastrophic event should occur. See the "Saving the Cool Stuff" section in this chapter for more information on saving.

Getting Caught in the Web

Here are some points to ponder that can save you loads of time and a few gray hairs:

✔ If images are loading too slowly, deselect Auto Load images in Communicator's Edit⊅Preferences (Advanced) menu. When deselected, images are replaced by small icons, and you click the Images button in the toolbar to view the images. If you've got Auto Load turned off, you can still see selected images by double-clicking them (Mac) or right-clicking and choosing View Image (Windows).

✔ If at first you don't succeed . . . try, try again — sometimes the third time's the charm. Web servers can get lots of traffic and sometimes they get overwhelmed.

To speed things up with Communicator, you can deselect unneeded features. Here's a list of options to consider deselecting (from Communicator's Preferences [Advanced] menu) if things are moving too slowly:

✔ **Enable Java:** Allows *Java applets* (small programs that add functionality to pages) to run automatically.

✔ **Enable JavaScript:** Allows *JavaScript* (commands that add functionality to pages) to run automatically.

✔ **Enable style sheets:** Displays pages formatted by style sheets as the author intended. If unselected, author's formats aren't included.

✔ **Enable Autoinstall:** Allows Communicator software to automatically be updated over your office or organization's network. (In some organizations, this is predetermined by a system administrator.)

✔ **Send email address as anonymous FTP password:** Transmits your e-mail address automatically when you log on to a public FTP site. (Grab more info about FTP in Chapter 15).

Saving the Cool Stuff

Navigator offers you the ability to save the contents of Web pages to your computer's hard drive and to save your bookmarks, address book(s) and preferences so that you can trade them with your friends, save bookmarks from one computer to use on another, or just back them up on a floppy. You can spend a good deal of time customizing Communicator — you don't want to have to do all that again every time you switch computers.

Here's a great tip, Communicator lets you save multiple bookmark lists in case you want to have one for each class in your computer lab, or your own personal bookmark set that you don't want saved to every machine in the school! To save a bookmark list:

1. **Choose Communicator⇨Bookmarks (Mac) or Bookmarks⇨Edit Bookmarks (Windows).**

   The bookmark file in the active window is the one that will save.

   The Bookmark window appears as shown in Figure 7-6.

2. **Choose File⇨Save As.**

   Enter the name of a bookmark file. Be sure to choose a unique filename so as not to overwrite or confuse files later. Press Return to save. This saves your current bookmark list as an HTML-formatted file.

To open a list and use it:

1. **Choose CommunicatorÍBookmarks (Mac) or BookmarksÍEdit Bookmarks (Windows).**

   The Bookmark window appears as shown in Figure 7-6.

2. **Choose File⇨Open Bookmarks File.**

   The file you open determines what you see in your Bookmarks menu. Your old bookmarks are safe and sound (hopefully!) in the default file called "bookmarks.html" or something similar on your hard disk.

Printing Web Pages

Raise you right hand and repeat after me: "Electronic resources on the Web save paper and hard drive space. There is no need to save or print the entire Internet." Okay, good. The obvious message here is to resist (and have your students resist) the urge to save or print every bit of info you see on the Internet. Believe me, doing this leads to a black hole of deforestation from which you cannot escape. Concentrate on bookmarking the sites you want to revisit later instead of printing them (see the "Dog-Earing Your Pages with Bookmarks" section earlier in this chapter).

That said, if you must print, I guess I should share tips and tricks for doing so. Printing a Web page is as easy as printing a document from your word processor. Just click the Print button in the Communicator Toolbar or choose File⇨Print. (⌘-P/Alt+P also works!)

The tricky part of printing Web pages is that some Web authors use a design technique called *frames*. Frames subdivide a Web page into several independent sub-pages. Subdividing the page helps organize the display and make it easier to work with. Because each sub-page displays a separate page, they may be changed and scrolled independently. Usually, Webmasters use frames to display menus or "contents" of a site across the top or left-hand margin of each page in the site.

To print a specific part of a home page that's divided into frames, just make sure to click inside the sub-page to let your printer know what you want to print. You can also Control-click (Mac) or click the right mouse button (Windows) and choose Open a new window with this link to display just the frame you wish to print and then print as usual.

Sometimes, the width of a home page is wider than your printer will support. When this happens, your "one" home page will likely print multiple sheets, which you must then cut and paste together. Yuck. Luckily, you can change your print setup preferences to squeeze things a bit for easier printing.

1. **Choose File⇨Page Setup.**

   The Page Setup window appears.

2. **Change page layout options.**

   Type a number in the Scale box to reduce the size of the printed page (this is useful to get a wider than usual Web page to fit on one page). I usually print pages at 85%. That'll do the trick to get it on one page (at least width-wise).

Smart Browsing

From the "really cool feature" department, the good folks at Netscape delivere Smart Browsing, which helps you quickly find what you want on the Internet and filter out what you don't.

It includes:

- ✔ **What's Related:** A list of URLs (addresses) for home page sites related to the page you're currently viewing. To view related sites, click the What's Related button on on the far right of the Location toolbar and select from the list.

- ✔ **Internet Keywords:** A shorthand way of typing addresses into the Location box. Typing apple for example, whisks you to `http://www.apple.com`. Type **www.whatever.com** and Communicator automatically adds the `http://` prefix.

- ✔ **NetWatch:** Navigator's built-in, password protected feature lets you control the type of Web pages that can be viewed on your computer. To enable NetWatch, Choose Help⇨NetWatch. A Web page appears like the one shown in Figure 7-7.

  NetWatch is Netscape Navigator's built-in ratings protection feature. It lets you control what kind of home page pages can be viewed on your computer using an Internet rating standard known as PICS (Platform for Internet Content Selection). PICS is designed to help parents, teachers, and employers screen out material they feel is inappropriate for children or employees. PICS gives home page publishers a standard way to describe the content of home page pages, and browsers like Navigator a standard way to read the description.

  NetWatch recognizes two independent PICS-compliant ratings systems, RSACi and SafeSurf. Each system employs a different method to describe in as much detail as possible the levels of potentially offensive content on Web pages.

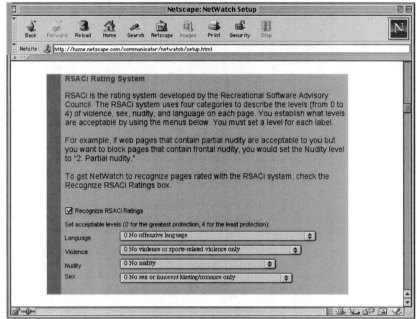

Figure 7-7:
Filter Web
content with
NetWatch.

Web site publishers sometimes voluntarily rate their pages using one of
these systems. You can choose one or both of the rating systems and
decide which levels are acceptable to you in the NetWatch setup
process. Of course, those sites that don't get rated don't get filtered out!

Setting up Smart Browsing is super simple:

1. **Choose Edit⇨Preferences.**

   The Preferences window appears.

2. **Select the Navigator category from the list down the left side of the
   Preferences window and choose Smart Browsing from the Navigator
   submenu.**

3. **Make sure there's a check in the Enable What's Related and Enable
   Internet Keywords check boxes to enable these features.**

Chapter 8

The Search Is On

In This Chapter

▶ Searching 101

▶ Tricks of the Trade

When I think about searching the Internet, I have to look no farther than my own recent journey to find out more about my family. My father is Welsh/English, my mother Norwegian/English, and my last name is Williams. More than 30 years ago, my great-grandfather began work on a family tree (well, more specifically, one branch of a family tree). This labor took him most of his life, and when he died, he left behind a simple one-page chart, meticulously hand drawn and lovingly mailed to his children. After more than 50 or so years of research, he uncovered three generations of the family.

When I moved to Boston in 1996, I had a coworker who was "into" genealogy. Donna introduced me to a wonderful software program called "Reunion" (www.leisterpro.com) and gave me a list of URLs she used to search for her family's roots. She also gave me the dial-up phone number for the computers at the mother-of-all genealogical libraries: the Family History Library of the Church of Jesus Christ of Latter-day Saints, a wonderful resource for starting your own geneological search.

I logged on to the geneological library and, using great-grandpa's chart, found six more generations of the Williams family and began to explore other branches of the family — unveiling more than 100 other possible connections. I put these names and birth/death dates into the program and printed a stunningly complex and useful chart. Then I had lunch. I'm not sure about the reliability of the information I located, or whether that Williams family in Cardiff are really long-lost relatives. (Now my father's got the program for his Mac and he's probably going to end up with a book of his own.)

Whether it's your genealogy or the latest satellite images from planet Mars, finding things on the Internet is much easier than it's ever been. Search engines abound and are available 24 hours a day.

Internet Search 411

If you use only one search engine, say the popular Yahoo! (www.yahoo.com), chances are you're missing a significant amount of content that's posted to the Web. That's right, all search engines aren't created equal. In fact, no single search engine can index the entire Internet. And to top it all off, Yahoo! isn't a search engine at all, it's actually a *directory*. Confused? It's really not that complex. Read on!

The main ways of searching the Internet are

- ✔ **Search engine:** An amazing software program backed by a bank of computers with lots of processing power and electronic storage capacity. These programs take a *keyword* or (or *keywords*) you enter and jump out to the Internet, blasting through millions of sites in seconds and returning a list of URLs containing the keyword you entered while you wait. Altavista, shown in Figure 8-1, is an example of a search engine.

  Other top search engines include: AltaVista (www.altavista.com), Excite (www.excite.com), HotBot (www.hotbot.com), InfoSeek (www.infoseek.com), and Lycos (www.lycos.com). Some search engines, called *metasearch engines,* actually search other search engines, Beaucoup (www.beaucoup.com) is an example of a metasearch engine, as is the benevolent Dogpile (www.dogpile.com).

- ✔ **Directory:** A man-made list of links that someone sorts by topic and stores on some behemoth computer. Like seach engines, directories are keyword-searchable. The main difference between a directory and a search engine is that the directory searches through the links that have already been added to the directory rather than the Internet at large. Directory services use powerful programs called *spiders* that run during off-peak hours to collect and categorize Web sites to make the directory a better resource for your searching needs. The wildly popular Yahoo! and the spin-off Yahooligans!, shown in Figure 8-2, are popular directories.

  The 800-pound gorillas of the directory world include: Yahoo! (www.yahoo.com), Education World (www.education-world.com) — a must-surf education resource — the Magellan Internet Guide (www.mckinley.com), Yahooligans! (www.yahooligans.com) especially for surfers ages 8–14, and The Awesome Library (www.neat-schoolhouse.org/awesome.html)

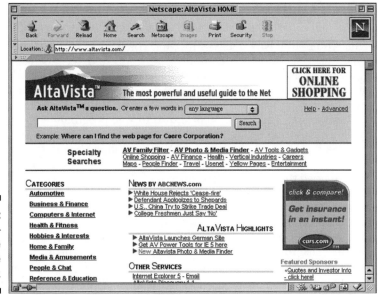

Figure 8-1:
AltaVista —
a must-use
on the
infoway.

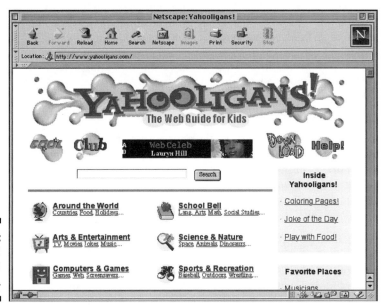

Figure 8-2:
Yahooligans!
— Yahoo!
for kids.

WYSINWYG

(What you search isn't necessarily what you'll get). No directory or search engine is perfect. Most use complex algorithms to determine which URLs show up first in your results listing. Usually this involves the back-end computer doing frequency counts for words on selected sites, or searching keywords (included in each Web site's HTML), or looking at the "title" of pages (also in the HTML code). Each method is known to Web programmers and a culture of slick webmasters trying to "fool the engines" to move their sites to the top of the list has made the search engine programming teams go crazy. One trick, which no longer works (because the search engine teams got savvy), was to embed thousands of keywords as colored text on a like-colored background (invisible to the surfer) to get engines to think that their site was more relevant (the term more frequently occurred in regular content) than others. One 'infamous' men's magazine even hid "invisible text" containing almost every noun in the dictionary on their front page and suddenly soared to the top of the search list for almost any word you searched for. The Internet community caught on quickly, however, and put measures in place to avoid such tricks. Of course, there are many, many smart people out there who've found other ways. This cat and mouse game has yet to be played out.

What does all this mean to your students? It means that now you can explain what some unscrupulous Webmasters will go through just to get your eyeballs to their site. It also explains why an occasional not-so-nice site pops up as a result of an innocent search attempt.

As the computing power of desktop computers increases, so do the possibilities for new, more powerful and fully-featured browser technologies. The latest versions of Communicator and IE have some nifty new features to make your browsing and searching easier.

You can use Communicator's Smart Browsing feature by typing keywords right into the Location box. For example, you can type **goto *firstword secondword*** to jump to a Web site that those words suggest or **search *firstword secondword*** to search for those words using, a popular search engine. If you don't type **search** or **goto**, but type the keywords, Communicator assumes that you've typed **goto**.

Another new feature that first appeared in Navigator v. 4.06 is the What's Related button that appears to the right of the Location box in the top right of your browser window. When you click this button, the browser sends the URL in the Location box to Netscape headquarters and returns a list of pages similar to the one you typed, based on pages other people have visited in the past.

Microsoft's approach to smart browser technology is a bit different. Keywords in the Address box jump you to the mother of all directories, Yahoo! and displays a list of similar pages. IE also has a Search button in the menu bar— the button that looks like a magnifying glass. Clicking this button reveals a cool

Search window that lets you search for pages, people, and businesses quickly and easily. To start over with new keywords, click New. You can also choose your favorite search engine by clicking the Customize icon, the litter hammer and gear, at the top of the Search window.

When you search for Web pages, the Search Assistant in Communicator sends your keywords to one of several search engines. If you don't like what comes back, click the Next button at the top of the Search window and the Search Assistant tries another.

The Great Search Engine Myth

Most beginning Internet explorers (no pun intended) think that each and every search engine does an equally thorough job of searching the Internet and returning information — actually, nothing could be further from the truth. In fact, most of us sit down at our computer and enter search terms in several search engines and directories until we find what we want. Wouldn't it be great if there was some type of technology that would allow you to search multiple search engines *at the same time*?

Personal search detective on the case

Sometimes being a Mac user really pays off. A little program that comes with Mac OS 8.5 called *Sherlock* is a tool that Apple calls a *revolutionary personal search detective.* Born out of the education research and development team at Apple, Sherlock allows you to search multiple sites concurrently, saving you and your students hours of valuable time by quickly zeroing in on the exact information you're looking for.

Sherlock can send your query to several leading search engines at the same time, and in a few seconds generate a list, ranked by relevance, with duplicate sites removed. You can view them all in one convenient window and link to any result instantly with a single click. Clicking the link opens your default browser and whisks you to the site. This powerful tool can even summarize a document into a couple of paragraphs before you see it, and you and your students can save search criteria and results for

later use.

Sherlock can also search within documents on any storage device your computer has access to — even through hundreds of thousands of files. Simply tell it what you're looking for (in plain English) and Sherlock does the rest. Whether your students are distilling large amounts of information for their latest class project or you're building an abstract for a dissertation, Sherlock's on the case.

The Basic Search

Searching the Web is really a simple process because virtually all search engines work the same way. Here are the basic steps:

1. **Log on to the Internet and the start your Web browser.**

   If you're a Mac user using Mac OS 8.5 or higher, take a look at the "Personal search detective on the case" sidebar and save yourself about a zillion hours.

2. **Choose a search engine.**

   This means entering a URL, like www.excite.com, into your browser window. See the Internet Search 411 section for a list of some popular search engines.

3. **Enter search terms or visit pre-determined keyword lists.**

   Type the term or terms into the Search box online. You may have to press the Return key (Enter key in Windows) on your keyboard after you type, or click a button that says "Go," "Search," or (ugh, what a term) "Execute."

4. **View the results. If they don't make sense, then go back to step 3 and reenter or refine your search.**

   The results appear in a listing, sometimes ranked by relevance, sometimes sorted alphabetically, and sometimes sorted by URL.

   If you find a site that's almost, but not quite, what you want, most search engines have a "more like this" (or "find similar sites") function to help you hone your search.

Specialized Searches

There will come a day when one of your students will have a need to find a psychiatrist for Trixie, your class Iguana (you know, the one that hides every time a child comes close?) or when you really want to relive your college memories and search for a long-lost friend. Enter specialized search engines.

Specialized search engines typically focus on some small subset of the information on the Internet, but offer much more extensive and customized searches. Suppose you want to find the address and phone number of your long-lost college roommate (you know, the one who owes you $50 and took your disco records). Jump onto the Net and search WhoWhere (www.whowhere.lycos.com), Yahoo's people search function, 411 (www.four11.com), and my favorite, Switchboard (www.switchboard.com), shown in Figure 8-3.

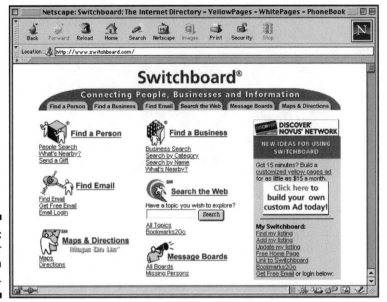

Figure 8-3:
Search for
people with
Switchboard.

Enter a name, e-mail address, state, and other information, and the service does the equivalent of thumbing through every telephone book in the US — all in about 5 seconds. Now you just have to get up the nerve to call them!

There are also some specialized search engines and directories perfect for the classroom. One of my favorites, Research-It! (shown is Figure 8-4) is particularly handy. Despite its wordy URL (www.itools.com/research-it /research-it.html), Research-It! offers searchable dictionaries, thesauruses, quotation databases, area codes, 800-number directories, a global currency converter, FedEx package tracking, and more — free!

You can also search for programs (software) to download using specialized search engines like Shareware.com (www.shareware.com) and CNET (www.download.com) These directories search libraries of public domain software (free) and shareware (try it and keep it for a modest fee) programs by keyword. These search engines are excellent places to search for software upgrades and nifty programs written by other educators, students, and hobbyists.

Figure 8-4:
Lots of Cool
tools at
Research-It!

The Tricks of the Trade

You may have already tried searching using the search engines in this chapter. You probably got about a zillion "hits," and most were links to sites you didn't want. Luckily I can pass along several tricks and tips to make your searches much more efficient. Although all these tricks don't work with every single search engine or directory, you may as well try. If they work, they'll save you and your students gobs of time.

Ifs, ands, and buts

Programmers and savvy librarians know about them. Mathematicians know about them. Here's what they know: Using *operators* such as and, or, and not, coupled with special characters such as *, +, and - can refine an Internet search. Known as a Boolean search, using operators between keywords in your search helps narrow, and therefore speed, your search.

Here's an example: Suppose you're searching for information about the care and feeding of horses. You'd fire up a search engine and enter: **horse**. Unfortunately, *horse* turns up about a thousand hits: everything from auto dealers (Mustang) to basketball (horse is a well-known round ball activity) to drugs (horse is a slang term often used to refer to heroin).

To narrow your search, you can use Boolean operators as follows:

```
horse and feeding
```

Most search engines assume an "and" between search terms, so you might get the same results typing: **horse feeding**. You can also try narrowing the search with a search like this: **Horse and feeding not drugs and not cars**. That should screen out the addicts and muscle-car sites.

You should be careful, however. It is possible to "confuse" a search engine with an improperly constructed Boolean search. Here's a no-no:

```
Horse and feeding not feed or horse shows
```

This search construction is a no-no for two reasons. One is that "feed" is a root word of the word "feeding". Horse and horse shows will look much the same to the engine, you'll need to put "horse shows" in quotes to give it a clue what you're looking for.

You can also use quotation marks around a search term to force a search engine to treat multiple words as a complete and unique search term. For example: typing in **"Ford Mustang"** returns only occurrences of the words "Ford" and "Mustang" that are used *together*. So this screens out horses, biographies of Henry Ford, and the Betty Ford clinic.

You can also use additional operators like "+" and "-" and "*" as in: **Ford Mustang +1998 –Cobra**.

These keywords return a search for Web pages containing the exact phrase "Ford Mustang", at least one occurrence of "1998" and then deletes from your search results any page containing the term "Cobra." (Cobra, for those uninitiated, is the name for Ford's performance Mustang.)

Finally, using an asterisk "*" after a search term enables a "wild card" search. That means if you search for **Must***, you're going to get mustang, mustard, must, musty — you get the idea.

Coming up with a list of examples like the ones above and challenging students to narrow their searches is a good exercise. Begin by having your students check the "help" information for their search engine to find out what kinds of operators and punctuation might be useful. Then, think about activities such as "who can construct a search phrase that returns information about what a mouse eats and not get information about computer mice or that funny cartoon guy from Disney." (This one's harder than you think!)

More tricks

Just in case you need even more tricks up your sleeve, here are a few tips and tricks that could be indispensable, or give you a headache.

- ✔ **Case matters.** Use lowercase in your search unless you're searching for a proper noun (*ding!* Grammar lesson time!).

- ✔ **Get near.** The "near" search term, which works in some browsers, only returns sites if two words are next to each other. Typing "Apple *near* computer" gives you the kind of apple you plug in and not the kind you eat.

- ✔ **List, Lizst, list.** Have your students create a list of keywords before you begin your search session in the classroom or lab. See who can narrow down a search for the topic to the fewest search attempts. Recognize the winner with the "Net Detective" award.

- ✔ **Use lots of bookmarks.** Why reinvent the wheel? Make a standard bookmark (or favorites) file containing your favorite search engines and content-rich sites and put it on every computer in your school.

- ✔ **Don't wait.** Slow connection? You can usually tell if the page you're accessing is helpful or not *before* the graphics have trickled in. If you hit a dud, go ahead and surf to the next site. Click Stop, enter a new URL, and hop to the next site.

- ✔ **Share.** Tell others when you find a useful site. In fact, write it on the wall in the teacher's lounge — that'll give folks something to talk about.

Chapter 9

Safe Surfing in the Schoolhouse

● ●

In This Chapter

▶ To serve and protect

▶ Filtering (if you must)

▶ Copyright law and the Internet

● ●

1 know something you don't know. I can go and look at it, but you can't. It's out there and that's all I have to say. Whatever you do, don't look for it. It's bad and I don't want you to see it.

Now, come on, aren't you the *least* bit curious? These are the types of messages that kids receive these days about objectionable content on the Internet. You know, the stuff that doesn't belong in class — from bomb-making to bestiality, the Internet has it all, just a URL away.

You can build walls, install filtering and blocking software, and scold. But I'm not sure I know of *any* creature on the earth more industrious than a middle-school student when it comes to translating curiosity into action. They'll find it. They'll print it. You'll find it on a locker, slipped into your gradebook, or crumpled up in the hands of a very embarrassed kid caught in the act.

So should you just look the other way and hope it doesn't happen? Certainly not. As you'll see in this chapter, I suggest you confront the issue head on; talk about it and make it a part of your discussions about using the Internet wisely. Create policy and enforce it — ruthlessly.

I also discuss the issue of copyright and the Internet. Does the Fair Use Doctrine cover Internet content? Read on!

The Filter Fallacy

In spite of all the scary talk about objectionable content on the Net, you may be surprised with what you're about to read. I have some pretty strong opinions about the use of filtering software and hardware in schools and libraries: I'm generally not in favor of them.

Filtering (or blocking) software can work in several ways. Programs can restrict access to Internet content by:

- ✔ Matching and screening content based on an internal database that comes with the filtering software

- ✔ Matching and screening content via a database maintained externally to the product, generally accessed via network or Web when the software is enabled

- ✔ Screening content based on certain ratings assigned to those sites by a third party (similar to movie ratings)

- ✔ Scanning and filtering content based on a keyword, phrase or text string

- ✔ Blocking based on the source (URL) of the information

You or someone in your school has probably engaged in a heated discussion about the use of filtering software to restrict access to Internet content. The fact is, there really isn't an easy answer to this argument. No matter what you do, someone will eventually get the idea that they can make lots of noise or sue to make their point, no matter which side of the issue they're on.

One place to look for guidance is the public library system. The American Library Association (ALA) has an Intellectual Freedom Committee that released a policy statement in 1997 that says that the use of filtering software violates the ALA voluntary Library Bill of Rights. More specifically, they say:

> *The use in libraries of software filters which block Constitutionally protected speech is inconsistent with the United States Constitution and federal law and may lead to legal exposure for the library and its governing authorities. The American Library Association affirms that the use of filtering software by libraries to block access to constitutionally protected speech violates the Library Bill of Rights.*

(See `www.apa.org/alaorg/oif/filt_stm.html` for the full text.)

That's right, the librarians at ALA — the very ones at risk for Johnny using their wonderful high-speed connection for downloading nudie-pix to take home and post on the refrigerator — don't think filtering software is the way to go either way.

The problem I see with filtering systems is that no matter what filter you use, your filter is probably different than someone else's filter. Software such as NetNanny, SurfWatch, and CyberPatrol take a stab at what most feel is controversial, but this criteria is (at least initially) set forth by the software manufacturer, not your community. And can you imagine what might happen if you held a town meeting to come up with a list of what to filter? (Can you say *career-ending decision?*)

The only effective filter is vigilance and close supervision. You can take simple precautions such as:

- ✔ Create bookmark pages (starting points) that feature carefully chosen sites.

- ✔ Talk to students *before* they hit the keyboard about what's appropriate in your classroom and where you want them to browse.

- ✔ Remind students that Internet access in school is a privilege that can be revoked; enforce this with an iron fist (or regional equivalent).

- ✔ Contact your local police department and report pornographic sites that break laws prohibiting the production or distribution of child pornography and obscenity; these laws apply to the Internet, too.

For more information on filtering check out: www.filteringfacts.org

Filtering When You Must

Okay. If you've read my carefully worded diatribe about filtering Internet content in the previous section and you still want to install some software, I'll give you some options. More and more products are appearing in the marketplace to help parents and teachers restrict and monitor usage of the Internet. These products filter Web sites based on fixed lists of URLs and selected keywords that each program's authors have deemed to be objectionable. When a student reaches an offending site, the student (or teacher) receives an onscreen "tsk, tsk," and access to the offending site is denied.

None of these programs tells you exactly what it blocks, and your idea of what's appropriate and inappropriate for your classroom may not be the same as the programmers'. Some software even blocks sites where political opinions are given. (Wait, I'm back on the soapbox. Okay, I'll stop.) Want to see what kind of sites are blocked? Visit SurfWatch fido.siv.spyglass. com/testasite/ (shown in Figure 9-1) and test the waters.

Most filtering and blocking software offer a "try before you buy" evaluation. These systems work both on client (desktop) systems and through networks run by filter-laden servers. I'd say if you're considering using filtering systems, check the education periodicals (like *Educational Leadership* and *Technology & Learning*) for reviews. Here's a list of a few of the biggies in the filtering/blocking world:

SurfWatch (Spyglass); phone 888-677-9452; www.surfwatch.com

Net Nanny (Net Nanny Software Intl., Inc.); phone 800-349-7177; www.netnanny.com

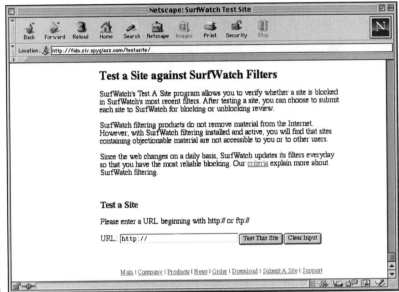

CyberPatrol (The Learning Company); phone 800-828-2608;
www.cyberpatrol.com

Cybersitter (Solid Oak Software, Inc.); phone 800-388-2761;
www.solidoak.com /cysitter.htm

As you can see by the teacher approved icon, my favorite is CyberPatrol,
which is the most flexible and the most *editable*. Want more info about filtering and blocking programs? Visit www.smartparent.com for a complete
listing and some dandy reviews — assuming you really want to use this stuff.

Copyright and The Internet

Before long, your students will begin generating heaps of new content based
on the information they've found by searching the Internet. That's about the
same time that you'll notice that most students don't have a clue when it
comes to copyright issues. I'm not a lawyer, but I've talked to a few.

Here's a primer on copyright that should do justice to the actual law.
Remember, just to be safe, consult your school media specialist/librarian
and/or your school attorney for more information or your school's policy on
the use of copyrighted works. I can't leave you hanging, though, so to help
you out, here's a basic look at copyright do's and don'ts.

Don't copy that!

Copyright law in the U.S. says that anything your create, such as pictures, text, audio files, multimedia, and so on is automatically protected as soon as you write (print) or save it to electronic media (disks, servers, CD, and so on). It's a simple, reasonable law that protects your work and the work of your students, too.

Basically, anything you or your students copy from the Internet is copyrighted material. So, you and your students should be aware of how to request permission for use of materials or the other statutes that apply to copying work for educational purposes.

What's fair is fair

Most educators area aware of the so-called Fair Use Doctrine. This provision, actually part of the Copyright Act, 17 U.S.C., Sec. 107, has some special language that suggests that in certain circumstances, some copying is not an outright infringement of copyright.

The Fair Use Doctrine allows for using copyrighted works for criticism, news reporting, teaching, scholarship, comment, and research. Before you get all excited about that "teaching" thing, note that there are four "tests" that legal-beagles use to decide if a work is fairly used:

- The purpose and character of the use, including whether such use is of a commercial nature or is for a nonprofit-educational purpose. (Schools generally fall into the nonprofit-education category.)

- The nature of the copyrighted work. (Schools generally copy works that are informational.)

- The amount and substantiality of the portion used in relation to the copyrighted work as a whole; generally, the greater the portion of the work, the less likely it falls under "fair use."

- The effect of the use upon the potential market for or value of the copyrighted work. (If your use prevents the author from realizing value, meaning cash, then it's not "fair use".)

If all this sounds like gobbledygook, you're almost right. Copyright law is a little tricky, and the better-safe-than-sorry approach is best, for sure. Messing with copyright can cost you your job.

The bottom line

Get permission, in writing, for everything you or your students copy from the Internet if you have a notion that it doesn't fall under your school's copyright policy guidelines. If you have any question, check with your school's librarian or media specialist or get your school board attorney to take a look.

In fact, having a copyright attorney visit your school and talk with your students about copyright and the Internet is a great idea. End this activity by working with the attorney and the librarian to draft a permission letter that can be sent via e-mail and returned with original signatures in regular (postal) mail format.

Hopefully I didn't scare you too much about this Internet copyright stuff. Just be vigilant and know your school's policy and you should be okay!

Chapter 10

Spinning Your Own Web

· ·

In This Chapter

▶ Why build a Web page?

▶ Weaving your own Web page

▶ Choosing the right tools

▶ Finding a home on the Web

▶ Showing the world

· ·

*F*or every educator, a special moment comes, usually within your first two years of teaching, when you get an idea. Not some run-of-the-mill idea that will excite your students for ten minutes — I'm talking about some *insanely great* idea. You know, the kind of idea that keeps you planning until 1:00 a.m. and gets you to the school an hour early just so that you can get things moving. Fortunately, for many educators, these ideas come frequently.

After you come up with the idea and experience the thrill of having your students excited about the learning journey you created, word gets around that something wonderful just happened in Mr. Jones or Ms. Smith's classroom and everyone wants to hop on the bandwagon. (An interesting and positive side-effect is the concurrent decrease in the number of times your name is written next to an expletive on the school's bathroom walls.) You usually spread the word about your great idea through notes in the school's newsletter, sharing handouts with your peers, or by being embarrassed and standing up in front of the faculty, playing show-and-tell. The sad part is that more often than not, the terrific product of teamwork between educator and student usually remains trapped inside the classroom, a victim of the long-standing tradition that some hidden "mortar monster" somehow defines and limits the spread of knowledge.

Fortunately, the Web offers an opportunity for you and your students to share your work with millions of people — all from within the safe confines of the mortar monster's influence. Now you and your students can gain well-deserved recognition for your hard work from lots of people you don't even know!

Seriously, education has given me much satisfaction over the years. (Maybe that's why I'm a professional student. Is there a degree beyond a doctorate?) Publishing on the Web gives you and your students an opportunity to give knowledge back to the body of humanity, to become *producers* as well as *consumers* of information. The reason so many terrific resources for educators and lifelong learners are already on the Web is that people like you took the time to publish their work. Believe me, the journey itself is part of the reward.

Why Web?

Answering the "Why Web?" question is kind of like answering the broader "Why Internet?" question. But just in case you need a few more reasons to get Webbed, think about these points:

- ✔ The Web is a very efficient way to present information — organized by nature, cross-platform, and very simple to maintain.
- ✔ The Web can be very interactive (take a look at Chapters 18 and 19), and folks are creating new tools for using it every day.
- ✔ The Web offers an easy way to transfer data from your PC and storage devices to someone else without clogging up their hard drive.
- ✔ The Web offers an opportunity to teach higher-order thinking skills (à la our buddy Ben Bloom).
- ✔ Creating for the Web can be fun. So what are you waiting for? Get your class Webbed!

You or your students can easily create your own home page. If you're connected to the Internet via a PPP account and your information provider has room on the server, you're well on your way. Your school's home page might include

- ✔ Links to home pages created by your students
- ✔ A picture of your school
- ✔ Links to favorite reference resources
- ✔ Information about your school and the surrounding community
- ✔ Links to other schools' home pages for sharing and learning

To learn how to create your own home page, visit Web 66 at the following URL, where you can find complete instructions on Web page building:

`http://Web66.coled.umn.edu`

With a standard word processor and a few special commands, you're in business. If Web 66 isn't enough, you can also try these:

`http://home.netscape.com/` (click on Education)

```
http://w3.org
www.microsoft.com/ie
www.terran.com
```

How Do I Weave a Web Page?

To move up the information chain from consumer to producer, you and your students need only four things:

- ✔ An idea
- ✔ Some concept of how to present the idea (a storyboard)
- ✔ A word processor or specialized Web page creation tool (even the Mac's Teachtext or your Windows Notepad will do in a pinch!)
- ✔ A place to post your Web page

Bodacious ideas

I leave the idea-generation part for you and your students to consider. Usually, schools begin with a simple page offering information about the school facility, programs, and faculty. Such information is a nice place to begin, but don't stop there. Remember that the purpose of the Web page is to communicate with an *audience.* That audience may be your students, faculty, and administration; your local community; or the whole beach-ball-of-a-planet. As you frame your idea for a Web page, think about your audience and provide content that compels people to want to visit your page. When I recently added a link to an Internet search site to my own home page, for example, traffic increased 10 percent within a week. (Of course, that increase challenges me to play with the rest of the page even more.)

If you want to see a few samples of Web pages created by schools around the world, drop in to Web66 at `www.web66.umn.edu` and search sites in your area.

Design and conquer

The design part of creating a Web page is great fun, kind of like designing a yearbook, except that it's more interactive. Rather than featuring mug shots and gratuitous photos of the football team, you're featuring original content, students' work, links to the outside world, and gratuitous pictures of your principal or department chairperson. I usually recommend sketching out the pages on a piece of paper, a sort of Web *storyboard*. Remember, though, content is king, design is secondary (but essential)!

You can read more specifics about Web design in my book *Web Publishing For Teachers* (IDG Books Worldwide, Inc.). If you're ready to take the plunge after reading this chapter, I encourage you to check it out.

What tools do I use?

After you've come up with a great idea and have thought about a design theme, it's time to get to work and actually build the Web page. There are basically two ways to create a Web page:

- ✔ Learn HTML (the scripting language of the Web) and use your word processor (any word processor will do, nowadays Microsoft Word, AppleWorks, and others even have basic HTML scripting templates built-in).
- ✔ Use a Web page creation tool like Claris Home Page, Netscape Composer, Microsoft FrontPage, NetObjects Fusion, Go Live!, CyberStudio or, for those that want every option imaginable, Macromedia Dreamweaver.

Both methods have their benefits. Learning (and teaching) a scripting language like HTML helps you and your students better understand and extend the possibilities of Web scripting. Sure, you have to learn codes and follow syntax, but you can also do some pretty amazing things by writing HTML raw code that you can't (yet) do with most Web page creation tools.

Web page creation tools like Dreamweaver, PageMill, Go Live!, Frontpage, or Claris Home Page remove the need to know HTML code. Instead, using these tools is more like using a word processor or page-layout program. All the commands are reduced to shortcuts, such as choosing commonly used commands from a pop-up menu that help you be more accurate. You can get from zero to Web page in a matter of minutes without knowing a single HTML tag. The downside to these tools is that they've not yet caught up with some of the "bleeding edge" tools like JavaScript and CGI script processing. For that, you need some HTML on your side. (Check out *HTML For Dummies,* 4th Edition by Ed Tittel and Stephen N. James, IDG Books Worldwide, Inc.)

Finding a home for your page

The last step in creating your own Web page is figuring out where you can post your new creation. If your school, town, or district has its own Web server, you're probably in luck. Just use an FTP (file transfer protocol) program to copy your Web page to the server and you're in business! If you don't have a server in-house, make a deal with your Internet service provider (ISP) for some space on its Web server and then use FTP to copy the Web page(s) you created to the ISP's server, as I describe in the "Publishing to the Web" section later in this chapter. In either case, remember to upload the page again each time it changes. (For more info on FTPing check out Chapter 15.)

A number of online services also offer the opportunity to create a custom Web page. AOL, for example, automates the process of building and posting a rudimentary page. If you or your students want to use a Web page primarily as a jumping-off point to search the Net, some nifty solutions are available. Some of the web sites that serve as directories also offer customized home pages. Check out www.excite.com for Excite's customizable home page "My Excite."

Publishing to the Web

After you and your students have a masterpiece of a Web page or *Web site* (a collection of Web pages) together, you can post your site so that the whole world can enjoy it. This last step involves copying your Web pages to your service provider's computer. (Remember, your service provider might be an online service like AOL, or your school district's server that's connected to the Internet.)

Basically, the steps to publishing a Web page are as follows:

1. **Log in to your service provider using your own login and password.**

2. **Launch your FTP program.**

   I usually use Fetch (Mac), but WS FTP, Cute FTP, BBEdit (www. barebones.com), or even your browser will do.

   If you are using your browser, type **ftp://username@ftp.whatever.net** into the Location (Address in IE5) box and enter your password when prompted. (Note that IE5 supports the use of a new prefix "upload" which the Net sees as "ftp.")

3. **Find the folder (directory) where your Web pages belong.**

   Double-click directories to burrow down and find the place for your files. The name is usually something like /pub/username/ or /pub/username/ www, where username is your name.

4. Upload your Web page(s).

Use ASCII mode for Web (HTML) pages and binary for graphics files. If you use your browser, just drag each file from your desktop into the browser window or choose File⇨Upload File.

If you are on your best Net behavior, you'll also remember to Log Out of the site. Some browsers leave the server on the other end waiting for a log out command to show you're finished with your upload/download session. Eventually (in a few minutes) they'll just "time out" and log you out automatically. If your browser (or FTP program) has a Log Out feature, use it.

After the upload (copy) is complete, you can access your Web page using a URL something like `www.whatever.net/~username/homepage.html`.

Note that browser makers have played a nasty trick on Webmasters — making their browsers interpret HTML in different ways. That's why testing your Web pages with a variety of browsers is important: test with Netscape Navigator and Internet Explorer.

Creating a Web page for yourself, your school, or your classroom represents the next logical step in the evolution of your learning about the Internet. You and your students are literally moving up the information chain from consumer to producer. Above all, don't be intimidated by the tools, HTML code, or anything else involved in Web page creation; they are all much easier to deal with than programming languages or even early word processors were. Web page creation is definitely a skill worth learning . . . and teaching. To borrow a well-worn phrase, it's like "thinking globally and acting locally" at 28.8 Kbps or greater.

Show the World

After you and your students enjoy the satisfaction of creating a Web page and posting it to the Internet (and well you should!), you have to think about whether anyone is going to know it's there. Because all search engines and directories don't automatically index your Web page and directories don't always add a link to their site (and because school's can't generally mount multi-million dollar ad campaigns plastering the URL on billboards), you'll have to go to Plan C (C for "cheap", but effective!). Here are a few ways to publicize your site:

✔ Print the URL everywhere (letterhead, business cards, school newspaper, on the gymnasium walls, and report cards).

✔ Surf the major search engines and directories (Yahoo!, AltaVista, Excite), and submit your pages for inclusion in their databases. Most have a link on their main page that says something like "Submit your site."

✔ Fork over some cash to the folks at www.submit-it.com and have them promote your site.

✔ Call all your friends (parents, school sponsors, and so on) and have them link to your site.

Don't expect big numbers overnight. If your site is dynamic (changing) and offers meaningful content, you'll soon be getting hits. Your service provider (or network administrator) can provide you with statistics about how often your web site is accessed, and who's visiting. Use these stats to improve your site. Oh, and don't forget to have a party the first day your site gets more than 1000 hits in a day. That's pretty good for any school! (No fair asking every teacher to visit the site 20 times!)

Part III
Communicate, Collaborate, Celebrate

The 5th Wave — By Rich Tennant

"Our classroom PCs have created a challenging atmosphere where critical analyzing, synthesizing and problem-solving skills are honed. I think the students have gotten a lot out of them, too."

In this part . . .

*I*n this part, you take your first steps onto the information superhighway. As your coach, I offer bunches of helpful tips and step-by-step instructions on how to use popular shareware and freeware programs (some included on the CD with this book) to make your journey on the Internet more pleasant and productive.

The Internet is a vast, lawless place, full of knowledge just waiting to be used. These chapters give you the basics, step-by-step, for becoming a top-notch knowledge navigator, plus a glimpse into the near future as multimedia meets the Web in the form of Web cams and much more.

Chapter 11

E-Mail: You'll Get Hooked!

In This Chapter

▶ Dissecting an e-mail

▶ Sending and receiving e-mail

▶ E-mail 101: Eudora Light

▶ Using Internet browsers for e-mail

▶ Automating E-mail functions

▶ Finding your friends on the Net

▶ Teaching and learning Netiquette

▶ Using Emoticons

*M*y teacher friend Cathy came flying down the hall one day, wildly waving a piece of paper containing a recipe for pecan fudge cookies. Big deal, you say? You bet! That recipe was her very first *e-mail* (electronic mail). The coolest part was that the message came from a home economics teacher in Alaska who teaches in a remote K-12 school with 20 students, and Cathy had never had any contact with her before. Great, huh? Great ideas are everywhere, and e-mail is a cool way to share them.

I have a prediction. The very first time you receive an e-mail message (perhaps from a fellow teacher hundreds of miles away), you'll be hooked, too. If you're like most educators, you spend precious little time communicating with other teachers. I mean, I'm not the only one whose ever felt a bit isolated in my classroom, am I?

Don't believe me? Try to call a teacher friend during the day. Bus duty, homeroom responsibilities, and faculty meetings (not to mention teaching five or six periods a day) leave little time for using traditional methods to communicate with the outside world. Just as mastering global communications is becoming a standard work skill for our students, the same is certainly true for teachers. E-mail is the grand equalizer that finally knocks down the walls of our classrooms and enables us to get to the resources we need. With access to e-mail through a classroom or media-center phone line, a schoolwide network, or from home, we can finally have a clear line of communication with parents, friends, relatives, and students.

What Is E-Mail?

Any message that travels over a network, regardless of whether the message stays in your school's local area network (LAN) or passes through an Internet provider to the Australian outback, is e-mail.

Think of e-mail as a sledgehammer that enables you to begin knocking down classroom walls. We teachers have been somewhat restricted to ideas and resources that are housed within our own school. Sure, we grab a moment now and then to discuss ideas with fellow staff members, visit the media center, and store classroom resources like pack rats. Still, historically our resource base has been pretty much confined within the walls of the school.

Using e-mail, you and your students can exchange ideas with people all over the planet. The fact that you can communicate directly with everyone from research scientists to rock stars through the power of telecommunications is awesome. In short, e-mail is a great way to begin your exploration into the Internet from your classroom.

What can I do with e-mail?

It slices, it dices, it . . . well . . . e-mail *is* versatile — just versatile enough to connect you with the world or to offer a grand opportunity for student mischief. But look on the bright side: With access to e-mail, you and your students can

✔ **Send and receive electronic letters.** Mail a note to a local politician or to your best friend. By using e-mail, you can reach virtually everyone on the Internet — all 23,000,000+ of them. The letter arrives almost instantaneously — complete with misspelled words (though most e-mail programs come with spell checkers nowadays) and happy thoughts. Oh, and by the way, you can send one letter to scads of different people with the click of a mouse. Wait . . . is that good?

✔ **Send and receive files.** I can whip up a lesson plan on my word processing program, attach it to an e-mail, and then friends all around the world can experience the wonders of my fifth-period science class. Save pictures from the Internet, too, and programs — even sounds. Most for *free*. Is this awesome, or what?

✔ **Receive regular mailings from topic-based mailing lists.** *Subscribing to* any one of a bunch of electronic newsletters and topic-based discussion groups is a snap if you use e-mail. See Chapter 12 for more information on mailing lists.

Okay! I'm convinced! What do I need to do first?

To send e-mail, you need a computer, a modem, a connection to the Internet (see Appendix C to explore your connection options), and access to a computer program that sends and receives e-mail. You can connect through a commercial online service such as America Online or Prodigy, a local *Internet service provider (ISP),* a college or university, one of several "free" mail services such as YahooMail or HotMail. The way you send and receive messages depends on how you connect to the Internet.

Your Internet provider or online service provides you a personal e-mail address when you make arrangements for Internet access. After you have your connection and your address, the rest is as easy as A-B-C. Read on!

What's my address?

Knock, knock. Who's there? Before you send a letter to someone else's e-mail address, you need to know your own address. An Internet e-mail address is assigned by your Internet provider and has three parts: the *username* (a series of letters and/or numbers that form your unique identity as an Internet citizen), the *domain name* (the name of the one [or more] computer[s] to which the account belongs), and the *top-level domain* (which describes the type of location from which the message is sent). An @ sign separates the username from the domain name and top-domain name. Here's one example of a standard e-mail address setup:

```
flintstone@bedrock.com
username@domain name.top-level domain
```

Your username (the information to the left of the @ symbol — flintstone in the preceding example) is assigned to you by your service provider. Depending on the size of your organization, usernames can sometimes get really lengthy. You may, for example, see something like this:

```
george%george.jungle@bananaman.com
```

Some usernames are strictly numeric, as in this CompuServe address:

```
72344.1234@compuserve.com
```

Moving right along, the first letters and/or numbers in the domain name (to the right of the @ symbol) describe the name of your Internet server. In the preceding address, The 72344.1234 is the user's ID and compuserve is the name of the online service.

Breaking the Internet's secret code

You may see any one of a number of different endings (called *top-domains*) at the end of an Internet address. Here are the six most common endings:

✔ **.com:** A commercial service (example: socrates@aol.com, an America Online address) or company (such as www.nintendo.com).

✔ **.edu:** An education or education-related organization (example: quarterback@uga.cc.uga.edu, which gets you a touchdown at the University of Georgia).

✔ **.gov:** Government and/or government contractors (example: president@ whitehouse.gov, one of the president's e-mail addresses — the mailbox is always full!).

✔ **.mil:** The military (example: patton@army.mil, one of our nation's finest).

✔ **.org:** Other organizations that don't really fit into another classification like professional associations (www.nea.org) or professional organizations (www.ascd.org).

✔ **.net:** Network resources (example: chiphead@mainframe.net, for chipheads only). Often e-mail accounts through larger Internet Service Providers, like Mindspring, or free online services (like Netscape mail) end in .net as in mindspring.net and netscape.net.

Now don't go sending a bunch of mail to the addresses in this sidebar — they're all figments of an occasionally fertile imagination — except for the president's address, that is.

Want to see more? There are proposals underway to create brand new extensions for businesses, people, and more. Check out Chapter 5 for the scoop.

If you connect through a commercial information provider, your address may have anything after the @ symbol, like this:

```
bananaman@bigshack.jungle.com
```

Finally, a period separates the top-level domain (.com in the preceding address) from the Internet computer's name. Looking at the letters that follow the last period helps you determine what kind of organization sent the mail (see the "Breaking the Internet's secret code" sidebar in this chapter). In some cases the top-level domain reveals the country of origin, such as .uk for United Kingdom and .fi for Finland. These endings are *Country Code Top-Level Domains (CCTLDs)*. Here's what a URL containing a CCTLD might look like: www.whatever.com.de (Germany).

Can we talk?

Well, you've gotten this far, and I know what you're thinking: "Wait! I have a Zebra 9000 computer, and my friend has a Peach 6150. Can we talk?" Luckily, the answer is yes. Because the Internet works in a *standard protocol* (that's techno-weenie for *common language*), virtually any machine can send and receive e-mail. The only hitches come when you exchange pictures, sounds, or programs, as discussed in Chapter 15. So don't worry; I've sent e-mail from an Apple IIe to an Apricot computer somewhere in Britain without a hitch. (They're nuts about computers over there, too.)

On occasion, someone will ask you for your Internet address over the telephone or in person. To sound like an Internet veteran, remember one rule: When you say your address, the familiar period becomes "dot." So, if your America Online e-mail address is socrates@aol.com, you say, "Socrates at A-O-L dot com." Isn't techno-babble wonderful?

Sending and Receiving E-Mail

Commercial online services and accounts furnished by Internet providers offer the easiest and most user-proof method of sending e-mail. The graphical interfaces and (more or less) intuitive commands are a bit easier to handle than *mailers* (programs running on a UNIX network that also enable you to send e-mail).

Mail anatomy

Before you learn to send a message, here's a little mail anatomy: E-mail has two parts, the header and the message.

The *header* contains information about you (the sender), the receiver's electronic address, the date, and a subject. The *subject line* is where you type in a brief description about the message's, well, subject. If you were writing to mom about your bad cat Fluffy, a good subject might be "Fluffy's foul temper" or something similar. The *message* area is where you expand on your subject line (in other words, where you write the body of your letter): Fluffy, your birthday wishes, requests for information about your spring break trip to Florida, or anything else you feel like writing about. See Figure 11-1 for an example of a typical e-mail interface. Easy as pie!

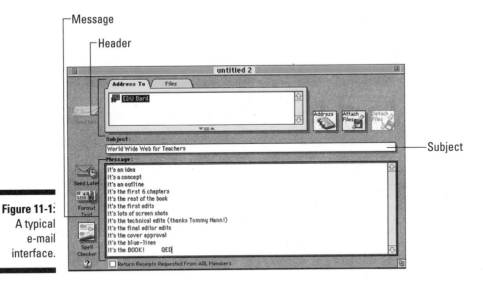

Figure 11-1:
A typical
e-mail
interface.

Sending and receiving Internet mail via an online service

All major commercial online services offer users the option of sending e-mail through the Internet. Most services only require you to enter a full Internet e-mail address (`username@domain_name`) in the To line and send the message on its way. Of course your message also needs a subject and some message text to actually *mean* something.

On AOL, for example, sending and receiving Internet e-mail is a cinch. Note that these examples are based on AOL Version 4.0 for both Macintosh and Windows 95. If you have an earlier Version of AOL (3.0 or earlier), some of these screens may look a little different. You can get a free upgrade to Version 4.0 of AOL by signing on to the service and entering Keyword: Upgrade.

Snail mail

People who use e-mail generally refer to the Postal Service's way of delivering a postmarked letter as "snail mail." In general, no matter where you send an e-mail message — to the front office or to Zimbabwe — it arrives much faster than a letter (usually). No stamps, no delays, no rain, sleet, or snow. It's a little hard to send your grandma's birthday present (that grand piano she's always wanted) through the Net, but who knows . . . someday it may be possible.

1. **Sign onto America Online.**

2. **Choose Mail⇨Compose (or Write) Mail or press ⌘-M (Ctrl+M).**

3. **Enter the full Internet e-mail address of the recipient (enter more than one if you would like to send the same e-mail to multiple recipients) in the Send To line and then press Tab to move to the Subject line.**

   Note: If you're sending e-mail to someone on the same online service, you don't need the @domain_name part of the address (for example, the @aol.com in socrates@aol.com). If you use the domain name, the mail still goes through, but it takes the long way, like calling your basement from your attic via Mozambique.

4. **Type a subject in the Subject line and press Tab to move to the next line.**

5. **Type your message.**

6. **Click Send Now (to send immediately) or Send Later (to ask AOL to send your message another time).**

Now, unless you've clicked Send Later, your e-mail message zips through America Online's Internet gateway computer out onto the Internet and roots around until it finds a destination. This long journey, by the way, takes milliseconds — that's faster than a teacher can duck a flying eraser (an important survival skill taught and practiced in teacher preparation programs everywhere)!

Other commercial online services, such as CompuServe and Prodigy, offer similar graphical e-mail interfaces. Incoming mail comes right to your e-mail inbox, and an audio or visual online cue alerts you when it does. On AOL, you see a mailbox and if your computer has sound capability, it proudly announces, "You've got mail!" and you see the flag go up on your online mailbox. Just select Mail⇨Read New Mail and double-click each message to read your mail.

Sending and receiving Internet mail via a university/UNIX network

If you're connected through a university network, you have access to server-based programs, called *mailers,* that have names that sound environment friendly, such as *Pine* and *Elm,* or names that sound technical, such as *x-mail* and *mail/mailx* (Berkeley mail). These text-based mail programs are just as functional as their online service counterparts, but you have to use somewhat cryptic commands to read and send messages instead of merely clicking an icon with your computer mouse.

Pine is one of the most common e-mail programs available for UNIX-class users. Someone once told me that Pine is an acronym that stands for *Pine is not Elm.* I guess Elm stands for *electronic mail,* but it could stand for *every-*

body's limited mail. Sorry, Elm-people.

To access a mailer from your computer workstation, sign onto your network and at the prompt type in your logon word (**elm** or **pine**, depending on which mail system your network uses). The rest is menu driven. Figure 11-2 shows a sample message ready to be sent using pine.

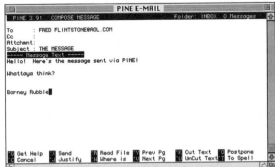

Figure 11-2:
Pining away
for a better
interface.

See what I mean? It's hardly as friendly or as full-featured as its graphics-based relatives, but it works.

Luckily, most information providers and some universities provide a great way to avoid the hassle of using Elm or Pine — these programs do little more than send and receive mail and have no easy way to attach files and manage mail like the newer e-mail clients do — say hello to Eudora Light.

Internet e-mail 101: Eudora Light

Eudora Light is a program that you can use to send and receive e-mail if you're connected to the Internet through a PPP account. (If PPP is Greek to you, check out Chapter 4.) Eudora Light and its big sister, Eudora Pro, are available for both Windows and Macintosh computers. The program has an easy-to-use interface for sending, receiving, and managing mail. As with most other graphical-based e-mail programs these days, it has lots of useful bells and whistles, too.

The version of Eudora Light included with this book is freeware for educators. The folks at QualComm, makers of Eudora, also have a commercial version, called Eudora Pro, which has an enhanced feature set. For purchasing information, send e-mail to eudora-info@qualcomm.com or check the Read Me file (in the Eudora folder) on the CD-ROM that accompanies this book.

The main user manual accompanying Eudora says that the program got its name when the programmer was inspired by Eudora Welty's "Why I Live at the P.O.". Isn't it wonderful that great writing still moves people . . . to write programs? Long live Eudora!

Okay. To get down to business, here are the basics. . . .

Sending mail with Eudora Light

You're in luck! Freeware versions of Eudora for the Macintosh and Windows are on the CD that comes with this book. Eudora for Windows operates very much like Eudora for the Macintosh, so the directions below work virtually identically for whatever computer you're using. You can use any FTP program (Fetch, WS FTP, and so on) to retrieve a more current version of Eudora Light for your computer via FTP from `ftp.qualcomm.com`.

Here's a set of step-by-step instructions for you to follow to send an e-mail message using Eudora Light:

1. **Open Eudora Light.**

   The installer program you ran from your Internet for Teachers CD gave you an option of where to locate the program folder (directory). If you've forgotten where the program is use ⌘-F (Find) or the Find program in your Start menu (Windows) to locate the program.

   Note: If this is your first time using Eudora Light, the configuration window pops up automatically on the Windows version and on some of the older Mac versions of the program. If the configuration window doesn't pop up when you first launch Eudora Light, choose Special⇨Settings; then choose Personal Information from the icons on the left of the dialog box and enter your account information in the screen that pops up (like the one shown in Figure 11-3).

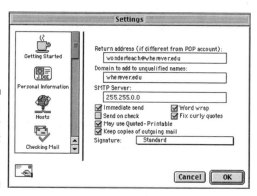

Figure 11-3: Enter your account information here.

2. Log on to the Internet.

You don't have to be logged in to create your message. You can complete Steps 4 through 8, log on (see Steps 2 and 3) then, and click Send. This is important for those who have billing plans that only allow them to be online for a certain number of hours a month.

3. Choose Message⇨New Message.

A window like the one shown in Figure 11-4 pops up.

Figure 11-4:
The Eudora
Lite
Message
window.

4. Click to the right of the word *To* and enter the full Internet address of the person to whom you're sending your letter.

(Example: `ashley.jordan@cook.com`).

You can type more than one Internet address in the To line. Just separate them with a comma, like this:

`addressone@domain.com, addresstwo@domain.edu`

Eudora also has a Nicknames option that enables you to save lists of frequently used e-mail addresses to save you time. Just think, you and your students can publish your own online newsletter and send it to hundreds of people as easily and quickly as sending to one person! Now there's a scary thought! Mass mailings border on "junk mail," which I discuss in Chapter 12.

5. Press Tab to move to the Subject line (or click to the right of the word Subject as above), enter what your message is about and then press Tab.

Note that the cursor "leapfrogs" over the From: line because it's already completed for you.

6. Enter one or more other Internet addresses in the Cc (carbon copy) or Bcc (blind carbon copy) lines if you like and then press Tab.

When you send a blind carbon copy, the BCC recipient does not know who else you sent the message to. Sneaky, huh?

Note that the cursor now jumps again, this time to the Attachments line, which enables you to send any file (a program, picture, sound, or text document) along with your e-mail message by inputing the name of the file in the line. To send an attachment, choose Message⇨Attach⇨Document and select the file you want to attach from the dialog box.

Attached files don't always translate properly between commercial online services and accounts with universities or ISPs, or vice versa. Sending files from one member of a commercial online service to another member on the same service, or sending an attached file from one university or ISP account to another, however, usually works without a snag.

7. Press Tab once more to move the message box, write all you want, and when your masterpiece is complete click the Send button to send it on its way.

A very long message (more than the equivalent to five pages or so) may be clipped or segmented when it is received by other Internet mail servers. Good Internet etiquette (or *Netiquette*) is to keep your e-mails down to a couple pages. Anything longer should probably be sent as an attachment to the e-mail if possible.

After you press the Send button, you see a dialog box containing a progress bar that lets you know the message is being sent. You can, by the way, press the Stop button in case you forgot to add something to a message or change your mind about sending it. The Stop button only works, however, while the message is being sent. Once it's gone, it's gone. (The progress bar is shown in Figure 11-5.)

Figure 11-5:
A progress bar keeps you busy while your message is being sent.

Sending Mail...	
Messages remaining to transfer:	1
Charles Brewer, Re : Opportunities...	
▉▭▭▭▭▭▭▭	Stop

8. After your message is sent, choose File⇨Quit.

Note that although you've just quit the Eudora Light program, your Internet connection is still active. You can relaunch Eudora Light to send or receive more e-mail, or you can use another Internet software tool, such as Netscape Communicator, Internet Explorer, or TurboGopher/ HGopher (which are discussed in Chapters 6, 7, and 16, respectively), or terminate your Internet connection from your PPP control panel (discussed in Chapter 4).

Now you can fool around with all those buttons that are displayed across the top of Eudora's mail screen and use them to get to other Eudora goodies. For example, the JH button (on the far right) enables you to add a customized signature (see Chapter 11 where I discuss e-mail signatures). Use other buttons to add a nickname, forward mail, and so on.

Getting organized

Stop right now and think about how you want to organize your list of favorite e-mail addresses. Because some e-mail addresses are pretty long, it pays to store them so you don't lose them. Eudora Light enables you to create "nicknames" that match e-mail addresses for your personal use, but a more visible record may be more appropriate for your class. Ask your students to begin a class list of the most helpful or interesting Internet e-mail addresses and post it prominently in your classroom. These addresses come in handy when you begin to put together Internet projects. Now, what was the president's address? (Try `president@whitehouse.gov`.)

Receiving and reading a message with Eudora Light

When someone else sends you e-mail, it automatically arrives in your Internet e-mail *Inbox*. Here's how to read your mail after it arrives:

1. **Launch Eudora Light.**

   Eudora talks to your computer, and if you're not already logged onto the Internet, it launches MacTCP/IP or WinSock and dials your Internet service provider.

2. **After you log in, you are presented with a dialog box where you can enter your password.**

   Use the password furnished by your Internet provider. Eudora Light enables you to automate the password entry function (see the Preferences menu).

3. **Choose File⇨Check Mail.**

   If you have no mail, Eudora Light presents you with a dialog box in which a happy little snake accompanies a `No new mail` message. Try sending e-mail to yourself so you can see how Eudora Light handles incoming mail. (To e-mail yourself just put your e-mail address in the To line of the message and maybe the word Test in the Subject line, and then press Send.)

   If you do have incoming mail, you see Eudora Light's Inbox, which looks something like Figure 11-6.

In			
newaccounts@wired.com	2:00 AM 2/7/95 +0	7	Welcome to HotWired!
BITNET list server at UNMUMA (1.8	6:52 AM 2/18/95 -	2	Output of your job "bardw"
BITNET list server at UNMUMA (1.8	6:52 AM 2/18/95 -	23	File: "TEACHER3 CONTACTS" 1/9
Netsurfer Digest	12:31 AM 3/3/95 +	7	Welcome to Netsurfer Digest
Netsurfer Digest	12:31 AM 3/3/95 +	10	Netsurfer Digest FAQ
Netsurfer Digest	12:31 AM 3/3/95 +	25	Your First Netsurfer Digest (HTML
R US Dept. of Education	2:08 PM 3/4/95 -0	2	Re: Your Input Needed! New Inter
R fred.flintstone@bedrock.com	8:33 AM 3/6/95 -0	3	Internet Book
R Wentworth Worldwide Media	4:42 PM 3/6/95 -0	2	back issues of Classroom Connect
• Internet for Teachers	4:16 AM 3/9/95 -0	5	Cover Art Ready to Go!
Scott Tyson	8:23 PM 3/13/95 -	1	We're Going to Disney World!

12/82K/0K

Figure 11-6:
Eudora's
way of
saying
"You've got
mail."

See all those messages? A round bullet in the message status column to the far left means that a message hasn't been read. An R means that a reply has been sent.

Here is a full list of the codes Eudora Light uses for both incoming and outgoing messages in the message status column:

- **Unread/Sendable:** Message ready to send (outgoing) or not yet read (incoming)

- **Read/Unsendable:** A blank space next to the message means the message has been read or that it isn't ready to be sent

- **R:** This message has been *replied* to

- **D:** This message has been *redirected* (passed along to someone else's e-mail box as if they were the intended recipient)

- **F:** This message has been *forwarded*: (sent along to someone else, even though you were the intended recipient)

- **Q:** This message has been *queued* (an electronic waiting room where messages wait to be sent)

- **S:** This message has been sent

- **–:** This message is waiting to be sent

4. **To read a message just double-click on it.**

   After you've read a message you may take no action, in which case the mail item stays in your Eudora Inbox, save it (choose Save from the File menu) or you can delete it by selecting the message (single click) and pressing the Delete key (or choose Message⇨Delete).

One word of warning about the Reply function. If someone writes you a note and copies it to 20 others and you choose Reply to All, Eudora also sends your reply to all 20 original recipients. You don't need to be a math whiz to figure out that everyone's mailbox can quickly be stuffed with a bunch of unnecessary "me too" messages. To avoid this sometimes embarrassing moment, always check the To line to make sure it contains only the e-mail address of the person or persons to whom you want to send a reply and be mindful of when you choose "Reply to sender" and "Reply to all."

See you at 4 p.m.

I once received a message that said simply, "See you at 4 p.m." Unfortunately, I had no idea what the message referred to. Was it a faculty meeting, a happy hour, or a tax audit? It's courteous to remind folks of their message to you when you reply. Just snip out the important parts of the message that you're replying to and paste them in your reply.

Eudora does this automatically when you choose Message⇨Reply. The "quoted" text is signaled with a greater-than sign (>). Feel free to delete parts that aren't important to the essence of your message before you add your reply and mail your letter.

Not too tough, is it? After you're comfortable with manually checking your mail, visit the Special⇨Settings to explore Eudora Light's automatic options such as the ability to poll your mailbox automatically and automating common message handling functions.

Eudora Light and Eudora Pro (the big-sister commercial application available from QualComm) have lots more features, such as a gong that sounds automatically when something is in your mailbox and the ability to snip off all the annoying extra information in the header of an e-mail message.

Eudora Light is a great compromise between the graphical interface of a commercial service and the kludgy server services. You can get updates to Eudora Light from www.qualcomm.com or get the commercial version, complete with a ton of new features, a 150+ page manual, and other stuff by sending e-mail to eudora-info@qualcomm.com or by telephoning QualComm at 800-2-EUDORA.

Okay. Now you're ready to e-mail the world. You can use Eudora or your favorite online service to reach out and e-mail someone with the click of a mouse. Because e-mail is quick and easy, it's a great way to introduce yourself and others to the Internet. Now, where is that Alaskan pecan fudge cookie recipe that was forwarded to my e-mail box?

Sending and Receiving Attachments via E-Mail

Wouldn't it be great if you could exchange lesson plans, desktop-published documents, and graphics with other people via e-mail? Well, yippee! You can! The Internet's techno-deities have smiled on us and even made it easy to do!

Receiving a file is even easier than sending one; Eudora does all the work! Follow these steps to view a file you receive via the Internet:

1. **Log on to the Internet and launch Eudora Light.**

2. **Choose File⇨Check Mail or press ⌘-M/Ctrl+M.**

3. **Double-click the line of the mail message that contains the downloadable file.**

4. **In the Save File dialog box that appears, choose the proper directory (this tells Eudora where to store the file you've received) and click Save.**

   The file is moved from your Internet host computer to your hard drive or floppy disk or other storage device.

5. **If a file compression program has been used to compress the file, unstuff (uncompress) the file by using StuffIt Expander or StuffIt Lite (if you've got a Macintosh) or WinZip (if you're using Windows).**

   You can tell if StuffIt has been used to compress a file because the file-name ends in the .sit extension. Both StuffIt Expander and WinZip are on the CD that accompanies this book.

6. **After you've uncompressed the file, sign off (if you want) and double-click the file's icon to open the file.**

Practice sending and receiving files by attaching files to e-mails addressed to yourself. Try it; it really works!

Commercial online services also enable you to send and receive files easily. On AOL, click the Attach File icon after creating your e-mail message, choose the file you want to attach from the dialog box, and click Send Now or Send Later.

Attached files don't translate well between different commercial services; the results are unpredictable, at best.

If you want to know more about downloading files (getting files directly from another computer), check out Chapter 15.

Using Netscape Communicator for E-Mail

Netscape Communicator features a built-in program called Netscape Messenger that supports sending and receiving e-mail. You can access Messenger from the Communicator menu or by clicking the Inbox icon on the Communicator Component bar (see Chapter 7 for more info on Communicator).

To prepare Netscape Messenger to send and receive your e-mail:

1. **Choose Edit➪Preferences.**

2. **Choose Mail and Newsgroups from the collapsible list in the left side of the Preferences window and then choose Mail Servers.**

3. **Fill in the blanks with information given to you by your ISP.**

   Figure 11-7 shows the Communicator Mail Server Preferences window.

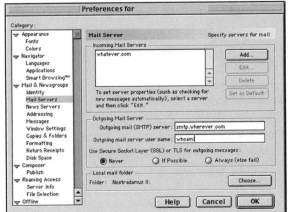

Figure 11-7:
Set your
mail prefer-
ences in
Netscape
in the
Preferences
window.

4. **Click Identity from the list at left.**

5. **Enter your name, e-mail, and reply-to address.**

6. **Click OK (or press Return/Enter) to accept your changes.**

Note that you have a ton of other related options to play with after setting the options I've mentioned above. Things like signature files (see the Identity Preferences window) allow you to add custom name and address information automatically to the end of your e-mail message.

You can send e-mail on the Web in two ways using your Netscape Navigator browser:

✔ Choose a link that automatically opens the e-mail response window (meaning you click on a mailto: command — HTML for *I'll supply the return address for you.* If you click someone's e-mail address on their Web page, the e-mail response window opens).

✔ Choose File➪New Mail Message (make a brand new mail message and send it to whomever or several whomevers).

Navigator's mail system works just like Eudora Light's — you simply "fill in the blanks" (see Figure 11-8 for a Netscape Navigator e-mail screen). Note that you can attach files, Cc to others, and use the address book, too (click on the Address button).

Receiving e-mail is easy. First, double-check to make sure you've entered Server and Identity information into the Mail and News Preferences dialog boxes (accessible through the Edit menu).

Next, click on the Get Msg icon in the top left corner of your Netscape Messenger window. Messenger logs on to your ISP's e-mail server and retrieves your mail.

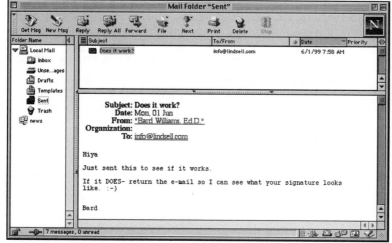

Figure 11-8:
Netscape's
Messenger
makes
e-mail easy.

Using Internet Explorer for E-Mail

Internet Explorer (IE) makes grabbing your e-mail easy because it features a helper application called Outlook Express that comes free with the full version of Internet Explorer. To prepare Internet Explorer to send and receive e-mail:

1. **Choose File⇨Preferences.**

2. **Scroll down and select General item from underneath the e-mail heading.**

   Figure 11-9 shows the IE General Preferences window.

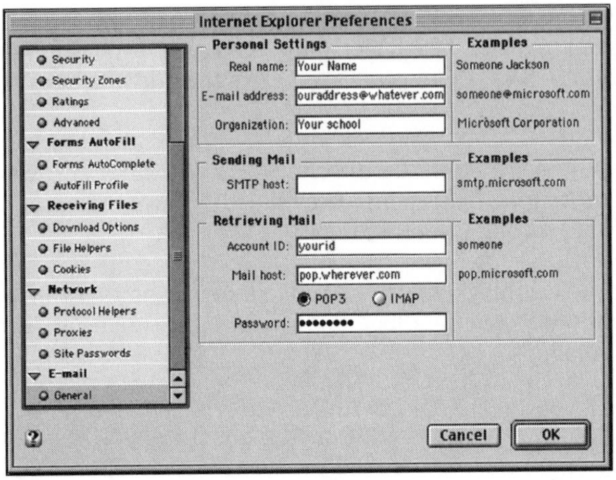

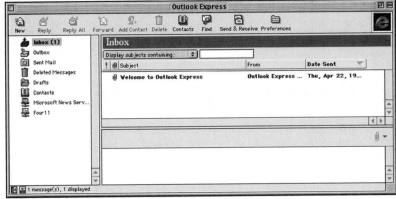

Figure 11-9:
Internet
Explorer's
Preferences
window lets
you person-
alize the
program.

3. **Fill in the blanks with information given to you by your ISP.**

4. **Click OK or press Return/Enter to accept your changes.**

IE's mail system works just like Eudora Light's — you simply "fill in the blanks" (Figure 11-10 shows IE's Outlook Express e-mail screen). Note that you can attach files, Cc messages to others, and use the address book, too (click on the Address button).

Figure 11-10:
The Outlook
Express
e-mail
window.

Receiving e-mail is easy. First, double-check to make sure you've entered Server and Identity information into the Edit⇨Preferences dialog boxes.

Next, click the Send/Receive icon on the menubar of Outlook Express and sit back and watch the files come in.

Worldwide shopping basket

Want to get an idea of how e-mail can be used in a classroom to gather information? Have your students come up with a list of ten common foods they like and create a short e-mail survey designed to compare prices. Send the survey via e-mail to a teacher you know on the Internet and ask that teacher's students to price each item and return the results via e-mail.

Next, ask them to pass the survey on to at least four other people. Ask each of those four people

to e-mail the survey back to you for tabulation. With a little luck, you'll have data for a nifty activity where you discuss economics and the usefulness of the Internet for gathering information quickly. One hint: Be sure to put a limit on the number of recipients because this electronic chain letter can quickly get out of hand!

Automating E-Mail Functions

After you're a bonafide *Netizen* (Net citizen), you'll find yourself constantly stopping what you're doing, running to the computer, and signing on to get e-mail you're expecting. In a classroom setting, where checking your messages all the time is impractical, wouldn't it be nice to have a little robot friend who grabs e-mail from all your e-mail accounts (I regularly answer five of them); sorts your mail by sender, subject, or content; logs off, and then, sit still patiently and awaits your next instructions? Well, the good news is you can!

Most e-mail clients, such as Eudora, Claris E-mailer, and Outlook Express allow you to customize how often your e-mail is checked (especially if you're connected full-time to the Net) and what happens to your mail after you get it (often called "mail actions"). Check your program's Mail Preferences to find out what timesavers are available to you.

Finding Your Friends on the Net

In the early days of the Internet (that would be about five years ago), finding your friends was very tough. You had to use *UNIX* (the operating system that forms the backbone for many parts of the Internet) commands such as "finger" to find people through a complicated process of list requests, or break down and call to ask them for their e-mail address.

As the Internet matured, people figured out that it made sense to post directories, and search engine gurus began to build ways to search for people the same way (generally) you search for curriculum resources into their sites. These days, not only can you find your friends, but you can also

- ✔ Obtain door-to-door directions to their home with Web-based mapping services
- ✔ Find out where they work (and play) by searching for Web pages that include their name
- ✔ Get their telephone number and e-mail address from online directories
- ✔ Find out who their neighbors are through reverse phone directories (to enter a phone number and get an address)

Uh oh. I can see some of you cringing out there. You're worried that there's all this information about *you* on the Internet, too, and that all these television marketing guys that show up on your TV at 3 a.m. hawking miracle food dehydrators will have a field day with it. If you're careful about where and when you give out personal information while online, you can control what people know about you. If you're really concerned about your privacy, you can even have your name excised from these online phone books.

No single resource exists on the Internet that is "all-knowing" about anyone or anything. Just as you should use multiple search engines and directories to find curriculum resources, you can also use multiple sites to sift through the zillions of bytes of information on the Internet to find your friends.

A wonderful (and humbling) exercise is to begin your search by finding someone you (hopefully!) know well — yourself. Visit each of the locations below and see what dirt you can dig up:

- ✔ **AltaVista** (www.altavista.com): Search here for your name (put it in quotes, like this: "Your Name"). This search can reveal not only personal web pages, but also anyplace on the Web your name is listed, such as in articles, reports, or directories. Try this with your friends and see who gets the most *search hits* (successful entries found by the search engine), and then you can all sit around trying to figure out if getting those hits is a good thing or not.
- ✔ **American Directory Assistance** (www.abii.com): Search for your name here, and if you find it, you can even ask for a street map of the address.
- ✔ **Bigfoot** (www.bigfoot.com): Search Bigfoot for people and get a free e-mail address for life. If you sign up for the free e-mail be careful to fill out only required information and turn off all of the marketing requests, or the marketeers will have you for life as well.
- ✔ **Netcenter's People Directory** (www.netscape.com/netcenter/whitepages.html): Find a person; then get a map to their house!

- ✔ **Sherlock:** A personal "metasearch engine" built-in to the Mac OS that searches Web directories and indexes, ranks them by relevance, and allows you to choose which sites your browser visits.

- ✔ **Yahoo People Search** (`http://people.yahoo.com`): Search here for addresses, phone numbers and e-mail addresses. If you don't like the way you're listed you can add, update, or delete your entry.

- ✔ **WhoWhere** (`www.whowhere.lycos.com`): Another "white pages" directory (like your telephone book).

The easiest way to find someone's Internet e-mail address is still to let your fingers do the walking: Call your friends on the phone, if possible, and ask them for their e-mail addresses. Yes, having to use the phone seems like a low-tech cop-out (the phone is now low-tech?), but you can save yourself a lot of time and frustration if you do!

Netiquette: Internet Dos and Donts

Nothing is more annoying than rudeness. In the real world, children everywhere learn certain rules to help make life easier and kinder: Raising their hands to talk helps (when they remember) and opening doors for other people shows good manners and kindness.

Because the Internet is relatively blind to the identity of the user, the only thing that comes across in Internet conversation is your words. That playful look in your eyes that tells someone you're just kidding is lost in the cold binary-digit world of an e-mail or chat room, so your manners have to shine. Because the Internet's inherent blindness and relative anonymity makes rudeness tempting at times, most Net surfers adhere to a basic set of manners that veteran Netizens refer to as *Netiquette* (short for Internet ettiquette).

In this section are several things that you should do, and some you shouldn't, during your visits to the Internet. Most of the following suggestions apply to e-mail, newsgroups, mailing lists, and other ways in which you and your students interact with the other people on the Internet.

Do create a custom electronic signature message for yourself or your school

In the Internet community it is customary to tag your outgoing e-mail messages with a brief unique signature. These user-created works of art relay more information about the sender and give you an opportunity to express a bit about your personality in a word, phrase, or quotation, or even a picture created from ASCII text characters.

Here's an example of an electronic signature that may accompany the imaginary Tim Buktu's e-mail messages:

```
*************************************************
Tim Buktu     nowhere@outtathere.com
Dean of Men, DoRight College, Anywhere, USA
"Carpe Diem, seize the day boys, seize the day.
Make your lives extraordinary."
Robin Williams, "Dead Poets Society"
*************************************************
```

See? Electronic signatures give you and your students a nifty way of signing your e-mail messages, and you can include all those witty quotations you've always wanted to use. Keep signatures under 40 character spaces wide with no special characters so that everyone can enjoy your signature tag without reformatting their screens. You can also include such information as your school or home phone number and *snail mail* (postal) address. Most software, including Eudora Light, enables you to append your electronic signature automatically to outgoing messages.

Some Net signatures are really creative. Have your students create their own Internet signature messages that reflect their own personalities. Use books of quotations or search for quotations on the Net. You can find searchable lists of quotations and more ready-reference resources by pointing your WWW browser (see Chapter 5) to www.columbia.edu/acis/bartleby/bartlett/.

Don't send anything through e-mail that you wouldn't write on your chalkboard

Because e-mail is sent from your computer to someone else's via an Internet gateway computer, someone may catch and read your messages as they pass through. Although most universities and commercial online services have some security, nothing is completely secure. A good guideline is to assume that any message that you send via the Internet may well be read by someone other than the intended recipient. As a result, you shouldn't send credit card information or personal information about yourself or your students through e-mail. Better safe than sorry!

Don't flame

You're already familiar with *flaming*. Some people flame in the real world. Have you ever walked into the teacher's lounge at the end of the day and heard a coworker blasting an administrator for interrupting class with a message on the PA system? Ever heard the football coach launch into a bench-kicking tirade about how rotten the officiating was at last Friday's game? *That's* flaming.

Flaming is the term for inflammatory messages on the Net. Basically, no matter how angry you or your students feel about what some other Internet surfer says, resist the temptation to "go off" on them, and instead use that energy to do something else. If you receive a flame or read one in a newsgroup, resist the temptation to reply. Replying to a flame usually doesn't work, whether your reply is calm or otherwise. The people who wrote the flame have already lost their self-control and are unlikely to regain it before they read your reply. Tell your students and peers that flaming is simply an uncool thing to do, and in any case a waste of time and energy.

Do talk to your students about what's appropriate to send via e-mail

Some things you don't want to discuss via e-mail because they are too personal, or are best said in writing (the old fashioned way) or in person. An e-mail wedding invitation is a social faux pas for sure, as would be an e-mail termination notice (gasp!) from your principal. With your students, brainstorm a list of appropriate and inappropriate uses of e-mail to help drive this point home.

Don't type in all capital letters

Capital letters leap off the screen and CAN BE REALLY ANNOYING; they're considered the cyberspace equivalent of screaming. Of course, sometimes using all capital letters is appropriate . . . such as when you're scolding your students via e-mail about not being good Netizens. Younger students in particular have a tough time remembering to turn off the Caps Lock key. Do the online world a favor and have your little ones practice locking and unlocking that key several hundred times (off-line!) so they'll remember.

Emoticons: Getting That Fuzzy Internet Feeling

One of the most interesting things about the Internet is the way people convey feelings and emotions.

Because face-to-face electronic chatting is still somewhat of a dream for the general public, creative humans have developed their own set of letters and symbols that represent emotions, feelings, and other things that are tough to express in Cyberspace. Those familiar with techno-speak call these symbols emoticons (emotional icons) or simply smileys.

Emoticons are oodles of fun. You can read most of them by tilting your head 90 degrees left and looking at the combined symbols as one. For example, a smile (sideways) looks like this: :-)

Table 11-1 shows some of the emoticons and abbreviations that you may see online:

Table 11-1	Some Emoticons and Abbreviations		
Emoticon	*What It Means*	*Abbreviation*	*What It Means*
:-) or <grin>	Happy	AFAIK	As far as I know
:-(or <frown>	Not happy	BTW	By the way
;-)	wink	BRB	Be right back
:-D	Big, goofy grin	CUL8R	See you later
[:-)	Wearing a Walkman	RTFM	Read The Friendly Manual
8:-)	Glasses on the forehead	IMHO	In my humble opinion
oO:-)7	Teacher, circa 1850?	LOL	Laughing out loud
?:-z	A clueless person	OIC	Oh, I see
[[]]	A hug	ROTFL	Rolling on the floor, laughing

Ask your students to brainstorm a list of famous people who are related to a specific subject area, or share some examples from the list that follows. Challenge students to design their own emoticon for the person of their choice. Present the final product to the class and then try them out on IRC (Internet Relay Chat, which is discussed in Chapter 18) or in live conference on a commercial service, and see what happens!

Running out of space

Grab the e-mail address of a teacher in another school and try this easy introductory activity.

1. Get your students to find a favorite poem, or have them write their own. (Go for the obscure; the more arcane the merrier.)

2. "Despace" the text — that is, remove all spaces between words and carriage returns so that the text is basically one very jumbled paragraph-length word.

3. Send this despaced disaster to another class and have students there "respace" the text to re-create what they think are meaningful lines and stanzas.

4. Finally, have the other class return the poetry to your students.

Voilà! You get as many interpretations as there are return letters. Warning: Lewis Carroll's "Jabberwocky" and anything by e. e. cummings will drive them nuts!

Chapter 12

Mailing Lists-R-Us

· ·

In This Chapter

▶ Stalking the wild mailing list

▶ Subscribing and posting to mailing lists

▶ Surviving mail storms and unsubscribing from mail lists

· ·

*I*f you're like most teachers, you're probably a magazine junkie. A glance at the overstuffed shelves in my home office reveals that my interests are a bit schizophrenic; I have everything from *Educational Leadership* and *National Geographic* to *Wired* and *Internet World*, with issues of *Southern Living, GQ,* and *MacWorld* nestled in between. My magazine rack is great whenever I'm in the mood to browse for a topic — I can usually find something there to explore.

A mailing list is, in many ways, like a magazine subscription: It enables you to select a topic of interest and read the thoughts and ideas of folks from around the world. What makes mailing lists so cool is that you can also add your own thoughts to the discussion! Your ideas can be published electronically to thousands of unsuspecting Internet users at the touch of a button. Ooooo . . . a scary and exciting thought, no?

Mailing Lists with Attitude

Mailing lists (a.k.a. maillists) are special kinds of e-mail addresses that automatically forward topic-specific discussions to your e-mail Inbox — just like a magazine subscription does, only much more quickly. Super cool, eh?

Mailing lists also enable you and your students to communicate with more than one person at a time. In essence, you're joining an online discussion. Mailing lists are sometimes referred to as discussion groups, because they are focused on a specific topic, such as elementary education or brewing beer in Wales. You also hear mailing lists referred to as *LISTSERVs*. LISTSERVs are the most common type of mailing list.

Some mailing lists are quite active; others mercifully aren't. Each mailing list has its own characteristics, whether its structure is rigid and formal with *topic police* hounding those that stray from the subject at hand, or more informal, where anything including the kitchen sink are fodder for discussion.

Mailing lists can be classified into four basic types:

- ✔ **Open:** Any subscriber can post a message. Topics are suggested by the name of the mailing list, but nobody gets too upset if you stray now and then. These lists tend to draw the most traffic since nobody feels like anyone is looking over their shoulder as they type.

- ✔ **Moderated:** Any subscriber can post a message, but before it gets sent to the entire list, a moderator reviews it. Moderators protect you from silly, off-topic, or redundant postings. This type of list is my favorite.

- ✔ **Announcement:** Basically a one-way list. Announcements come from only one source and only the mailing list owner(s) can post to the list.

- ✔ **Digest:** Moderated lists that take a week or so of postings, remove duplicates, and stick them all together in one e-mail. That makes all that information easier to . . . well . . . digest.

You can generally tell whether the group you've subscribed to is moderated by carefully reading the confirmation message when it returns from the LISTSERV. Encourage any student or teacher who uses your Internet account to question and verify information on any list, especially from mailing lists that are unmoderated.

Finding a Mailing List

You can locate the addresses that you need to subscribe to a mailing list in several ways. One method is to purchase a book or magazine that has a list of LISTSERV addresses. *The Directory of Electronic Journals, Newsletters, and Academic Discussion Lists*, which lists thousands of LISTSERVs and 250+ electronic journals, is available from the Association of Research Libraries (phone 202-296-2296) or check their Web site at `www.arl.org`.

Another place to obtain a "list of lists" is from the Internet itself — simply search the Web (Chapter 8 offers tips on searching the Internet). You can also send regular e-mail to `listserv@bitnic.educom.com`, leave the subject line blank, and type **list global** in the message field. Soon a lengthy list of mailing lists appears in your mailbox.

You probably noticed that I listed two different ways to get the list — this is pretty typical of the Internet. Just as you can choose from more than one way to get Archibald to do his calculus homework, you can get the same information on the Internet in different ways as well. The path that you choose depends on the type of Internet connection you have (online service, independent ISP, or other) and the tools you're using (browsers, and so on). If you get stuck, try a different method. You may be surprised at what works!

Subscribing to a Mailing List

After you find a mailing list that interests you, you have to subscribe to it before you can start receiving messages. To subscribe to a mailing list, all you usually have to do is send a message to the LISTSERV (the computer that controls, sorts, and distributes incoming messages on a particular topic). It's as easy as 1, 2, 3 (well, maybe 1, 2, 3, 4, 5, 6):

1. **Log on to the Internet and launch your e-mail program.**

   If you don't have an e-mail program, see Chapter 11 where I discuss e-mail programs (including Eudora Light, which is on the CD that comes with this book).

2. **Open a new mail message. Address your message to the LISTSERV computer that administers the list you're interested in subscribing to and enter the appropriate message in the subject line.**

   Because your subscription request is read by a big, stupid computer rather than by a bright, energetic human, you have to follow some strict rules about what you send.

3. **Enter the full Internet address of the LISTSERV computer in the To box.**

   The format of the LISTSERV computer's address will probably look something like this (doesn't always begin with LISTSERV, sometimes it begins with the actual name of the list):

   ```
   LISTSERV@bigdumbox.edu
   ```

4. **Leave the Subject line blank.**

   Some LISTSERV servers require you to enter text in the subject box itself. Don't worry if you do it incorrectly; the receiving server usually returns a nicely worded, slightly scolding message about where to and where not to type.

5. **In the Message (text) area, type the command** subscribe **and the name of the list to which you want to subscribe, followed by your full name (not your e-mail address).**

   Here's what a subscribe message to the macintosh-l LISTSERV (one of many Macintosh mailing lists) for user Joshua James looks like:

   ```
   subscribe macintosh-l Joshua James
   ```

6. **Click the Send button to send your message and then wait for a return confirmation. (It could take up to a couple of days for a confirmation although most come within a few hours.)**

Just so you know that you've got it right, Figure 12-1 shows a request message Fred Flintstone sent to subscribe to a LISTSERV called `rockbreakers-1` that was running on a computer located at `bedrock.edu`.

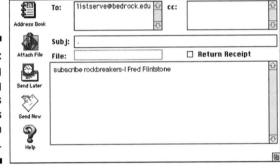

Figure 12-1: Subscribing to a mailing list is as easy as sending an e-mail.

Easy, huh? Sometime between ten seconds and a couple of days, you should receive a cryptic message from the big, dumb mainframe computer that looks something like Figure 12-2.

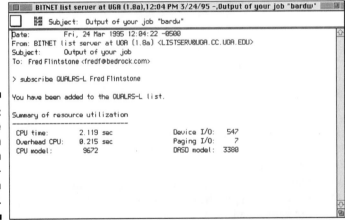

Figure 12-2: An example of a return confirmation of membership in a mailing list.

The Web: A new way to subscribe

Many Web sites now offer short forms you can fill out online that send all the necessary information to respective mail servers and subscribe you automatically to the list of choice. Generally, all you do is enter your e-mail address and click a Send or Subscribe button. Very convenient, no? Beware, however — always look for a way to *unsubscribe* (get *off* of the list). Three or four subscriptions can stuff your mailbox with thousands of e-mails!

 Your confirmation message may include specific information about canceling your subscription to the mailing list. It's a good idea to save this document or print it out so that when your mailbox gets overstuffed, you can stop the waterfall of e-mail from mailing lists.

Posting to a Mailing List

 Posting to a mailing list is as simple as sending an e-mail message. It pays to have some "list smarts" before your first post, though, because after you send the e-mail, you can't take it back. Because a mailing list can potentially be distributed to millions of people, your little boo-boo can turn into something pretty big, pretty quickly.

Before your first post, look at the header (see Chapter 11 for e-mail basics) that accompanies your incoming mailing list messages. Notice that the sender is the list name, followed by the domain name that identifies the sending computer. Be careful: If you reply to the message by using your e-mail client's Reply All command, your reply is sent to each of the zillion people who get mail on the mailing list.

If you want to remove yourself from a list or make a comment to the list's originating human, you have to use a different address. Check your mailing list subscription confirmation or the header or footer in your incoming mail for the list owner's address.

 The posting address is always different from the address that you use to subscribe to the mailing list. Use the `listserv@domainname` address only when you want to get on or off of the list. Otherwise, look for an address with the letter *l* appended to it. That address is the return address for mailing to everyone on the list. For example, you may use `listserv@bozo.edu` to subscribe, even though `cartoon-l@bozo.edu` is the actual posting address of the mailing list.

Warning: Traffic jam on the information superhighway!

As you and your students enter the information superhighway, you'll no doubt be tempted to subscribe to many mailing lists. Don't. A teacher friend of mine spent about twenty minutes online one night and subscribed to four popular mailing lists. By 8:00 the next morning, she had more than 200 e-mail messages. Interesting? Yes! But reading all those messages can consume your life. Choose carefully which lists you subscribe to.

A very challenging activity for students is to have them create a list of rules about what's appropriate and what's not appropriate to post on mailing lists. The discussion brings out new ideas and, after it's over, ensures that you and your students are all driving with the same superhighway road map.

Weathering the Mail Storm

The time will come when you no longer want to be on a mailing list to which you've subscribed. Although each LISTSERV computer requires a slightly different unsubscribe message, most unsubscribe messages look the same. Generally you must send an e-mail to a special "unsubscribe" address with the word "unsubscribe" in either the body of the e-mail or in the subject line. Figure 12-3 shows a typical LISTSERV e-mail with instructions for unsubscribing from a mailing list.

Some mailing lists deliver messages to your Inbox one at a time, as they are posted by the author. Others, called digest mailing lists (or just digests), save messages and send them in tidy bundles one or two times a week. Whichever type of list you happen to choose, know that some mailing lists are really, really busy. Thousands of college students who have lots of time on their hands begin discussions (for example, on "what's hot at the movies") that regularly produce more than 200 messages a day.

Watch your mailbox closely for a day or two after you've subscribed and see what the traffic is like. If messages jam up your in box, find out whether a digest of messages is available. If no digest is available, consider dropping all but the most important lists to which you subscribe.

With most mailing lists, it's possible to place your subscription on "hold" when you know you'll be away from your computer and modem for a while. The commands you need to hold (or temporarily stop) e-mail from arriving are usually spelled out in the confirmation message you receive shortly after you subscribe to a mailing list.

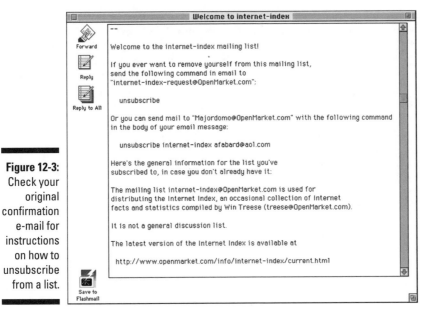

Figure 12-3:
Check your
original
confirmation
e-mail for
instructions
on how to
unsubscribe
from a list.

Mailing lists are a great way to keep up on trends and issues in education and educational media. Keep a file in your classroom with a list of your favorite mailing lists and the instructions for unsubscribing from them should the need arise.

If you can't find the instructions for unsubscribing from the list, check the footer of your messages. Often, the instructions will be included there somewhere.

Your First Subscription

Compose an e-mail message and subscribe to the very popular Library Media Network (Syracuse University). The LM-NET is a moderated list that offers tons of ideas and lots of information about using media and telecommunications in schools — a terrific first stop on your information highway mailing list tour!

Address your request to LISTSERV@suvm.syr.edu.

In the message (text) field, type subscribe LM-NET <your full name> (not your e-mail address!) and then send your message.

Be sure to print out or save the confirmation message when it comes via return e-mail so you can unsubscribe if your mailbox explodes.

If you don't like this mailing list and want to get buckets of opinions and information from somewhere else, fire up your Web browser and surf to the Liszt (bad pun) site at www.liszt.com or visit the "real time" version of lists on the Web: *message boards or bulletin boards.* Message boards are built into Web pages and offer *threaded* (indexed) message listings; they are called "real time" because the message sends instantly and often your replies are quick. These boards offer a bit more control over what and where you post, and make reading other postings easier, not to mention keeping your in box cleaner! Visit a few message boards at these sites:

```
www.apple.com/education/ali
www.parentsoup.com
www.sfgate.com
www.well.com
```

Chapter 13

Be a NewsGroupie

In This Chapter

▶ What's a newsgroup?

▶ Spreading the news with Netscape Communicator

▶ Changing your Outlook with Internet Explorer

▶ Extra, extra! Read all about it!

▶ Newsgroup etiquette

*N*ow that you have your students telecommunicating with Masai tribesmen and your Inbox is stuffed with the contents of a zillion mailing lists, you've seen all there is, right? Nope!

Welcome to newsgroups, the world's biggest corkboard.

Newsgroups 101

Like a mailing list (see Chapter 12 for more info on mailing lists), a newsgroup is a way to freely share information among Internet users. Newsgroups, also referred to as Usenet newsgroups, are like public access bulletin boards. Users float by and electronically tack messages into special message areas that are organized by topic, and while there they can read the hundreds of messages posted by other users.

As with unmoderated mailing lists, no one picks through the posted messages and looks for the kinds of words that you see scrawled on restroom walls. The contents are often off-topic, risqué, and disorganized. The upside is that newsgroups represent a cross-section of the planet; they're a great place to explore humanity.

Newsgroups are different from mailing lists in that the messages you read are not sent to your Inbox. Newsgroup messages are sent to community mailboxes whose home is on some server's huge hard drive (called a *news server*), where everyone can access them via the Web or special newsgroup-reader software. When you access a newsgroup server, you're presented with a list of newsgroups to choose from. Once you've chosen one that interests you, the index of the newsgroup (a list of posted message) is downloaded to your computer. Clicking on any message allows you to see the contents. Newsgroups are organized by topic and come chock full of messages and responses to those messages, offering a running dialog about a wide variety of subjects.

Figure 13-1 gives you a glimpse at just one of the information nuggets that you might find in the `misc.education.science` newsgroup. Education newsgroups like this one are a handy way to get questions answered or exchange ideas.

Figure 13-1:
Netscape's
Commun-
icator
newsgroup
interface.

Finding a Newsgroup

Newsgroups are organized according to the theme of the group and the category to which each group belongs. Currently, more than 35,000 newsgroups are available worldwide, about 80 of which are specifically related to teaching and learning.

The first word in a newsgroup name indicates the category to which the newsgroup belongs. In a newsgroup called k12.chat.junior, for example, you stumble on middle schoolers who are talking about what they do to their teachers each day. Need a movie review for a media class? Try rec.arts.movies (rec stands for recreation — see Table 13-1 for more prefixes). You and your students will never get bored; there are thousands of newsgroups out there.

Table 13-1 lists the Usenet categories you may find most useful. One category, the k12 groups, is generally posted by teachers, for teachers. Each day you can find new ideas and helpful hints for everything from lesson planning to the newest strategies for fund-raising. You encounter plenty more categories (prefixes) as you explore newsgroups, and new ones are added (and old ones removed) practically every day.

Table 13-1	Usenet Categories	
Top-Level Domain	*Description*	*Example*
alt (alternative)	Everything you can imagine, no matter how strange; a birthplace for many soon-to-be certified newsgroups	alt.pets.rabbits
comp (computers)	Discussions about the use of computers and their peripherals	comp.sys.powerpc
k12 (education)	Discussion for teachers by teachers	k12.library
soc (social)	Discussions about social issues	soc.college
news (network news/ software)	Relates to network news and Internet software	news.announce. newusers
rec (recreation)	Recreation and the arts	rec.music.beatles
sci (science)	Research and the sciences	sci.bio. microbiology
talk (idle chatter)	Arguments; organized chaos	talk.politics. mideast

Read All about It

You read newsgroups by launching your browser and surfing to a site containing Web-based newsgroup listings, or by using the Newsgroup functions built-in to your browser. This is a great improvement over the "old days" of the Internet (you know, four or five years ago?) when the only way to access newsgroups was a stand-alone newsgroup program called a newsreader. You can also log on to an online service, such as America Online and CompuServe, that give you access to newsgroups.

Whether you use a browser, a newsreader program, or an online service, reading newsgroups is now as easy as clicking an icon. Figure 13-2 shows what AOL's Newsgroups window looks like. Reading, adding, and searching are all choices on the newsgroup menu (AOL Keyword: **Newsgroups**).

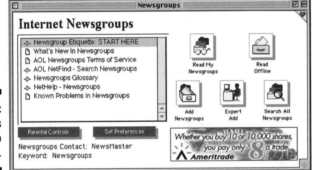

Figure 13-2: AOL's newsgroup interface.

If you're using another Internet Service Provider (*ISP*), your Netscape Communicator or Internet Explorer browser is the easy way to do things. There are newsreaders built-in that make the process practically transparent.

Navigating Newsgroups with Netscape

Netscape Communicator has a great newsgroup reader that's a viable alternative to using a stand-alone newsreader like NewsWatcher. Using the Communicator newsreader is convenient, too, because it's integrated with the Netscape Messenger mail client.

To ready your computer to read newsgroups using Netscape, you have to feed it a bit of information. The most important info is the name of your newsgroup server.

To add a newsgroup server or modify its information:

1. **Choose Edit⇨Preferences.**

2. **Choose Mail & Newsgroup Preference⇨Newsgroup Servers.**

3. **Enter the name of the newsgroup server and press Return.**

Once you've entered a server, if you'd like to change its properties (such as whether or not a selected newsgroup server will prompt you for a password or enter it automatically), here's what to do:

1. **Choose Edit⇨Preferences.**

2. The Communicator Preferences window appears.

3. **Select Mail & Newsgroup Preferences from the list at left, then select Newsgroup Properties and, finally, choose the server you wish to edit from the Servers box and click Edit.**

4. **Choose from the following options:**

   - **Always ask me for my user name and password**: Netscape always prompts you for your user name and password to add an extra level of security.

   - **Only ask me for my user name and password when necessary**: Netscape only asks you for your password if you need to log in before accessing the distant server (such as when you require a secure server connection).

5. **Click OK again.**

Accessing newsgroups

To access newsgroups with Communicator, click the Newsgroups icon on the Netscape Component bar (the same as choosing Communicator⇨Newsgroups) or click a newsgroup Web link. What's the difference between these approaches? Clicking a newsgroup Web link only allows you to read the newsgroup, whereas clicking the Newsgroups icon also allows you to subscribe to new newsgroups. With Navigator, you can also type a newsgroup URL (such as `news:alt.education`) directly into the Location box on the Location toolbar near the top of the Navigator window. This will automatically start your Netscape Newsreader. (This trick starts Outlook Express in IE).

Subscribing to newsgroups

Want to subscribe to a newsgroup? (As if you don't get zillions of e-mail messages already!) If so, follow thses easy steps:

1. **Choose Communicator⇨Newsgroups.**

   The main Messenger window appears (refer to Figure 13-1).

2. **Choose File⇨Subcribe.**

   The Subcribe to Folders and Newsgroups window appears, as shown in Figure 13-3.

3. **From this page you can both subscribe and unsubscribe from newsgroups.**

   To subscribe to a newsgroup, enter its name in the Newsgroup box and press Enter/Return.

   To unsubscribe from a newsgroup, select the newsgroup you wish to unsubscibe from and click the Unsubscribe button (you can also do this in the regular Messenger window by selecting a newsgroup from the left pane and clicking Delete).

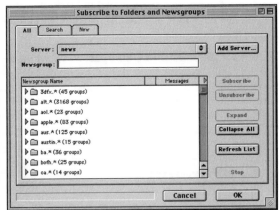

Figure 13-3:
Netscape makes it easy to subscribe to newsgroups.

Newsgroups with Internet Explorer/Outlook Express

Internet Explorer uses a helper program called Outlook Express (free with your copy of Internet Explorer) to access newsgroups and e-mail. Newsgroup information is displayed in the same windows Outlook Express uses to display e-mail messages, making managing newsgroups as easy as managing your e-mail. Like Communicator, you can use IE to surf to a site containing a portal to newsgroups on the Web, or you can use Outlook Express as a newsreader program. If you wish to use Outlook Express as a newsreader, you have to configure it first.

Prepping Outlook Express to read newsgroups

1. **Find out the address of your newsgroup server from your ISP.**

   It looks something like this: `news.whatever.com`, or it might be a "dotted quad" like this: `255.255.0.0`.

2. **Log on to the Internet.**

3. **Launch Internet Explorer and click the Mail icon in your toolbar; then choose Read News to get to your default news server.**

   You can also launch Outlook Express directly by double-clicking the Outlook Express program icon on your desktop or by choosing Start➪Programs➪Outlook Express.

Figure 13-4 shows the Outlook Express interface newsgroup.

Figure 13-4:
The Outlook Express newsgroup window.

4. **Choose Edit➪Preferences (Mac) or Tools➪Accounts and click the News tab to display the Internet Accounts dialog box (Windows).**

   A Preferences dialog box like the one shown in Figure 13-5 appears.

5. **Select News from the Accounts submenu and click New Server.**

6. **Enter a name for the news server and click OK.**

   This name will be used to identify the news server in the folder list and can be anything you can dream up.

7. **Type in the server address.**

   Get this info from your ISP.

8. **Check the This Server Requires Authentication check box (Mac) or the My News Server Requires Me to Log On (Windows) and type your user name and password in their respective boxes.**

   Some servers don't require a user name and password; if your provider doesn't, ignore this step.

9. **If you want to make this your default news account, click Make Default (Set as Default for Windows users).**

10. **Click OK.**

Subscribing to a newsgroup

Now that you've gotten your server identified, all that's left is to grab a list of available newsgroups, then subscribe to and read one (or more). Follow these steps to subscribe to a newsgroup:

1. **Click a news server from the left-hand window in Outlook Express.**

   If you don't receive a list of newsgroups automatically and you're using a Mac, choose View➪Get Complete Newsgroup List. In Windows choose Tools➪Newsgroups and click the All tab. The complete list of newsgroups appears on the right side of the window.

2. **Choose a news server from your Outlook Express mail/news window.**

3. **Select a newsgroup from the list and then do one of the following:**

   - To subscribe to the selected newsgroup, choose Tools⇨Subscribe. Each subscribed newsgroup is displayed in the folder list beneath the news server. (In Windows, choose Tools⇨Newsgroups, select the newsgroup from the All tab, and then click the Subscribe button in the Newsgroups dialog box).

   - To unsubscribe from the selected newsgroup, choose Tools⇨Unsubscribe. (Windows users choose Tools⇨Newsgroups, choose the newsgroup from the All tab, and then click the Unsubscribe button.)

Reading a newsgroup message

Reading a newsgroup message is easy — just click on the message from the list. If you need step-by-step instructions, I've got you covered:

1. **Choose a news server from the folder list on the left-hand side of your Outlook Express window, then click the newsgroup that you want to read.**

   A list of the newsgroups to which you've subscribed appears.

2. **Choose File⇨Open Newsgroup.**

   Your newsgroup messages begin to download. You can continue to do other things while you're waiting for the download, if there are a lot of messages it takes a minute or so.

3. **Click the message you'd like to read to view the message in the pre-view pane or double-click to view the message in a separate window.**

   You'll likely see message threads (a series of responses to an individual message). These are denoted by a triangle to the left of the original message. Just click the triangle to reveal the threaded messages.

Now, don't be a _lurker_! Lurkers read newsgroups and never post anything. Go ahead, try posting yourself! Add to the knowledge of the Internet. Posting a message is as easy as choosing News Message from the Outlook Express File menu and typing in the info, and then clicking Send to post it.

That's the basic course in Outlook Express newsreading. Like most Microsoft programs, you'll find a zillion more bells and whistles for managing and organizing newsgroups attached to the newsreader program. Outlook Express allows you to filter messages and set up custom colors to help you know what you've read and what you haven't. Check out the Help menu in the Outlook Express menu bar and search for "Newsgroup rules" for more info.

Spreadin' the (Deja) News

The DejaNews Web search engine is not only a great search engine but also the mother of all Newsgroup search engines to boot. DejaNews is an easy way to find newsgroups that interest you. Here's how to use it:

1. **Start your browser.**

2. **Go to the DejaNews web site (**www.dejanews.com**).**

   Figure 13-6 shows the DejaNews home page.

Figure 13-6:
The
DejaNews
home
page.

3. **Click Browse Groups.**

   A list of popular newsgroups appears, divided into broad categories.

4. **Click one of the top-level groups, like edu (education).**

   The Browse Group Results screen appears and presents a list of subdivisions. Each subdivision corresponds to an individual newsgroup or collection of newsgroups.

5. Click one of the folder or branch links like *Society & Culture/Education* to see a list of forums, as shown in Figure 13-7.

6. Click a subgroup to read the threaded messages.

Figure 13-7:
DejaNews
education
groups.

 DejaNews also offers an Interest Finder that allows you to search newsgroups by interest area. A quick reminder: you'll find anything and everything in these newsgroups, even in the relatively "safe" education environment, so watch your students closely!

Newsgroup Rules

Wash your hands before you eat. No food in the computer room. Don't run in the halls. Don't scrape your fingernails on the chalkboard. Say please and thank you.

Rules and manners are important, whether in the classroom or while surfing the Internet. If you and your students mind your (newsgroup) manners, people

ON THE CD

Honoring the old ways: NewsWatcher

In addition to a browser, you can also use a separate *newsreader* program to find and read newsgroups. Basically, these programs enable you to create a list of newsgroups that you want to read so you don't have to hunt for them every time you log on, much the same as the integrated browser features explained earlier in the chapter, only without the integration. You might want to use one of these programs if you don't have access to Netscape or Outlook Express or AOL, or if you just want to challenge your students with something different.

NewsWatcher is an easy-to-use and feature-rich newsreader for the Macintosh. This nifty freeware enables you to create a customized newsgroup list and easily read and post messages to Usenet newsgroups. You can get a copy of NewsWatcher via FTP (see Chapter 16 for details on using FTP) from the following address:

> ftp.halcyon.com

If you use Windows, I've included a copy of Free Agent on the CD. Free Agent works much the same as NewsWatcher and has a very reasonable learning curve. For Mac users, I've included Nuntius, which is also a useful — and free — Usenet newsgroup reader.

Another alternative for Windows users is Trumpet, an excellent shareware newsreader and e-mail program available via the web from www.download.com in the Internet Newsreaders directory. Trumpet also works the same way NewsWatcher does and is so full-featured that it has its own chapter in *MORE Internet For Dummies*, 4th Edition, by John Levine and Margaret Levine Young (IDG Books Worldwide, Inc.), which you should check out if you need more information after exploring the program on your own.

If you are using AOL or another online service, all this stuff is built in and easy as pie to use. Just go to the Internet forum (Keyword: **newsgroups** in AOL) and choose Newsgroups.

like you better. Some advice is timeless. Because newsgroup postings often originate from packed college computer labs at midnight or from K-12 students who are trying out the newest toy while the teacher is looking the other way, the atmosphere on the Internet is pretty much one of anything goes.

In general, the newsgroup rules are

- ✔ Be brief, but complete and to the point.

- ✔ If you don't have something nice to say, don't say anything. (Yes, Mom was right.)

- ✔ Pay attention to the topic — don't put square pegs into round holes.

- ✔ Watch your tone of voice. Yes, it comes through even in e-mail. Sarcasm, as a rule, doesn't work because you can't see the facial expression of the sender. It usually comes off as just rudeness.

Just the FAQ files, Ma'am!

Many newsgroups feature information about, or directions to, a group of downloadable files known on the Internet as FAQ files. FAQ is a TLA (three-letter acronym) that stands for *frequently asked questions*. Someone has taken the time to pull together all the questions that *newbies* (new Internet users) ask and put them in one place. FAQ files are generally well written and informative. Read them and have your students read them, too, before posting questions to the newsgroups.

  ✔ DON'T USE ALL CAPITAL LETTERS! (It's the Net equivalent to shouting.)

  ✔ Look for FAQ files and read them! (See the sidebar on FAQ files.)

Saving Your Job

You probably don't condone censorship. You probably believe in free speech. But let's get real. You really like your job, and your job is working with other people's children. You will no doubt come to realize that some things found in Cyberspace aren't appropriate in most school settings.

One target of criticism is the much misunderstood alt. (alternative) newsgroups. These groups aren't subject to the same scrutiny as other newsgroups, and often they come and go on a daily basis. Anyone can create any topic he or she wants — any topic — no matter how crazy, lewd, or mischievous. Newsgroups represent the ideas and opinions of every person posting — whether genius or maniacal. You'll find postings from every part of that spectrum in the alt. groups.

Some newsgroups in the alt. series are just plain fun, some are strange, and some might make the Board of Education tear up your teaching contract. A brief (and, yes, censored) glance at a small sampling from the alt. newsgroups listed in Table 13-2 gives you the idea.

Table 13-2	A Sampling of alt. Newsgroups
Newsgroup	*Topic*
`alt.fan.mst3k`	An online shrine dedicated to the "Mystery Science Theatre 3000" TV show
`alt.spam`	Celebrating a luncheon meat as a national treasure
`alt.sport.lasertag`	Indoor game where nervous people zap each other with infrared lasers
`alt.sports.baseball.atlanta-braves`	Atlanta Braves major league baseball
`alt.support.divorce`	A frank discussion about tough times
`alt.games.doom`	A very popular PC game that's no doubt the cause of countless wasted hours in schools and the workplace
`alt.humor.best-of-usenet`	Someone's idea of what's funniest on the Internet
`alt.society.generation-x`	Lifestyles of those born when we wish we were (maybe)
`alt.fan.heinlein`	The prolific science fiction author
`alt.fashion`	Everything from bell-bottoms to bustiers
`alt.folklore.computers`	Weird tales about possessed hardware
`alt.politics.democrats`	Discussion in support of the president

And you wouldn't believe some of the groups that I didn't list. Suffice it to say that the `alt.` groups are as varied as the humans on our planet are. The `alt.` groups are often the place where budding newsgroups first see Cyberspace.

Several `alt.` newsgroups are great sources of rumors and gossip that are so close to reality that you'll feel like a swami. Ask your ISP whether users can control access to `alt.` groups if you're concerned.

Extra, Extra! Read These Newsgroups!

Hundreds of newsgroups are packed with information for educators. Log onto the Internet, launch a newsreader or browser, and subscribe to one of these:

```
k12.chat.teacher
k12.chat.elementary
k12.chat.junior
k12.chat.senior
k12.ed.special
```

To help spread the word, print a few of the messages that you receive and share them with colleagues. You'll get them hooked in no time!

Newsgroups Anonymous

Every day, Usenet users pump upwards of 40 million characters into the system — roughly the equivalent of half the information in a large encyclopedia. You'll find that if you're not careful, you can spend countless hours reading newsgroups and posting messages, such as, "I'm looking for a company that makes chalk in 30 colors."

Chapter 14

Chatting on the Net

• •

In This Chapter

▶ IRC: Chatter at Cyberspeed

▶ Chatting on AOL

▶ Immediate gratification: Instant Messaging

• •

*H*ello? (Send; then wait an hour.) Hello. (Send; then wait a day.) How are you? (Send; then wait a minute.) E-mail is a marvelous way of keeping in touch, but is it a good way to have a conversation? Zipping out an e-mail to an expert helping you teach your students about National Parks and awaiting a response is certainly a good use of the Internet, but wouldn't a live, one-on-one question-and-answer session be more exciting?

Online chat is the Internet version of real-time communication. A chat lets you communicate instantly with other people logged on to the Internet by typing messages back and forth. Assuming you can type, chat's much faster than *snail mail* (postal mail), and more interactive than e-mail. Chat is most useful when you need to get immediate information or feedback about an idea or subject, or when you'd like to bring a technology into the classroom that allows a more personal communication than e-mail. Now you can invite a real, live Park Ranger into the classroom and have your students type questions and get immediate answers.

Chatting on the Net

Here are two types of online chat you and your students might find useful:

> ✔ **Group chat in chat rooms** (online channels): This is the electronic equivalent of a class discussion in which a whole bunch of people (some of whom you may not know that well) express their opinions online. When you enter the chat room (or join a channel), you can read on-screen what people are saying and add your own comments by typing them and pressing Return (Enter in Windows).

✔ **One-to-One**: This is a private conversation between you and another person whom you invite to chat online. Only you and the person to whom you're typing (and the 28 students looking over your shoulder) can see the text on-screen. These one-to-one conversations can take place in special private chat rooms (channels you create yourself or those designed specifically for only two people) or through *instant message* tools such as AOL Instant Messenger and ICQ.

Chat is easier than ever on the Internet these days. You can conduct group or one-to-one chat sessions on the Internet using *IRC* (Internet Relay Chat) or on online services such as AOL.

IRC: Chatter at the Speed of CyberSpace

Internet Relay Chat (IRC) is a software-dependent method of holding live online conversations with people around the world. IRC kind of reminds me of a global CB radio network that you access via computer — a free-for-all place where people speak their minds to whomever will listen. Like a CB, the IRC interface contains many different *channels,* which (in the case of IRC) are chat areas that cover particular topics.

After you log onto the Internet, launch your chat software (or enter a Web page where the software is embedded as a Java applet), and join a chat, you can type words that all the other people sharing your chat can see instantly (assuming, of course, anyone shows up — remember you have to invite them and they must join your chat). At any one time, hundreds of channels (chats) are buzzing with chatter. You can either join a channel or create one of your own.

After you learn how chats operate, you can make your chats private or by invitation only and assign yourself and your students a nickname (critical for participation in public or uncontrolled chats).

If you and your students want to study humanity, IRC is a great way to begin. IRC chats are raw, uncensored, mile-a-minute dialog, and spelling doesn't count! As with any free-form medium, you are likely to see things that will curl your hair. I recommend using IRC (or any kind of online public chat) *very cautiously* with your students and only with a *specific purpose* in mind.

The best use of IRC may be to begin your own private chat and invite other classes from across the country to participate. Use e-mail or newsgroup and mailing list postings to invite them (see Chapters 12 and 13).

In the next section, I discuss how to use one of the popular IRC chat *clients* (local software on your computer). Nowadays, though, with the spread of *Java* (a computer language used to write special programs called *applets* that run in your Web browser), many people and businesses offer chat clients built into their Web sites. Just point your browser to the site, click "chat,"

and the host computer copies a Java applet to your computer) or uses special HTML commands that open a new window within your browser (like the one shown in Figure 14-1) containing chat tools that will have you chatting in seconds. Because the programs are stored in your computer's memory (RAM) and not on your hard drive, when you leave the site, or log off of the Internet, the Java applet is erased.

IRC is not very pretty, but it can be a very powerful collaborative tool in a classroom, breaking down classroom walls to connect students with peers and experts around the world. IRC can also be a part of the solution to the problem of extending learning to your community. Read on to find out more about extending your reach with IRC.

If you are connected to the Internet via an Internet service provider, you can chat live by using a software application that supports IRC. You can access IRC from your own computer either by using telnet to connect with another computer that is running an IRC client, or by using IRC client software.

Two of the best shareware IRC programs are:

   ✔ IRCle for the Macintosh (`http://www.ircle.houseit.com/`)

   ✔ mIRC for Windows (`www.mirc.co.uk`)

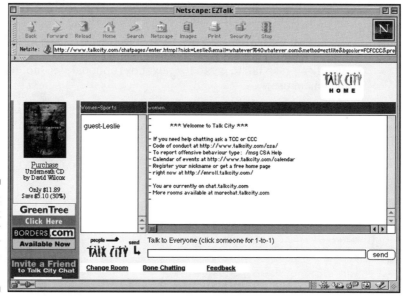

Figure 14-1: Visit Talk City for html- or Java-based chat.

Because this technology is so useful, and a bit addicting, there are new IRC programs popping up practically weekly. If you want updates or would like to check out other chat programs, visit one of the many shareware sites on the Internet like CNET (www.download.com) or visit the home pages for each product listed above.

Here's how IRCle (Mac) works. (Windows users note that mIRC works pretty much the same way — look for the Windows-specific instructions following Mac instructions.

1. **Log on to the Internet and launch your IRC client.**

   A dialog box appears, asking for information about the IRC server that you want to contact.

   Windows users: Use your Program Manager or Start button to run mIRC.

2. **Choose Open Connection from the File menu and choose a server from the pop-up menu. (Any server will do!)**

3. **In the Nickname box, enter a unique name (by which you'll be known during the chat) and press Tab to get to the next box.**

   The name that you use is kind of like a CB handle. It's important not to reveal personal information, so come up with something that doesn't give information about who and where you or your students are.

4. **If your IRC program prompts you for an e-mail address, you don't have to enter one (for school, leave it blank).**

   If you wish to enter an address, though, enter an e-mail address in the format e-mailaddress@domain (for example, Flintstone@bedrock.com) and then press Tab to get to the next box (optional step, not recommended for school use).

   Almost ready ! So far, your IRC setup box should look like the one shown in Figure 14-2.

Server:	irc.colorado.edu
Port:	6667
Nickname:	BeachBum
Mail address:	rocky@bermuda.net
Real name:	

Auto-Exec (write auto-exec commands into the

Notify from inactive window ☒ Blinking ☒ Audible

Notify from background ☒ Blinking ☒ Audible

[Cancel]   [OK]

Figure 14-2: The IRC setup box.

5. **To get a listing of what chats are already under way, choose Channel List from the Windows menu in the menu bar or use ⌘-L.**

   mIRC users, just click the List Channel icon, the sixth icon from the left on the toolbar.

All IRC commands begin with a forward slash (/). The slash tells the computer that you are about to enter a command, rather than a message. Enter commands in the command field, as shown in Figure 14-3.

	#education

```
#education :@Fred
> Hello!  Welcome to the Education chat!
> Today we'll talk about Technology in the classroom
```

```
Fred talking to <nobody>          irc.funet.fi              07:27:14
/join #education
```

Figure 14-3: The command field is at the bottom of the IRC screen.

A complete list of currently running chat rooms appears. (It will be a *long* list that contains every conceivable name — some quite naughty!) Note that these rooms could have been created by a user anywhere on the globe. Neat, huh?

```
*** Channel  Users  Description
*** #schools         School CA$H
*** #oboes 1 My favorite instrument!
*** #irp 1
*** #zoosrus 1
*** #wonderkids      2         The MacMillan School Online
*** #comix 4
*** #macintosh       3
*** #barney  1       Dedicated to bashing a purple creature
         Snip! I just spared you the other 3,455 chats that
         were listed.
```

Just like other places on the wild Internet frontier, some chat channels have names that'll raise more than a few eyebrows and make you nervous. As with any Internet session, *supervision* is the key when you are working with students. Proceed with great caution!

6. **To enter a room, choose Join from the Commands pull-down menu, type** `/join #channelname` **in the command box or double-click the channel name.**

The UNIX command `/join` appears in the command box.

For example, you use the command `/join #windows` to enter the room called *windows* from the listing. (If you enter a name that's not on the list of currently running chat rooms, you create a new room.)

A window opens with the room name on the title bar. You're in! (A second window opens behind the current window, showing the status of your connection and lots of other information for techno-brains.) Now all you have to do is invite someone else to join in or begin typing in the command box. As you type and press Return, your text is distributed so that everyone in your room can see it.

Figure 14-4 shows an Education chat that I participated in recently. Note that the names of all the participants are at the top of the chat and that each person's name automatically appears next to comments he or she makes. You also see system commands, such as `***Signoff` or `***Entered`, indicating someone leaving or entering your channel.

Figure 14-4:
A sample
IRC chat on
education
issues.

```
On IRC via server jello.qabc.uq.oz.au :University of Queensland, Australia
idle for 130 seconds
Topic is: #Education :Yippee!
#Education :Bard Boppo Pug Demi Gradu Gavel TFool MacS Acne Fred
Teacher Kidz Banshee Scotter @Master
Mode is +tn

*** Candice [Trustee@iquest.net] has joined #Education

Boppo changed the mode on #Education to "+o Boppo"

<Bard> What kind of multimedia do you use in your school?
<Pug> Mostly CD-ROM and some videodisc.
<Scotter> HyperStudio is great for videodisc stuff.
<TFool> really, Scotter?  Is it easy?
*** Signoff: Gavel
*** Signoff: Kidz
<Pug> It's so easy my third graders are making multimedia so much I had
to buy a 1 GB hard drive!
```

For more information about using IRC, check the newsgroup `alt.irc` or FTP at `cs.bu.edu` in the `/irc/support` directory. (For more information about newsgroups, see Chapter 14.)

If you join a very busy channel, the chat window is quickly filled with messages. Each message starts with a person's IRC nickname, followed by the message.

IRC chat seems awfully confusing at first, kind of like homeroom on the first day of school. Just be patient and read as much of the text as you can. When your students are online, typing speed becomes a factor. Be sure to warn other users if the typist is a bit slow.

7. **To quit your IRC session, click the close box in the open IRC window and choose File⇨Quit (⌘-Q). For Windows 95 and later, right-click on the icon in the system tray (right side of the task bar) and choose Disconnect.**

Remember that quitting IRCle doesn't mean that you've severed your Internet connection. You may have to visit your Control Panel (MacPPP/WinSock) to do that.

The error message `TCP Connection status open failed` means that the server is busy. Just wait a minute and try again or choose another IRC server.

Table 14-1 provides some useful commands for IRC chat.

Table 14-1	IRC Commands Put You in Control		
Command	*What It Does*	*Example*	*Comments*
/join #*channel*	Joins the specified channel	`/join #irchelp`	Joins the IRC help channel
/part #*channel*	Leaves a channel	`/part #irchelp`	Leaves the IRC help channel
/list [#*string*] [**-min** #] [**-max** #]		`/list`	lists all available channels
		`/list-min 5-max 20`	lists channels with names between 5 and 20 characters long
		`/list #love`	lists channels with *love* in the name
/msg *nickname message*	Sends a private message to this user without opening a query window	`/msg StudyBuddy Your students seem very bright! How about a pen-pal exchange?`	The message is visible only to StudyBuddy
/whois *nickname*	Shows information about someone	`/whois StudyBuddy`	Find out who the person who goes by StudyBuddy is
/nick *nickname*	Changes your nickname to whatever you like	`/nick Another SillyName`	Your nickname is now Another SillyName

(continued)

Table 14-1 *(continued)*

Command	What It Does	Example	Comments
/quit [*reason*]	Disconnects you from IRC and gives the optional message as the reason for your departure	`/quit That's all folks!`	Leaves with the message "That's all folks!"
/topic #*channel newstopic*	Changes the topic for the channel. (*Note:* You must be a channel operator to use this command.)	`/topic #friendly Oh what a beautiful day!`	Changes the topic of the channel called "friendly" to good weather
/invite *nickname* #*channel*	Invites another user to a channel	`/invite Study Buddy #K12chat`	Asks Study Buddy to head to the K12chat channel

Live Chat Via AOL

If you've chosen to surf the Internet on America Online (AOL), you can converse live online in electronic conference rooms. The intuitive interface makes chatting easy and fun. The online hosts, real-live volunteers that work for AOL part time, keep order and facilitate discussions. AOL also allows voting, comments, and even rolling dice.

To "go live" on America Online, log on and choose an electronic conference room. Find conference rooms on AOL by clicking the Keyword icon (or press ⌘-K/Ctrl+K) and using keyword: **Chat** or keyword: **People Connection**, The Schoolroom, located in the Electronic Schoolhouse (keyword: **ESH**), is a great place for teachers to get together. There's also a kind of a teacher's lounge in cyberspace (keyword: **Teachers' Lounge**) where you can find plenty to chat about.

After you've found a chat room, you'll see a screen much like the one in Figure 14-5. At the top right of the screen, you'll see a listing of how many people are currently in the chat as well as their screen names. Icons at the bottom right of the chat screen let you find people (keyword: **Member Directory**), report naughty chatters (keyword: **Notify AOL**), engage in a private, one-on-one chat, set the preferences (such as whether you wish to be notified when someone else enters or leaves the room), and more.

People behaving badly

In the old West there were sheriffs to get the bad guys. Unfortunately, in the new frontier of the Internet you're pretty much on your own. The good news is that you've got several options for dealing with people behaving badly in a chat room.

✔ **Leave the chat room.** Create a new one of your own and send e-mail or an Instant Message to your friends asking them to join you there.

✔ **Complain to the offender's ISP.** Sending e-mail to `postmaster@service-provider.xxx` (insert the name of their service provider and a ".com", ".net" or whatever as necessary). On AOL you can report offenders by clicking the Notify AOL button. When you press the button, a window pops up to help you gather all the information to file your report. You're also asked to copy and paste offensive dialog into the form provided. AOL deals swiftly

with these reports and has the power to terminate (cancel) user's accounts for violations of their Terms of Service agreement. (For more information, log on to AOL and use keyword **TOS**.)

✔ **Ignore them.** Remember when your mother told you if you ignore bullies and they would go away? Well, the real world tells you this really works — sometimes.

✔ **Filter them.** On AOL, double-click the screen name of the offender in the room list and click the Ignore check box. Their name and comments won't show up in your chat window.

Whatever scheme you choose, do not, repeat, do not engage in a conversation mirroring their behavior. *You* could end up being the one reported, and engaging in the action with the person most often just escalates the situation.

Figure 14-5:
AOL chat is easy and reliable.

ON THE CD

Talk and see?

I guess it was a matter of time before some brilliant person figured out a way to actually speak and be heard over the Internet. Using a small video camera and a software program called CU-SeeMe (see the demo on your IFT3 CD) you and your students can hear *and see* another person. There are other video chat clients as well. Microsoft's Netmeeting will also do the trick. It has less features, but it's free (www.microsoft.com).

Imagine taking virtual field trips through your computer screen. The technology is not quite perfect though, and everyone kind of looks like TV's Max Headroom, mostly because the pipeline (speed of connection) isn't quite large enough. Jerkiness (the image, not the people) aside, it's an emerging technology that has much promise. My prediction is that within five years, we'll all be using our computers as videophones anyway. Guess I've got to buy a new bathrobe.

Clicking on a member's screen name in the chat list brings up a menu that gives you three helpful options:

✔ **Ignore:** Checking this box makes that person disappear from your screen (they're still in the chat room, you just don't see what they type). The ignored person can still see what you type, however, unless they ignore *you*. (To "un-ignore", just double-click the person's name and click the check-box again.)

✔ **Send message:** Brings up an Instant Message that allows you and another chatter to type back and forth privately. The main chat continues in the background.

✔ **Get profile:** Displays the member's current profile. If your students are chatting, be sure they don't reveal any personal information in the profile. Profiles are set at keyword: **Profile** or by choosing My AOL↪ My member profile.

To enter a message and participate in the chat, all you have to do is type in the box at the bottom and click the Send button. You'll also find some other icons that allow you to control the font size, color, style, and more just above this message entry box.

HEADS UP

Join educators in AOL's Schoolroom for weekly electronic chats on education-related topics such as the Internet and critical thinking. Check the schedule in the Electronic Schoolhouse (keyword: **ESH**) for more information.

Instant Message Systems and the Classroom

Driven largely by our seemingly insatiable urge for immediate gratification, the wizards of the Internet have created the ability to find out if someone else is online (logged into the Internet) and send and receive *real time* (live and immediate) messages. They call these wonders of technology *instant messages*.

Instant message systems differ from chats in that you're generally talking to one person at a time (one to one). There's really not that much difference in instant message (IM) systems, so your decision about which to use in your classroom may boil down to whether to allow the use of such technologies at all. IMs can be distracting and, worse, offer opportunities for "inappropriate communication" that's potentially more difficult to control than e-mail or chat rooms. On the other hand, it's handy if you have a "guest speaker" because you'll know immediately when they're available and you may not want to search for an IRC or AOL chat room.

The two most popular entries into the Instant Message arena are ICQ and AIM (AOL Instant Messenger). The next couple of sections give you a glimpse of each program and tell you how to get a free (yippee!) copy.

ICQ

ICQ (which stands for "I Seek You") is shown in figure 14-6 and is the grand-daddy of instant message systems with tons of features and options; it's available for Mac and PC, and it's very easy to set up and use. Normally, ICQ runs in the background all the time when you're online in a minimized (Windows) or background (Mac) window. ICQ tells you when other ICQ users are online, as well as their status — for example: Free For Chat, Do Not Disturb, and Away (from the computer) and even has a built-in real-time chat function. Grab a free copy at www.icq.com).

AOL Instant Messenger

The AOL instant messenger (AIM) is based on AOL's highly successful (and sometimes annoying) "Instant Messenger" (keyword: IM) feature that AOL users have enjoyed since the early days of online communication. AIM (available at www.aol.com/aim/) lets you communicate with other AIM (and AOL) users through a password protected chat system when they're online. Because AIM is an Internet messaging program, you don't have to have an AOL account to use the stand-alone program. Figure 14-7 shows the AIM Sign On window.

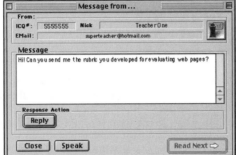

Figure 14-6:
Chatting
away
with ICQ.

Figure 14-7:
AOL Instant
Messenger
is chat on
the run.

If you are a "no-frills" IM user, then AIM is the program to use. All it does is let you type messages back and forth. It even lets you exchange files. AIM is also much easier to set up and more stable than ICQ.

More instant messaging options

You can find plenty of other systems that you can use to send instant messages. You've probably already realized that AIM and ICQ users can't talk to each other. Trying to talk to ICQ from AIM or vice versa is like having a BetaMax video tape in a VHS world. This will no doubt change since the 500-lb gorilla (AOL) purchased ICQ. Watch for a new standard (courtesy of AOL) to emerge soon!

You'll find other systems like Yahoo Pager (www.yahoo.com) that are just as fun and proprietary. There is, of course, a standard system — called e-mail — that is universal. But instant messaging is soooo trendy; it's just fun to use.

A Meeting of the Minds

For your first foray into the world of online chat, I suggest using a commercial service. It's easier to access than IRC and, by and large, online services offer more control over who wanders into your chat and whether they abide by the rules of the information superhighway. This activity works for any kind of electronic chat, whether you choose IRC or an online service.

Send an e-mail message to two or three of your teacher friends across the country and invite them to an online chat or IRC chat on a topic relating to education or technology. (How about the Internet?) During your chat, share ideas, talk about issues, and think about how you can use this medium with your students.

Some helpful hints for your electronic discussion:

✔ Arrange for a dress rehearsal beforehand if you intend to invite administrators or other visitors.

✔ Be sure to pay attention to time zones so that everyone shows up at the right time.

✔ Always have a moderator, preferably an adult, to ensure good taste and on-task behavior are the rules, not the exceptions.

✔ "Log" or "trap" the incoming text for later reference. (Both IRCle and real-time conferencing on commercial services enable the user to capture the text of a real-time session and save the resulting conversation to a text file for later use. This is referred to in Internet-speak as *logging* or *archiving* text.)

My guess is that you'll really enjoy chatting with experts, peers, and other sundry people across the Internet. Whether you're enriching a lesson on weather by talking with someone from the National Weather Service or chatting with your grandma, chat really does have some interesting uses. What's next for chatting? Can you say v-i-d-e-o? That's right, now they can SEE you, too! Check out Chapter 18 for info on Webcams for more info.

Chapter 15

I Want My FTP!

In This Chapter

▶ FTP: files for (almost) nothing
▶ Finding files on the Internet
▶ Decompressing
▶ Capturing the Flag

A student and I once spent a full hour searching our school's media center for a picture of a *tapir*. The report had long since been written into a well-planned HyperStudio stack featuring everything any human could want to know about the strange creature — everything, that is, except a decent picture. We found a tapir peeking around a tree and a tapir peeking out of the swamp, but no tapirs eating. No tapirs smiling for the camera.

(For those of you who, like me, think of a candle's taper when you hear its homonym *tapir,* a tapir looks like a cross between a pig, an elephant, and a miniature rhino, hangs out in swamps, and is nocturnal. It has a short trunk that it swings out of the way when it eats, instead of using the trunk to pick up food the way an elephant does. The tapir weighs more than 500 pounds at full maturity. If all this is too much to believe, visit one in South America — or at the zoo.)

Luckily, FTP came to our rescue. The student (while I wasn't looking, of course) logged on to the Internet, found a graphics library online that had a plethora of strange creatures' pictures, and *downloaded* (transferred the file from the host computer to our classroom Macintosh's hard drive) a most magnificent "two-shot" of a mom and baby tapir. A bit grainy and definitely not something for a Christmas card, mind you, but perfect for the report.

The moral of the story: If you can find a picture of a tapir on the Internet, you can find almost anything.

What Can I Do with FTP?

FTP (short for *File Transfer Protocol*) is a protocol (set of rules) for data transfer, allowing files such as applications, pictures, sounds, movies, and so on to be exchanged between computers without regard to how they are connected or what operating system they are running. With FTP, you can transfer files from a host computer to your computer's floppy or hard disk drive, or transfer files (like your class or school Web page) to other computers (like your Internet Service Provider's server) over the Internet.

The Internet provides access to zillions of files. Whether your students are searching for a picture of the White House or a sound file of Martin Luther King's "I Have a Dream" speech, you can probably grab one with FTP.

You can download files from an FTP site using your Web browser by entering `ftp://www.whatever.com/filename`, using special software like Fetch (Macintosh) or WS-FTP (Windows), or by using ftp directly.

To understand what people mean when they talk about FTP, you have to get out your parts-of-speech manual. You use the noun FTP when you refer to the actual File Transfer Protocol, as in "That file is available via FTP from Microsoft." When you describe the process of sending or receiving files on the Internet, you use FTP as a verb, as in "You ftp that file from Harvard's server."

FTP is sometimes referred to as anonymous FTP because the host computers don't require the user to have an account to log in and access information. Anonymous FTP sites allow anyone to enter publicly accessible directories, so you and your students can (legally!) sneak in and access the files.

Using FTP is a little like going to a flea market. You can find nearly anything there you can imagine, but not all of it is high-quality stuff. As you browse the Internet, you and your students will develop lists of favorite FTP sites and the resources found there. Luckily, there are plenty of files to browse.

Hundreds of systems connected to the Internet have file libraries, also called *archives,* that are open to the public. These libraries offer many free or low-cost computer programs for all types of personal computers.

Here are a few samples of what you can download by using FTP:

- ✔ A QuickTime movie of JFK's inaugural address
- ✔ A wave file of the sound of a dog barking
- ✔ A program that strips unnecessary carriage returns from a text document
- ✔ MP3 files, which allow you to download and listen to CD-quality music tracks
- ✔ A picture of a tapir

FTP: The Basics

Regardless of what type of computer you're using, the process of using FTP is similar. The speed of your file transfer varies, of course, based on the speed of your Internet connection and the server you are downloading from.

A typical FTP session consists of these seven steps:

1. **Launch your FTP software.**

   Using a Web browser, such as Netscape Navigator or Internet Explorer is a good solution, if you know where you're going and you just want to download, but for heavy-duty FTPing and especially uploading files (such as when you build a Web page), Fetch, WS-FTP, or another dedicated FTP client is best.

2. **Tell your FTP client the address of the computer you're seeking.**

3. **Tell the FTP server who you are (usually *anonymous*).**

   If you're using a modern browser (such as Netscape or Internet Explorer 3.0 or above), this part is automatic if the site is public.

4. **Enter the password when prompted.**

   Again, if you're using a browser, this part is automatic.

   Most of the time, entering a password is optional for public sites. It's common Net courtesy to enter your entire e-mail address instead of just leaving the field blank.

5. **Browse the directories for files you want.**

   Figure 15-1 and 15-2 show you what browsing the `ftp.info.apple.com` site looks like using Fetch and Internet Explorer, respectively.

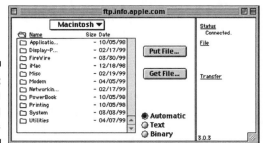

Figure 15-1:
Visiting a
site using
Fetch.

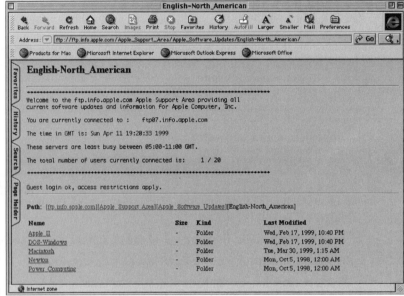

Figure 15-2:
The same site using Internet Explorer for Mac.

6. **Download the files you want.**

In browsers, you just click a hyperlink of the file you want. In Fetch or WS-FTP, you click the Get button to retrieve a file. In the Mac OS and Windows 95 and up, you can also drag and drop the file from the active window to your desktop or hard drive.

Are Internet programs really free?

Some are; some aren't. You can sort the files on the Net into three categories: public domain software, freeware, and shareware.

- ✔ Public domain programs and files carry no copyright and have no limits on redistribution, modification, or sale.

- ✔ Freeware programs and files are free for you to use and give away, but not to sell or modify. The author retains the copyright.

- ✔ Shareware programs and files allow you to road-test programs for a short evaluation period and then either pay the author a small fee or erase the program from your computer. The author retains all copyrights; although you can give shareware programs to your friends, all shareware information must accompany the program, and they have to pay the author, too.

You can set a good example for your students by always paying shareware fees and by discussing the issue of intellectual property rights with them. Most of the programs that come with this book are programs that wouldn't be available if there weren't lots of honest computer users like you out there.

7. **Log off (this is automatic when you surf to another site or Quit your FTP program).**

   After you log off the server, you can open the files you've downloaded by using a word processor for a text file (even a free one, like Microsoft's Wordpad, will do), or a multimedia tool like QuickTime for digital movies or pictures.

Finding Files on the Internet: Old and New

In the old days of the Internet (that would be like five years ago), we used to use specialized search software like Gopher and Anarchie to search for downloadable files. Nowadays, we can use our browser to surf to popular download sites like CNET's "Download.com," (see Figure 15-3) a fabulous source of downloadable shareware and software updates. You don't even have to type the `ftp://` thing — the Web site handles all that for you.

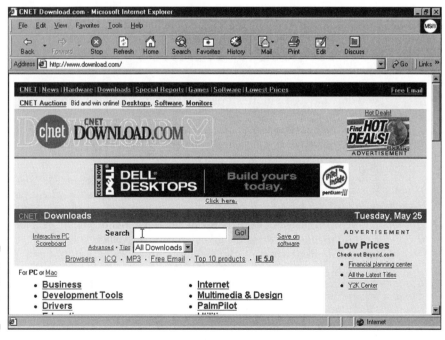

Figure 15-3:
CNET's
Download.
com.

Of course there are lots of other sites, too. Here are some of my favorites:

- ✔ **TUCOWS** (`www.tucows.com`) stands for The Ultimate Collection of Windows Software and has Windows 3.1, Windows 95, Windows 98, and [gasp!] even Macintosh software in their libraries.

- ✔ **File Mine** (`www.filemine.com`) has tons of great downloads for all platforms and includes lists of favorite downloads, daily jewels, and more.

- ✔ **Shareware.com** (`www.shareware.com`) is a searchable interface similar to CNET's download.com. An easy place to find a program that someone's told you about. Also includes information on the reliability of FTP sites and several links to try based on geographic location.

I'd be remiss if I didn't return to the roots of FTP searches and mention Archie. Archie is an Internet search resource that runs on selected Internet host computers. Archie gets its name from *archive* because it looks through hundreds of different FTP sites and tells you where the files that you want are located. A shareware program called Anarchie (available at `www.umich.edu/~archive/mac/util/comm/anarchie1.60.sit.hqx`) runs as stand-alone software on your Macintosh and allows you to find downloadable programs. For Windows users, check out `www.internet-connections.net/ftp/win3/winftp.html`.

Got the File, Now What?

After you ftp the file to your classroom computer's hard drive or floppy disk, you only have two more steps to make the software usable:

- ✔ **Uncompress the file.** Sometimes your browser software is smart enough to do this for you. Other times you'll have to run decompression software (you won't get the bends here).

- ✔ **Install the program.** Most programs (a.k.a. "executable files") need to be installed before being used. Luckily, most software downloaded on the Internet these days comes with self-install programs that do the work for you. In the case of pictures or text files, of course, all you and your students have to do is double-click the file, which should tell your computer to automatically launch the application that can view them and open the relevant file for you to enjoy. If this is not the case, you may need to launch the program yourself and open the file manually from within the application.

Some programs and files, especially pictures, take quite a while to download. Things could be worse. Most files are squeezed (compressed) by using data-compression software before storage on the host computer. The good news is that downloading a compressed file takes less time. The bad news is that you have to uncompress the file before you can view it, run it, or read it.

Watch that computer virus!

Unlike the files you download from an online service, files from the Internet have probably not been screened for computer viruses. That means you have to screen them yourself.

Stop what you're doing right now and do two things:

- Establish a school policy on screening downloaded files for viruses.

- Visit an online service, search the Net, or go to a local computer store and purchase a virus protection and screening program. (Some great freeware, shareware, and commercial virus protection programs are out there.)

If you work in a school, you've probably already had to deal with infected computers. It's not fun. Now you have to worry about files coming into the school from _all over the planet_ instead of just all over your community. A virus released in early 1999, named Melissa (after the virus creator's girlfriend?), attached itself to Microsoft Word files and spread via the Internet to an estimated four million Windows computers in less than three days. Never fear, though, the virus scanning programs work very well. Just be proactive.

Most of the files on the Internet look a little different from the files on your hard drive. They have extra letters attached like .ZIP (for Zip files) or .SIT (for Mac Stuffit files). Some of the letters indicate the _file type,_ and some cue the user about how the file was _compressed_ (packed) before sending.

Here's an example:

```
outcomes.txt.hqx
```

In this example, .TXT indicates that the file is a _text file,_ readable by most any word processor. The extension (suffix) .HQX shows that the file is in _BinHex format._ BinHex is a special cross-platform format that allows files to be accessed by almost any computer, regardless of the hardware or software installed. You'll also see the extension .BIN that indicates a binary file. Binary files are often (but not always) picture files.

Most Macintosh files are compressed by using a program called StuffIt. When the files are compressed, the author (or the program) appends the letters .SIT to the end to let you know what kind of compression was used. Here's an example of the way you write the name of a file that was compressed by using StuffIt:

```
roadrunner.gif.sit
```

After downloading the file, Macintosh users can unpack it by using a program such as StuffIt Expander, which is freeware on the CD accompanying this book, or the commercial full-featured program StuffIt Deluxe. Windows users can use WinZip (or PKUNZIP for DOS users), which is also on the CD.

Literally hundreds of compression formats are out there. A few possible extensions (suffixes) are listed in Table 15-1.

Table 15-1	Compressed file extensions
Extension	*Type of Format*
.ZIP	A file created by PKZIP or WinZip
.Z	A file compressed by UNIX
.SHAR	UNIX, shell archive
.TAR	Another UNIX compression routine
.ARJ	A DOS compression scheme; created by ARJ
.SIT	A Macintosh file created by StuffIt
.SHK	Apple II format; created by Shrinkit

Sometimes folks get really crafty and use more than one compression scheme on a file. In general, StuffIt and WinZip can handle those, though.

Chapter 16

Webcams in the Classroom

● ●

In This Chapter

▶ Webcasting

▶ What is a Webcam?

▶ How do I get started?

▶ What about HTML?

▶ Examples and Resources

● ●

*Y*ou are now entering another dimension — a place where the visual takes control of your "Internet senses." A place where live action is the rule and where anyone's "15 minutes of fame" can quickly turn into a lifetime. Welcome to the Webcasting zone!

Turning On to Webcasting and Webcams

Webcasting is the term for the process of using a camera, your computer, and special software to broadcast pictures from your classroom, computer lab, or anywhere directly to the Internet. The pictures can be *streaming* (continuous live video) or *real-time delayed* (live shots taken once a second, once every 30 seconds, or at other intervals and then broadcast). Visitors to your Website can see you and your students live (or nearly live) — a very inexpensive way to extend communications from your classroom to the "outer limits."

A *Webcam* (short for Web camera) is simply a device that, when plugged into your computer, takes still or live motion pictures and, using special software, broadcasts them to your Web pages for the world to see.

I'd be remiss if I didn't warn you that Webcam sites, like any other kind of mass communication on the net or anywhere else, have their share of "objectionable content." A simple search of "Webcam" on the Internet will no doubt reveal more than a few sites offering the kind of "education" that's inappropriate for classroom and school. If you visit Webcam sites with your students, be sure to "surf ahead" and build a bookmark list of safe Webcams you can use for illustrative purposes.

Note that I'm drawing a distinction between Webcams, Webcasting, and Web conferencing. Web conferencing (with software tools like White Pine Software's CU-SeeMe (www.wpine.com) is using the Internet like a video telephone with audio *and* video images. The Webcams featured in this chapter are *video only.* (And you'll find this can be a blessing in disguise!)

To get an idea of some wonderful Webcams, fire up the Web browser and surf to these sites:

- ✓ **NASA Live Mission:** A snapshot of NASA's Web camera site: Keep up on the latest NASA mission — Earth orbit and beyond (www.ambitWeb. com/nasacams/nasacams.html).

- ✓ **The Puppy Cam!:** A live look at the latest candidate for adoption (www.humanesocietymiami.org/petcam)

- ✓ **Defiance Middle School Computer Center:** A super example of what happens when schools and Webcams meet (nwoca.ohio.gov/ ~def_ms_www/webcam.html)

Webcams are one of the hottest things on the Net right now — perfect for spicing up your school Website. The result is definitely worth the effort!

Getting Started

First, you need to think about what it is you want to Webcast using your Webcam. Will it be your classroom, a field trip, your school's cafeteria or the next football game? Content is king, so think carefully about why you're Webcasting and what messages you want to convey — a live camera shot from inside Fred's locker just doesn't work.

Next, visit other (classroom appropriate) Webcam sites and figure out how best to display the resulting image(s) from your Webcam. Some incorporate the image into their main Website, others choose to have "channels" where visitors can switch between different Web cameras for different views.

Creating your own Webcam site isn't that tough, but it might take a little bite out of your media or technology funds. The following sections tell you what you need to build your Webcam toolkit.

Computer

Any computer that has ports (places to plug in connectors) that support the exchange of video images works nicely. It's also a good idea to have at least 64MB of RAM — that's so you can use your computer for other things *while* you're Webcasting. Not sure if your computer has the right ports? Spin it around and take a look. You don't need but one of the following connection types. You connect a Webcam to any of the following:

✔ A USB port (Universal Service Bus – found mostly on newer computers like Macs and some Windows PCs) This is my preferred connection method since USB provides power and connection is easy

✔ A parallel or serial port (the same port where you plug in your modem or printer)

✔ An ADB (Apple Desktop Bus) port (the place where you plug in your keyboard or mouse on older Mac products)

✔ A FireWire port (a new port available on Macs and some other computers where you plug in video cameras or way-fast hard drives and other stuff)

✔ A video card that has an "RCA" or "S-video" input and output port

If your computer doesn't currently have one of the connectors above, or if your computer has a connector different than the type your camera has, all is not lost! You can usually add a *video capture card* or *"AV card"* to your present computer if you have an open slot. Check with your local computer store for your options.

Web camera

Many types of cameras are appropriate for use with your computer. Your choice depends on how you will connect the camera to your computer, how high a resolution you require, what special features (like zoom, wide-angle, and auto-focus) you want, and how much money is in your school wallet. You can buy a camera made especially for Webcasting (around $100–$250) or use a video camera that you or your school may already have!

Note: You really don't need fancy features like wide angle, solarization, and so on, unless you wish to use your camera for something else (like videotaping your school play).

Here are a couple more camera options in case you're ready to jump from beginner to big-time Web camera producer:

✔ **Motorized armatures** (tripods) are available that allow viewers to control (pan, tilt, and zoom) your Web camera (it takes some HTML pizzazz to make that happen on the Web end, though).

✔ **Server cams** are a new technology that require no computer hardware on the video end, just a phone line that's connected to someone else's computer anywhere else in the world.

Webcam software

Webcam software captures the images from your camera through your computer and sends it to your Web host. The software you use depends on how many bells and whistles (camera control functions) you want to have, how much RAM (memory) your computer has, and how much you'd like to spend. The following list includes some of the more popular flavors of Webcam software:

✔ **CamRunner** by Digital Camera Network for Windows 95/98 (`www.dcn.com`): CamRunner automates the real-time capture and transmission of live images (JPEG, GIF, BMP, PNG) to your home page and operates over either a dedicated Internet connection or a dial-up modem. Scheduler, time/date stamp and other features.

✔ **FrameServer** by Roal Vertegaal shareware for Mac (`reddwarf.wmw.utwente.nl/pub/www/persons/vertegaal/software/aboutframeserver.html`): FrameServer is a full-featured Webcam utility that actually works with your Web cam software and provides your Web pages with some unique (and functional) options. When someone logs into your Web page, you'll actually hear a "knock" from your computer's speakers! FrameServer then waits 2 seconds, then renders a still Webcam photo. The photograph is automatically saved as a JPEG file on your hard disk and is then transmitted to the visitor via your Web page. FrameServer can be used with any CGI-compliant World Wide Web server (such as WebStar or WebCenter) running on any Macintosh computer.

✔ **Oculus** by Poubell Software and International Web for Mac (`www.intlWeb.com/Oculus2/index.html`): Oculus allows you tremendous control in setting up your Webcam. It features a very easy setup, time and date captioning, image captions with alpha channels (you can send two images from two different cameras, or the same image to two servers — for really popular sites) and effect filtering. It also relies on the powerful QuickTime graphics software for speed and functionality. Oculus also has support for FTP and local image saving. It also has a nifty feature that only captures images if there's motion (that is, frame differencing).

✔ **SiteCam 3.0** by Rearden for Mac (`www.rearden.com`): A full-featured Webcam program for putting live images and time-lapse movies on the internet. SiteCam can integrate into your Web site in minutes.... whether you want a new image every 5 minutes via FTP or you want to stream live video (if you use a Mac server and WebStar). SiteCam is reliable, inexpensive, easy-to-use and has the features that professional Webmasters want. It does a time stamp (places the current time on the image), you can save sequenced files ("last 10 frames") to QuickTime movies. There's a free trial version included on the CD that comes with this book.

> ✔ **WebCam32** by Kolban for Windows (www.kolban.com/Webcam32/): The most popular software for PCs running Windows (up to Windows 98). The software stamps the time and date on your image, automatically uploads images to your Web server, has tons of special effects, and lots more.

Before purchasing any software, see if you can download a "demo" version first. Otherwise you might end up wasting your money on something that you don't like. Most capture software will have a "time-limited" or "limited edition" version that you can try before purchasing.

Modem

You will need to have a modem to dial to the Internet if your school doesn't have a direct (network) connection. Modems can be internal (inside the computer) or external (outside the computer plugged into the modem port). Modems also come in different speeds, usually anywhere from 14.4Kbps to 56.6Kbps. The faster the modem you have and the "cleaner" your local phone lines are, the faster you will be able to upload your captured image. Modems can be purchased at almost any computer store and cost anywhere between $50 and $200.

Connection to the Internet

First and foremost you need some way to connect to the Net. This can be a *direct* connection (through your school-wide network), a cable modem, a DSL (digital subscriber line) connection, or a dial-up account through your phone line via a modem. Depending on where you are setting up your Webcam you might need to get an ISP (Internet service provider). An ISP will give you a

---

Bandwidth hog

If your site is very popular, and many users visit your Web site and request your Webcam feed, your ISP may get really testy. That's because each user logs into your site and then their browser automatically polls your server for the camera image at intervals you predetermine. Imagine 100 users, each hitting your Web server once every 10 seconds. You can quickly eat up 50GB per day of your ISP's bandwidth (the size of their transmission pipeline). Whoa, Nellie!

To keep them happy (and to avoid some seriously huge charges), try setting your camera software's refresh rate to 1 minute or take the camera offline during peak hours of Internet use. You can also monitor traffic (number of visitors) and bandwidth carefully using tools provided by your service provider to ensure you're not a bandwidth hog.

"dial-up" account where you can dial up from your modem to the Internet using a phone number, user-name and password. You can also get access to a *Web host* (a server on which to post your Web page) if your school doesn't have one. There are many different ISP's out there. (We've conveniently included a Mindspring sign-up kit on the CD that comes with this book). ISP's usually cost from $20 to $200 a month depending on your requirements for speed, bandwidth, and storage.

Web page

The Webcam image gets incorporated into your Web page much like a static (still) image or a movie would. You make the page using HTML (HyperText Markup Language), the code used to design Web pages. To learn more about creating your Web pages with HTML, check out Chapter 10 or try *Web Publishing for Teachers,* by yours truly. Later in this chapter, I share exact HTML needed for posting your Webcam images, so even if you're a novice, you can copy and learn!

Web host

This is a computer that is constantly (in a perfect world!) connected to the Internet and stores your Web pages so visitors can always see your pages. This is where you will be uploading your Webcam image. Check with your school to see if you already have a Web server that can host your Web pages. Some universities may also offer free Web hosting allowing you to create and upload your pages. If your school does not allow this or doesn't have a Web host, then you can usually get a Web host through one of the many ISP services. See "Connection to the Internet."

Setting Up a Webcam

Once you've begged and borrowed all the pieces, it's time to hook everything up. Here's a step-by-step to getting all these pieces to work together.

1. **Connect your Webcam or video camera to your computer.**

   Depending on your choice of camera, doing so is probably just a matter of using a serial, USB, or FireWire cable to make a physical connection between camera and computer. If your camera (like the QuickCam or Apple's QuickTake camera) was also shipped with software, you'll want to install that now was too. If your installation also involves adding a video capture card, make triple-sure you read all the instructions before installing.

2. Install and configure your capture software.

After you decide which software to use, you need to configure it to work with your modem, network, service provider and computer. To make sure you have all you need, ask your school or district network administrator (or ISP) for the following information:

- **Host Name:** (www.hostname.com or a number such as 204.16.16.4).

- **Username:** For logging into your service provider or network.

- **Password:** Goes with the username, should be at least six characters. Mixing numbers and letters ensures the most secure password.

- **Pathname:** The exact location on your computer or the host computer where you'd like the images to be stored) — for example `www.school.edu/www/Webcam/images.`

- **The URL of your Website:** You need to tell people where to go to see all your students' fabulous images, right?

3. Connect to the Internet.

Now that you have your camera set up and hooked up to your computer and you've tested your capture software, you are ready to connect to the Internet and upload your image to your Web host. Connect either through a direct Internet connection (your school's network) or through your modem dial-up account.

4. Launch your capture software (double-click the program icon) and enter the information that your ISP provided for you.

Make sure you read the instructions on how to enter this information for your type of capture software. You need to decide where on your computer you will store the uploaded images and what to name them. Upload your image either in the top folder of your Web host or create a new folder. Make sure to remember the pathname to the folder and what you named it.

You also need to name the image that you are uploading. Depending on the file format you use: GIF or JPEG, you will need to name it appropriately — for example: myimage.gif or myimage.jpg.

5. Test your setup to make sure you uploaded your image successfully.

6. Launch your Web browser.

7. Type in your Web page URL.

Go to the URL that your ISP gave you and enter the pathname for your Webcam image. It will probably look something like this:

`www.school.edu/myfolder/myimage.jpg`

8. Now for the fun part. Work with your students to build the Web page that will become the home of your Webcast image.

In the next section, I share some HTML code you can (with my permission) "liberate" and type right into your Web page to make your Webcam live!

Using HTML for Webcams

The HTML code for including Webcam images on your Website is really pretty straightforward. There are several methods for displaying and refreshing your Webcam images (note that these methods are for displaying still images, not streaming):

- ✔ Using META refresh
- ✔ Using JavaScript
- ✔ Using Java
- ✔ Using JavaScript to open a "remote window"

The method you choose really depends on how much you understand about HTML and if you want to use Java in your site. Use META refresh if you don't want to mess with Java right now.

Refreshing your Webcam image

You will need to include some extra HTML code that will allow the image from your Webcam to be *refreshed* (updated) on your Web page. This code will allow for images coming from your camera to be presented and updated automatically. Each visitor to your site will keep getting updated images as your camera captures them and your capture software uploads them to your server.

What follows is some example code you can place on your page.

META (morphic) refresh

The simplest way to refresh your image on a Web page is with the META tag. (If you're lost in the HTML-speak already, pick up a copy of *Web Publishing For Teachers* by yours truly and published by IDG Books Worldwide, Inc. and learn to tell your METAs from your "tags." Shameless plug alert! <grin>)_META tags are HTML code tags that instruct your computer to take a specific "global" action automatically or according to some set of rules.

Between the <HEAD> and </HEAD> tags (tags that signal the beginning and end of the HTML content on your Web page) include the following code:

```
<META HTTP-EQUIV="pragma" CONTENT="no-cache">
<META HTTP-EQUIV="Refresh" CONTENT="30">
```

Make sure that they are in the same order as you see them above. Leave the first line as you see it; don't make any changes. This will allow for the browser to be able to refresh a new image without loading it from cache. Sometimes Netscape 4.*x* and above will only load the image from cache (local memory) and your image will not refresh.

The second line of code sets how often your image changes on the screen:

```
CONTENT="30"
```

Put in a number value equal to the number of seconds between each refresh.

For example, if you want your image to update every 60 seconds, instead of the 30 second refresh in this example, enter **60**. Most Webcams update about once every 30 seconds.

Note: Some browsers, such as WebTV, may have a problem with refreshing images. To solve this problem add the attribute RELOAD="60" to the <IMG> tag further down the page (anywhere between your <BODY>....</BODY> tags) where your Webcam window shows up (not in the META tag). For example:

```
<IMG SRC="myimage.jpg" RELOAD="60">
```

If you add this and the META tags above, you can support all types of browsers and solve both problems with refreshing.

Here's a tip for experienced HTML'ers. Set the RELOAD time to a little less than the META reload time, say by 10 seconds; then the WebTV visitors will be able to get a new image right before the META reload happens, giving them a new image.

JavaScript refresh

Java, invented by Sun Microsystems, is a computer language that can run on many different kinds of computers, making it easier to deliver application programs and instructions that add function to your computing environment via the Internet.

JavaScript is a user-friendly front end to the Java programming language. JavaScript is a scripting language that looks a great deal like Pascal or one of the other "scriptable" languages you may have seen. JavaScript is fairly straightforward, but, like most languages, it's a stickler for correct syntax.

JavaScript gives you lots of options for displaying your Webcam images that you won't get using the META-tag method described previously. The downside? Some older browsers don't support JavaScript, so those users won't see anything but the first image sent; the autorefresh won't work.

To create a JavaScript refresh window, include the code exactly as written between the <HEAD> and </HEAD> tags on your Web page:

```
<script LANGUAGE="javascript">
  <!--
  camImage = new Image(320,240)
  camImage1 = new Image(320,240)
  camImage.src =
  "http://www.hostname.com/folder/myimage.jpg"
  function reloadImg()
  {  uniq = new Date();
    uniq = "?"+uniq.getTime();
    newImage = document.imgToLoad.src;
    index = newImage.indexOf("?", 0);
    if (index > 0)
      {
        newImage = newImage.substr(0, index);
      }
    camImage.src = camImage1.src;
    camImage.src =
    "http://www.hostname.com/folder/myimage.jpg"+uniq;
    camImage1.src = camImage.src;
  }
  function ends()
  {    document.imgToLoad.src = camImage.src;
      reloadImg();
  }

  // -->
</script>
```

Note the italicized text. This is the only place where you will be editing the script. All other information of the script should look the same.

The first italicized code describes the width and height of the image. Enter the width and height (in pixels) of your Webcam image here. (Most graphics programs have a ruler built in so you can see the dimensions of your image.)

The next italicized text in the code requires you to fill in is the URL of the place on your server where your image is located. It will look something like this:

```
http://www.school.edu/myfolder/myimage.jpg
```

Make sure you use the full pathname (URL): You must put in http:// and the full address of your site, foldername, and image name.

Next, include the `<IMG>` tag with the reference to the script in the `<BODY>` . . . `</BODY>` tags as shown here:

```
<BODY>
  <img name="imgToLoad" onload="setTimeout("ends()", 15000)"
  onerror="setTimeout("ends()", 3000)"
  onhalt="setTimeout("ends()", 1000)"
  alt="my image" BORDER="0" WIDTH="320"
  HEIGHT="240" RELOAD="30">
</BODY>
```

The only thing you change here is the `ALT` attribute value to be something like "myimage.jpg" or "My Webcam page" and the width and height of the image (in pixels) to match the previous code. You can also include the `RELOAD="30"` to support WebTV visitors. See the META refresh example in the section entitled "META (morphic) refresh" section.

Include these in your Web page and you're set and ready to Webcast!

Creating remote windows

Another fancy JavaScript option is to open a new (remote) window containing the Webcam image when visitors click on your Webcam link. This leaves your original page intact and users can easily return there by closing the Webcam window. To include a remote window containing your Webcam image:

In the `<HEAD>` and `</HEAD>` tags include the following script:

```
<script language="javascript">
   function mycam() {
  myWindow =
  window.open("http://www.hostname.com/folder/mypage.html",
  "mycam","toolbar=0,location=0,directories=0,
  status=0,menubar=0,scrollbars=0,
  copyhistory=0,width=350,height=425");
  myWindow.location =
  "http://www.hostname.com/folder/mypage.html";
  }
  function fetch(url) {
    rootWin.location = url;
  }
</script>
```

The only things you need to edit in the code are what's italicized; the URL to your Web page, the size and name ("mycam") of the new window containing the image, and whether you want to show/hide scrollbars and so on.

In the <BODY> area of your Web page add the following code to your Anchor tag to refer to the code that brings up the remote window:

```
<A HREF="javascript:mycam()">click for remote window</A>
```

Where you named your remote-cam window name you'll also want to refer to it here in the Anchor tag. (See italic "mycam".)

That's it! Play around with it a bit. If all else fails, surf to another Webcam site and take a look at the way it enters the code. After you reach a site you would like to review the source code for choose View⇨Page Source (View⇨Source in Internet Explorer).

Examples and Resources

I know you'd like to see some examples of good uses for this exciting new medium. Here are some of my favorites:

- ✔ **EarthCam — Times Square, NYC** (www.earthcam.net/nycams). Get a taste of Manhattan via the Web.

- ✔ **Moscow and Russian Web Cameras** (www.paratype.com/camera). A catalog of cameras across Russia.

- ✔ **The Puppy Cam!** (www.humanesocietymiami.org/petcam). At the Humane Society of Greater Miami. You won't be able to resist a peek at this site. The puppies featured are up for adoption.

- ✔ **GhostCam** (www.flyvision.org/sitelite/Houston/GhostWatcher). Can you spot the ghost? I think I saw one at this site once, but it was after a four-hour writing session <grin>.

- ✔ **The FamilyCam** (www.ionetWeb.com/familycam). And you thought your family was interesting? Try this one!

- ✔ **Steve Wozniak's Classroom Camera** (http://wozcam.woz.org). As shown in Figure 16-1. Steve Wozniak, co-founder of Apple Computer, now teaches in California. Want a glimpse of his office and classroom?

- ✔ **WHS ScienceCam!** (einstein.wsd.wednet.edu/ScienceCam.html). Wenatchee High School science department. A superb example of a school Webcam.

- ✔ **False Pass Java Web Cam Classroom cam** (www.multigrade.org/wolverines/Webcam2.html). Multigrade (K-6) Aleutian Islands, AK. It's not cold there all the time. This camera offers a virtual field trip to a fabulously scenic region.

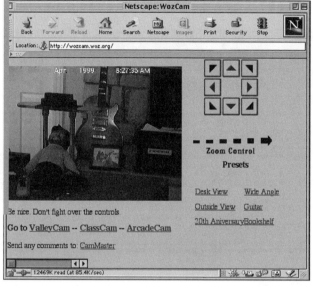

Figure 16-1:
Here's a
peek at
Woz's
remote-
controlled
Webcam!

And here are some great sites to visit to find out more about Webcams. Be sure to visit these and try them out *before* you use them in your classroom. Remember, Web cameras can broadcast *anything*.

✔ **Internet Global's Justsurfit.com Live Web Cameras and Development** (`www.justsurfit.com/liveWebcam.shtml`). Tutorials, software resources and more.

✔ **QuickTime** (`www.apple.com/quicktime/`). Learn how to incorporate video into your Web pages.

✔ **WebcamWorld** (`developers.Webcamworld.com`). Find other Web cams and use them as an example. (You'll also find a few you probably shouldn't use as an example.)

✔ **Camcentral** (`www.camcentral.com`). An ever-growing list of Webcams.

There you have it, all you need to go from idea to broadcast. As pipelines (data bandwidth) increase over the coming years, my guess is you'll see more and more sites jumping on the Internet with live, or almost live, Webcam images. Who knows, perhaps the progression of instructional video in the classroom that jumped from filmstrip to 16mm projector to video tape will jump to the Internet next?

Avoiding the perils of live broadcasts from your school

Remember that you should always inform people visiting your classroom that there's a camera present. Put up a really big sign. ("You're on candid camera?") You should also get express, written permission from each and every parent of every student who could potentially end up on camera.

Some sites offer chat (two-way typed communication) alongside their camera images. This allows real-time communication between the person watching your camera, and your classroom. If you enable this feature, watch the students carefully. Ensure that nobody give out any personal information or information about your school — ever. Better safe than sorry!

Chapter 17

New Net Tools and Issues

● ●

In This Chapter

▶ Intranet basics

▶ Intro to HTML

▶ Dealing with new Net issues, challenges

▶ New Internet tools

● ●

*W*ith all the technologies and tools surrounding the Internet changing faster than we can edit these books, I just can't resist the opportunity to give you a glimpse into what's new on the Internet (probably what's not-quite-new-anymore by the time you read this book) and some prognostications about some of the new issues raised by all this fast-moving technology.

The jargon (unique vocabulary) of the Net continues to expand with the introduction of new spins on networking (intranet) and new tools for trans-mitting and receiving multimedia on the Net (VRML, Shockwave, Java, and RealAudio, for example).

The material that follows stems from a conversation I had with a 16-year-old computer whiz after a meeting to plan a recent *Macworld* convention. You'd have to meet this kid to believe he's 16; he's helping me configure a Net server, add JavaScript to my Web page, and figure out a way to add full-motion video to a Web page at a local school. Lest you think this kid is spending all his time exercising his fingers on the keyboard, he's also on the state gymnastics team and can throw a baseball so far I'd need a telescope to follow it.

Sigh. Just another reminder of how far behind we feel sometimes. Don't worry, though; I've condensed our conversation down to a few points that may help keep *you* on the cutting edge of educational technology.

What's an Intranet?

Just when you thought you'd mastered technospeak, here's yet another word to ponder — *intranet*. An intranet is really nothing more than an internal network, a LAN (Local Area Network) or WAN (Wide Area Network), that uses Internet tools like browsers and e-mail programs to organize, present, and archive information. *Intranet* is becoming a word you hear a great deal as more and more schools become "wired." Some schools are using Netscape Navigator and mail programs like First Class as the main communication and storage tools on their file servers. Teachers post everything from the lunch menu to after-school activities to classroom rolls using a Web-page format. Intranets can act just like the Internet, too, but the only people who can see that site (or sites) are those connected to the intranet. Another thing that makes the idea of an intranet so cool is that you use the exact same tools (Web browsers) when you search for information or access resources outside your school — on the Internet.

All you need to set up an intranet, then, is a couple of computers; a way to connect them to one another; some software tools, (such as a browser, e-mail program, word processor, and perhaps a Web page-making tool); and some knowledge of HTML . . . Uh oh, a four letter word! Sorry.

HTML — Is That All There Is?

Like any other innovation, the Internet carries its own load of jargon that delights and confuses. *HTML* is an acronym that you see everywhere these days because it's the name for a simple scripting language (HyperText Markup Language) that's used to make all those fancy Web pages you visit. Working in HTML is much easier than programming in languages such as BASIC and Pascal, because most commands are in "plain English" and the structure is pretty straightforward. HTML was derived from SGML (Standardized General Markup Language — eek, another chunk of jargon!) as a way for developers to quickly create Web pages that can be accessed by a variety of different computers.

In Chapter 10 of this book, you discover that learning HTML code isn't the only way you can build your own Web page. For an up-close-and-personal understanding, however, you need to jump to *Web Publishing For Teachers,* written by yours truly (published by IDG Books Worldwide, Inc.), where you can find hundreds of Web sites to emulate and a whole bunch of strategies for working with your students to produce content for the World Wide Web.

New Issues, New Challenges

If I were a betting person (as if educators had any money to bet!), I'd wager that within the next five years, the bickering about whether to use Windows 2000, Windows 95, or Macintosh OS will ease. It's certainly possible that HTML, Java, and other Internet tools will become the foundation for the operating systems of tomorrow. You'll still need those driver thingies and special programs to get your computer going, of course, but most of the overhead stuffed into today's bulging operating systems may be handled by programs that come from the Internet. Here are three reasons I think this prediction will come true:

✔ The Internet is a better place to store information than your hard drive. Just how large do you think they can build these drives before it doesn't make any practical sense? It's kind of like a school bus that seats 250 kids. It's very convenient, but it's way too hard to find Johnny or Sue quickly, and you can forget about navigating the thing around town. Why not use the vast "Cyberspace" accessed by the Internet? You'll need your local hard disk only for storing documents and such that you create from resources out there on the Net.

✔ Data types are changing faster than your PTA's focus. We used to deal with text and pictures (graphics). Now we have QuickTime movies, QuickTime VR (virtual reality), VRML (Virtual Reality Markup Language), JavaScript, and much more. Making easy, compact tools for reading these data types, rather than going through an upgrade every time a new data type comes along, makes better sense.

✔ Desktop computers as we know them may become obsolete. Instead, you may navigate the Net using something dubbed an *information appliance*. It may sit on your TV or your desk, or you may wear it on your wrist. It accesses the Net spectacularly, but it doesn't do Windows. Information appliances are already being developed, like Microsoft's WebTV box that brings the Internet to your television, leaving the PC sitting in the corner wondering what the TV will do next.

So is it time to throw all those computers in the trash and start over? Not hardly, while we're awaiting the hand-held supercomputer, desktop computers are becoming smarter, too. With software developers racing to create a more personal computing experience with software that learns from you, the user; the future heralds new ways to communicate and compute.

So, don't give your Macintosh away or pitch your Windows PC out the window. Watch for a "transition period," when technologies that can run on your desktop machine ease the move from bulky memory-hogging programs to "compartmentalized" or specialized mini-applications. Kind of like trying to step off a moving train, no? You can't jump off — so you may as well stay on for the ride.

Addressing Tough Internet Challenges

Go and look in the mirror. Right now. Look at yourself and decide whether you're one of those people who sits around worrying about how the Internet may lead to the inevitable degradation of human values or, more apocalyptic, the extinction of the human race. Or do you see a bigger picture and realize how the Internet, used effectively, can bring the world closer together and keep us Cro-Magnons from reinventing the wheel every day or so? Some people can find lots of negatives to point out about the Net these days. Sure, some issues challenge many of us, but do each of these concerns really make sense in your community? Here are a few I've heard. What do you think? (You're obviously an open-minded, wonderful person, because you so kindly bought this book.)

Too-tough URLs

Several months ago I was driving down the Massachusetts Turnpike (where the Bard tolls) and spied a large billboard for a popular brand of blue jeans. Terrific billboard, by the way, except for one thing . . . down below the very distracting picture was a URL that looked something like this: `http://www.jeans.com/~blue/pictures/catalog/` . . . I didn't get the rest. After all, I was doing 65 m.p.h. (give or take 10 m.p.h.), and I couldn't do the Exorcist maneuver (the 360-degree head-twist) without hitting the car in front of me. Did this manufacturer really expect folks to pull off the highway and copy this long-sentence length Web address down? Sigh.

Everyone's got a Web page — it's the new status symbol. Some companies are smarter than others, though, selecting URLs that are short and sweet, like `www.apple.com` or `www.ibm.com` or `www.classroom.net`. These I can remember. Some folks think URLs are too complex, but that's what bookmark programs are for! Complex, sure, but watch for graphics and bookmark programs to shield you from those URLs someday soon.

Telephonus interruptus

Sometimes the phone just hangs up. You know: You're in the middle of a huge demonstration for a gym full of students, and just as you click a link, the line drops, leaving you making pheasant and doggie shapes with your hands in front of the overhead projector screen. Phone lines, especially those old phone lines run to schools back in 1820, are not very dependable. Luckily, help is on the way. Phone companies are working hard to upgrade the nation's phone system. Also, dedicated lines, like high speed T-1 or T-3 lines, are always "on," so you don't have to hold your breath as you wait for the modem to connect anymore. Whew!

Porno pandemonium

Yep. You can find plenty of stuff on the Web that you may consider porno-graphy. The hitch is that some people don't consider naughty what you consider naughty. Some folks even like the stuff. The challenge is that there's a huge "beware of unacceptable content in your classroom" between free speech and what kids may jump into while mining the Internet from your classroom. What do you do if Sarah finds an underwear-clad Marky Mark while she's supposed to be looking for a current map of Bosnia? Read the chapter on Internet responsibility one more time. If you're really worried, you can dig up acceptable use policies, hardware, and software solutions, and get more information from sites on the Net. (Search Yahoo! or your favorite search site for keywords: **acceptable use** or **filter**.) You can also watch Sarah more closely and make sure she feels some time pressure to get what she was after. No time for surfing for porno. Nothing is as effective as watchful eyes (the four every educator has — two in the back, of course).

High tech or high touch?

Many people think that with the many opportunities for entertainment and education on the Net, we'll all retreat into our homes and end up seeing folks only via our computers. Gone will be the "high touch" — the intimacy, the feeling of being near someone, and the occasional pat on the back, so rare but welcome. Hmmm. I'm really not sure about this one. I know I can't stand to write for more than about four hours at a time or I get really nuts. I gotta see and be with other people. Alvin Toffler, author of *Future Shock, The Third Wave,* and a few other brain-busters, believes a balance is needed between high-technology tools and opportunities to do what humans do by nature — namely, have occasional physical contact. I think Alvin's got a point, don't you? Okay. Put the book down and go find somebody to hug.

Gender-centric

Statistics show that most of the people on the Net these days are male. The number is more than a majority — it's a regular landslide. Why? Probably because surfing the Net and sending e-mail is what many in the mostly-male world of computers and technology do most of the day when they're sup-posed to be working. Inevitably, this situation must change. When activities like stock portfolio management, real estate transactions, home control, and bill payment via computer become a regular fixture, everyone, male and female, will *have* to log on.

One-way street

Internet use is kind of a passive experience these days. Most of what people do is click from hyperlink to hyperlink. But some new technologies, like NetPhone, Shockwave, QuickTime, Flash, and others (see Chapter 29) are changing that. Look for the Net to get extremely interactive as it continues to mature. Already you can watch movies, hear speeches, or talk on the phone via the Net. The border between the Internet of today and that of tomorrow is clearly broadband Internet services, and they're coming soon. The Internet's just begun to crawl these days. If you're like me, you can't wait to see it walk!

The information access gap

Imagine, for a moment, that you have no computer skills, no access to technology of any kind, and although you've heard of the Internet, you really don't know what it is. Those "dot com" addresses have no meaning. You hear commercials advertising computers on TV, but you wonder how people afford them. Welcome to reality folks — this scenario describes almost half the population of the U.S. and the majority of the people on planet Earth.

Because teachers live and work in a learning environment that often gives us access to new technologies and also because we are typically well-educated and talk about technology with our friends, we may forget that millions of people don't understand or have access to the same technology we take for granted.

As the information age matures, interpersonal communication is becoming increasingly more digital. Soon, you will be able to receive postage stamps from your laser printer. Many more of us will pay taxes, learn, shop, and maybe even vote using a computer. We continue to learn more, read more, and explore more — but there are many who don't. If this information access gap continues to grow, then we will emerge as a society of the wired and unwired — of the digital and analog; a society of those who rely on just-in-time information for their livelihood and those who die because they don't have information they need to save themselves.

As educators, our duty is to ensure equity of access to the knowledge and technologies that make our lives better. Whether it's your grandmother, your foster child, or the street person on the corner of Mission and Market, somehow the quality of their lives will be effected by technology in the coming years — for better of for worse. It's incumbent upon teachers to help people learn and have access to the information and technologies that can enhance the quality of their lives.

So (as I climb off my soapbox) my action item here is to encourage you to teach one other person about technology. Go ahead, think of one right now and make a personal commitment to help him learn what we have already come to take for granted. The narrowing of the ever-widening information access gap is within our control, and the digital future will be brighter and richer if *all of us* participate.

Lost in the mall

A student once described the Internet as a "shopping mall without directories." A common criticism of the Internet is that it is difficult to navigate. Simply too much information is out there.

Just as mall managers have taken to constructing easy-to-use maps and kiosks complete with the all-important "you are here" dot, Internet guardians are coming up with new, easy ways to navigate the Net. Soon you'll have no excuse to get lost. Now, where did I put my car keys?

Warp Ten on the Info Highway

If you think the rate at which new information is being posted on the Internet is incredibly fast, wait until you get a glimpse at the speed with which new tools are being developed. Practically every week, three or four new mini-programs, called "plug-ins," that work with your Web browser are thrown out to the world, creating new opportunities and fueling lots of ideas on the Internet.

What follows is a short-and-sweet summary of what some of the emerging tools are and what they're for.

What's Java?

It used to be that Java was what you had with cream and sugar. Nowadays, Java is also the name of an Object Oriented Programming (OOP) language similar to C++ used to create stand-alone applications that can be incorporated into a Web page. JavaScript, a descendent of Java developed by Netscape Communications and Sun Microsystems (which created Java), is a scripting language that's easier to use than Java because it has more built-in functionality, easier, more intuitive syntax, and is somewhat forgiving. JavaScript can make text appear to dance (animation), create an automated form that works like an up-to-the-minute stock ticker, or any number of very interesting multimedia enhancements for a Web page. The Java world also includes small programs called *applets* (which are automatically downloaded to your computer) to control your Web browser and make great things happen on the screen — everything from smart information agents that retrieve information at the click of an on-screen icon to interactive games.

For an overview of Java and lots of great examples, visit Sun's site at http://java.sun.com or see one of several books on Java, such as *Java For Dummies*, 3rd Edition, by Aaron E. Walsh (IDG Books Worldwide, Inc.).

Here's an excerpt of some JavaScript code that makes text jump around on your screen. It's only an excerpt, however, and it won't work if you try to type it in.

```
[lots of JavaScript mumbo-jumbo here]
if (seed > 100) {
  seed@hy;
  var cmd="scrollit(" + seed + ")";
  timerTwo=window.setTimeout(cmd,100);
}
else if (seed <= 100 && seed > 0) {
  for (c=0 ; c < seed ; c++) {
      out+=" ";
  }
  out+=msg;
  seed@hy;
  var cmd="scrollit(" + seed + ")";
    window.status=out;
  timerTwo=window.setTimeout(cmd,100);
}
[more JavaScript mumbo-jumbo follows]
```

Some folks are concerned that Java can allow unwanted programs, messages, or viruses to be downloaded into your computer or unscrupulous users to access information from your computer or network. Several large companies have encouraged employees to disable Java on their Web browsers (check your Preferences menus) until Java becomes more secure. I think the security issue with Java is a bit overblown, so don't freak out and de-Java your computer just yet. Just beware, especially if your school's network isn't separated (physically or by a software firewall) from the network you use to access the Internet. You make the call on this one!

Java may have more to offer than similar languages such as Pascal and C++. However, lots of teachers are learning the easier JavaScript with their students, and together they're creating some amazing projects.

Getting shocked

From the folks at Macromedia comes Shockwave: a terrific innovation that enables anyone to add animated graphics, sound, and multimedia to Web sites. Shockwave sites offer interactivity, such as moving from screen to screen, zooming, and panning, as well as presentation-quality slideshows that you can use to wow your audiences.

For educators, Shockwave may be just the ticket to bring auto-instructional learning to the Net, and also offers an opportunity to provide real-time presentations related to key curriculum areas on your school's *intranet*. (Look back to the intranet section in this chapter if you haven't mastered the jargon yet.)

To create these Net-wonders, you use Macromedia's Director (available at an educator's discount, by the way). To view your amazing creations, however, all you need is the Netscape Navigator plug-in called Shockwave (a *plug-in* is a software program that goes in your browser's plug-ins folder and adds functionality to the browser). For information about both of these tools visit www.macromedia.com.

Audio-R-Us

One of the early challenges of the Internet was to find a way to transmit sound so that folks with all kinds of computers and all kinds of speakers could hear and understand it. Enter tools like QuickTime (www.apple.com/quicktime) and RealAudio (www.realaudio.com). Both programs allow the transmission of sounds, now even supporting CD quality, from a remote location on the Net to your computer, and also *streaming audio* (audio that begins almost immediately, without waiting for a large sound file to completely download first) and create a very usable method for transmitting large sound files.

Motion on the Net

Now you can watch movies on the Internet. Sheesh . . . there goes another 20 hours a week! We've come a long way from filmstrips in the classroom, no?

With powerful tools like Apple Computer's QuickTime (available for Macintosh and Windows computers) and it's built-in QuickTime VR (virtual reality-like movies), you can now use your Web browser like a movie projector, as shown in Figure 17-1. Of course, the faster the connection, the better your picture. Using today's 28.8 kbps modems is a little like yesterday's TVs with *rabbit ears*. Fast network connections allow for transmissions that are smooth as silk. Grab info about QuickTime at www.apple.com/quicktime and QuickTime VR at http://qtvr.quicktime.apple.com.

Figure 17-1:
QuickTime
offers
access to
more than
200 data for-
mats on the
Internet.

For Windows users, Microsoft offers the Windows Media Player. It offers full control of video files transmitted on the Internet. Explore the Windows Media Player at www.microsoft.com/windows/mediaplayer.

Phone home

Telephone companies are not smiling these days. In fact, they're madder than wet hens. First, the cable TV people stepped on their feet by offering Internet access through your TV, and now some crafty lads and lasses have created programs that allow you to make the equivalent of a long-distance phone call on the Internet — for free. (Can't you just see the phone folks quivering now?) I'll go out on a limb, though, and declare that the folks at Ma Bell will either figure out how to optimize this technology (and charge for it) or figure out how to use your telephone to get cable TV. They're very creative and don't sit still when it comes to innovation.

You can get more information about telephone software (sorry, Ma) at www.netphone.com.

Conferencing

Somebody really creative finally figured out how to allow users to see and be seen (and heard) on the Net. Using a small video camera and a Net program called CU-SeeMe (it's on the CD accompanying this book), you and your

The Internet For Teachers Directory

The 5th Wave   By Rich Tennant

"I'm not sure — I like the mutual funds with rotating dollar signs, although the dancing stocks and bonds look good, too."

In this directory . . .

*T*he *Internet For Teachers Internet Directory* serves as a helpful reference for tracking down the best educational resources available on the Internet. This directory includes more than 150 of the best Web sites to help you integrate technology into the curriculum.

The site listings are divided by subject into categories. Most listings include a brief description to help you quickly determine if the site offers content you're interested in checking out.

The Internet For Teachers Directory

•••

In This Directory

▶ Brushing up on the best online art and music sites

▶ Helping kids gear up for college or vocational school

▶ Getting technical with the best computer and Internet sites

▶ Keeping up with current events

▶ Getting grounded with the best general education sites

▶ Helping kids stay safe and active with health and fitness sites

▶ Taking care of two of the three Rs at the best language arts sites

▶ Addressing the third R with great mathematics sites

▶ Helping parents help kids with great sites for parents

▶ Going methodically through the best science sites

▶ Teaching kids about the world with the aid of the best social studies sites

▶ Finding out how technology can benefit kids with special needs

▶ Adding stuff to your bag of teaching tricks at the best teacher resources sites

•••

*T*hink back to the thickest and heaviest textbook you ever had to carry. Maybe it was that 1,200-page behemoth you lugged around for your 10th-grade World History class. To put the Internet's enormity into context, consider that it contains 500 million or so more pages of information than that textbook did. (Your arms are getting sore just thinking about that, aren't they?) Fortunately, none of this information weighs an ounce, and all you need to access it is an Internet connection, a Web browser, and an inquisitive mind.

Of course, not all of the material to be found on the Internet is educational or even interesting to students and educators. But a lot of it *is*. This Directory points you to the best sites the Internet has to offer — sites housing a wealth of facts, figures, learning tools, maps, photos, audio files, and other helpful resources for teachers and their students.

I've sorted the sites into 12 handy categories, beginning with Art & Music and ending with Teacher Resources. I include each site in only one category, although some sites could conceivably fit in more than one category.

I chose the sites in the directory by asking the following key questions:

✔ Does the site contain information useful to enrich or enhance the classroom experience?

✔ Is the site published by a reputable, credible source?

✔ Does the site contain contact information for content authors useful for resource verfication?

✔ Does the site represent the "best available" information about the subject?

✔ Is the site easy to navigate and well organized?

I've probably left out a few of your favorites (so much content, so little space!). Visit www.dummies.com and submit your ideas for our next edition.

The CD includes a list of just about all the Web sites I reference in this directory and elsewhere in this book. Each listing consists of the name of the site and an HTML link to the site's URL or Web address. So if you want to get to a site in this directory quickly, you can just pop the *Internet For Teachers* CD into your CD-ROM drive, launch your Web browser software (usually Netscape Navigator or Internet Explorer), open the LINKS.HTML file from the CD, find the category in the left-hand pane, and click on the link in the right-hand side. Okay, these instructions are a bit abrupt; for step-by-step instructions on these steps, see Appendix D.

Give the listings in the directory a quick scan and you will notice that most of them include miniature icons (a.k.a. *micons*). Don't worry, these micons aren't aliens from the planet Internet; they're just little signposts on the information highway that give you more information about each site. Here's your micon menu:

This site has resources that are appropriate for preschool teachers and students.

This site has resources that are appropriate for elementary teachers and students.

This site has resources that are appropriate for middle-school (or junior-high-school) teachers and students.

This site has resource that are appropriate for high-school teachers and students.

This site contains a searchable database.

You can send your students to this site to help them with your assignments.

Art & Music

There's nothing like the first day when students in the band pick up their instruments and blast out that first scale or the first time students realize that paint can be used for something other than walls. The Internet has much to offer the many among us who enjoy art and music. The following sites can contribute to a greater appreciation and understanding of these popular artistic pursuits.

All-Music Guide

www.allmusic.com

Comprehensive database of music: All-Music Guide is an excellent resource for students interested in Bach, rock, and everything in between. This site is dedicated to reviewing and rating all music ever recorded (with the possible exception of that tape your younger sister recorded of you singing "Yackety Yak" in the shower when you were fifteen years old).

ArtLex

www.artlex.com

Dictionary of art terms: Whether you're looking for the meaning of *eshi* ("in Japanese tradition, a painter") or the correct pronunciation of *oenochoe* (eh-nuk'oh-ee), ArtLex is the site for you. It offers definitions of over 2,800 art terms. Also includes illustrations, quotes, and links to other great sites.

ArtMuseum.Net

www.artmuseum.net

Internet-based art museum: Presented by Intel Corporation, this site expands access to great art exhibitions by presenting them online. A recent exhibit featured the works of Van Gogh in 3D.

ArtsEdge

artsedge.kennedy-center.org

Linking the arts and education through technology: ArtsEdge strives to help teachers, students, and artists share resources and ideas that support the arts as a core subject in the K-12 curriculum. Contains helpful links for students writing papers on arts-related topics. For teachers, the site offers plenty of lesson plans.

Crayola FamilyPlay

www.familyplay.com

Hundreds of activities for kids: Need to keep the kids busy with some fun and creative activities? Head to Crayola FamilyPlay for scads of ideas — certainly enough to make use of all 128 crayon colors, a giant tub of glue, and a thick ream of construction paper.

The Minneapolis Institute of Arts

www.artsmia.org

One of the best museum sites on the Internet: You don't need to take students on a field trip to Minneapolis to enjoy this museum. The site includes images of works of art in the permanent collection as well as those in special exhibits. Numerous categories are offered, ranging from 20th-Century Art to Period Rooms to Textiles.

The Mr. Holland's Opus Foundation

www.mhopus.org

Donates musical instruments to schools and students: Know of an aspiring tuba player who possesses great potential but no tuba? The Mr. Holland's Opus Foundation can help. The foundation partners with businesses, communities, and schools to provide new and refurbished musical instruments to qualified schools and individual students.

Music Education Online

www.geocities.com/Athens/2405/index.html

Music education resources: Here's a site for educators, students, and parents who are looking for music education resources on the Internet. Music Education Online includes a wealth of articles, an interactive bulletin board, and links to other music-related sites. Perhaps the site's best feature is an online search engine that allows you to specify an instrument and find an instructor that teaches it in your area.

The Music Technology Learning Center

www.mtlc.net

Discover how computers are changing music: This site keeps educators, students, and musicians up-to-date with the latest information on the constantly changing world of computers and music. Learn about MIDI, digital audio, and all the new music software and hardware. Participate in discussion forums and online chats. Also offers information on college-level music programs.

National Museum of African Art

www.si.edu/nmafa/exhibits/currexhb.htm

Detailed information on current African art exhibits at the Smithsonian Institute: Terrific resource for students interested in learning more about past and contemporary African art.

Other Sites Worth Visiting

Americans for the Arts
www.artsusa.com

ARTtalk
www.arttalk.com

Association for the Advancement of Arts Education
www.aaae.org

Incredible Art Department
www.artswire.org/kenroar/

Indiana University School of Music
www.music.indiana.edu

Mozart's Magical Musical Life
www.stringsinthemountains.org/m2m/1once.htm

College Prep & Vocational Education

Preparing for college and selecting a career can be quite stressful and confusing. The Internet eases the burden by making the process of registering for standardized tests, accessing college and vocational school information, and researching career options simpler and faster.

ACT

www.act.org

Nonprofit provider of educational services: Best known for its college admission test, ACT has several other products and services, including EPAS (Educational Planning and Assessment System), a program that allows schools to track a student's progress in educational and career planning from the eighth grade through high school. At the site, students and parents can complete the ACT's Financial Aid Need Estimator, allowing them to get a better idea of how much college at their school of choice will cost them.

College Board Online

www.collegeboard.org

All-in-one site for high-school students preparing for the jump to college: College Board Online offers a daily sample SAT question; online SAT registration; SAT, AP, and CLEP test dates; and financial aid information. Also featured is an online store where students can purchase videos and books geared toward helping them do their best on college-prep tests.

Kaplan

www.kaplan.com

Leader in the field of educational services: Kaplan is a big company, offering a wide range of services, and its Web site is reflective of its size and its diverse offerings. Visitors can find information on standardized tests, colleges, financial aid, distance learning, and just about everything else related to getting an education and the job you want.

RWM Vocational School Database

www.rwm.org/rwm

Database of vocational schools: This site lists hundreds of postsecondary vocational schools in all 50 states. An excellent resource for high-school students wanting to explore their career options.

Other Sites Worth a Visit

apprenticeship USA
www.apprenticeship-usa.com

The Educational Testing Service Network
www.ets.org

The Princeton Review Online
www.review.com

Test.com, Inc.
www.test.com

Computers & Internet

If you're searching for information on computers and the Internet, there is no better place to look than the Internet itself. At the sites below, you can discover the best educational software, find out how to get free and discounted hardware for your school, read about the history of computers, learn how to create a Web site for your class or school, and more.

Apple Computer Education Page

www.apple.com/education

Information about Apple's educational products and software solutions: Check out special deals for educators or visit the Apple Learning Interchange and chat with friends. Includes an extensive K-12 section.

Computer History

www.si.edu/resource/tours/comphist/ computer.htm

Online tour of the Division of Computers at the National Museum of American History: You can find a wealth of information here, all tied to the history of the computer and the Information Age. An Oral/Video History section features interviews with many leading figures in the history of computing, such as Bill Gates and Steve Jobs.

Computers for Learning

www.computers.fed.gov

Federal program that donates computer equipment to schools and educational non-profit organizations: Founded by Vice President Al Gore, this site can be used to register to receive donated computers, learn how to best assess your classroom's computing needs, find National Tech Corps volunteers who are willing to lend their tech skills to a good cause, and more.

Education World

www.education-world.com/

Where educators go to learn: About a zillion resources for teachers and students including lesson plan libraries, chats, online games, and much more.

KidsClick

sunsite.berkeley.edu/kidsclick!

Internet search engine for kids by librarians: A kid-friendly search engine created by a group of librarians at the Ramapo Catskill Library System. Search results categorize each site's reading level — a very helpful feature.

Linux Online

www.linux.org

Site dedicated to the Linux operating system: Discover why everyone in the computer world is talking about Linux, the revolutionary operating system created by a young Swedish programmer, Linus Torvalds, with some assistance from developers around the globe. The site offers Linux history, news, downloadable software, hardware information, and links.

Web66

web66.coled.umn.edu

Working to bring technology into schools: At Web66, you can find an exhaustive list of school Web sites from around the world. The site also offers a plethora of computing resources and information, empowering teachers with the knowledge to make use of the latest technologies in their classrooms.

Webworks

**hyperion.advanced.org/16728/ie5/
index.html**

Resource for aspiring Web developers:
Webworks features an HTML tutorial along
with instruction on more advanced Web
technologies like CGI, ActiveX, and Java. A
powerful and visually appealing site,
Webworks was created by three students,
ages 16, 14, and 13.

Other Sites Worth a Visit

Children's Software Revue
www.childrenssoftware.com

**PEP Directory of Computer
Camps for Kids**
www.microweb.com/pepsite/
Camps/camps_index.html

Sites by Kids
kidswebsites.miningco.com/mbody.htm

ZDNet
www.zdnet.com

Current Events

The Internet has transformed the way we
keep track of current events, providing us
with immediate access to breaking news
and, in cases such as John Glenn's recent
Space Shuttle launch, the ability to watch
events unfold in real time on our computer monitors.

CNN Interactive

www.cnn.com

News supersite: Want to read, hear, and see
the latest news? You can at CNN
Interactive. The site features local, national, and world news along with special
sections for Science and Technology,

Entertainment, Health, and several other
fields of interest. Many stories include
sound and video files.

The New York Times Learning Network

www.nytimes.com/learning

News site for Grades 6-12: All the news
that's fit to print — for students, teachers,
and parents. Read the day's top stories,
take the news quiz, make use of vocabulary
-enriching tools, tap into an archive of
lesson plans, and do a special crossword
created just for students.

Time For Kids

www.pathfinder.com/TFK

Popular magazine's kids-only version: Get
up to speed with what's going on in the
world with *Time For Kids*. Features two
editions: one for grades 2–3 and one for
grades 4–6.

The Times of London

www.the-times.co.uk

*Internet edition of world's oldest daily
broadsheet newspaper:* Get a non-American
view on world events. This sleek site
demonstrates that the generations-old
newspaper can change with, you guessed
it, *the times*.

Other Sites Worth a Visit

Awesome Library: Current Events
www.neat-schoolhouse.org/Classroom/
Social_Studies/Current_Events/
Current_Events.html

Chicago Tribune
www.chicagotribune.com

MSNBC
www.msnbc.com

General Educational Reference

Looking for all-purpose educational sites that are chock full of great information and cover a wide range of subjects? These sites are for you.

Ask Jeeves For Kids

www.ajkids.com

Innovative search engine: Need fast answers to tough questions? Ask Jeeves; he has all the answers — or at least most of them. Ask Jeeves For Kids is a search engine with a twist. You type in a question (such as What is the population of Nepal?), and Ask Jeeves follows up with a group of questions of his own (such as, Where can I find demographic information for the country of Nepal? and Where is Nepal?). Click on the most appropriate follow-up question, and Ask Jeeves then takes you to a site that will most likely have the answer you're looking for.

Bonus.Com the SuperSite For Kids

www.bonus.com

Online activities for kids: Keep younger students busy with hundreds of fun and mentally stimulating activities at Bonus.com. For teachers and parents, there's a section with activities for use in the classroom and at home.

ePALS

www.epals.com

Connect with classrooms from 100 countries: This site connects classrooms from 100 countries speaking many different languages. ePALS allows students to correspond with their peers around the world.

Super Tutor

www.supertutor.com

Direct students to homework help on the Internet. This cool site features an online learning center for high school students and the ultimate download center for educational software called "Super Tutor." The folks at Super Tutor also offer a huge, ever-growing archive of step-by-step lessons, reference material, animations, streaming video tutorials, and interactive quizzes created especially to help your students with their homework!

Virtual Museums

www.icom.org/vlmp

Directory of online museums: You don't need to leave your house to visit the Fine Arts Museum in Hungary, the National Museum of Namibia, and Japan's National Science Museum — all you need to do is access the many museum links at this great site!

Other Sites Worth a Visit

Berit's Best Sites For Children
db.cochran.com/li_toc:theoPage.db

Biography.Com
www.biography.com

Encyclopedia Britannica Online
www.eb.com

The National Association for the Education of Young Children
www.naeyc.org

Kids' Space
www.kids-space.org

SchoolHouse Rock
genxtvland.simplenet.com/SchoolHouseRock/
index-lo.shtml

Texts Educational Network (TENET)
www.tenet.edu

Health & Physical Education

Using the Internet may be a sedentary activity, but that doesn't mean that you can't use it to improve your physical condition. Explore these health and physical education Web sites from a comfy chair, then get on your feet and use what you've learned to lower that cholesterol, bulk up those biceps, and whiten those teeth.

Infection Detection Prevention

www.amnh.org/explore/infection/
index.html

Magazine about the cause and prevention of infectious diseases: Check out the "Bacteria in the Cafeteria" and find out "How Lou Got the Flu" at this site from the American Museum of Natural History. The site features interactive games and adventures. Requires Macromedia Shockwave plug-in for full effect.

KidsHealth.org for Kids

kidshealth.org/kid

Expert health information for students and parents: KidsHealth.org makes learning about health fun. Created by The Nemours

Foundation Center for Children's Health Media, the site offers separate sites for kids, teens, and parents, each with its own focus and design.

KidzGolf

old.golf.com/kidz

Site for golfers under the age of 12: At KidzGolf, colorful illustrations and games make discovering the game of golf fun for kids. The site includes explanations of golf rules and lots of playing tips.

Safety City

www.nhtsa.dot.gov/kids

Safety tips from the National Highway Traffic Safety Administration (NHTSA): Vince and Larry, the NHTSA's crash test dummies, give kids a crash course on safety.

Sports Illustrated for Kids

www.sikids.com

Popular sports magazine's just-for-kids site: Articles about today's greatest athletes, along with interactive games and animated cartoons, make this a must-visit site for young sports fans.

Youth Sports Network

www.ysn.com

Online center for youth sports: Find a sports camp in your area, access loads of playing tips, read about ways to improve your health and fitness, and play online games — all at this site! From baseball to water polo and every sport in between, Youth Sports Network covers them all with useful, up-to-date information.

Other Sites Worth a Visit

American Dental Association's Kid Site
www.ada.org/consumer/kids/youth.html

Black Belt for Kids
www.blackbeltmag.com/bbkids

The Locker Room, Sports For Kids
members.aol.com/msdaizy/sports/locker.html

Language Arts

Is the written word — be it in English, Italian, or Swahili — near and dear to your heart? If so, this is the category for you. The Internet is a fantastic tool for publishing your own writing as well as reading the writings of others. Reading a work online may lack the comforting heft in the hands a book can provide, but at least you don't have to worry about paper cuts! A number of excellent sites out there can also help you hone your foreign language skills.

The Complete Works of William Shakespeare

www-tech.mit.edu/Shakespeare

The Web's first edition of the complete works of William Shakespeare: Here thou can search the genius playwright's complete works, participate in a discussion group, and find links to many other Shakespeare resources.

Creative Writing For Kids

kidswriting.miningco.com

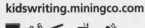

Guide to writing-related sites for students and teachers: This site lists hundreds of helpful writing sites. A sampling of categories includes Parts of Speech, Spelling, and Teach Poetry.

KidPub

www.kidpub.org/kidpub

Over 30,000 stories written by children worldwide: At KidPub, kids can publish stories they've written or read stories written by other children. For children wanting Internet pen pals, the site offers the KidPub KeyPals section.

The Mother Goose Pages

**www-personal.umich.edu/~pfa/
   dreamhouse/nursery/rhymes.html**

Nursery rhymes and children's songs: Fee! Fi! Fo! Fum! Here's a site that's loads of fun! Dozens and dozens of nursery rhymes and children's songs can be read at The Mother Goose Pages.

Vocabulary University

www.vocabulary.com

Puzzles to help students enrich their vocabularies: Vocab U. offers three different levels, one each for elementary, middle-school, and high-school students. The puzzles serve as excellent supplementary learning tools to classroom instruction as well as an effective way to prepare for the SAT and other college entrance exams.

Other Sites Worth a Visit

Basic Punctuation and Mechanics
www.duq.edu/facultyhome/lindstrom/
grammarpages/hndbk.html

German-English Dictionary
www.tu-chemnitz.de/urz/netz/
forms/dict.html

GrammarNow
www.grammarnow.com

Japanese-English Dictionary
 enterprise.ic.gc.ca/cgi-bin/j-e
Poetry for the Elementary Classroom
 www.cis.yale.edu/ynhti/curriculum/units/
 1991/4/91.04.06.x.html
Poetry Pals
 www.geocities.com/EnchantedForest/5165
Reading Rainbow
 www.pbs.org/readingrainbow
The Young Writers Club
 www.cs.bilkent.edu.tr/~david/derya/ywc.html

Mathematics

Two plus two equals four, and a computer plus an Internet connection equals the ability to check out plenty of fun — *and* educational — math-related Web sites.

A+ Math

www.aplusmath.com

Helps students improve their math skills: A+ Math features interactive math games, flash cards, and a Homework Helper section. The site also offers a message board that can be used to get math help from others.

Algebra Online

www.algebra-online.com

Free algebra help online: If you're looking for help with those quadratic equations, Algebra Online is the site for you. Here, you can get free private tutoring, as well as access live chats and message boards to get answers to difficult quadratic equations and other algebra problems.

Math Baseball

www.funbrain.com/math

Play baseball and sharpen your math skills at the same time: A fun game that pitches a math question, which the batter then swings at with an answer. Can be played by one or two players.

Math Brain Teasers

www.eduplace.com/math/brain

Challenging math word problems: Broken down into three categories — Grades 3-4, Grades 5-6, and Grades 7+ — these brain teasers help students gain a better understanding of how math skills can be applied in real-world situations.

Other Sites Worth a Visit

Algebra.Help
 members.aol.com/algbrahlp/index.htm
Geometry
 tqd.advanced.org/2647/geometry/
 geometry.htm
MEGA Mathematics
 www.c3.lanl.gov/mega-math/index.html
U.S. Department of the Treasury
 www.ustreas.gov

Parenting

For parents, monitoring a child's Internet usage can be quite challenging. But the Internet itself has a number of useful sites for making sure kids are exposed to the best the Internet has to offer rather than the worst. Sites are also dedicated to helping parents better understand their children and improve their parenting skills.

D-14 Science

KidsPsych

www.kidspsych.org

Help children develop their cognitive thinking skills and deductive reasoning: A very impressive multimedia experience, complete with endless animations and sounds. The site features games for children ages one to nine. The purpose of the games is to help children with cognitive thinking skills and deductive reasoning, give parents the opportunity to better understand their child's development, and have a boatload of fun in the process.

Librarian's Guide to Cyberspace For Parents and Kids

www.ala.org/parentspage

Resources for parents from the American Library Association: Discover how to raise a reader, choose the best books for your child to read, and use the Internet to increase your child's appreciation of reading.

A Parents' Guide to the Internet

www.familyguidebook.com

Keep your children safe online: This site offers easy-to-understand instructions on using computers and the Internet along with much helpful advice on teaching your children the safe way to explore online.

Parent Soup

www.parentsoup.com

Online community for parents: Parent Soup is a resource-rich online community for expecting parents and parents of children of all ages. Use the site to get parenting advice as well as hear others' parenting experiences and share your own.

SafeKids.Com

www.safekids.com

Tips on making your family's online experience more safe, fun, and productive: This site's primary concern is making certain your kids' online experiences are safe ones. SafeKids.Com offers lots of information on parental-control software, rules for online safety, and child-safe Web sites.

Other Sites Worth a Visit

CyberAngels
www.cyberangels.org

Expect the Best From a Girl
www.academic.org

Safe Surfin'
www.safesurfin.com

SafeTeens.Com
www.safeteens.com

Science

You don't have to worry about blowing up the chemistry lab when you conduct a science experiment online! The Internet is beloved by science students and teachers; explore this long list of sites to find out why.

Bill Nye The Science Guy

disney.go.com/disneytelevision/billnye

Multimedia science lab: Popular science guru Bill Nye brings his lab online, providing visitors an extensive collection of video and audio files. The site also offers a Demo of the Day — a daily science demonstration that students can try at home.

Cool Science for Curious Kids

www.hhmi.org/coolscience

Science experiments, facts, and images: Here's a site where you can discover the connection between butterflies and caterpillars, get an up-close look at the air we breathe, read about how monkeys are like moose, and find many more interesting science factoids.

Dinosaurs at the National Museum of Natural History

www.nmnh.si.edu/paleo/dino

Virtual tour of this museum's dinosaur exhibit: Ever wonder what a centrosaurus skull looks like? Check out this site and wonder no more! You can find many great images and informative descriptions here, thanks to the National Museum of Natural History's extensive dinosaur collection.

Earthquake Information: United States Geological Survey

quake.wr.usgs.gov

Earthquake facts, preparedness tips, and links: You don't have to be a seismologist to appreciate this tremor-endous site from the United States Geological Survey. The site offers information on the most recent earthquakes, feature projects, maps, preparedness tips, and links to other earthquake-related sites.

The Franklin Institute Science Museum

sln.fi.edu

Online tour of science museum: A variety of exhibits can be explored at this Philadelphia museum's site. Visitors can also browse the museum's monthly magazine, *inQuiry Almanack*, and learn about the life and work of the museum's namesake, Benjamin Franklin. There's also a special section called Wired@School that details the work of nine teachers who are pioneering the use of the Internet in K-8 schools.

Global Online Learning Adventures

www.goals.com

Help students concentrate on reaching goals. The educational uses for this site go beyond the science, technology, nature, and adventure themes that run through it. You can create lots of great lesson plans that revolve around the goal-setting and goal-accomplishment stories that abound at this site.

I Can Do That!

www.eurekascience.com/ICanDoThat/ index.htm

Go on an online tour of DNA: Looking for a way to make learning about DNA fun? I Can Do That! does just that by delivering a bevy of fun facts on DNA, RNA, cells, protein, and cloning. The site presents the information with good humor, an easy-to-understand writing style, and numerous color illustrations.

Kinetic City Cyber Club

www.kineticcity.com

Adventure-like science experience online:
Kids can join the Kinetic City Super Crew
in cracking cases that involve scientific
puzzles, such as why plate tectonics could
be mistaken for underwater ghosts. The
colorful interface and the adventure
theme may remind teachers of software
favorites such as *Where in the World Is
Carmen Sandiego?* To take full advantage
of the site, teachers should get a login and
password for kids to use.

Kratts' Creatures

www.pbs.org/kratts

Associate animals and their habitats: The
Kratt brothers' Web site includes a great
map of the world that allows kids to zoom
in on the habitats of many interesting animals. Also included are fun and interactive
animal activities and a guide of the various episodes of the *Kratt's Creatures* TV
show on PBS for teachers.

MAD Scientist Network

www.madsci.org

Answers to science questions: Do you have
a pressing science question? Why not
pose the question to hundreds of professional scientists around the world? At the
MAD Scientist Network, you can! The site
brings together the collective cranium of a
network of scientists worldwide who have
volunteered to answer questions submitted by students, teachers, or anyone else.
Before you submit a question, be sure to
first check out the Archives section —
your question may have already been
asked and answered. The site also features a MAD Labs section, where you can
find lots of experiments that can be con-
ducted at home or in the classroom.

The Museum of Paleontology

www.ucmp.berkeley.edu

*Museum dedicated to the study of fossils
and modern organisms:* Paleontology is the
study of fossils. If that sounds boring to
you, give this site a look and you'll quickly
discover that the subject can actually be
quite fascinating. For example, dinosaurs
— everyone's fascinated by these prehis-
toric beasts, and this site has plenty of
them to see and read about, from the
Carnosaur to the Tyrannosaurus rex. The
Museum of Paleontology offers much
more, including online exhibits on plants,
the different time periods, and geology.

National Aeronautics and Space Administration

www.nasa.gov

Space exploration and related sciences:
Without a doubt, one of the best sites on
the Internet, NASA's site serves as proof
that the government *can* do something
right. From the site's home page, visitors
have the option of blasting off to four separate sites: Mars Global Surveyor, Earth
Observatory, Spaceflight, and ESE Kids
Only. The latter is for students of all ages,
offering image-intensive, information-rich
articles on topics such as El Niño, tropical
rainfall, the ozone, and careers in earth
science. There's also a Teacher Guides
section, which makes available material
created by NASA for use in teaching earth
science. The material is in PDF format, so
you need Adobe Acrobat Reader (downloadable for free at www.adobe.com) to
open it.

O. Orkin Insect Zoo

www.orkin.com/html/o.orkin.html

Virtual tour of an insect zoo: At the O. Orkin Insect Zoo, you can discover the important role insects play in our delicate ecology and how humans and insects are, in fact, interdependent. The site offers plenty of up-close images of beetles, millipedes, spiders, and other insects that many of us flee from offline. The O. Orkin Insect Zoo is part of the National Museum of Natural History, and, such being the case, the site includes links to many other exhibits at the museum.

San Diego Zoo: Animals at Large

www.sandiegozoo.org/apps/animals/
    index.html

Descriptions and images of animals: The San Diego Zoo is widely regarded as one of the best zoos in the world, so the similar excellence of the Zoo's Web site should come as no surprise. Point and click your way to exotic animals like the Chinese leopard, the white rhinoceros, the sulawesi hornbill, and the Galapagos tortoise.

Sci4Kids

www.ars.usda.gov/is/kids

Fun and informative site from the Agricultural Research Service: Sci4Kids features interesting stories about all things agricultural, such as "Nightmare On Elm Street, The Happy Sequel," which tells how scientists are successfully battling Dutch Elm disease. This site also has classroom resources, such as quizzes and other activities, that can be used to teach students about agriculture.

Sport! Science

www.exploratorium.edu/sports/
    index.html

Examining the role of science in sports: Ever wonder why a ball bounces or, in some cases, fails to bounce? Or how, in baseball, a curve ball is thrown? If so, this site has the answers you're looking for. With easy-to-understand explanations, Sport! Science reveals the laws of nature that control the games we play. There's even a reaction time exhibit where you can find out if you have what it takes to hit a 90-mph fastball from a big-league pitcher. This site proves that learning about science can be fun.

UCARweb Weather

home.ucar.edu/wx.html

Weather forecasts, issues, links: UCARweb Weather is one of many sites that offers weather reports and forecasts. But this site is much more than just a place to find out if it's raining in Reykjavik or hailing in Halifax. Here, you can also read articles about important weather topics. Probably UCARweb Weather's best feature is its extensive list of links, ranging from The Weather Channel (www.weather.com) to The Tornado Project Online (www.tornado-project.com) to satellite imagery sites like Real-Time Data (www.ssec.wisc.edu/data).

WebElements

www.webelements.com

Periodic table online: WebElements should appeal to chemistry students and teachers alike. Created by a chemistry professor in England, the site presents the elements in a comprehensive periodic table, chock full of details about each element. For example, click on element number 54, Xe, and a page quickly appears listing its name, Xenon, along with its spelling in four other languages, its atomic weight, its color, and many other bits of information. There's even an audio file that, when clicked upon, speaks the correct pronunciation of the element — very helpful!

Other Sites Worth a Visit

American Veterinary Medical Association Kid's Corner
www.avma.org/care4pets/avmakids.htm

The Best Paper Airplane in the World
www.zurqui.com/crinfocus/paper/airplane.html

Biology4Kids
http://www.kapili.com/biology4kids/index.html

Butterflies at The Field Museum
www.fmnh.org/butterfly/default.htm

How Things Fly
www.aero.hq.nasa.gov/edu/

Kid's Valley Garden
www.arnprior.com/kidsgarden/index.htm

Museum of Science and Industry
www.msichicago.org/exhibit/exhome.html

The Nine Planets
www.seds.org/billa/tnp

OwlCam
members.aol.com/owlbox/owlhome.htm

Plants and Our Environment
tqjunior.advanced.org/3715

Science Daily
www.sciencedaily.com

U.S. Fish & Wildlife Services: Kid's Information Central
www.fws.gov/r9endspp/kid_cor/kid_cor.htm

Virtual Frog Dissection Kit
www.itg.lbl.gov/ITG.hm.pg.docs/dissect/info.html

Social Studies

Don't know much about history? Spend some time perusing the sites below and you'll not only know a lot about history, you'll also know plenty about politics, geography, and anthropology.

ArchNet

www.lib.uconn.edu/ArchNet

Virtual library for archaeology: Those interested in archaeology should definitely bookmark this site. ArchNet features archaeological facts and figures, definitions, news, links, and more!

CIA Kid's Secret Zone

www.odci.gov/cia/ciakids/safe.html

Learn all about the CIA (Central Intelligence Agency): Did you know the CIA was created when Harry Truman signed the National Security Act in 1947? Or that the CIA's Canine Corps was established in 1991 during the Persian Gulf War? You can discover these factoids and many others at the CIA Kid's Secret Zone.

How Far Is It?

www.indo.com/distance

Distance calculator: Enter two locations, anywhere in the world, and this site calculates the distance between the two and provides a detailed map of both locations. A fun site, sure to stimulate student interest in geography.

Let's Go: Around the World

www.ccph.com

Global exploration: Virtual adventures around the world await visitors of this site. Meet the children of the Amazon, take an African safari, or listen to the call of exotic birds. Teachers can sign up for The Connected Teacher, an e-mail newsletter listing site updates.

THOMAS: Legislative Information on the Internet

thomas.loc.gov

Legislative information from The Library of Congress: THOMAS, a service, the site proclaims, "in the spirit of Thomas Jefferson," enables visitors to access bill summaries and texts, Roll Call votes, the text of the *Congressional Record*, committee reports, government links, and more.

Trusty's Kids Corner

www.trustkids.org

Games, puzzles, and quizzes educating kids on the importance of preserving historical landmarks: From the National Trust for Historic Preservation comes this fun site, featuring interactive activities (or *interactivities*, if you prefer). Requires Macromedia Shockwave plug-in.

The United Nations CyberSchoolBus: Elementary Planet

www.un.org/Pubs/CyberSchoolBus/
menuelem.htm

Games, animations, and quizzes await those who travel aboard the UN's CyberSchoolBus. Learn all about the

world we live in and its many different cultures — and have a whole lot of fun in the process! The site can be accessed in three different languages: English, French, and Spanish. It also offers information on the popular Model UN program.

White House For Kids

www.whitehouse.gov/WH/kids/html/
home.html

Join Socks and Buddy on a tour of the White House: Find out about the history of the White House and its occupants, including the First Children and First Pets. There's even a section where you can send a message to the President.

Other Sites Worth a Visit

Empires Past
library.advanced.org/16325/indexie.shtml

Greatest Places
www.sci.mus.mn.us/greatestplaces

Kids Can Make a Difference
www.kids.maine.org

United States Postal Service For Kids
www.usps.gov/kids/welcome.htm

Special Needs

For people with disabilities, such as the blind, the Internet is not always a friendly place. Fortunately, there are sites like the ones below working to ensure that all sites are accessible to everyone.

Bobby

www.cast.org/bobby

Analyzes sites to determine if they are accessible to people with disabilities: Terrific Web-based tool, from the Center for Applied Special Technology. Simply input a URL and click on Submit, and Bobby displays a report showing accessibility and browser compatibility errors found on the page. Analysis is based on the World Wide Web Consortium's Web Content Accessibility Guidelines.

National Attention Deficit Disorder Association

www.add.org

Information on Attention Deficit Disorder (ADD) for parents and children: A comprehensive ADD site that offers info on treatment and research, expert articles, a list of support groups, and a Kid's Area.

The Road to Special Education

thelinkto.com/Road

Newsletter for families who have children receiving Special Education services: Feature articles, laws, Q&As, and links — all related to Special Education and all in one site.

Sighted Electronics

www.sighted.com

Adaptive technologies for people with blindness or visual impairments: Sighted Electronics offers a wide range of software and hardware, such as braille printers, embossers, and displays.

Web Accessibility Initiative

www.w3.org/WAI

Information on the World Wide Web Consortium's efforts to make the Internet accessible to persons with disabilities: The World Wide Web Consortium (W3C) wields much power and influence in the Web-development community. This site details the W3C's Web Content Accessibility Guidelines and what Web developers can do to ensure that their sites are accessible to everyone.

Other Sites Worth a Visit

Access-Ability
www.access-ability.co.uk

Deaf World Web
dww.deafworldweb.org

Electronic and Information Technology Access Advisory Committee
www.access-board.gov/notices/ eitaacmtg.htm

National Federation of the Blind
www.nfb.org

Office of Special Education and Rehabilitative Services, U.S. Department of Education
www.ed.gov/pubs/TeachersGuide/osers.html

PACE: Parenting Autistic Children Effectively
www.ncnow.com/pace

Special Education Resources on the Internet
www.hood.edu/seri

What Teachers Can Do About Learning Disabilities
www.ldonline.org/ld_indepth/ teaching_techniques/teaching-1.html

Teacher Resources

Looking for a new lesson plan? Need funding for a special project? Point and click your way to these sites and find lesson plans, curricula, grants, funding, and other invaluable teacher resources!

ArtsEdNet

www.artsednet.getty.edu

Online services supporting arts education: Searching for a lesson plan on, say, Navajo art? Look no further! This site, from the Getty Education Institute for the Arts, includes many different lesson plans and curriculum ideas for all grade levels. The site also features extensive image galleries.

Arts Education and School Improvement Resources for Local and State Leaders

www.ed.gov/pubs/ArtsEd

Find out about funding options for arts programs: An online guide directed at local and state leaders, art educators and practitioners who want to learn about funding for arts education programs through the U.S. Department of Education. The guide includes, among other things, a description of each program, its intended use, and specific program contact information.

CNET Download.com for the PC — Teaching Tools in Education

www.download.com/pc/list/ 0,339,0-d-10-16-d- 1,00.html?st.dl.cat10.subs.sub16

Download scads of software for teachers: Want to create, say, computer-based tests for students but don't know where to begin? Head to Download.com's Teaching Tools section and download A+QuizMaster 3.0 — shareware that enables you to create those computer-based tests. Download.com features hundreds of applications for educators, most of which is either freeware or shareware.

EdWeb

edweb.cnidr.org

Hyperbook exploring educational reform and information technology: From Andy Carvin comes this resource-intensive site, a continuing work in progress offering information on the role of the Internet in education, a tutorial on HTML and creating Web pages, radical school-reform ideas, and a list of K-12 Internet resources.

Institute for Learning Technologies

www.ilt.columbia.edu/k12

A gateway of K-12 resources: A great place to discover revolutionary ways to integrate the Internet in the classroom. Check out the site's many K-12 resources and read about the projects being supported by the Institute for Learning Technologies.

PBS MATHLINE

www.pbs.org/teachersource/math

Resources for mathematics teachers Grades K-12: Get up to speed on new instructional techniques at PBS MATHLINE. The site offers lesson plans and video clips for use in classrooms.

United States Department of Education

www.ed.gov

One-stop site for education news, grants, financial aid, and statistics: No matter what you're searching for, if it's related to education, this is a good place to look first. Teachers will most appreciate the Funding Opportunities section; students and parents can benefit from the Student Financial Assistance section.

Other Sites Worth a Visit

Community of Science, Inc.
www.cos.com

Corporation for Public Broadcasting: Education and Technology
www.cpb.org/edtech/index.html

E-Education on the WWW
indy.cs.concordia.ca/e-edu/main.html

How to Offer a Course Over the Internet
www.edgorg.com/course.htm

students can interview scientists across the globe in real-time. Sure, everyone looks like Max Headroom because the connection isn't quite fast enough, but you can see an emerging technology that's going to improve quickly.

Find out more about CU-SeeMe videoconferencing via Net at www.cuseeme.com and Apple's QuickTime video conferencing at www.apple.com.

Part IV
Teaching with Terabytes

"Children- it is not necessary to whisper while we're visiting the Vatican Library Web site."

In this part . . .

*I*n this part, you can discover some specific ways to use the Internet to enrich and enhance what goes on in your classroom. This section most typifies what makes the *...For Teachers* series a useful tool for you and your students.

Find out strategies for learning the Internet and for monitoring your students as they progress in their use of the Web. Discover how your role can change as you move from "sage on stage" to "guide on the side." Also new in this third edition are brand-new CyberJourneys and a few ideas about assessing student progress.

Chapter 18

CyberTeachers, CyberLearners

● ●

In This Chapter

▶ Planning an online experience

▶ Managing time, materials, and kids

▶ Teaching students (and yourself) about the Internet

▶ Special-needs students and the Internet

▶ Changing roles for teachers and students

● ●

Get ready for *the feeling*. You know *the feeling,* the one you get when something exciting is going on in your classroom, the students are enthusiastic and on task, and the lesson plan that you spent three hours writing is working. You and the students are on an educational roll, rocketing toward that mystical state of the *meaningful educational experience.*

With a little planning and a smattering of good luck from the technology gremlins, educational expeditions via the Internet can be among the most rewarding and motivating activities you'll ever experience.

Planning an Online Experience

How many thousands of lesson plans have you written? You know the drill: objectives, materials, procedures, evaluation, and so on. Planning an online experience isn't all that different, although you need to consider some things that can make the difference between a great lesson and a technological disaster.

I want your first (and every) experience of using the Net with students to be a positive one, so I'm gonna share those deep dark planning secrets that I've gleaned from peeking around classroom doors and watching my mentors teach. Shut the curtains, lock the doors — here are Bard's 12 Steps to Planning and Implementing Successful Internet Projects (and pardon me if I sometimes seem to state the obvious):

✔ **Think about your goals for the lesson.** What do you want to accomplish? What outcomes would constitute *learning* for this lesson?

✔ **Consider whether the Internet is the best way to accomplish your goals.** Sometimes, using more, uh, traditional media (paper and pencil, a protractor, a workbook, garden tools, a test tube) makes more sense than using the Internet. The Net is like any other classroom resource: There's a right way and a wrong way (and a right time and a wrong time) to use it. Let the curriculum drive the use of technology, not the other way around.

✔ **Identify and analyze the Internet resources that your students may use.** Do they need access to e-mail? FTP? Preconstructed bookmark lists for quick starts? Tools for downloading, unpacking, and decoding files? What are the pitfalls that they may encounter?

✔ **Check out your stuff.** Check your hardware and software, including your telephone or network connections, before class begins. Murphy and his law are alive and well and living in an Ethernet hub near you.

✔ **List the steps necessary for success.** Follow the KISS (keep it simple, stupid!) rule and establish a step-by-step procedure if that's the way your particular group learns best. The Internet is *huge;* your students can, and probably will, get lost there more than once. The more specific you are at the beginning, the better your students will become at navigating on their own.

✔ **Set parameters for time.** You need to consider not only how long completing the project may take, but also how much lead time you need to give your fellow teachers or collaborators on the Net. If you're planning an online writing project, for example, think about how long students may need to wait for a reply. Things happen, and sometimes delays can be excruciating. Guess what? Your kids will be as anxious as you are.

✔ **Build in opportunities for feedback.** When are students on target, and when are they just surfing aimlessly around the Net? How will you let them know where they stand?

✔ **Think about the final product.** What should the final report, document, or outcome look like? What constitutes success? How will you grade it? Some possibilities include rubrics, an analysis of printed documents, and evaluating reflective writing in journals.

✔ **Use mentors.** Identify how and when students should, can, or must use their fellow students, teachers, parents, and so on as resources.

✔ **Think about your role.** How closely do you need to supervise the students? Should you answer questions?

✔ **Try it yourself.** As a beginning teacher, I once showed my middle schoolers a science film without previewing it. The film, entitled something such as "Man, the Incredible Machine," featured an opening sequence where a camera panned a young woman's body from the top of her head to the tip of her toes. I saw my life, and my teaching contract, flash before my eyes well before the camera reached the toes.

(Thankfully, the film skipped the parts that would've been the end of teacher Bard.) I vowed never to make that mistake again. The potential for chaos/disaster/bizarre stuff is just as high on the Internet. Try the project yourself *first*.

✔ **Make time to look back and debrief.** You'll find that there's more than one way to accomplish nearly every task on the Internet. Leave it to the students to startle you with new ways to link to information and to locate new resources you'd never imagined.

How to cite electronic media

After your students find information on the Net, how do they properly give the author credit when they use material? Here's a set of standards modeled on the APA guidelines. These guidelines are based upon those available via the APA at:

```
www.uvm.edu/~xli/reference/apa.
html
```

In the examples below, you (or your students) should replace the text in italics with the appropriate information from the document to be cited. In each case, the date represents either the date of the document or the date the resource was downloaded if the document date is not available:

✔ **Electronic mail messages:** *Author, (year, month, day). Subject of message [sender's e-mail address],* [Online]. Available e-mail: *receiver's e-mail address.*

For example: Templeton, P.K. (1999, June 5). Project Deadline [templeton@ed.com], [Online]. Available e-mail: phikap@aol.com.

✔ **Articles available on the Web:** *Author. (Date of document or download). Title of Item.* [Online] Available http://*address/filename.*

For example: Doe, Jane R. (1999, March 5) The Internet in the Classroom. [Online] Available www.somewhere.com/document.html.

✔ **Articles available via mailing lists:** Root, C. (1997). ESL and learning disabilities: A guide for the ESL practitioner. TESL-EJ 1. Available e-mail: LISTSERV@CMSA.BERKELEY.EDU. Message: GET TESLEJ01 A-4 TESLEJ-L F=Mail.

✔ **FTP or telnet:** Kehoe, B.P. (1994). Zen and the Art of the Internet (4th Ed.), [Online]. Available FTP (Telnet): quake.think.com. Directory: pub/etext/1992. File: Zen10.text.

✔ **Computer programs:** Sandford, J.A. & Browne, R.J. (1985). Captain's log: Cognitive Training System (Version 1.0), [Computer program]. Indianapolis: Psychological Software Services, Inc.

✔ **Online databases:** The educational directory. (1992). [Online]. Available: Knowledge Index File: The Educational Directory (EDUC6).

✔ **Online image:** The Interior of Walker Elementary School Café. (1999). [Online Image] Available http://www.walkeres.edu/caf♪.gif.

✔ **Online video:** The First Flight of Karen's Model Airplane. (1999). [Online Video] Available http://www.walkeres.edu/plane.mov.

✔ **Online sound:** Baby Josh's First Words. (1998). [Online Sound] Available http://www.wilsonfamily.com/googoo.au.

Managing Time, Materials, and Students

Okay, let me guess. You have one computer and 30 kids. You're teaching in a room the size of a closet, and if you can't complete your lesson in 50 minutes, the fifth period teacher will put out a contract on you.

Never fear. There *is* hope for Internet activities in your classroom! The good news is that if you plan well, activities involving research and the exploration of the Internet can be easily segmented into bite-sized (class period-sized) pieces.

Here are ten tips for managing time, materials, and students:

- ✔ If you're doing a live (real-time) project with other people on the Internet, don't forget to think about time zones and the cultural differences of the groups with which you're communicating. The information superhighway covers all times zones — now was that two hours' or three hours' difference?

  In case you and your students get time-confused, point your Web browser to `http://weather.yahoo.com` for the current time and weather anywhere on the planet!

- ✔ Plan to supplement your Internet activities with a variety of print, video, and computer software resources. The information superhighway is rich with resources, but it's only one tool!

- ✔ Think about using a contract or acceptable use policy (AUP). (See Chapter 3 for some tips for creating a contract for your school.) Surfing doesn't have to be hazardous to your health.

- ✔ Always have a backup plan, or "escape route," as a teacher friend of mine refers to it. If you haven't given the proper oblations to the techno-gods, you could end up as road kill on the information superhighway. Your hard drive could fry, or the phone company may choose to service the school's phone lines in the middle of your class time.

- ✔ Be sure that students have some kind of directions for where to start and, generally, how to proceed, or road map, before they travel the information superhighway.

- ✔ Make sure that students obey the road signs on the highway: Be nice, and don't go where you're not supposed to go or where the resources that you need aren't located.

- ✔ Periodically take time to ask students what they've accomplished. Are they surfing aimlessly? Are they drowning? Or are they shooting the Internet waves like a pro?

- ✔ Every classroom has a supersurfer or two. Be prepared with enrichment (extra credit) activities or have students create their own.

Beyond pen-pals . . .

E-mail can be a very powerful tool in your classroom. The first thing you probably think of is simply finding an electronic pen-pal for your students. That's interesting, but I've found (particularly with K–8 students) that the quality of pen-pal writing often degrades to something such as the following excerpt from a fifth grader's pen-pal writing:

How old are you? What do you look like? Which is your favorite Star Wars action figure?

Wouldn't you rather have this excerpt from a fifth grader's essay on "A Special Person in My Life"?

My grandmother is the nicest person I know. She cares about me, about my mom, and about my puppy, Joker. I like the way her cheeks turn red when she laughs. That always happens when we play together on the porch. She always takes time for me. She must have been a great mommy.

As you think about using the Internet with your students, you'll discover many projects that focus on higher-order thinking skills, such as analysis and evaluation. A teacher in New York developed a writing project that featured autobiographies of the "everyday person on the street." She exchanged them with teachers at other schools using e-mail and together, they created a "Profile of America." A media specialist from Canada built a database of children's book reviews collected from students all over the world via e-mail. The final product was posted to a Web site that features children's literature and other resources called The Children's Literature Web Guide at

```
www.ucalgary.ca/~dkbrown/
index.html
```

Sigh. I had a nice grandma, too. Think about moving your students *beyond* pen-pals and toward more pithy outcomes such as collaborative writing or lesson exchange.

✔ Think about using a timer to encourage kids to focus on the activity at hand and not to stop at every roadside diner.

✔ Remind students to *think* before they telnet, Gopher, ftp, e-mail, or Web-surf: What is the right tool for the information superhighway journey of the day?

Students with Special Needs and the Internet

A wonderful teacher named Dr. Elizabeth Garrett gave me a virtual slap on the face one day — a wake-up call that every educator should one day experience — when she invited me to visit our school district's special needs center. Before that day, I thought of the special needs center as the place where they keep "those kids" that we couldn't handle. I knew that kids with severe physical challenges were there, along with those placed there because we, for one reason or another, weren't able to meet their needs in a regular classroom. Still, as I walked up to the door of the building that day I really didn't know what to expect.

What I saw changed the way I look at education, at students, and at myself. I saw some of the most attentive, caring professionals coaching some of the brightest-eyed, most energetic kids you can imagine. I saw what happens when these children have access to technology. I saw computers with adaptive aids change the very quality of life for those kids. Without access to this technology, many of these kids simply could not communicate, create, explore, or have fun. And then I saw one of them type "I love you" to his mom on a keypad with a foot-long pointer clenched between his teeth — that did it.

If I had a zillion dollars in the bank, I would make sure that each and every student around the planet had a computer and the adaptive aids necessary for teaching and learning.

The bottom line is that it's important to consider students with special needs when thinking about using the Internet in your classroom. Here are a few suggestions from the experts for using the computer to access the Net with kids who have special needs:

✔ Set your browser for larger font sizes for visually impaired students.

✔ Investigate alternative devices (switches, sip & puff devices, and wands) to substitute for the mouse.

✔ Explore screen-readers (like the Ultimate Reader from The Center for Applied Special Technology (CAST) that can read the text from a Web page or any other source. Go to www.cast.org to visit them on the Web.

✔ Think about low-tech help, like placing nonskid materials under keyboards and mousepads, using monitors that swivel and tilt, and built-in adaptive aids, like the Mac's built-in Universal Access (Easy Access and CloseView) and on Windows 95 in the Accessibility Options control panel.

✔ Set aside extra time for students with special needs to use the computer; try to pair them with understanding, patient partners.

✔ Explore using Braille output for printout of information from the Net for blind students.

✔ Check out speech recognition (voice input) software or Dragon System's "Naturally Speaking" or "Voice Power Pro" (Mac/Windows).

✔ Use At Ease (a student management program from Apple), Foolproof (Mac/Windows), or another powerful tool to automate the process of logging onto the Net.

Thanks, Liz, for that cyberslap. It worked. There will forever be a special place in my heart for the teachers of students with special needs and their equally special students.

Staff Development and the Internet

The Internet learning curve is a bit steep, but you can overcome it easily. The best way to learn is to ask someone who's already an Internet surfer to show you the way. And guess what, these mentors don't even have to be in the same country as you! They can be anywhere in cyberspace. You can use telecommunications such as e-mail, real-time chat, LISTSERVs, and so on to communicate. Someone recently called this relationship *telementoring,* which I think is a nifty way of saying, "Find an online mentor and have that person teach you about the Net."

I like to think of Internet tools as "stumbleware." One of the best things about the Internet is that you often stumble onto resources or ideas that you never dreamed of finding. The best way to learn about the Net is just to dive right in and try it. An easy introduction through a commercial online service is a great way to begin.

During your first visits, focus on one tool or type of information. Think about how you can make your next visit more productive as you explore. As with any technology, the more you use it, the better you become. Happy surfing!

Launch your Web browser and go to the Classroom Connect site (http://www.classroom.com), where you can find lots links to valuable education sites on the Web like articles, lesson plans, professional development opportunities, and even some home page links to schools on the Internet. This group of folks also publishes what I believe to be the best monthly education resource for Net-surfers, the *Classroom Connect* newsletter (available through a paid subscription). There's also the free *Classroom Connect* mailing list, send an e-mail to connect@classroom.com. *Classroom Connect* also has a free mailing list with daily mailings (send an e-mail to crc-request@listserv.classroom.com and type **subscribe digest crc** in the body of your message). Did I mention they have great conferences, too? Call *Classroom Connect* at 800-638-1639 or visit www.classroom.com/pd/ for more information.

Their newsletter has a total of nine newsletters for $39.00. All you have to do is e-mail them to get on their mailing list. Call 800-638-1639 to place your order.

Keeping Up with Changing Roles

Carolyn, a 12-year-old student of mine, sat quietly at the computer, hunting-and-pecking away for more than an hour. Every once in a while, you'd hear a strange noise or the sound of a video tape being rewound. Once she came over to the group of students I was helping with a science lab and asked, "Do you like programs that read to you or ones that you just read yourself?" I told her that I liked both, particularly the kind that reads to me if the things I was learning were new or complicated.

Another 20 minutes later, Carolyn called me over to see her finished product. In the next few minutes, she introduced me to the "Creatures of the Georgia Coast," one at a time. I saw sea gulls, starfish, even a turtle — each with a stunning photo and voice narration. Some even had rudimentary animation and background music. Her last frame read, "Carolyn Baxter, Age 12." I admit it, I was totally humbled. Not only was I amazed at Carolyn's ability to synthesize information, but Carolyn had no formal training in the program she used — Knowledge Adventure's HyperStudio.

A few years have passed since I saw Carolyn's project and realized that the use of technology was dramatically changing my role in the classroom — along with my students' roles.

The good news is that after you realize that your role as a teacher is changing, a whole new world of possibilities opens for you. The Internet simply provides a wide, endless avenue for you to explore. Perhaps technology, and specifically the Internet, can help more students move toward higher-level learning goals.

How is the role of the student changing as technology becomes an easily available tool? Think about these roles as you peruse Table 18-1.

Table 18-1	Students' changing roles
The Student That Was/Is	**The Student That Will Be**
A passive listener ("Today we heard about climate.")	An active learner ("Today I used the Internet to study climate photos of our state.")
A doer of teacher-prepared tasks ("Read page 23 and do questions 1 through 44.")	A teacher of others ("Can anyone explain how to telnet to NASA to access the pay load list?")

The Student That Was/Is	The Student That Will Be
A slave to the curriculum ("If it's March, it better be Chapter 2.")	A researcher student, who works toward a goal at his or her own pace ("I'd like to finish by Friday.")
An examiner of the textbook ("It has nice pictures.")	A knowledge navigator ("I found information in 21 places, but the best one was...")

By now you're probably thinking "Uh oh, we're not in Kansas anymore, Toto." Well, you're right. Many of you have already changed the way you teach as you incorporate technology into the curriculum. Think about the changing roles of teachers and read over Table 18-2.

Table 18-2	Teachers' changing roles
The Teacher That Was/Is	The Teacher's That Will Be
A deliverer of information, a sage on stage	A coach; a guide off to the side
A teacher of the textbook	A teacher whose lessons are driven by reality and up-to-date information resources
A coordinator of group work	An information manager
A dictator in a controlled democracy	A knowledge navigator
An educational island	A member of a learning team (technology coordinator, media specialist, teachers, administrators, parents, and students)

So, what's the bottom line in preparing for the use of the Internet in your classroom? The answer's the same as for any lesson: Plan. Try things out yourself beforehand. Head off potential problems before they arise.

Oh, and did I say relax? Have fun? Smile?

Chapter 19

CyberJourneys: Learning Expeditions into the Net

● ●

In This Chapter

▶ Exploring a day in the life . . . (K–5)

▶ Getting spaced out (6–8)

▶ Conducting the great scavenger hunt (9–12)

▶ Fighting for a cause (college and up)

▶ Cyberplanning for the teacher

▶ Spinning your own Web

● ●

*W*hen I sent a request over the Internet for cyberjourney ideas (a cyberjourney is an Internet learning activity) I received more than 120 replies in less than two weeks. After sifting through them, I have chosen a few that I think you'll like. Here they are — teacher-tested and ready for your classroom — a few cyberjourneys to get you started integrating the Net into your curriculum. Planning these activities can take a bit of practice, but the payoff can be huge.

Each journey begins with a short description and ends with a starting point, an address or tip that will help you and your students begin in the fast lane of the information superhighway. Even though the exercises are presented by grade level, you can adapt most of them for use with any student from kinder-gartners to adults. Happy motoring!

Don't forget to spend some time talking with students about citing electronic resources. For a standard format, see the sidebar in Chapter 3.

A CyberJourney for K–5

This activity — perfect for younger students' first excursions into the Internet — comes from Frances Kinsey, an elementary teacher from Topeka, Kansas. The idea for the activity, called "A Day in the Life" . . . is based on the popular *keypals* project, in which students from various places around the world write to each other about a topic that's predetermined by the teachers on the project team.

Enjoy "A Day in the Life. . . ."

Remember when you'd come in from school and your parents would ask, "What did you do in school today?" I'd usually shrug and give the obligatory "Nothin'" response. Here's a chance for your students to find out what other people do, both at school and in the workplace and respond with "Somethin'" good.

Ask students to conduct short interviews, either in person or via e-mail, of other students, parents, teachers, or community members and create a short story describing one day in the life of their subject. It can be a short paragraph, and may be supported with pictures, video, or audio. Before they begin, be sure to help students generate a few "who, what, when, where, why, and how" questions, and also discuss how to ask questions.

Subscribe to newsgroups (such as k12.chat.elementary) or write to your teacher friends on the Internet and set up an exchange. Send the stories via e-mail to another school for response and comment.

As an extra bonus after a couple of exchanges, try linking the two classes via real-time chat by using IRC or ICQ (see Chapter 16) or by using the conference room of an online service. (AOL's Electronic Schoolhouse is a great place for this activity, if you've got an AOL account, of course.)

Starting Point: Visit Classroom Connect (www.classroom.net) or the Apple Learning Interchange (www.apple.com/education/ali) and organize a chat.

A CyberJourney for 6–8

Bob Chris, a techno-wizard from a private school in Atlanta, offers this out-of-this-world activity that he uses with his eighth-grade earth science students. In an activity he calls "Spaced Out," Students locate information, download graphics, and surf the World Wide Web searching for information about the U.S. space program.

Have students pretend they are reporters for a major newspaper or magazine. Their assignment editor has just received word that funding may be cut for the U.S. space program. The students' "assignment" is to collect information from the Internet to answer the question, "Is the U.S. space program extra or essential?"

Instruct the students record where they visit and what information they find as they hunt. Work with the class to decide whether the final product is a news, editorial, or a feature story. Have students present their findings (through story, presentation, and so on) to the rest of the class after the Web surfing portion of the exercise is complete.

Be sure to review the use of Web browsers, and FTP tools (Fetch or WS FTP) — they'll need to pull out all the stops to find information about this one!

Set a reasonable time limit (based on the students' ability to access the Internet) for the project, or it could go on for days!

Starting Point: Try these Web pages: www.eb.com/ or www.nasa.gov/.

Need a great resource for facts and figures? Call the CIA! Have your students point their browser to the CIA World Fact Book at http://www.odci.gov/cia/publications/factbook/index.html.

A CyberJourney for 9–12

One of the best ways to help students learn about and identify resources available on the Internet is to serve up a scavenger hunt for them to chew on that's both fun and challenging. You'll be amazed at how many different sources students tap as they answer questions.

This doozy of an activity comes from Terry Mansell, a journalism teacher from Tucson. At the time, she had been using the Internet for less than a year but was already a supersurfer. Here's a list of 10 questions, appropriate for grades 9–12, that encourage the use of a variety of Internet resources and the tools to access them.

CNN on the Web: The ultimate starting point for cyberjourneys

I admit it. I'm a CNN junkie. There's simply no better place to go for up-to-the-minute news. Now CNN offers a suite of Internet services for you and your students to use as a starting point for your Internet research journeys. CNN has a whole division dedicated to helping you in your classroom, too, at:

    http://learning.turner.com/

Here are a few must-see sites to visit:

Internet CNN Newsroom

    www.cnnewsroom.com

This is the home page for choosing which day's programming you wish to view. Programs are listed by date, and you'll find links to archives and daily lesson plans on this page also.

CNN Electronic Field Trips

    http://learning.turner.com/tal/
       index.html

This site is a repository for the popular CNN Field Trips. Take your students (virtually) around the world, under the oceans, and more.

CNN's Main News Site

    http://www.cnn.com/

So point those browsers to CNN, the world's most important (Inter)Network.

How about "The Great Internet Scavenger Hunt?" Turn students loose with a Web browser (Netscape Navigator, Internet Explorer, and so on) and see how they track down the following information. Be sure to ask them to record and share the sources that they use to locate each answer.

1. What is the first line in L. Frank Baum's *The Wizard of Oz?*

2. In how many movies did both Martin Sheen and his son Charlie star?

3. How old was artist Salvador Dali when he did his first painting?

4. Who discovered the element lithium? What is lithium's atomic number?

5. What is the destination of the Voyager Probe? (Hint: use WebCrawler.)

6. The MARVEL server offers lots of information from the catalogs of the Library of Congress. What does the acronym MARVEL stand for?

7. What's the zip code for Pig, Kentucky?

8. What is the WWW address (URL) for *Peanuts* (the comic strip)?

9. How many sailing magazines are on the Internet?

10. List four education-related businesses that have home pages on the Web.

Starting point: Excite: `http://www.excite.com`

Don't miss this 9–12 Web site that features CNN Newsroom and other news resources. Point your browser to CNN News at `http://learning.turner.com/newsroom`.

A CyberJourney for College Students and Educators

One of the neat things about the Internet is that you can find sources of information that represent virtually every imaginable point of view. This activity, designed for pre-service or in-service teachers, focuses the learners' attention to using Internet resources to collect and analyze information about an issue that they feel strongly about. The lesson title is "Fighting for a Cause."

Think about an issue that you feel strongly about. The issue can be related to education, the environment, politics, or students' rights. Surf the Net and collect ideas and facts that help you put together a presentation about Internet resources that are available on your subject. Present the final results of your search to your classmates. As you make your presentation, cite the sources and explore the issue of information bias.

Starting point: Here are some Web stops (use Netscape or another Web browser) that you might visit to help you get ideas:

Site	Web address
Developing Educational Standard	`http://putwest.boces.org/Standards.html`
Greenpeace International (Amsterdam)	`www.greenpeace.org`
LD Online	`http://ldonline.org`
Thomas Congressional Database	`http://thomas.loc.gov`

The folks at NASA have put together a special Web page called "Internet in the Classroom" that offers pre-service and in-service teachers hundreds of online activities. Point your browser to NASA at `http://quest.arc.nasa.gov`.

CyberPlanning for the Teacher

It's 4:30 p.m. on a Friday afternoon and I've just spent nearly two hours separating pebbles, sand, gravel, and stones from a marvelous stream-table experiment that dazzled and educated my students earlier that day. Just as I seal my last container, the principal comes in smiling like the cat that ate the canary.

"Have a good day?" she asks, still grinning.

"Sure! Great experiment; we all learned something. Third period even made little boats and sailed them down our model stream," I repy, knowing that these social visits from the principal at this hour of the day are often followed by the dreaded "we really need to . . . " speech.

"How wonderful. You're such a good teacher," she says, grinning even larger now.

"Uh-huh," I say, blushing maybe a bit.

"You know, we really need to update our technology plan," she says, now looking more seriously at me amid the gravel, pebbles, and sand containers.

Aha! I knew it! Even though we just worked on the plan last summer, five months later she presents this huge task again. Sheesh.

Ready-made cyberjourneys?

Merely having a physical connection to the Internet isn't enough for effective K–12 use. What else is there? A company called American Cybercasting Corp. offers a dynamic content package of ready-made cyberjourneys that it calls Educational Structures. Educational Structures is designed to serve as an up-to-date curriculum component for most subject areas. The program provides more than 70 commercial print publications in hypertext format, ranging from resources suited to the very young (*Ranger Rick*) to those read mainly by older students (*The Washington Post, Discover*, and *Beijing Review*, plus several encyclopedic references).

The company also offers customized organization of Internet-based resources for a school or district, making it easy to incorporate Internet resources into the curriculum. These services include customized lesson plan support and a variety of online activities for students. The product is competitively priced and requires multiple Internet connections at each site for optimum use. For more information, send e-mail to k12@americast.com.

Okay. So I'm a little dramatic. Actually, I really welcomed those visits from my principal. I knew the technology plan needed to be updated. Technology plans go stale faster than the bread in your pantry. Luckily, I planned for this. I'd been doing three things as a "personal cyberjourney" over the last few months that are likely to make the update much simpler:

- ✔ Collecting articles from magazines and newspapers about trends
- ✔ Collecting samples of other school's technology plans
- ✔ Collecting sites on the Web that offered information about technology planning

So, here's a personal cyberjourney that helps you update your school's technology plan. Hopefully, you'll take this as an ongoing task and be ready when the grinning principal shows up at your door!

Starting point: The U.S. Government Department of Education has published a technology plan that's packed with great statistics, research reports, and a sensible set of steps that can be very helpful at: `http://www.ed.gov`.

One more hint. Visit AltaVista (`www.altavista.com`) or Yahoo! (`www.yahoo.com`) and use "technology planning" and "education" as keywords. My last search found more than 10,000 potential links (information overload)!

You'll also discover that many schools now share their tech plans on their school's Web sites. Visit Web66 (`www.web66.coled.umn.edu/`) for a list of schools on the Net.

A CyberJourney for Your School

Here's a Cyberjourney that can benefit your community: Develop _your own_ Web site.

A Web site gives you the freedom to teach something you're interested in, share creative writing, post class assignments, tell about your family, and much more. To establish a Web site, you need two things: disk space on your Internet service provider's host computer and your own customized home page. A home page contains one or more screens of hypertext-linked graphics and text. Other Internet users reach your home page by using a Web browser such as Netscape Navigator or Internet Explorer.

Most Internet service providers will grant schools space on their host computer to use for storing a limited amount of WWW information. Some provide the space for free, and some charge a one-time fee. You can create your own home page by using a word processor or a number of software tools that are available on the Internet. Get set for this activity I'll call "Spinning Your Own Web." (Chapter 8 gives you an overview about how to create a site.)

Starting point: You can find all you need to start your own site from the World Organization of Webmasters site at http://world-webmasters.org.

In case you or your students need a break, it is now possible to order pizza (and many other junk food goodies) online some places around the U.S. (and Australia). Check out www.pizzaonline.com/. They're still working on a way to feed the pepperoni through the phone lines to places other than California, though.

Chapter 20

Rockin' Rubrics and Web Page Evaluation

In This Chapter

▶ Believing what you read

▶ I found it on the Net

▶ Evaluating student-created Web resources

There are two major evaluation needs when planning projects that use the Internet as a resource — evaluating the credibility of Web sites and the information contained therein; and evaluating the final product, if that product is a Web page. I'll start you off by getting your brain cells focused on the credibility issue and then cap off the chapter with talk of evaluating student-created Web sites.

Believe It or Not

Most people believe what they read on the Internet. In fact, some studies suggest that some believe the Internet to be *more* credible than other, more traditional, print media. There are people out there concocting and ingesting home remedies and treating illnesses based on information randomly collected from the Web. Is that amazing, or what? Just because it's digital, it's true? Hardly. In this case, your life could literally depend on your ability to know what's credible and what's not.

Our students are no exception, of course. They're even more gullible than we are, as a rule (probably because we've had more time on the planet). It pays, then, to have a serious discussion about verifying resource credibility.

I Found It on the Internet

There are more than 400 million documents available on the Internet. That's more grains of sand than in your school's sand volleyball pit and way more than what's stuffed into Tommy's locker in the front hall. Assuming you and your students manage to find the info you need (see Chapter 8 for more information on searching) the really difficult part remains. Can you *trust* the information presented? Is the information biased, misleading, or maybe even downright false? How do you know if it's "good" information?

Evaluating research resources

I scoured the Internet and found more than 100 pages dedicated to the evaluation of Web content, and most seemed pretty reasonable. Generally, they asked the searcher to consider these areas when trying to decide if a site is accurate:

✔ Is the site trustworthy, that is, is it from a recognized and familiar source? Does the site offer direct links to the author of the information for verification purposes? (National Geographic is a whole lot more credible than "Joe's Alligator Page" when trying to find out what kind of alligator ate the school's prize football.)

✔ Is the site up to date? Are the resources the most current available? (Okay, so it may be more up-to-date than your textbook, but is that good enough?)

✔ Does the author site bibliographic information useful in finding the primary source of information? (Watch for phrases like "research says" and "virtually all" that are unsubstantiated — journalists call those "weasel words.")

✔ Is the site really a clever advertisement or sponsored by an organization that might directly or indirectly bias the information you're collecting? (I once did a simple activity that asked students to use the Internet to figure out how far a specific hotel was from Disney World. I got five answers from five different sites. The hotel, not surprisingly, gave the shortest distance estimate.)

✔ Does the information make sense? Is there other conflicting information available on the same topic? (Do cacti really make good socks?)

✔ Does the site ask for personal information in order to give you information? (Remind students never, never, never to give out personal information on the Internet.)

It'd be very easy, should you so choose, to create a *rubric* (loosely defined as a measurement tool in the form of a checklist or other subjective measure) with each of the items above and pass this document out to your students for use each time they find something "good" on the Internet.

Here are a few sites (very credible) to check for more information about evaluating Web sites:

WWW CyberGuide Ratings for Content Evaluation

```
http://www.cyberbee.com/guide1.html
```

Evaluation of World Wide Web Sites: ERIC

```
http://ericir.syr.edu/ithome/digests/edoir9801.html
```

Critical Evaluation Surveys (from Internet guru Kathy Schrock)

```
http://www.capecod.net/schrockguide/eval.htm
```

Evaluating Student-Created Content on the Web

Recently I had the pleasure of creating and organizing a rather large contest on the Web. Students had to create Web pages based on the theme "A Student's Look at the Future of Technology" and include at least one appropriate example of QuickTime video. The judges represented education, graphic design, Web development, multimedia production, and, um, Hollywood. (I couldn't resist!)

As my team worked to create the contest evaluation tool, we struggled most with how we could bring this highly motivated, creative, and intelligent group to consensus about whether a Web page submitted for the contest was, well, good.

We tried an A, B, C, D, F grading system, a Likert-type (rate 1–5) scale, checks and x's, even happy faces/sad faces. Then we realized we were missing the point. Someone ran to the white board and wrote "It's the content, stupid." Point taken.

The result was that the judges used a simple rubric that focused on content first (adherence to the theme), then appropriate use of tools (the process), then design (aesthetics), and finally the execution of the whole thing (the technical aspects and whether the thing worked or not). After only two rounds of judging literally hundreds of sites, the team decided on the same 20 or so award winners. The rubric looked something like the one in Table 20-1.

Table 20-1	Chart for Student Web Page Evaluation			
Site	*Content/Theme*	*Technical Execution*	*Originality/ Creativity*	*Process*
School 1	5	2	4	5
School 2	4	5	4	5

The values 1–5 were based on benchmarks like the ones below (I've just given you part of the items to save space):

- ✔ Content/theme: (5) The student(s) chose accurate content that enriched and enhanced a clear theme.

- ✔ Technical execution: (5) The page/site was pleasing, easy to read and understand with intuitive navigation. The site functioned well 100 percent of the time.

- ✔ Originality and creativity: (5) The site/page presented a unique approach to the theme, including appropriate and creative use of technologies like multimedia, graphics, and design.

- ✔ Process: (5) There is demonstrable evidence of planning and organization during the process of site development. Benchmarks and feedback loops were employed during the testing phase.

Each of the aforementioned items had a list of "did they, didn't they" rules that corresponded with various point totals. All the judges had to do is find the right place on each continuum and issue points. Every judge wrote a note suggesting that this was the way we should measure the success of all student programs. (I, of course, confessed that rubrics have been used for some time in education and that they could find far better ones on the Net. I also thanked them for making me feel good.)

Of course, it makes sense to tip students off about the evaluative measures *before* they begin working so that they can measure themselves along the way to make sure they're staying on track. It's very easy when it comes to creating Web content to get so focused on design, layout, navigation, and fancy code that you forget that the real intent of the page(s) is to accomplish a specific goal, give a specific message, or elicit a certain response.

So, now the bottom line. How do you evaluate students who complete projects using the Internet or who create Internet-based projects? The answer depends on your goal. Think about whether the goal of your lesson is to do one or more of the following:

✔ Teach something *about* the Internet

✔ Teach how to *use* the Internet

✔ Teach something by *using information gained from* the Internet

Check out this site to see how George Washington High School (Pittsburgh, PA) does it (well!):

```
http://georgew.gw.pps.pgh.pa.us/rubrics/hprubric.html
```

Regardless of whether you're focusing on the Internet, the process of using this new medium, or the way the resulting information is used, you can use the same techniques of evaluation that you use for other classroom projects. Checklists, rubrics, peer-evaluation, pen-and-paper exams — they all work just fine.

Part V
The Part of Tens

The 5th Wave   By Rich Tennant

"I don't care what your e-mail friends in Europe say, you're not having a glass of Chianti with your bologna sandwich."

In this part . . .

Okay. Here's where I admit it. I am an avowed Internet junkie. When the editors suggested I come up with some short lists for this part, I figured a couple of thousand tips and techniques wouldn't take that much space. Alas, I was forced to choose a Top Ten in each category (but I crammed more in there anyway!). You'll find tips on e-mail exchanges, professional development (release days, yea!), some cool online projects, a few geek-speak terms (just for fun), and some net-trends that'll keep you at the bleeding edge of technology.

It's worth noting that lots of the tips in this part were inspired by teachers just like you. I tried soliciting business leaders and politicians, but their ideas about using the Internet in the classroom were about as exciting as riding on the team bus after losing a football game.

Chapter 21

Ten (-Plus) Ideas for E-mail Exchanges

. . . .

In This Chapter

▶ Conducting a survey

▶ Reporting the news

▶ Issuing an Olympic challenge

▶ Having e-mail buddies figure out where you are

▶ Spinning a yarn

▶ Gleaming the cube

▶ Gathering newsletter information

▶ Sponsoring a scary-story contest

▶ Sending multimedia

▶ Writing to the president

▶ Finding out about a senior citizen

▶ Exchanging ideas with other teachers

. . . .

Electronic mail makes for a great way to manage your students' time on the Internet because they can do most of the work offline (without a live Internet connection). Students can use any word processor to create and edit their work, and then you or a student assistant can compile and mail the resulting files. You also can use electronic mail to share ideas with other educators.

Be sure to save your Internet-ready files as *text* (ASCII) files so that anyone can read them, regardless of whether they're using a Macintosh, a computer that uses DOS or Windows, or another kind of computer. Almost any word-processing program can read ASCII files.

Survey Says . . .

Collect e-mail addresses for schools around the country. (Check out `http://web66.coled.umn.edu` for a place to begin.) Have your students design a survey related to a topic of interest and e-mail it to your list. As responses are returned, mark a map to show which part of the country is represented.

Go wild! Possible survey topics might include the following:

- School nutrition
- Attitudes about the use of computers in schools
- Voter registration
- Community history
- Favorite clothes, foods, school subjects, famous persons, and so on
- Most vivid memory
- Favorite periodical
- Best Internet World Wide Web (WWW) site
- . . . and lots more!

News Hounds

Challenge your students to become reporters and provide perspective on local events for e-mail pals around the world. Find an issue in your community of national or global interest and have students write a news story explaining what's happening.

Encourage students to use other Internet resources to help them research their topics before writing. When you send the articles, request that the receiving student give the author constructive and specific feedback, accompanied by their own opinions about the issues or events presented.

Olympic Proportions

Have students develop Olympics-related math stumper questions and challenge their peers, via e-mail, to solve them. See who wins the first gold medal in Internet problem-solving.

Here's one to start you off: How many Olympic track and field events involve having the athlete travel more than 15 feet? (Be sure to think vertically *and* horizontally.)

Play Guess Where

Create a geographic scavenger hunt. Have your students prepare a list of geographic features and prominent landmarks in your area and challenge other schools across the Internet to identify the location of your school. If students get stumped, have them visit one of the many geographic servers on the Internet. These geographic servers help students match landforms and other characteristics with specific locations; you even learn the latitude and longitude. (Point your Web browser to `www.altavista.com` and use the keyword search term *geography* to find one.)

Story Starters

This tried-and-true activity works on the Internet, too. Simply generate 8 or 10 thematically based story starters (prompts) and trade them via e-mail with other schools. For a really interesting twist, have each recipient add only one or two sentences (or paragraphs) and pass it along to the next student. The result is a sort of global effort.

Gleaming the Cube

The phrase *gleaming the cube* is known to skateboarders everywhere. It's part of a language born of California culture and skateboarders' wit. The Internet is a particularly good place to explore the jargon of skateboarding and any other of an amazing variety of sports, professions, industries, and activities. Challenge your students to build their own skateboarder's dictionary illustrated with information from the Net and from more traditional magazines.

Newsletter Swap

Offer to cross-publish newsletter articles with a school from another area. Have your students create and exchange general interest stories for publication in a special column in your school newsletter. Be sure that in the byline you list the writer's name, e-mail address, and the tag ". . . from the Internet!"

Don't forget to send a copy of your completed newsletter back to the other school via snail mail for inclusion in the school's or class's scrapbook.

Things That Go Bump

Sponsor a scary-story contest via the Internet. Write to several schools and work with teachers and students there to design criteria for the story and the contest. Make arrangements with a local newspaper to publish the winner. Be sure to request a short biography from the winner that includes the author's city, state, and school.

Project-rich site for students and teachers

It's amazing what some people can do with a little time and a great idea. While surfing around for sites for this edition of *Internet For Teachers*, I stumbled across a site created by a guy named Dave Leahy. It's called "Connecting Students" (see the figure below) and it's a rich link list, by category, of tons of useful resources.

My favorite is his listing of quizzes on the Internet. I burned an hour of so of precious writing time trying my hand at some of them — a totally humbling experience, but I learned a lot! Visit Dave's site at

```
http://www.connectingstudents.
com/interact.htm
```

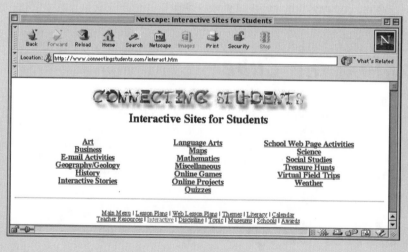

Multimedia Mania

Text isn't the only thing you can send via e-mail. You can attach files, too! (See Chapter 11.) Schools everywhere are harnessing the power of multimedia, putting together QuickTime movies and HyperStudio stacks to exchange around the world. How about a digital snapshot of your town or school for sharing with others? Who's to say that your next school yearbook won't include some input from international friends!

Send a Letter to the President

Ask your students to draft letters to the president of the United States. As you're reminding them to dot their *i*'s and cross their *t*'s, discuss how to write a persuasive letter. Mail their masterpieces to president@whitehouse.gov. They get a response from an automated e-mail answering machine or, occasionally, a real person. Word has it that the president actually sees a few of these electronic letters.

Note that you can also contact most of the folks in Congress via e-mail. Call your congressional offices or check the Internet for their addresses.

Interview a Senior Citizen

Arrange for students to develop a list of questions to ask the oldest person they know. Have them try to find out as much as possible about the person's life and times. Enter the resulting raw data into an e-mail message and zip it off to another classroom somewhere on the Internet. The receiver's task is to create a short biographical sketch, based on the data they've received, and return a finished product to its owner. Publish the results in your school or community newspaper or on your own Web site.

Start a Lesson Plan Chain Letter

Sending lots of mail to folks you don't know is a no-no on the Internet. A couple of lawyers plastered the Net with an advertisement once, and they're still getting complaints.

You might try a variation of a multiposted, or chain, letter, though. Simply create a mail message to two of your friends asking for their favorite teaching idea. Mail it along with a note to pass it on and a request to have each subsequent letter sent to your address. Before long, you have more ideas than you can fit on your hard drive. Be sure you include a cut-off date in your letter so you don't still get mail ten years from now.

A Few More Ideas from Other Net-Teachers

I'm warning you, this Internet stuff can get out of hand. Try one project and you and everyone around you are suddenly clamoring for more access and more time to do projects online. There are so many possibilities that you could literally plan an entire curriculum focused on Net-projects like the preceding ones. Below are a few more snippets of activities I've picked up from fellow net-surfing teachers. They tell me that the response from students and participating teachers was overwhelmingly positive. Use them at your own risk. :-)

- ✔ **Research exchange:** Exchange research from the Internet on a given topic.

- ✔ **Literature swap:** Exchange literature that represents the students' own culture or environment.

- ✔ **Poems plus:** Create poetry on a chosen theme and exchange it for illustration by the students who receive it.

- ✔ **Electronic park:** Swap descriptions of the world's first electronic dinosaur and have recipients create a name and illustration for each creature. (No fair writing about your first computer — even though it's a dinosaur. One of my first computers, a Mac 512K, is now a real-live fish tank in my den. I'm a firm believer in recycling.)

Chapter 22

Ten Tips for Teaching Others about the Internet

In This Chapter

▶ TTOM

▶ Rounding up resources

▶ Sharing your ideas

▶ Going cybercamping

▶ Taking a surfin' safari

▶ Getting to the princip(al) of the thing

▶ Exploring e-commerce

▶ Sleuthing elementary-style

▶ Brainstorming bookmarks

▶ Creating a wacky Web site

*I*n the next decade, more than 2 million new teachers are expected to join the workforce. In 1999, fewer than 10 percent of teacher preparation programs required a working knowledge of the Internet as part of a pre-service program. Couple that with an aging (aren't we all) in-service force for whom an Internet course, or even a computer course, during their teacher preparation programs was rare or non-existent and you get into some pretty thorny issues. Namely, we're pouring millions of dollars into instructional technology and frantically wiring classrooms, and then plopping equipment in front of educators who haven't had the time or opportunity to learn what to do with it.

The good news is that education has risen to the challenge of "teaching their own" through innovative staff development courses, education trade shows, instructional media, and more. Over the last few years, professional development in technology has blossomed into a full-blown industry and has become an obsession for many schools that are serious about getting the most for their money.

Here are my favorite ideas for helping to give a technology booster shot to your friends and colleagues. Have fun with this and don't be afraid to try a few of these ideas — I think you'll be delighted with the results.

TTOM

Everyone likes a party. Why not celebrate every month of the school year by recognizing a Technology Teacher of the Month? Grab an old CD, paint it and mount it to a plaque or thread it on a shoelace, and award it at your monthly faculty meeting to the one faculty or staff member who has demonstrated innovative thought in the use of technology with students, parents, or peers. Make sure to have nomination forms and keep an idea book that everyone can share. Sit back and watch the competition begin!

Resource Roundup

Pop down to the hallway outside the principal's office before school one day and snag the first 20 or so people you see. Coerce them with coffee and doughnuts (after the activity!) to visit the computer lab for a 15-minute activity that will change the way they look at the Internet.

When the class is assembled, have each one of them fire up a browser and search for the ten best sources for information about their subject matter of choice (or for a unit or topic they're currently teaching). Teach them how to bookmark the files. Save the files (using the File⇨Save As command) into bookmark files and distribute them throughout the school. Do this three or four times and you'll have quite a bookmark library! (But don't forget the doughnuts and coffee!)

Gettin' Tricky with It

Challenge teacher-friends to log on to the Internet and share at least one lesson plan with the rest of the planet. If you don't want them logging into adult sites (ha!), you can suggest that they visit www.apple.com/hotnews and subscribe to the Learning Interchange, a rich community of educators and educational activities, or stop by Classroom Connect's site at www.classroom.com.

Talk to the participants in this activity about how the Web is becoming more personalized and how there are increasingly more opportunities for two-way communication. Challenge them to return to one of the aforementioned sites and share more ideas of their own.

CyberCamping

Arrange with a local camping spot (scout or 4H camp with electricity) to hold a technology camp for educators. Bring in the best staff development providers, ideas, and people together for a week-long immersive camping and computing experience. This idea works well with kids; why not with adults? A little silicon and marshmallows never hurt anyone.

Surfin' Safari

Everyone loves a contest. Imagine picking up your daily bulletin one day and reading:

"Win a dinner for two at <insert really cool restaurant name> just by finding an ocelot. Details in the media center after school today."

When they arrive, tell them that you have a box of topics (related to your school's current curriculum). Each person draws a topic (ocelots could be one of them!) and has 24 hours to use the Internet to find as much information as they can on the subject. The twist? The information must be presented as a list of statements like "I found out that . . ." or "I discovered that . . ." written on poster board and accompanied by a bookmark list. Post the final posters in your teacher work room, media center, or classroom. Draw from the participants for the grand prize. (By the way, I've never come across a restaurant yet who wouldn't donate a meal for the cause of educational technology. Perhaps that's why I could lose a few pounds?)

It's the Princip (al) of the Thing

During one memorable staff development course that introduced principals to computers (back in the very early days), I watched a principal pick up a mouse, turn it around, point it at the computer monitor, and click the mouse button furiously. He turned to his neighbor, an equally clueless administrator, and exclaimed, "How do you turn this thing on?" (To this day, I get a chuckle out of that one!) That same administrator, by the way, now runs a school whose teachers are some of the most prepared to integrate technology of any I've ever seen.

Moral of the story — construct and deliver a professional development course "for administrators only." Begin with helping them discover how the Internet can bring research and other useful tools to their desktops, and remind them how useful this information can be in decision-making. Unfortunately, we've left out many administrators in our zeal to offer professional development to classroom teachers. A more informed administrator will make better decisions that will make a big difference in teaching and learning with technology in your school or district.

Let's Go Shopping

Give everyone in your professional development course $100,000 "e-dollars" and have them visit online shopping establishments and see how they'd spend it. Start at www.amazon.com and explore what happens when specialized search engines and e-commerce meet. Visit real estate sites, hardware manufacturers, and so on to give the participants a real feel for shopping on the Net. Discuss site security (see Chapter 9) and the benefits of buying through the Net. *Caution:* At no time should a credit card ever leave *your* wallet!

It's Elementary

If you have a Macintosh lab, corral your staff and have them poke around using the built-in Sherlock search engine. (Choose Sherlock from the Apple menu.) Practice entering plain English phrases like:

- Why is the sky blue?
- How many legs does a millipede have?
- Who is the political leader of Afghanistan?

You'll be impressed with the results. Discuss the merits of using different search engines and indices in your classroom activities.

Bonzai Bookmarks

This one works with teachers *and* students. It's pretty simple. Just write a topic on the chalkboard and have everyone in the classroom (with a computer) or computer lab focus on building a site list (bookmark or Favorites list) based on that topic. Before you begin, create a list of criteria participants should use to decide if a site is worth for inclusion.

Wacky Web

There's nothing like home-cooked meals. There's nothing like the experience of baking your own Web site, either. Nowadays you can create Web pages in minutes using Claris Home Page, Go Live! CyberStudio, and most word processors. It's easier than you think. Check out Chapter 10 for some tips on getting started. For an in-depth activity, surf to www.amazon.com and buy a copy of *Web Publishing For Teachers* (published by IDG Books Worldwide, Inc.). My accountant will thank you!

Chapter 23

After Recess: Ten Net Trends You Should Know

In This Chapter

▶ Sharing one box, one connection

▶ Learning anywhere, anytime

▶ Finding information needles in the Internet haystack

▶ Building a customized Web home

▶ Shopping from the sofa

▶ Going online with SIS

▶ Maximizing screen time

▶ Grabbing "just-in-time" information

▶ Learning 24/7

▶ Talking with your toaster?

I'm no soothsayer, but I do read a lot. I also get to attend lots of technology conferences both inside and outside the field of education (including the National Educational Computing Conference, www.necc.org, and Internet World, the megaconferences for those of us who spend all our time wired). I love to talk with lots of people and get ideas about what may be the next great thing in the world of the Internet and educational technology. I use that information when I talk with school districts about teaching and learning and when I get the pleasure of talking with folks like you at my event keynotes.

Whether you're planning technology or just learning things for yourself, you may find these snippets of a possible future useful. Watch closely over the next year or so as these concepts turn into reality. If I'm right, you can say you read it here; if I'm wrong, please carefully rip out this chapter and feed it to your intelligent shredder.

One Box, One Connection

The pundits call it *convergence*. I call it *one box does it all*. As companies merge and buy each other out and people figure out new ways to combine technologies like the Internet, your TV (digital video), your trips to the mall (online shopping), and your classroom (online curriculum), you'll see more technology sharing between the oddest couples.

Wherever/Whenever Technology

Some of the hottest technologies are PDAs (personal digital assistants), little computers that can contain records, calendars, and small programs and can keep you connected (via e-mail and Web browsing). In schools, portable computers (laptops) and other devices are creeping in as budgets allow. Many colleges and universities have been requiring the purchase of laptop computers for some time now. The day will come in our lifetime (unless you're 99 going on 100) that each student will carry some kind of portable learning device that'll probably connect to the world via wireless networking (or have 300 foot cables). They're getting more rugged, more fully featured, and less expensive. All these things make these devices perfect for the classroom. Watch for this trend to get a kick-start when wireless networking goes to school.

Finders, Keepers

Nothing is quite as confusing as entering a search term in an online search engine on the Web (see Chapter 8) and getting 2,000 possible choices of places to find information. Enter smart search engines. These Web-based programs allow plain English phrases and actually *learn* from your browsing habits. One example of the current systems that works well and is a peek into the future is Sherlock, a search engine built in to every Mac running Mac OS 8.5 or higher — see Figure 23-1 for a glimpse.

Plain English queries give a list of relevance-ranked results that you can save, summarize, or, with a click, launch your browser and see the site. It's so easy, it's scary. Watch for search *assistants* to get more intelligent, easier to use, and more integrated into the baseline tools we all use.

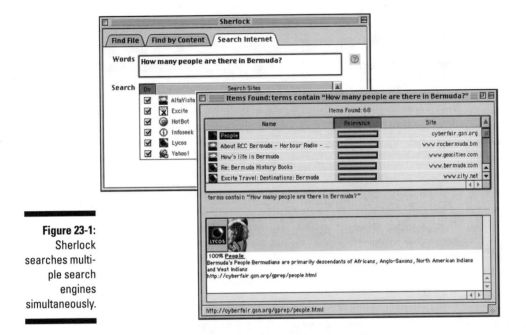

Figure 23-1:
Sherlock searches multiple search engines simultaneously.

Find It Your (Net) Way

When I sign on to Amazon (www.amazon.com) to buy books (yes, I'm a word junkie), the Web site greets me with my name and a customized listing of books, music, and video (based on items I've bought in the past). The accuracy of the profile is amazing. After I choose my book, video, or CD, I click Add to My Shopping Cart and proceed to check out. The system already knows my billing address, credit card number, and more (it's a secure system). With one more click (and one or two days' wait), I get more goodies for rainy days. I've found the same wonderful options at Apple's Online Education Store (www.apple.com/education/store), Nordstroms (www.nordstroms.com), 1-800-Flowers (www.1800flowers.com), and more. What a delightful way to spend all your hard-earned cash and be a hermit at the same time!

Other Web *portals* (entry points), like Excite (see Figure 23-2) and Yahoo!, also offer customization options based on what kind of information you'd like to see when you sign on to the Internet each day. You can get stock reports, weather, TV listings, news, and other things delivered right to your desktop — and *you* choose how much and how often you wish to view the info. It's free, too! Here's to personalization!

Figure 23-2:
Excite offers a cus-tomized portal to the Web.

The Global Shopping Network

Just when you thought you were safe by avoiding shopping malls and the Home Shopping Network, along comes electronic commerce (e-commerce). In the next few years, e-commerce is likely to surpass traditional catalog sales in volume and may, ultimately, actually pass in-person shopping. Educators aren't left out, either. Folks like IDG Books Worldwide, Inc., (the publishers of the *...For Teachers* and other series) even have a place for you to purchase online (www.idgbooks.com). Watch for e-commerce to be the retail place to be in the coming millennium.

SIS Goes Internet

Most schools use some type of computer software to track academic progress, keep student records easily accessible, and manage everything from lunch counts to who's in third-period class. Nowadays, companies that make such student information systems (SIS) are racing to bring the power of their programs to intranets (internal networks) everywhere. Watch for secure internal information networks to grow and flourish in schools in the next few years. The one that makes the transition from current systems to these new systems easiest and more affordable wins.

Screen Time

First it was television; then video games drew kids' eyeballs from networks to chasing digital space aliens. These days, kids are drawn to the Internet. Now they not only get virtually limitless channels and multi-player games, but they also get person-to-person communication and a wild and wacky world of information about anything their heart desires. Our challenge, of course, is to help them understand and evaluate what they've seen. (See Chapter 22 for more information about credibility and source analysis of Internet content.) Watch for more emphasis in your professional development courses on understanding and assessing the value of Internet content. You'll also find lots of people vying for your student's eyeballs with commercial-laden "curriculum" sites.

I Want It Now!

Letters take a week; phone calls a few seconds. Enter the Internet, with its seemingly limitless forms of interpersonal extravaganza — Web cameras, instant messages, e-mail, personal Web pages, chats, and more. Watch for an increasing reliance on the Internet as a communication tool. Just-in-time communication will meld with just-in-time learning. Your school will rely on the net more to communicate with students and parents; you'll soon vote, pay taxes, and even order meals over the Internet. Yum!

Learn 24/7

One of the biggest issues for incorporating technology in to the curriculum is that your students often have more time to learn about the Internet and other technologies than you do. Professional development takes time, usually before or after school, and missing your classes to attend seminars takes lots of extra time-consuming planning. Enter the Internet and the world of online professional development. Folks like Apple Computer (www.apple.com/education/staffdev) and Classroom Connect (www.classroom.org) now offer online courses 24 hours a day, 7 days a week. It's easy and inexpensive, and on occasion you'll even get credits (or even work toward your degree) at major colleges and universities. Watch for this business to really take off in the decade to come.

Talking Toasters?

I guess it's inevitable that things with chips in them will begin to talk to each other. Your refrigerator will order a new gallon of milk when you've drunk it all, your toilet will call the doctor if something's wrong, and your personal digital assistant will alert a parent when little Johnny skips class. I guess technology is both scary and wonderful. Hold on; it's going to be an interesting ride!

So there you have it. My prognostications for what will happen with the Web. Of course I have lots more, but I have to save something for the 4th edition.

Chapter 24

Ten Cool Sources for Online Projects

In This Chapter

▶ Terra Fermi?

▶ Tammy's Tips

▶ The Learning Interchange

▶ Connected Classrooms

▶ The Project Center

▶ Globe Trotting

▶ The Headbone Zone

▶ The Quest, NASA Style

▶ Kids Connect

▶ Weather, Or Not?

▶ Sister, Sister

*I*f you read this chapter, or even skim through it, you'll be stuck by the vast creativity that educators and others around the world have shown in building classroom activities. However, as a result of reading these ideas, you must make a promise to think of one great idea and find a way to share it on the Internet with other educators. The medium is only as powerful as the message, after all.

This chapter gives you ten of my favorite starting points for classroom activities on the Web. Each site has been tested by educator friends and is certified as kid energizing. Try them; you'll like them.

Terra Fermi?

`http://www-ed.fnal.gov/trc/projects/project_index.html`

Designed to demonstrate principles of engaged learning and effective use of technology by K-12 teachers who participated in staff development programs at Fermi National Accelerator Laboratory, a U.S. Department of Energy National Laboratory, in Batavia, IL.

Tammy's Tips

`www.essdack.org/tips/projects.html`

A whole bunch of great activities for the Internet, ClarisWorks (AppleWorks), HyperStudio, and more. This site is a product of ESSDACK (Education Services and Staff Development Association of Central Kansas).

The Learning Interchange

`www.apple.com/education/ali`

Apple Computer's repository of online professional development and more. Don't worry, Windows users are welcomed with open arms.

Connected Classrooms

`www.classroom.net`

Connected Classrooms is a library of amazing resources for educators of all stripes. Created for teachers, by teachers, this is a must-stop in your collection of activities on the Internet.

The Project Center

`www.eduplace.com/projects/index.html`

Houghton-Mifflin's entry into the online curriculum fray. Well done, dynamic, and worth a visit.

Globe Trotting

www.globe.gov/

Global Learning and Observations to Benefit the Environment (GLOBE) is a worldwide network of students, teachers, and scientists working together to study and understand the global environment. Students and teachers from more than 6,500 schools in more than 80 countries work with research scientists to learn more about our planet.

The Headbone Zone

www.headbone.com/

You can find two major resources for your classroom at Headbone. And they're both free! If you are looking for a structured and engaging way to teach your students Internet research skills, check out the Headbone Derby series. (The Derby Teacher's Guide has all you need to get started.) Or if you're looking to use the Internet in conjunction with a local newspaper, try the site's NIE (Newspapers In Education) Cyber Extension: Hispanic Heritage.

The Quest, NASA Style

http://quest.arc.nasa.gov/

NASA continues to have some of the best educational materials available on this planet (and perhaps several others). NASA Quest is a compendium of online projects, mailing lists, and lots more.

Kids Connect

www.ala.org/ICONN/kidsconn.html

Kids Connect is "a question-answering, help and referral service to K-12 students on the Internet" with a worthy goal — to help students access and use information on the Internet effectively and efficiently. KidsConnect is a component of ICONnect, which is a technology initiative of the American Association of School Librarians (AASL), a division of the American Library Association.

Weather, or Not

http://school.discovery.com/lessonplans/programs/wonder-sofweather/activities.html

If you're an Earth Science or General Science (or any science) teacher, you'll love this site. The good folks at the Discovery Channel have created a ton of activities that compliment their video and live broadcast offerings, including this site featuring cool ideas for studying the weather that will lift your students to the stratosphere of learning. (How corny can I get?)

Sister, Sister!

www.siss.org/Welcome.html

Leave it to the good folks at The Society for International Sister Schools to come up with the ultimate source for International keypals. The SISS connection helps students develop a sensitivity toward other cultures and develop a world view in a safe environment.

Chapter 25

Ten Virtual Field Trips

In This Chapter

▶ It Takes a Village

▶ A Bridge Too Far

▶ Interview with a Rock Star

▶ Cool Breezes

▶ For Your Health

▶ Ramblin' Runes

▶ Walkabout

▶ How'd They Do That?

▶ You Were There

▶ Web to the Edge

*E*ver been to Wales? I went several years ago with my father. We traversed castles, hoisted a few brews in more than one local pub, and dodged sheep in the one-lane country motorways. As I was brainstorming ideas for this book, I decided to use the Internet to see how much I could find about Wales — a somewhat vain effort to revive my memory about a beautiful experience.

The good news is that I found maps, pictures, Welsh language studies, satellite images, travel movies, and even audio files (my dad loves to sing Welsh hymns). So was this the next best thing to being there? Well, not quite. It's *high-tech* without the *high-touch*. The online experience didn't become truly magical until I shared it (again) with my dad. The lesson? As you work with Web-based activity, be sure to have some kind of personal (high-touch) interaction that follows. Sharing your experiences enriches the learning and offers the learner an opportunity to reiterate learned knowledge during the sharing process. To this day, my dad still signs his e-mails with a Welch "caru" — that, for those that don't know the Cardiff lingo, means love. <grin>

The inspiration from Wales lingers, so I've included an opportunity for you and your students to share knowledge in each of the Virtual Field Trips below.

It Takes a Village

Propose to your students that it's their job to collect information on the Net necessary to build, from the ground up, a small village like those (still) found in the most untouched regions of South America or Africa. After groups of students get an idea about what info they'll need, have them search for the particulars — things like "How do I build a thatch hut?" and "How much does it rain in Ecuador?"

Share: Find a way for your students to illustrate what they've learned — either on the computer (by using HyperStudio, a Web page, or a presentation program) or through an art activity. Be sure to spend some time talking about what info could not be found and where else (besides the Net) they could get the necessary information.

A Bridge Too Far

Brainstorm a list of famous bridges with your students. (I'll bet most students can't create a list longer than two or three.) Challenge them to use the Web to find other bridges and answer the following questions about each one:

✔ What makes the bridge unique?

✔ What impact would removing the bridge have on the surrounding community?

✔ How was the bridge built?

Ask students to exchange information and pictures (and bookmarks) and come to a consensus about the bridge that they would most like to visit.

Share: Have students build a replica of a favorite bridge from Popsicle sticks, toothpicks, or any other building material.

Interview with a Rock Star

Chances are your students have used the Internet to search for information about their favorite singer, actor, musical group, or equally famous (or infamous) person. Here's their chance to get to know their favorites *for class credit.*

Have students select a favorite celebrity and search the Net for information with the ultimate goal of producing, either in print or on video, an interview with the person or group. Encourage students to check both "official" and "unofficial" sites (discuss credibility of online info!), look through online tabloids, and search news engines (Wall Street Journal, USA Today, CNN, and so on) for the skinny.

Share: Crank up the role-playing engines and bring the event to life in your classroom. Make sure to roll the videotape!

Cool Breezes

It's everyone's dream: Cool breezes on a tropical island. Wait — do those really exist? Have students use the Net to plan a trip to the most remote island you can find. Challenge them to find airfares and hotels (if it's so remote there are no hotels, have them find out where to shop for a really huge tent).

Share: Ask students to create a travel brochure or Web site enticing other visitors to their deserted island.

For Your Health

Feed a fever, starve a cold? Or is it the other way around? Medical information is abundant on the Internet. Some of it not very credible, and some is downright dangerous. Drive this point home by asking students to research the question:

"What should you do for a fever?"

Finish the activity with a discussion of evaluating sites (see Chapter 9 for more on that) and the inherent dangers of getting medical advice from anyone other than a personal physician.

Share: Invite a local doctor to your classroom for some "Is it really true that . . . ." Q&A based on the info your students find during this activity.

Ramblin' Runes

There are no less than 20 sites on the Internet where students can read about, or participate in, "virtual" archaeological digs. I suggest this activity because the quality of these sites, in general, and that of the activities suggested there, is very high.

Begin this activity by searching the Net for the words "archaeological dig" and finding three or four sites with activities; then, turn your students loose.

Share: Grab a whole bunch of sand and dump it onto your classroom floor. Embed (when students are not looking) lots of little artifacts (big ones, too) in the sand and have them sift through, noting the position of each find. Suggest they present their findings in an HTML-based presentation. Throw in some digital pictures of them working to make the activity really shareable.

Walkabout

The Aussies have a way of looking at things that is truly unique. One curious and awe-inspiring native tradition is the Walkabout. First, get students excited by having them watch one of the terrific instructional films recounting Walkabouts in the Australian outback or read the interactive book *From Alice to Ocean: Alone Across the Outback*, by Rick Smolan & Robyn Davidson (Against All Odds Productions). Then, have students study Australia through the Web and plan their own.

Share: It's possible, of course, to do a "Yankee walkabout" in your own town or city. Now I'm not suggesting you or your students ditch school for a week to get in touch with nature, but you could have them ask their parents or others about experiences they've had that helped them become more enlightened. This should be a very interesting activity, don't you think?

How'd They Do That?

I always wanted to know how an M&M was made. It's not so much how the chocolate gets inside, it's how do they do it without creating a seam or visible "holding point." The candy shell is absolutely flawless, save the m emblazoned on top. (Can you tell I was eating M&Ms while writing this chapter? They melt in your mouth, not on your keyboard.)

Ask students to choose a common candy and search the Internet to see what they can find out about the manufacturing process.

Share: Have students write a short description of their understanding of the process. Compile the writing and send it along to the candy company. If they send you extra M&Ms, of course, send them directly to Bard Williams, care of IDG Books, Worldwide, Inc.

You Were There

This is a twenty-minute activity I tried with students in a summer Boy Scout Explorer camp. It worked. Brainstorm a list of the 10 or 15 most important events of the last millennium and write them on separate slips of paper. Fold each paper and stuff them in a bag and have students choose one. Start the clock and have small groups find out everything they can about the event in ten minutes of Web search time. Wait! Where did the other ten minutes go? That's the twist — the first ten minutes is spent *before* students begin to research; they develop a search strategy (keywords, starting points, and so on).

Share: Some role-playing or simulated newscasts can jazz this activity up.

Web to the Edge

What does the future hold for technology? Will your next computer be named for a Life Savers flavor and be small enough to wear on your wrist? Challenge students to create a Web page called "A Student's Look at the Future of Technology." This one was inspired by a successful Web-creation project by Apple Computer in 1999. See the results of the competition on the Apple Web site at `www.apple.com/education/k12`.

Share: Post the Web sites on your school's server for all to see and enjoy. You'll think back on one or more ideas ten years from now when your students have made their second million.

Part VI
Appendixes

The 5th Wave — By Rich Tennant

"A BRIEF ANNOUNCEMENT, CLASS — AN OPEN-FACED PEANUT BUTTER SANDWICH IS NOT AN APPROPRIATE REPLACEMENT FOR A MISSING MOUSEPAD."

In this part . . .

I once asked a 6th grade Life Science student, "What does your appendix do?" His reply was, "I don't know, but my mom just had hers taken out, and we're waiting around to see what doesn't work anymore." (You should've heard what the same kid said when we talked about the brain!)

These appendixes are designed for those of you who, like me, occasionally stare at the computer and think, "It doesn't work anymore." I've stuffed into these chapters some helpful hints in case you're one of a bunch of people who still don't have an on-ramp to the infoway. There's also a list of things to do when things go wrong, some cyber-terms defined in plain English, and a nifty description of what's on the CD.

The only thing certain about the Internet is that it will change. Thanks again for buying this book; it's nice to see you're changing, too!

Appendix A

When Things Go Wrong

• •

Murphy's law is alive and well in the classroom. From time to time, hardware and software seem to become possessed by mischievous spirits that are bent on making your life miserable.

When using the Internet and Internet tools, you find that some things are unavoidable — problems such as busy signals and data that just doesn't move from place to place the way it should.

Here are a few basic tips that can save you some trouble. I've divided the tips into the Internet, hardware, software, and a special section for modems *(Nightmare on Internet Street)*.

The Internet

You guessed it. Sometimes there's absolutely nothing wrong with your hardware or your software — it's the network. This situation may be the most frustrating kind of problem, because you're pretty helpless to do anything about it. Caution: These errors usually occur right in the middle of a major project, presentation, or anytime your principal or superintendent or department chairperson signs on to the Net.

Is it busy, or is it dead?

Web browsers like Netscape Navigator often display a message like this:

```
A network error occurred: unable to connect to server [TCP
Error: EBADF]  or "Error 404 - Server not available." The
server may be down or unreachable.
```

Arggghhh! Receiving messages like this can mean one of four things:

- ✔ The server is too busy. Your connection's fine, but a couple thousand folks are ahead of you, clicking their hearts out to get to the site.
- ✔ The server is temporarily or permanently "sick" because of technical problems.
- ✔ The pipeline is clogged (the network's just too busy).
- ✔ You mistyped the URL (this one you CAN do something about!).

In general, if you get an error similar to the one described above, try retyping the URL or waiting a few minutes before you try logging on again.

Picture pains

Sooner or later you run into an icon that looks like a broken picture (in Navigator) or a white box with a red x in it (Internet Explorer). This means the images are unreadable because of bad or missing data, or because your connection is flaky.

Usually, you can just click the "broken picture" icon and the picture reloads. Sometimes you can also click the "re-load" button in Netscape and it reloads the entire page, "fixed" graphics and all.

Cold as Ice

The browser began to download a page and then . . . nothing. The computer froze. The mouse is dead. Nothing's happening. Those are the symptoms, what's the cause?

Usually the reason a browser freezes a computer is that your RAM memory is full. In plain English, this means that the chips inside your computer that temporarily hold information sent to them by programs or through networks like the Internet are full, and there isn't even a byte or bit left over to process transactions like displaying an error message or allowing you a graceful exit from the program.

To combat the freeze-monster, you've got several options:

- ✔ Dump your browser cache: The *cache* is a certain amount of space set aside by your browser program for downloading and temporarily storing the contents of Web pages (graphics and text). The cache improves browser performance because if you visit the site again before the images *expire* (are pushed out by newer images) from your cache, your computer doesn't have to download all those images again. Although the cache is technically a *disk cache*, (that is, the images are saved on your hard drive) if it gets too full, it takes too much memory (RAM) to sort through it all and your computer just gives up. Dump the browser cache (this can be done through your browser's Preferences).

✔ Raise the memory allocation on your application: Some programs tell the computer how much memory to "reserve" just in case they want to expand and do something crazy. Sometimes the amount set aside isn't enough for the action you've requested and things just crash. On a PC, protected memory usually takes care of this automatically (theoretically). On a Mac, you can click on the original application icon and choose Get Info from the Edit menu. Bump up the bottom number (Preferred memory) a bit and relaunch the program. (You can also Control+click the program icon and choose Get Info from the resulting pop-up menu.) For more info, see "Crash & Burn" later in this appendix.

✔ Get more RAM for your computer: Memory is a hot commodity and goes up and down in price faster than kids exit the building during a fire drill. Watch for sales. Buy the memory, and install it yourself (in most cases it's very easy).

✔ Run fewer programs at one time: If you are like me, you'll launch Microsoft Word, your Web browser, and a couple more programs all at once because you have a short attention span and lack the ability to instantly access other information. Unfortunately, even though you're not using these programs, they eat up RAM space and can cause computer crashes just by being open.

Troubleshooting Hardware

If you've been teaching for any time at all, you know that the number-one rule in troubleshooting a classroom computer is to check for mischief. Curious students who are well meaning (and especially those you are not so well meaning) can wreak havoc with the click of the mouse or a kick of a plug.

Its dark in here!

When nothing shows up on your monitor, make sure that everything's okay with the power plug and the physical computer-to-monitor connection. Also, check the display controls to make sure that someone hasn't put you in the dark with a twist of the brightness or contrast knobs.

Crash and burn

Sometimes your computer will "freeze" while it's connected to the Internet; this problem usually indicates some kind of memory conflict or a corruption in your software. The solution varies according to what type of computer you're using and how you're accessing the Internet.

If you are using a PC that is running Windows and it freezes, the best thing to do is to press Ctrl+Alt+Delete, which brings up a dialog box that allows you to close programs that aren't responding. If you can't find the offending program, click the Shut Down button. Turning your machine off breaks the telephone/network connection and frees up whatever was blocking your transmission. If a simple reboot doesn't work, the next step is to try reinstalling your Internet software program. Still having trouble? Check to make sure that you're not running too many programs at the same time.

If crashes or screen-freezes happen frequently and you're using a Macintosh, try increasing the memory allocation for the program.

Here's how to increase the memory allocation for a Macintosh program (application):

1. **Single-click the program's icon.**

2. **Choose File⇨Get Info.**

3. **Increase the number in the bottom Preferred size box by 200 or so.**

4. **Close the dialog box.**

5. **Double-click the program's icon to restart the program.**

Ultimately, the solution may be to purchase more RAM for your computer. I recommend a minimum of 16MB for today's Internet applications, and 32MB or more is optimum on a Power Mac or a PC running Windows 95.

Troubleshooting Software

If things just aren't going well as your Internet journey begins, you should examine your software and the settings that enable you to make a connection to the Net. Check to make sure you've entered the correct IP address and other information into your PPP or network connection software (Dial-Up Networking in Windows 95/98). (The Cheat Sheet in the front of this book gives you a good idea of what questions to ask.)

If you're connected to the Net through a commercial online service, visit the online support areas or call the toll-free help lines for assistance. If you're connected via a commercial Internet service provider (*ISP*), give them a call and seek their advice. Because much of the software for PPP connections is freeware or shareware, ready assistance from the programmers may not be available. Your ISP has probably heard your question a thousand times before and can probably help you.

Undeliverable mail

Four things can cause your mail to be returned. Look for the reason in the "bounce" message that you receive from the host computer. Here are the most common reasons that mail doesn't get through and some ways to correct the problem.

- ✔ **Host unknown:** The Internet doesn't recognize the domain name that you entered. Check to make sure that you entered the correct address. Check your spelling, spacing, and punctuation!

- ✔ **User unknown:** The mail made it to the host computer but not to the person's address in the memory banks. Again, check to ensure that you haven't made a spelling boo-boo and resend the mail. Also, try sending a request for a correct address to `postmaster@domain` (see Chapter 10 for information on how to do this e-mail stuff).

- ✔ **Can't send:** Something's up, and the host is down. The best way to fight this problem is to wait an hour or so and try to resend your mail.

- ✔ **Service unavailable:** You've addressed your mail correctly, but the electronic postmaster is out to lunch. Sometimes this message means that the postmaster is just too busy to pay attention to your mail. Resend it later.

Network nasties

If you're connecting to the Internet through a computer that's in a network, problems accessing the Internet may be the result of improperly configured network software. Network problems can occur if you abort a program unexpectedly (thunderstorms, children tripping over cables, or turning off your computer after it freezes). Check with your network administrator to make sure that you have all the software, as well as rights and privileges, that you need to make the connection.

The Modem and the Phone Line

Several problems can ruin your day when it comes to working with your modem and phone lines. Call-waiting, noise on the line, and software that's configured incorrectly for your modem are a few of the more common problems.

Custom calling features

If your school has call waiting, you can temporarily disable it by adding *70 or 1170 before the phone number. The resulting dial-up number may look like this:

```
1170,555-1212
```

This trick disables call-waiting only for the time that you're online. After you hang up, call-waiting resumes as usual.

Can't connect

If your dial-up connection doesn't seem to work, check the software settings described in the documentation for your modem. Do they include a set of configurations (drivers) for your specific modem type? If so, are those configurations properly set up on your computer?

If you're connecting via PPP, check to see that all the numbers (IP address and so on) look correct (after you get the information that you need from your ISP). Double-check to see that your modem cable is plugged into the correct port on your computer.

If you're using a dial-up connection that's made via a telecommunications program, problems with software settings can often be signaled by random characters transmitted to your screen. That on-screen gibberish usually indicates that something in your modem setup is incorrect. Compare the settings with those provided by your ISP and correct them before you redial.

Noisy things

Noise can come from poorly installed wiring; cheaply constructed modems, interference from radios, TVs, and other electronic equipment; or even from the phone company itself. Now, everyone knows that schools traditionally have the highest quality phone wiring, right? If you're always getting dropped (or in computer terms, *punted*), you can ask the phone company to check for noise on your lines. The faster the connection speed, the more important a clean (noise-free) line becomes.

Phone extension roulette

If more than one phone in your school uses the same line, consider purchasing an in-use indicator box. These handy boxes are available at most electronics stores and can save you lots of grief. When someone else in the school is on the line, an indicator light shows that the line is unavailable.

Moving too slowly

Sometimes things just don't seem to be moving fast enough. In that case, your software may not be set to recognize your modem or connection speed. Dial-up numbers are different for some modem speeds. A 28,800 bps number, for example, sometimes won't support faster connections. Check with your ISP or commercial online service to make sure that the dial-up number you're using matches the speed that you want to use.

No dial tone

If you have everything connected but can't get a dial tone when your modem attempts to dial, something's up with your phone line. If you have an in-line switch that controls who accesses your telephone line, make sure that it's switched so that your extension is hot (or live).

If you are dialing out for the first time and can't get a dial tone, your school's phone system may not support direct dialing out. Check with the maintenance folks; you may need a dedicated phone line. Or you may just have to dial 9 to get out.

Appendix B

Glossary

address: A bunch of letters and/or numbers that tell the world who you are, followed by more letters and numbers that tell them where you are. Your Internet address looks something like this: username@domain_name. The username is your login name or account number. The domain name is the name of the computer through which you're connected to the Internet. The domain name can be a few words strung together with periods. An Internet address usually doesn't have any spaces between words or symbols, but when there are spaces, they are indicated by an "underscore" character, as in mailto:fredf@bedrock_slate.com.

AIM: America Online (*AOL*) Instant Messenger. Allows you to send and receive real-time text messages from other people on the Internet. See also *ICQ*.

alt: A newsgroup that deals with "alternative" topics; often thought of as the place where topics are born. When they grow up, they move to other classifications. Beware when you are stomping around in alt. territory; some things hiding in the bushes shouldn't be in your classroom.

America Online (AOL): A public online service that provides access to the Internet. AOL has the largest U.S. subscription base (currently over 17 million) of any of the commercial online services. Many of its subscribers are educators. AOL owns Netscape, ICQ and Compuserve.

Anarchie: A Macintosh shareware FTP program that does Archie searches. Find it on most commercial online services, or check popular FTP sites.

anonymous FTP: When you log on to someone else's computer, you may need to provide a login name and password. On some systems, logging in as "anonymous" and using your e-mail address as a password are enough to give you access to public files.

applet: A tiny computer program written in the Java programming language. The applets work with your Web browser to extend its capabilities. You can control whether or not you wish to use Java applets in your browser's Preferences.

Archie: A bunch of servers that keep track of files that are available for downloading on the Internet. It's also the name of a program that you use to search these servers. After Archie finds a file, you can get it by using FTP.

ARPAnet: The granddaddy network of the Internet. An acronym for Advanced Research Project Administration Network.

ASCII: American Standard Code for Information Interchange. Another word for characters (letters and numbers) in a text file.

attachment: Any file that accompanies an e-mail message.

bandwidth: The capacity of any electronic channel (such as a phone line) that carries data. The higher the bandwidth, the more data can pass through. This term has crept into the vocabulary of Silicon Valley folk and now also refers to a human's capacity to handle incoming data as in "I just don't have the bandwidth to complete that project right now."

baud: A unit of transmission speed. The greater the baud rate, the faster data moves from point to point.

BBS: Bulletin Board System. A system that lets people post messages and read others' messages. Usenet newsgroups are kind of like the world's largest distributed BBS.

binary file: A file that may contain words, sounds, pictures, and even movies in "raw form." Because binary code is the most basic form of digital information interchange, it can be read or executed by many different types of computers.

binhex: A program that converts a binary file, specific to a particular machine, to a text file so it can be transferred over the Net. The program can then be used to convert it back to binary for use on your computer.

bitnik: One who logs onto Cyberspace using a "pay to surf" computer terminal in a coffeehouse (a.k.a. Cybercafe).

bookmark: A Netscape Communiator term for saving a URL to a special list, accessible within the Navigator browser, that makes revisiting the link later easier. Internet Explorer refers to this link list as *favorites*.

bounce: When you send e-mail and it comes back marked as undeliverable it is said to have bounced back.

browser: A program that enables you to explore the World Wide Web (WWW). See also *Netscape Navigator* and *Internet Explorer*.

CGI (Common Gateway Interface): A programming standard used by Web servers for handling user input in forms. A CGI is an extension to a Web server that gives the server some functionality that it doesn't already have (such as database access).

chat: The electronic equivalent of CB radio. Person-to-person real-time conferencing. See also *AIM, ICQ,* and/or *IRC.*

client: A computer that uses the services of another computer or server. Technically, when you dial into the Internet, your computer becomes a client on the network known as the Internet.

communications program: A program that enables you to dial through a modem and access another computer. Examples are Microphone and Z-Term for Macintosh computers and CrossTalk and Procomm Plus for Windows computers.

cookie: A file used by browsers to save your user preferences for sites around the Internet. Cookies allow for the personalization of Web sites and make e-commerce painless. You can turn off cookies in you browser's Preferences.

CoSN: The Consortium for School Networking. A non-profit organization that supports networking in education. See www.cosn.org for more info.

Cyberspace: The digital world of computers and the information that passes between them. The term comes from the sci-fi novel *Neuromancer* by William Gibson.

Cybrarian: One who makes a living doing online research and information retrieval. Also known as a *data surfer* or a *super searcher* (Source: *Wired* magazine).

dial-up connection: You've got one of these if you access a network or the Internet by dialing a telephone number. The opposite, a *direct* connection, means the computer is always hooked into the Net.

digest: A compilation of a bunch of messages posted to a mailing list. The mailing list's moderator puts all the messages together periodically, by topic, and sends them out to all subscribers.

DNS: Domain Name Server. Geek-speak for converting Internet IP addresses, like 182.156.12.24, to Internet addresses like mit.edu. If you have your own DNS server, you can subdivide your site into your own unique domain names (phs.edu or maryvillemiddle.edu, for example).

domain name: Internet-speak for a computer on the Net. The part of an Internet address that comes after @.

dotted quad: The techno-weenie words that describe a numerical Internet address such as this one: 128.33.43.55.

download: To move data from another computer to yours. Opposite of *upload.*

e-commerce: Electronic commerce. Buying and selling stuff on the Internet. The new milleneum's threat to shopping malls.

e-purse: Short for "electronic purse" — an electronic monetary transaction card. Also e-Cash, e-Credit, and of course, e-Debt and, ultimately e-Bankruptcy.

edu: An Internet identifier for a college, university, or K–12 school.

Elm: A UNIX mail program. See also *Pine.*

e-mail: Electronic mail. Messages sent via modem or over a network.

ERIC: Educational Resources Information Center. A U.S. Department of Education entity and a clearinghouse of general information for education. Check out AskERIC at `www.askeric.org`.

Eudora: A terrific e-mail program for Macintosh and Windows computers. Both a shareware and a commercial version are available.

FAQ: Frequently Asked Questions. Commonly asked questions about a variety of topics, including learning the Internet. Reading FAQs saves you a great deal of time and embarrassment. You find FAQs in public areas of most FTP and Web sites and in the Internet areas of commercial online services.

favorites: Internet Explorer's term for saving URLs to a special list, accessible within the browser, that makes revisiting the link later easier. Netscape Navigator refers to this link list as *bookmarks.*

Fetch: A handy Macintosh FTP program from Dartmouth that enables you to transfer files.

Finger: A program that displays information about people on the Internet. If you're on a UNIX network, the finger command tells you who's currently using the system. On an Internet host computer, running Finger lets you know a user's full name and the last time that user logged on to the Net.

firewall: A computer or software program that forms the link between your network and the Internet. Firewalls can be configured to filter, screen, and monitor traffic traveling in and out of the network. Schools use firewalls to secure information that shouldn't be transmitted outside (or inside) your classroom or building-wide network.

flame: A sarcastic, critical, or obnoxious message posted to a newsgroup or sent via e-mail. Flames are neither nice nor necessary.

FTP: File Transfer Protocol. A method of transferring files across the Internet from one computer to another. Also refers to the name of a program that transfers files.

gateway: A computer that connects one network with another when the two networks use different protocols.

geek: Anyone who knows RAM from ROM or spends more time in front of a computer screen than sleeping. A term of affection (and big paychecks) in Silicon Valley.

GIF: Graphics Interchange Format. A kind of universal picture file that Macintosh and Windows computers, as well as most other computers running other operating systems can read by using a program called a GIF Viewer (pronounced "JIF" or "GIF").

Gopher: A program that runs on Internet host computers and helps you find information on the Net. The results are displayed via menus and can include documents and links to other computers. To get to Gopher, either launch a program such as TurboGopher, telnet to a Gopher server, or use your browser.

Gopherspace: That great area that Gopher searches on the Internet.

HGopher: A Microsoft Windows program that enables you to gopher information in a graphics-based environment.

hacker: Someone who knows a lot about computers and spends a lot of time on programming, surfing the Internet, and other computer-related activities. Don't confuse hackers (usually a witty, intelligent, thoughtful bunch) with _pirates_ who (often illegally) break into computer systems, usually to extract information or simply to cause trouble.

home page: The first page you see when you launch your Web browser.

host: A computer that offers resources that are usable by Internet users. You can access a host computer via telnet, FTP, or the World Wide Web. Technically, in TCP/IP, any machine connected via IP is considered a _host_ computer.

HTML: HyperText Markup Language. The language used to create a page for the Internet. The commands enable users to specify different fonts, graphics, hypertext links, and more. You can use a word processor to create a Web page if you know the HTML commands to embed.

HTTP: HyperText Transfer Protocol. The way Web pages are transferred over the Internet. Every Web address begins with `http://`.

HTTPS: HyperText Transfer Protocol-Secure. Like http but with security functions that encrypt the information sent and received. One way to check to see if a site is secure before completing on online transaction is to check for the `https://` address.

hypertext: Text found on Web pages that you can click to go to another location, page, or document, or to be linked to sounds, graphics, or movies.

ICQ: "I Seek You." Allows you to send and receive real-time text messages from other people on the Internet. See also *AIM.*

information superhighway: This is a goodie. It means lots of things. Most people think that the Internet *is* the information superhighway. They're mostly right. Stuff such as cable TV and phone company networks also qualify, though.

Internet: A bunch of computers hooked together by high-speed telephone lines and networks. The whole is greater than the sum of the parts.

Internet Explorer (IE): Microsoft's entry into the browser wars. IE contains a browser, e-mail program (Outlook Express) and more.

IP: Internet Protocol. Techno-speak for the language that computers use to route information from computer to computer on the Internet.

IRC: Internet Relay Chat. A system that enables Internet users to *chat,* or talk in real-time, by using an Internet link (rather than after a delay, as with e-mail messages).

Internet service provider (ISP): A company that supplies you with the connection that you need to access the Internet.

Java: A programming language invented by Sun Microsystems that gives your browser added functions (such as animated icons and text) and that can also be translated to your computer's hard drive in the form of little programs (called *applets*) that make Web pages "live" and interactive. Java's cool because it can run on many different kinds of computers.

JPEG: A compressed file format for pictures (pronounced: "JAY-peg").

Jughead: A program that helps you search Gopherspace. Compare to *Veronica.*

k12: A type of newsgroup that contains lots of great stuff for educators.

Killer App: The still-elusive "killer application," which will inspire even the techno-terrified to plug into new technology. The "killer app" for the Internet's first generation was probably the Web browser. Who knows what'll be next?

link: a.k.a. *hypertext link* or just *hyperlink*. The Web's way of moving with or among pages on the Internet. Links usually show up as underlined text, colored text, and are sometimes hidden behind images. Click everything!

LISTSERV: A family of programs that automatically controls, sorts, and distributes incoming messages on a mailing list server.

Lurkers: People who read message boards or discussions online but don't post any messages of their own. (These are the same people who never speak up at faculty meetings.)

MacTCP: An extension that enables your Macintosh to connect to the Internet. (On newer Macintosh computers, this control panel is replaced with TCP/IP.)

MIME: A standard for attaching binary files for sending across the Internet. MIME stands for Multipurpose Internet Mail Extensions.

mirror site: A duplicate of a Web or FTP site. Mirror sites help reduce the traffic by enabling users to choose from sites geographically closer to them.

modem: A marvelous piece of electronics that translates what you type and create on your computer into a signal that can be sent through a phone line and recreated by another modem on the other end.

moderated: In newsgroups and mailing lists, it means that someone's watching the list or newsgroup to ensure that people don't go crazy and get off the topic or start flaming other users.

MPEG: A compressed file format for movies.

Netscape Communicator: Communicator contains other programs that make Web work easy, including Navigator (the Web browser), Messenger (the mail program), and Composer (the Web page editing application).

Netscape Navigator: Netscape's entry into the browser wars. Available alone or with the larger Communicator (see *Netscape Communicator*) suite of programs.

'Netting: The act of logging online and surfing or chatting it up.

network: Basically, a bunch of computers strung together by wire. They could be wired together at one site (local area networks, or LANs) or connected via telephone or satellite (wide area networks, or WANs).

newbie: Someone who's new to the Internet. I must still be a newbie, because I discover something new every time I log on.

newsgroup: A bulletin board system on the Internet that's organized by topic.

newsreader: A program that enables you to read and respond to newsgroups on the Internet easily.

node: A computer that's hooked to the Internet.

NREN: National Research and Education Network. An effort to bring high-speed computing to schools everywhere.

pdf: Portable Document Format. A document type that retains formatting and graphics when transmitted over the Internet to Macs and PCs alike.

Pine: A UNIX mail program that's based on Elm. See also *Elm*.

ping: A program that searches to see whether an Internet site is still active.

Plug-in: A tool that works with your browser to display different data formts such as video, audio, pdf, and animation.

PKZIP: A file-compression program for DOS and Windows.

PPP: Point to Point Protocol. An alternative to SLIP for dial-in access to the Internet. It's more reliable, and sometimes faster, than SLIP.

protocol: A set of rules that controls communications on or between networks.

shareware: Software that you download and try out. If you keep the software, you're honor bound to send the author a small fee.

Shockwave: A Web browser "plug-in" (add-on tool) that enables you to view, in real-time, animation and movies made with Macromedia Director. (Visit http://www.macromedia.com for more information on Director.)

SLIP: Serial Line Internet Protocol. A way to connect directly to the Internet so that programs you download come to your local hard drive and not to your ISP. If you have a SLIP account, your computer is actually *on* the Internet; it's not just a dumb terminal. If you're SLIP (or direct or PPP) connected, others can telnet to *your* computer, too. A control panel called MacSLIP or InterSLIP is used to connect to the Internet if you have a dial-in connection.

spam: Posting commercial messages to lots of unsuspecting users. A huge no-no (and an equally huge problem) on the Internet. (Also a mysterious luncheon meat and the topic of Monty Python skits.)

StuffIt: A Macintosh file-compression program. Creates files often tagged with the suffix .SIT. Compare *WinZip*.

StuffIt Expander: A Macintosh file-decompression program.

tag: Text added to an HTML document so that Web clients (like your browser) can format the document on your computer's screen. Tags usually come in pairs, surround or introduce text and look something like this: <B>your text here</B>. (This particular tag makes text between the tags **boldface** on a Web page.)

TCP/IP: Transmission Control Protocol/Internet Protocol. The system or language used between computers (hosts) on the Internet to make and maintain a connection.

telnet: A way to log in to someone else's computer and use their computing resources.

terminal: A stupid, brainless front-end machine that relies on the computing power of a host computer. You can run programs on your computer that make it act like a stupid, brainless computer to enable you to dial in to some host computers.

TurboGopher: A program that enables Macintosh users to access Gopher servers by using a friendly point-and-click interface.

UNIX: A computer operating system that is often called the backbone of the Internet. LINUX is a "flavor" of UNIX.

upload: To move data from your computer to a host computer. Opposite of *download.*

URL: Uniform Resource Locator. Basically, the address of any Gopher, FTP, telnet, or Internet (including WWW) site. URLs for Web pages look like this: `http://www.domain.top-domain`; for a Gopher site, it might be `gopher://domain.top-domain`.

Usenet: User's Network. A collection of thousands of newsgroups.

Uuencode/uudecode: Programs that encode and decode newsgroup (and some other) files for sending over the Internet.

Veronica: A Gopherspace search program.

VT100: The thing you enter when a host computer asks for "terminal type."

WAIS: (Pronounced *wayz*). Wide Area Information Server. A system of servers that enables you to search for documents on the Internet.

Web: The World Wide Web (WWW), the graphical front-end of the Internet.

Webcam: Web camera. Any camera connected to your computer that transmits images seen on a Web page.

WebTV: Microsoft's online Internet service that allows you to surf the Net through your TV set.

Wetware: The third component needed for person-to-person communication online. Hardware, software, wetware. In other words, you.

WinSock: A program that conforms to a set of standards called the Windows Socket API. WinSock programs control the link between Windows software and a TCP/IP program. You need this API if you're using a computer running Windows to connect to the Internet.

WinZip: A file-compression/decompression program for computers running the Windows operating system. Creates files tagged with the suffix .ZIP. Compare *Stuffit*.

World Wide Web (WWW): Also known as WWW or simply as "the Web." A graphics-rich hypermedia system that enables you to move from site to site with the click of a mouse, collecting great (and some not-so-great) information at every step.

Appendix C

Getting Connected: You've Got Options

In This Appendix:

▶ Choosing your Internet connection

▶ Speeding on the I-Way: direct connections

▶ Dialing for resources: dial-up connections

▶ Locating an information provider

▶ Swimming with the sharks

Choice is good. Whether you're choosing a vegetable in the school cafeteria — why do they always serve corn with pizza? — or a new style for the football team's jerseys (Be sure to consult the student fashion police before trying that one!), it's nice to have plenty of options.

As with any other choice, you need to know the facts before you make a decision about the best way for your school to access the Internet. Doing some research can keep you from getting caught in the bog of administrative bureaucracy. The decision about how your school will connect to the Internet boils down to three things:

✔ Money: How much money does your school or district want to commit to an Internet connection now? In the future?

✔ Speed: How fast do you want to travel the superhighway? Is speed an issue? (Also, see preceding entry for determining this one.)

✔ Need: What do you need, in terms of information, access, and support, both now and in the future?

Direct or Not?

The two ways to get connected to the Internet are by either a direct connection or by a dial-up connection. These connection methods vary widely in cost, ease of access, and the amount of support needed to maintain the connection.

Before you read on, I should tell you that I've provided a table toward the end of the chapter that gets right to the heart of Internet "connectivity." If you have only a minute before your technology committee meeting, check out the table. Otherwise, read on for some hints, and hazards, that will help with your choice of connection to the Internet.

Go direct

In a direct connection, your computer or your local area network (LAN) is connected to the Internet all the time. To achieve a direct connection, your computer or LAN is connected to a magical box called a router, which carries a signal that has been translated from your computer's language into the official language of the Internet, TCP/IP (which stands for Transmission Control Protocol/Internet Protocol — just a term to throw around to impress your friends). The router is then connected via special high-speed telephone lines to the nearest Internet gateway, usually a university, research institution, or commercial Internet service provider *(ISP)*.

Why choose a direct connection?

A direct connection has many benefits. Because you're always connected, the Internet becomes just another resource on your network. A direct connection is also very fast, so you don't have to wait for files to transfer, and your e-mail zips along faster than you can lick a stamp.

Another benefit is that a direct connection supports multiple users at the same time. This means that you and several other users in your school can gain access to the Internet over the same single high-speed line. Because you control the network, you can easily control which Internet resources are available to users. This feature is especially nice for restricting certain newsgroups or limiting those inevitable naughty-file transfers.

What's the bad news? Cost. Direct Internet connections cost big bucks in the short term but may save you money in the long run. You have to buy the router (which can cost several thousand dollars) and get the thing installed (more money). But the biggest cost is the installation and maintenance of the high-speed lines. These lines are priced according to the speed of the connection. A 56K (acceptable) ISDN connection costs much less than a T-1 or T-3 connection (very fast). Of course, your school system may have used their e-Rate (telecom infrastructure) bucks for getting ahead on this one.

Over the long haul, however, a direct connection may be the most cost-effective route for most schools. Not having bunches of phone lines saves some money. You're also not paying a service provider a monthly fee for each Internet account as you do with most dial-up accounts.

Also, don't forget to consider the potentially large hidden cost of a direct connection: support. With other types of connections, the Internet provider is responsible for troubleshooting the system. With a direct connection, you need a Net-savvy person to maintain the gateway, assign and maintain user accounts, and troubleshoot. Luckily, the technology is moving toward easier-to-manage and more trouble-free connections.

Take a good, hard look at this type of connection if you're looking at ten or more connections from your school or at some type of county-wide or district-wide network. Think about what you'll need now and in the future.

With a direct connection, by the way, you can request your own domain name. The domain name is the part after the @ symbol in an Internet address, and it tells the receiver of your message where your computer is located. If you hail from Somewhere High School, for example, your address could be

```
yourname@somewhere.edu
```

The edu is called the top-level domain name and identifies the address as one for an educational institution. (For more information about domain names and addresses, see Chapter 11.)

Establishing a direct connection

Here are the general steps to take if your school decides to establish a direct connection to the Internet:

1. **Determine your school's needs.**

   How many concurrent users do you want to be able to support, and how fast do these connections need to be?

2. **Contact the operator of the nearest Internet gateway host.**

   Call a local university's computer center or your school district office.

3. **Plan and design your Internet connection.**

   Get help from the university or from another school that has been through this procedure. Don't forget to think about how you'll handle the maintenance and support of equipment and Internet accounts.

4. **Apply for an IP address.**

   You need to fill out a form or two; find out how from your university or school district contact. Note that the ISP can probably do this for you or you can do it yourself. (See www.w3.org).

5. **Have an experienced person install the hardware, networking, and phone lines.**

   Make sure the system integrator/installer has worked in educational institutions before. Schools are different than businesses! As a general rule, you can never have enough gurus around for the tough parts.

6. **Set up your Internet gateway accounts, do some general housekeeping, and set up an acceptable use policy (see Chapter 9).**

   Surf's up!

Remember money, speed, and need? A direct connection to the Internet makes sense if you have a good size startup budget (including money for monthly lease fees), want the fastest available connection, and need to support many simultaneous users.

Dial it up

The second type of connection is a dial-up connection. In a dial-up connection, you use your computer to dial another computer or server where your account is established. That host computer is directly connected to the Internet. It's kind of a direct connection, once removed.

Dial-up connections can be made through an ISP, or a commercial online service (COS — I just made up that acronym because these acronyms are everywhere!) like AOL or Prodigy.

A dial-up connection is great because it has a very low initial cost. You can use all the dandy graphical interface tools that directly connected users do, too. Dial-up connections are also very handy for home users and occasional surfers.

The downside to dial-up connections is that because a dial-up connection uses POTS (plain old telephone service), it's slower than a direct connection. You can still whiz along at 28,800, 33,600 or 56,000 bps though, and that's plenty fast for most of us . . . for now.

Another problem that you'll occasionally run into with a dial-up service is a busy signal. Depending on the time of day, it can get mighty frustrating. You know the drill — 40 students sitting on the floor impatiently waiting for you to dial into the Net for a demonstration. You get a busy signal. Luckily, most ISPs limit the number of subscribers based on a ratio of subscribers to phone lines. Check this ratio when you choose an ISP. (For more about wheeling and dealing with service providers, see the "Locating an ISP" section later in this chapter.)

Because you are dialing into another computer, you may not have as much access control as you would in a direct-connection scenario. ISPs and most of the online services offer some kind of parental control options.

Need another "pro" to balance the "cons"? With a dial-up connection you can rely on someone else (the service provider) to troubleshoot when things go wrong. Because you're not maintaining your own Internet server or gateway, those nightmares fall to someone else. Mighty convenient if you don't have time to teach six periods, grade papers, and manage a network node.

Welcome PPP

Yep. Another acronym. This is a pretty simple one, though. I'll spare you the techie-talk and get right to the point.

If you're dialing into the Internet through an ISP, you'll most likely be offered a choice of what type of dial-up account you want. Remember, choice is good if you're an informed decision maker. You'll want to set up what's called a PPP (Point to Point Protocol) account.

A PPP account is the next best thing to a direct connection. You can use all the software tools, such as World Wide Web (WWW) browsers and e-mail packages, very easily. You also can immediately store transferred files on your local hard drive. Other connections, such as those usually provided through a university dial-up account, first store files on the host computer — requiring an extra step to move them to your home or school computer.

PPP accounts are cost effective, too. You can get an account for about $20 per month with unlimited online time. A bargain! Remember, however, that you need one phone line for every account.

If you have a PC that is running Windows, you can run a dandy program called WinSock (Windows Sockets), a standard way for Windows programs to work with PPP. WinSock applications, such as Trumpet and Chameleon, are great for Net-surfing. Several PPP options are built into Windows 95 and Windows 98 (and probably future operating systems).

If you have a Macintosh, the TCP/IP control panel (built-in to the more recent Mac OS's) or the PPP control panel (on older Macs) will do the trick.

What about an online service?

Commercial online services, such as America Online (AOL) and CompuServe, offer a dial-up option that's also attractive to schools. Not only do you get Internet access through a single, easy-to-use interface, but many other resources are available through the service itself. If you're a casual user or want a great way to learn to Net-surf, try an online service. They're easier to install, and, in general, easier to use than some other Internet software programs.

Another plus is the number of educational activities and resources that are available through the online services. America Online offers tons of online projects, ready-made for teachers, in its online education forums. The service also makes contacting other educators very easy. The Internet isn't so friendly.

What's the downside of a commercial online service? It could be expensive and you may not need all the fancy features. In order for you to assign different accounts to different people (AOL offers five 'screennames' per subscription), you may have to buy *lots* of subscriptions for your entire district or school.

As with the dial-up service, you may also get a busy signal from time to time. America Online runs more than 8,000,000 sessions a day. Not even Alexander Graham Bell could have prepared for that. Remember, too, that you need one phone line for each connection unless your online service provides for direct TCP/IP connection (which AOL does).

One glance at a newspaper and you no doubt see AOL is the leader in the online service world. Lots of folks, like the Microsoft Network (MSN) and WebTV (also Microsoft) are trying to steal "eyeballs" away from AOL. Where will it end? Will McDonald's become an ISP? (Just think, drive-thru Internet!) We'll see.

Accessing the Internet via a university network

If you use a telecommunications program to dial into a university computer for Internet access, you have what's generally referred to as a shell account. When you dial in (using a software protocol called *telnet*), you get only a computer letter (like a DOS prompt) or a symbol prompt such as % or >. You can do most anything other Net users can do, but the environment is strictly a text environment, and you have to deal with UNIX, a computer language that only a serious computer programmer could love.

This kind of dial-up access enables you to do FTP (file transfer), telnet, search for documents on the Web, and do e-mail just like with regular ISPs and commercial online services, but it's a little different, too. In some cases, files you download get sent to your host computer and not directly to your own hard drive or floppy. Then you need to go through the extra step of transferring the file from the host computer to your computer at the end of your session. It's a bit confusing, but it works. (All Internet traffic used to work this way.)

Sometimes, local university networks offer users a limited tier of Internet services, like e-mail, Gopher, and telnet. This kind of account (sometimes referred to as a Limited shell account) is the one that's the least expensive (often free) and most restricted. But, if the price is right . . .

Establishing a dial-up connection

Here are the general steps to take if your school decides to establish a dial-up connection to the Internet:

1. **Determine the needs of your school.**

   How many concurrent users do you want and how fast do these connections need to be?

2. **Install phone lines (one per dial-up connection needed).**

3. **Buy a modem and a computer (any computer and the fastest modem you can afford).**

4. **Sign up with an ISP or a commercial online service.**

   They'll give you the details, such as the number you should dial and your account name.

5. **Build a collection of freeware, shareware, and commercial Internet tools, or request front-end software from a commercial online service.**

   Note that many of these online service start-up kits come with a bit of free time for you to use in evaluating the service.

6. **Do some general housekeeping and set up an acceptable use policy (see Chapter 3).**

7. **Dial, and you're in!**

Decisions, Decisions

Is your head spinning yet? That's okay. A friend of mine once spent two hours in a teacher supply store trying to figure out how to cover a classroom bulletin board with a colorful background and border for less than $5.00. She came out with a roll of decorative trim ($4.95) and 30 shopping bags (marked "ABC & Me") donated by a generous store clerk. (Don't laugh, it worked!) The decision about what type of connection your school needs may require just as much ingenuity, especially since your budget might be just as tight.

I'll sum up all the stuff for you. Table C-1 compares dial-up accounts to direct accounts.

Table C-1	Dial-Up versus Direct Internet Accounts	
Factors Connection	*Dial-Up Connection*	*Direct (dedicated)*
Capacity	Limited to number of telephone lines	Unlimited
Short-term cost	Low	High
Long-term cost	High	Lower (the more users, the more savings)
Access control	Information provider allows limited control	You determine what resources users use
Speed	28,800 to 56,000 Kbps	Faster than a speeding bullet (usually 56 kilobytes and up)
General Recommendations	Great for single-user (you) and limited school use (until you can afford a direct connection)	Great for school-wide connection to the Internet

Locating an ISP

After you decide what route to take to connect to the Net, you will need to contact a service provider. If you've decided to use an online service, all that's left for you to do is to make a phone call to the online service's toll-free number and request your software.

If you need to locate a service provider, point your browser to THELIST (thelist.iworld.com) on someone else's computer. There you find an extensive list of providers and lots of statistics to help you make an informed decision.

Now, if you've made the decision to use an ISP, as opposed to jumping onto the information superhighway via a commercial service such as AOL, or if you've been unable to weasel some free accounts out of a local college or ISP, you need to put on your wheelin' and dealin' hat and go to town.

Choosing an ISP

Choosing an ISP is a little like choosing food in the school cafeteria. Most of the choices look good, but when you get around to actually sampling them, you're liable to get something that's hard to swallow. Somehow, that lunch that the fifth grade teacher down the hall brought from home always looks much better. Fact is, the number of ISPs is growing quickly, and each of them is dangling a carrot — although some dangle tastier carrots than others.

The moral to this food-filled story (are you getting hungry?) is buyer beware! If you're careful, and note the Wheeler-Dealer's questions that follow, you're much more likely to end up with something that's easy for you and your administration to enjoy.

The Wheeler-Dealer's top ten questions for an ISP

Think of yourself as a reporter on the information superhighway. Get a comfortable seat, your best #2 pencil, a telephone, and go to work. Get the names of service providers by searching current magazines or your local telephone book, or by dialing into a commercial online service and using THELIST. (See the preceding section for how to access THELIST.)

1 How many toll-free telephone lines do you control?

A busy signal is the electronic equivalent of a traffic jam on the information superhighway. The number of telephone lines that a service provider controls is very important. That $15 per month "unlimited access" won't do you much good if you spend all your time redialing and listening to Ma Bell's busy symphony. Ask the ISP how often users can expect a busy signal. If they get really quiet, then run, don't walk, to another provider.

Several providers offer Internet access via a long-distance phone call. They promise you the world, as long as you pay 90¢ per minute. The best providers offer local access or access via a toll-free number. (Note that toll-free access is often accompanied by a "convenience surcharge.")

Don't be too concerned if an ISP says that it has only 10 or 20 phone lines. If you're a bit antsy, remember that the Internet is an ever-changing beast, so be sure to follow up your inquiry about phone lines with the obligatory "What are your growth plans?" question. It's really the ratio of phone lines to users that matters. (See the following section for ratio information.)

2 How many users currently use your service?

Think of what the hallway in your school looks like seconds after the last bell of the day rings. Hundreds of book-totin' bodies running for the nearest door, pushing and shoving. If your ISP has more users than its phone lines can accommodate, sooner or later you'll end up as the last one out the door and miss your Internet bus!

A good way to quantify "how many is too many" is to think about the relationship between the number of users and the number of free phone lines. A reasonable ratio is about 1 phone line for every 10 users. 1 to 100 might sound like an awful lot, but remember that every user won't log on at the same time on the same line.

3 What kinds of accounts do you offer?

Here's your chance to recall those TLAs (three-letter acronyms) you read about in the rest of this book. Most Internet carriers offer three types of accounts: e-mail, web hosting, and commercial/e-Commerce accounts. If you're just looking for e-mail, go cheap, otherwise you'll need a web hosting account (usually e-mail with about 10MB of space on the ISP fileserver to host your school website). Commercial accounts are typically for the big-guys (companies large and small). They're more than you probably need.

4 What does establishing an account cost?

The fine print is what often kills a sweet deal. Whether you're negotiating for yourself or your school, watch for hidden fees. Although most Internet service providers charge a fee to cover the establishment of the account, the amount they charge varies greatly. I've seen initial charges of from $10 to $75. An average is about $30. Most providers even throw in a dandy book (like this one!) or some handy software.

5 How much time do I get for my monthly fee?

Imagine for a moment that you've been waiting all afternoon to see the sun set over the waterfront. You spend all afternoon finding the place you want to sit where the viewing is best. Seconds before the big event, everything goes black. A booming voice comes from nowhere and says, "Sorry, your time is up."

Unless you and your students want to experience the unsettling and inevitable "information interruptus," go for an unlimited use account. The few extra dollars per month saves you much heartache and many heated discussions with the teacher down the hall who surfs more than Gidget at Malibu.

6 How many and what kind of newsgroups do you carry?

Because the number of newsgroups you can access has to do with the capacity of the equipment that your ISP owns, some services don't offer many newsgroups. If you and your students rely heavily on this information, you want to maximize the number available. Most providers give you access to 500 or more.

Some ISPs choose not to carry certain eclectic newsgroups, such as the notorious alt groups. (Chapter 11 has a discussion of the potential and some of the pitfalls of newsgroups.) Look for the section on saving your job. Get the hint?

7 Can I spin my own Web (page)?

Want to build your own Web page? Many providers offer you space on their hardware to create your school's own Web page. Often they even give you a template to fill in with your school information until you've had time to discover HTML (hypertext markup language), the scripting language that enables you to create really cool Web pages.

Be sure to check to see how much space the provider will allow. Depending on the number of graphic images that you include, you can use up a few megabytes of memory very quickly. Try for about 10MB of Web space in the beginning. Most providers allow you to pay a bit more and get a bit more space.

8 How is your customer support?

Don't you just love the commercial where the lady calls the customer support line of a major aerospace and appliance company and asks how to remove the elephant from her dishwasher? Like any technology — especially technology where students and newbie teachers are involved — things are bound to go wrong.

Just for fun, don your best British accent and call the customer support number of your ISP with a question such as, "What's the URL for that Coke machine at Carnegie Mellon University?" or "What do Archie and Veronica have to do with the Internet?" If they answer correctly, they're doing their job. If you get a recording asking you to leave a message, go to another provider. A recording just doesn't cut it when you're demonstrating Internet access to your class, with the principal sitting quietly in the back of the room conducting your evaluation, and the thing doesn't work. A voice mailbox won't get you tenure.

Oh, and be sure that when your elephant gets caught in the dishwasher you only have to make a local call to customer support!

9 Do you have any special deals for educators or schools?

Ever see educators at a trade show? My favorite thing to do is get freebies. You know, those nifty pens, disks, magnifying glasses, posters, catalogs, and, of course, the mother of all freebies, the umbrella. Everyone likes free things — especially when money is tight.

Many companies know that we're using the Net and related technology to help children just like theirs, so they're very often glad to cut you a deal. Having your district office do the negotiating can also bring the price down. Remember, negotiating for a few bucks off the per month fee is, in the long run, better than getting a complimentary sign-up fee. Don't be shy. If you don't ask, they aren't likely to offer!

10 What kinds of front-end and tool software do you supply?

Entering the Net without tools is a little like trying to teach without books and paper. A lot of great Internet tools are available, many for free on the Internet itself. Check to see whether your ISP provides you with tools; it will save you the trouble of downloading them. Of course, we've included lots of the tools you'll need on the CD that accompanies this book, so maybe you can put a check-mark next to this one right away.

Most service provders nowadays save you a few gray hairs by giving you a disc (as part of your sign-up fee) that comes preconfigured and makes your first Internet sign-on a breeze. Configuring your software initially can be at least twice as confusing as programming your VCR, so having it all done for you means a lot. You and your students merely copy the software, click the mouse, and start surfin'!

Appendix D

About the CD

● ●

*W*e've worked hard to get the "best of the best" software for this third edition of Internet for Teachers. We've even added a nifty interface to make navigating the software titles quick and easy. On the CD, you'll find software tools to:

- ✔ Get you connected to the Internet (Getting Connected)
- ✔ Help you create content for the Internet (Creating Content)
- ✔ Enhance your experience on the Internet (Enhancing the Net)
- ✔ Ensure your computer operates safely and efficiently (Utilities)
- ✔ Help you learn more about the Internet. (Tutorials)

Here's some of what you can find on the *Internet for Teachers,* 3rd Edition. CD-ROM:

- ✔ Mindspring, a popular Internet service
- ✔ Dreamweaver 2.0, a powerful Web site editor for creating your own Web pages
- ✔ SiteCam, a freeware program that turns your digital camera into a Webcasting camera

System Requirements

Your Apple Macintosh, PC, or reasonable facsimile thereof needs to meet the following system requirements. If your computer doesn't meet at least most of these requirements, you may experience problems using this CD.

- ✔ A PC with a 486 or faster processor, or a Macintosh OS computer with a 68030 or faster processor.
- ✔ Microsoft Windows 3.1 or later, or Macintosh OS system software 7.5 or later.

✔ At least 16MB of total RAM installed on your computer. For best performance, we recommend that Windows 95 or 98-equipped PCs and Macintosh OS computers with PowerPC processors have at least 32MB of RAM installed.

✔ At least 138 MB (184 MB on Windows machines) of hard drive space available to install all the software from this CD. (You'll need less space if you don't install every program.)

✔ A CD-ROM drive — double-speed (2x) or faster.

✔ A sound card for PCs. (Macintosh OS computers have built-in sound support.)

✔ A monitor capable of displaying at least 256 colors or grayscale.

✔ A digital camera (optional; needed for video conferencing and Webcasting software).

✔ A microphone (optional; needed for video conferencing and software).

✔ An Internet connection. (MindspringService setup software is included on the CD as a sign-on option.)

✔ A modem with a speed of at least 28,800 bps (56,000 bps is recommended).

Before using this CD, I recommend that you install Adobe Acrobat Reader and StuffIt Expander (WinZIP for Windows users). These programs make it easier for you to install some programs and read the manuals for some of the software. See the installation instructions for StuffIt Expander and Adobe Acrobat Reader in the following section, *"What You'll Find."*

If you need more information on the basics, check out *PCs For Dummies,* 7th Edition, by Dan Gookin; *Macs For Teachers,* 3rd Edition by Michelle Robinette; *Windows 98 For Dummies* by Andy Rathbone; or *Windows 3.11 For Dummies,* 4th Edition, by Andy Rathbone (all published by IDG Books Worldwide, Inc.).

How to Use the CD Using the Macintosh OS

To install the items from the CD to your hard drive, follow these steps:

1. **Insert the CD into your computer's CD-ROM drive.**

   In a moment, an icon representing the CD you just inserted appears on your Macintosh desktop. Chances are, the icon looks like a CD-ROM.

2. **Double-click the CD icon. The CD's contents window appears.**

3. **Double-click the Read Me First icon.**

   This text file contains information about the CD's programs and any last-minute instructions you need to know about installing the programs on the CD that we don't cover in this appendix.

4. **To install most programs, just drag the program's folder from the CD window and drop it on your hard drive icon.**

5. **Some programs come with installer programs — with those you simply open the program's folder on the CD and double-click the icon with the words "Install" or "Installer."**

   Once you have installed the programs that you want, you can eject the CD. Carefully place it back in the plastic jacket of the book for safekeeping.

How to Use the CD Using Microsoft Windows

To install the items from the CD to your hard drive, follow these steps:

1. **Insert the CD into your computer's CD-ROM drive.**

2. **Windows 3.1 or 3.11 users: From Program Manager, choose File➪Run.**

   Windows 95 users: Click the Start button and click Run.

3. **In the dialog box that appears, type** D:\SETUP.EXE.

   Most of you probably have your CD-ROM drive listed as drive D under My Computer in Windows 95 or the File Manager in Windows 3.1. Type in the proper drive letter if your CD-ROM drive uses a different letter.

4. **Click OK.**

   A license agreement window appears.

5. **Since I'm sure you'll want to use the CD, read through the license agreement, nod your head, and then click the Accept button. Once you click Accept, you won't be bothered by the License Agreement window again.**

   From here, the CD interface appears. The CD interface is a little program that shows you what is on the CD and coordinates installing the programs and running the demos. The interface basically lets you click a button or two to make things happen.

6. **Click OK on the CD Launcher message box.**

   If you do not want to start the interface at this point, you can click Cancel. This message box is just to let you know that the interface is opening up — after the first time you use the CD and agree to the license, this box is the first thing you see when you start up the CD.

7. **The first screen you see is the Category screen.**

   This screen lists the categories of software on the CD.

8. **To view the items within a category, just click the category's name.**

   A list of programs in the category appears. You can click the Go Back button to return to the Category screen. You can always return to the previous screen by clicking the Go Back button. This allows you to browse the different categories and products and decide what you want to install.

9. **For more information about a program, click the program's name.**

   Be sure to read the information that is displayed. Sometimes a program might require you to do a few tricks on your computer first, and this screen will tell you where to go for that information, if necessary.

10. **To install the program, click Continue. If you don't want to install the program, click the Cancel button to return to the previous screen.**

    Once you click the Continue button, the CD interface drops to the background while the CD begins installation of the program you chose.

11. **To install other items, repeat steps 7, 8, 9 and 10.**

12. **When you're done installing programs, click the Exit button to close the interface.**

    You can eject the CD now. Carefully place it back in the plastic jacket of the book for safekeeping.

What You'll Find

Here's a summary of the software on this CD. If you use a Macintosh OS computer, you can enjoy the ease of the Macintosh interface to quickly install the programs. If you use Windows, we've added the CD interface to help you install software easily.

The Internet For Teachers Links Page

The links page (Links.html) saves you time and effort in accessing the great Web sites in the Internet For Teachers directory. This handy Web page includes all the links in the directory in an easy-to-access format that makes educational surfing a snap, without typing in all those URLs! Simply look in the left-hand pane for the section the hyperlink falls under and click that hyperlink, and then scroll through the right-hand pane and click on a link. What could be simpler?

MindSpring Internet Service

For Macintosh OS and Windows. In the Getting Connected category. In case you don't have an Internet connection, the CD includes sign-on software for MindSpring Internet Service, an Internet service provider.

Visit the MindSpring Web site: www.mindspring.com.

If you already have an ISP, please note that MindSpring Internet Service software makes changes to your computer's current Internet configuration and may replace your current provider's settings.

Adobe Acrobat Reader 3.02, and 4.0 from Adobe Systems, Inc.

For Macintosh and Windows. In the Enhancing the Net category. Adobe Acrobat Reader is a free program that opens portable document format (PDF) files. PDFs are handy ways to publish electronic documents that contain the same formatting and graphics of a printed document.

Visit Adobe's Web site at www.adobe.com/acrobat.

Anarchie 3.0, from Stairways Software

For Macintosh. In the Enhancing the Net category. Anarchie Pro is a fast, efficient shareware FTP client that is useful for downloading batches of files together. Some users prefer Anarchie's interface to Fetch's. Anarchie Pro can download, extract, sort, and list the links contained in a Web page or enable you to maintain your Web or FTP site from a local folder while Anarchie Pro uploads only the changed files and deletes files that are no longer used. This latest version of Anarchie Pro contains many features and bug fixes, including a Macintosh OS 8 appearance, Web browser-like windows with an editable Address field (if you are running Macintosh OS 8.0 or later), support for searching Sherlock-compatible Internet Search Sites, a Commander window, a Show Document Kind command from the listing window, support for command-double clicking to open Web pages in your browser, and support for VMS servers.

Visit the Web site at www.stairways.com.

BBEdit Lite

For Macintosh OS. In the Creating Content category. BBEdit Lite 4.1, from Bare Bones Software, Inc., is a Macintosh freeware text editor with powerful features that make creating HTML scripts for your Web pages easy. The current commercial version of this program, BBEdit 5.0, has stronger HTML editing features. We've included a demo version of BBEdit 5.0 on the CD. This demo is fully-featured except that it cannot save files.

Visit the Web site at www.barebones.com.

Convert Machine, by Rod Kennedy

For Macintosh. In the Enhancing the Net category. Convert Machine to any of six standard formats (AIFF/AIFC, AU, WAVE, MacOS Finder sound files, QuickTime Audio and Sound Designer II); to mono or stereo; and to an arbitrary sampling rate and drop any format sound file onto its icon and, voilá, you get it copied to the required form.

Visit the Web site at www.kagi.com/rod/.

Cool Edit 96, by Syntrillium Software

For Windows. In the Enhancing the Net category. Shareware. Cool Edit is a digital sound editor for Windows. You might think of it as a paint program for audio—just as a paint program enables you to create images with colors, brush strokes, and a variety of special effects, Cool Edit enables you to "paint" with sound: tones, pieces of songs and voices and miscellaneous noises, sine waves and sawtooth waves, noise, or just pure silence.

Visit the Web site at www.syntrillium.com/.

CuteFTP, from GlobalSCAPE

For Windows. In the Enhancing the Net category. CuteFTP is a Windows-based File Transfer Protocol (FTP) client that allows users to utilize the capabilities of FTP without having to know all the details of the protocol itself. This shareware package also includes CuteHTML.

Visit the Web site at www.globalscape.com/.

Dreamweaver 2.0, by Macromedia

For Macintosh and Windows. In the Enhancing the Net category. A 30-day trial version of this tremendously powerful yet easy-to-use Web page development application. Designed for novice and professional alike, Dreamweaver combines a graphical design environment with templates for quick and easy development.

Visit the Web site at www.macromedia.com/software/dreamweaver/trial/.

Note: This software contains a 30-day timeout feature.

The Mac version of Dreamweaver 2.0 requires a Power Mac with 24 MB of RAM and a color monitor capable of 800 × 600 resolution.

Enhanced CU-SeeMe 3.1, by White Pine Software

For Macintosh and Windows. In the Enhancing the Net category. Enhanced CU-SeeMe 3.1 is a nifty program that lets you use the (relatively free) Internet to talk to and see other Internet users. To use this software, you need at least a microphone, a Macintosh (or PC with a sound card), and speakers. If you like, you can attach a digital camera to your computer. You don't need a camera to see other users with cameras, however. The software is good for a 30-day trial.

Visit the White Pine Software Web site at http://www.wpine.com

Note: Enhanced CU-SeeMe also comes with a copy of Adobe Acrobat Reader. If you choose to install Acrobat Reader during this process, you won't need to install Acrobat Reader again.

If you are asked to enter a serial number, type **DCBE01100KDCWWCA**

Eudora Light 3.1.3, from Qualcomm Inc.

For Macintosh and Windows. In the Enhancing the Net category. Eudora Light is a popular freeware Internet e-mail program. The latest version of Eudora Light and more information on its commercial sibling, Eudora Pro, can be found at the Eudora Web site at www.eudora.com.

After you have Adobe Acrobat Reader installed, you can read the Eudora Light manual EUL3MANL.PDF.

Fireworks2, by Macromedia

For Macintosh and Windows. In the Creating Content category. A peek at a powerful program for professional Web graphics design and production (Evaluation version).

Visit the Web site at www.macromedia.com/software/.

First Aid 2000, from Network Associates, Inc.

For Windows. In the Utilities category 30-day trial version. The most comprehensive diagnostic and repair application for PCs. First Aid 2000's self-healing technology automatically diagnoses and repairs thousands of computer problems, checks for and fixes Year 2000 issues, and prevents system crashes.

Visit the Web site at www.networkassociates.com/.

F-Secure Anti-virus, by Data Fellows, Inc.

For Windows. In the Utilities category. 30-day trial version. F-Secure Anti-Virus is the most comprehensive real-time and on-demand virus scanning and protection system for all Windows platforms.

Visit the Web site at www.datafellows.com/.

HotDog Professional 5 Webmaster Suite (Trial), from Sausage Software

For Windows. In the Creating Content category. This Web development software is aimed primarily at professional Webmasters boasts a new interface, enhanced performance, increased flexibility and functionality, and improved Web site management capabilities.

Visit the Web site at www.sausage.com.

Internet Coach, from APTE

For Macintosh and Windows. In the Tutorial category. Internet Coach for Netscape Navigator and Communicator makes it easy to know how to browse, search, send mail, join LISTSERV's and more. Learn all about Netscape Navigator's newest features such as: multimedia Web content like Java and VRML, Messenger, and Composer. For quick answers and shortcuts, Internet Coach also features extensive reference modules. No wonder Internet Coach is the most popular software for mastering the Internet. No Internet connection necessary because Web simulations are used.

Visit the Web site at www.apte.com.

Internet Explorer 5, by Microsoft

For Macintosh and Windows. In the Enhancing the Net category. Netscape's Communicator includes the Navigator Web browser, Messenger (Communicator's integrated e-mail client), and Composer for Web page editing and design. You can find the latest versions of Communicator as well as important updates on the Netscape support site: www.netscape.com/browsers/index.html.

Note: For Windows 3.1. users, we are including Netscape Communicator 4.06, which is the latest version for that operating system.

Visit the Web site at home.netscape.com.

Netscape Communicator 4.5, Netscape Communications

For Macintosh and Windows. In the Enhancing the Net category. For Macintosh and Windows. In the Enhancing the Net category. Netscape's Communicator includes the Navigator Web browser, Messenger (Communicator's integrated e-mail client), and Composer for Web page editing and design. You can find the latest versions of Communicator as well as important updates on the Netscape support site: www.netscape.com/browsers/index.html.

Note: For Windows 3.1. users, we are including Netscape Communicator 4.06, which is the latest version for that operating system.

Visit Netscape's Netcenter at http://home.netscape.com.

QuickTime 3.01, from Apple Computer, Inc.

For Macintosh and Windows. In the Enhancing the Net category. View movies you download from the Internet, play sound files and more with this powerful multimedia engine. Includes plug-ins for use with your favorite Web browser. Want real-time media streaming and MPG3 movies? Be sure to grab a free upgrade to QuickTime 4.0 at `www.apple.com/quicktime`.

Sherlock Plug-ins, courtesy of Apple-Donuts

For Macintosh. In the Enhancing the Net category. Approximately 300 plug-ins designed to work with Macintosh OS 8.5 (and higher) and Sherlock, the personal search detective (free with Macintosh OS 8.5 and higher) from a couple of mighty talented guys who built a Web site especially to collect these things.

Visit the Web site at `www.apple-donuts.com/`.

Shockwave, from Macromedia

For Macintosh and Windows. In the Enhancing the Net category. Shockwave Player is a great tool for entertaining, engaging, rich media playback. It lets you view interactive Web content like games, business presentations, entertainment, and advertisements from your Web browser.

Visit the Web site at `www.macromedia.com/shockwave/`.

SiteCam, by Rearden Technology

For Macintosh. In the Creating Content category. Demo. SiteCam 3.0.1 is a full-featured Webcam program for putting live images and time-lapse movies on the Internet. SiteCam can integrate into your Web site in minutes . . . whether you want a new image every 5 minutes via FTP or you want to stream live video. SiteCam is reliable, inexpensive, easy-to-use and has the features that professional Webmasters want.

Visit the Web site at `www.rearden.com`.

Sound Machine 2.7.1, Rod Kennedy

For Macintosh. In the Enhancing the Net category. SoundMachine is a user friendly sound file player for common audio formats such as m-law (mu-law), AIFF and WAVE. It supports a simple interface and is well suited to Web browsers or as a stand-alone application.

Visit the Web site at `www.kagi.com/rod/`.

StuffIt Lite 3.6, from Aladdin Systems

For Macintosh. In the Enhancing the Net category. StuffIt Lite 3.6 is a very popular freeware file decompression utility for the Macintosh. It can also decode some Internet binary formats. Aladdin Systems makes many other file management products, primarily for the Mac.

Visit the Web site at `www.aladdinsys.com`.

Web Painter, Totally Hip Software

For Macintosh and Windows. In the Creating Content category. Create the smallest, high quality animations in GIF, QuickTime movie, AVI and other formats with this easy to use tool. Demo.

Visit the Web site at `www.totallyhip.com/`.

WinZip 7.0, from Nico Mak Software

For Windows. In the Enhancing the Net category. WinZip is a shareware file compression utility which creates and extracts files saved in the popular PKZIP file compression format. For Windows 3.1, the latest compatible version of WinZip is version 6.3 has been included on the CD.

Visit the Web site at `www.winzip.com`.

WS_FTP LE 4.6, from Ipswitch, Inc.

For Windows. In the Enhancing the Net category. WS_FTP is a powerful Windows FTP program designed for the novice user. This evaluation edition has a 15-day free trial and comes in Windows 95 or 98 and Windows 3.1 versions.

Visit the Web site at `www.ipswitch.com/`.

If You've Got Problems (Of the CD Kind)

I tried my best to compile programs that work on most computers with the minimum system requirements. Alas, your computer may differ, and some programs may not work properly for some reason.

The two likeliest problems are that you don't have enough memory (RAM) for the programs you want to use, or you have other programs running that are affecting installation or running of a program. If you get error messages like `Not enough memory` or `Setup cannot continue`, try one or more of these methods and then try using the software again:

- ✔ Turn off any anti-virus software that you have on your computer. Installers sometimes mimic virus activity and may make your computer incorrectly believe that it is being infected by a virus.

- ✔ Close all running programs. The more programs you're running, the less memory is available to other programs. Installers also typically update files and programs. So if you keep other programs running, installation may not work properly.

- ✔ Have your local computer store add more RAM to your computer. This is, admittedly, a drastic and somewhat expensive step. However, if you have a Windows 95 PC or a Macintosh OS computer with a PowerPC chip, adding more memory can really help the speed of your computer and allow more programs to run at the same time. This may include closing the CD interface and running a product's installation program from Windows Explorer.

If you still have trouble with installing the items from the CD, please call the IDG Books Worldwide Customer Service phone number: 800-762-2974 (outside the U.S.: 317-596-5430).

Index

• A •

A+ Math site, D-13
abbreviations, 156
acceptable use policy (AUP), 40-41
Access-Ability site, D-20
ACE, 34
ACT site, D-7
ADB port, 207
address, 297
administrators, 267–268
Adobe Acrobat Reader (on the CD), 323
ADSL lines, 54
Advanced Research Projects Administration Network. *See* ARPAnet
Algebra Online site, D-13
Algebra.Help site, D-13
All-Music Guide site, D-5
alt newsgroups, 38
AltaVista, 152
American Cybercasting Corp., 248
American Dental Association's Kid Site, D-12
American Directory Assistance, 152
American Veterinary Medical Association Kid's Corner site, D-18
Americans Communicating Electronically (ACE), 34
Americans for the Arts site, D-6
Anarchie, 202, 297
Anarchie 3.0 (on the CD), 323
anonymous FTP, 198, 297
AOL (America Online), 48–51, 297
  channels, 49
  content, 50–51
  cost, 51
  interface, 49
  keywords, 51
  online chat, 190–194
  organization, 51
  resources on, 50

AOL instant messenger (AIM), 193–194, 297
Apple Computer Education Page site, D-8
applets, 225, 297
apprenticeship USA site, D-7
Archie, 202, 297
ArchNet site, D-18
.arj files, 204
.arpa extension, 67
ARPAnet, 11, 298
ArtLex site, D-5
ArtMuseum.Net site, D-5
Arts Education and School Improvement Resources for Local and State Leaders site, D-21
.arts extension, 67
ArtsEdge site, D-5
ArtsEdNet site, D-20
ARTtalk site, D-6
ASCII, 298
Ask Jeeves For Kids site, D-10
Association for the Advancement of Arts Education site, D-6
attachment, 146-147, 298
audio, 227
author credit, electronic media, 235
autologin program, 47
AV cards, 207
Awesome Library: Current Events site, D-9

• B •

bandwidth, 209, 298
Basic Punctuation and Mechanics site, D-12
baud, 298
BBEdit Lite (on the CD), 323
BBS, 15, 298
Berit's Best Sites For Children site, D-10

Best Paper Airplane in the World site, D-18
Bigfoot, 152
Bill Nye the Science Guy site, D-14
binary file, 298
binhex, 298
Biography.Com site, D-10
Biology4Kids site, D-18
bitnik, 298
Black Belt for Kids site, D-12
Bobby site, D-19
Bonus.Com the SuperSite For Kids site, D-10
bookmarks, 18, 100–101, 298
  adding, 100
  deleting, 100
  editing, 100–101
  setting, 100
  teacher education, 268
bounce, 298
browsers, 18, 298
  Back button, 69
  display, 68
  exiting, 71
  Forward button, 69
  home page, 70
  Internet Explorer. *See* Internet Explorer
  navigating with, 69
  Netscape Communicator. *See* Netscape Communicator
  Opera, 66
  Sherlock, 66
  sites, accessing, 70–71
budgeting, telecommunications, 58–60
bulletin board service, 15, 298
bulletin boards, 166
Butterflies at The Field Museum site, D-18

• C •

cache, 48, 290–291
CamRunner, 208
Carr, Sherah, 35

CD
  Adobe Acrobat Reader, 323
  Anarchie 3.0, 323
  BBEdit Lite, 323
  contents, 322–329
  Convert Machine, 324
  Cool Edit 96, 324
  CuteFTP, 324
  Dreamweaver 2.0, 324–325
  Enhanced CU-SeeMe 3.1, 325
  Eudora Light 3.1.3, 325
  Fireworks2, 325
  First Aid 2000, 326
  F-Secure Antivirus, 326
  HotDog Professional 5 Webmaster Suite, 326
  installing, 320–322
  Internet Coach, 326
  Internet connection, 46
  Internet Explorer 5, 327
  Internet sign-on kit included on, 56
  MindSpring Internet Service, 323
  Netscape Communicator 4.5, 327
  QuickTime 3.01, 327
  Sherlock Plug-ins, 327–328
  Shockwave, 328
  SiteCam, 328
  Sound Machine 2.7.1, 328
  StuffIt Lite 3.6, 328–329
  system requirements, 319–320
  troubleshooting, 329–330
  Web Painter, 329
  Web sites on, list of, D-4
  WinZip 7.0, 329
  WS_FTP LE 4.6, 329
Center for Media Education (CME), 34
CGI (Common Gateway Interface), 298
chat, 299
chat rooms, 183
Chicago Tribune site, D-9
Children's Software Review site, D-9
CIA Kid's Secret Zone site, D-18
citing electronic media, 235
Classroom Connect, 239
classrooms, Internet, 15

clients, 46, 299
CME, 34
CNET, 113, 201
CNET Download.com for PC-Teaching
    Tools in Education site, D-21
CNN Interactive site, D-9
College Board Online site, D-7
.com extension, 67
commercial Internet providers, 12–13
communications program, 299
community
  convincing to use Internet in school,
    27–30
  guidelines, 33–35
  introduction to Internet, 32–33
Community of Science, Inc. site, D-21
Complete Works of William Shakespeare
    site, D-12
compression formats, 204
Computer History site, D-8
computer viruses, 203
computers, 221
  memory, 46
Computers for Learning site, D-8
conferencing, 228–229
Connected Classrooms, 278
content
  control of, 35
  controversial, 32
  inappropriate, 37
contents, 322–329
convergence, 272
Convert Machine (on the CD), 324
cookie, 299
Cool Edit 96 (on the CD), 324
Cool Science for Curious Kids site, D-15
Copyright issues, 120–122
Corporation for Public Broadcasting
    Education and Technology site, D-21
CoSN, 299
Crayola FamilyPlay site, D-5
Creative Writing For Kids site, D-12
credibility issues, 251–253
curriculum, Internet integration, 35–36
customization of information, 273

CuteFTP (on the CD), 324
cybarian, 299
CyberAngels site, D-14
cyberjourneys, 243–250
  college students, 247
  educators, 247–249
  grade 6-8, 244–245
  grade 9-12, 245–247
  K-5, 244
  ready-made, 248
  updating school technology plan, 249
  Web sites, developing your own, 249–250
CyberPatrol, 120
Cybersitter, 120
cyberspace, 299

• D •

data types, 221
Deaf World Web site, D-20
Defiance Middle School Computer Center,
    206
DFN, 34
dial-up connections, 299
  commercial online services, 311–312
  described, 310–311
  direct connections versus, 314
  establishing, 313
  PPP accounts, 311
  university networks, 312–313
Dial-Up Networking, 55
digest, 299
Digital Freedom Network (DFN), 34
Dinosaurs at the National Museum of
    Natural History site, D-15
direct connections, 308–310, 314
Discovery Channel, 280
discussion groups, 17
disk cache, 290–291
DNS, 299
domain name, 299
domains, top-level, 67
dotted quad, 299
downloads, 18, 300
Dreamweaver 2.0 (on the CD), 324–325

• E •

Earthquake Information: United States Geological Survey site, D-15
e-commerce, 268, 274, 300
edu, 300
.edu extension, 67
education, Internet and, 11–12
Education Services/Staff Development Association of Central Kansas, 278
Education World site, D-8
Educational Testing Service Network site, D-7
EdWeb site, D-21
E-Education on the WWW site, D-21
EFF, 34
Electronic and Information Technology Access Advisory Committee site, D-20
electronic commerce, 74
Electronic Frontier Foundation. *See* EFF
electronic mail. *See* e-mail
electronic signature, 153–154
Elm, 139–140, 300
e-mail, 16, 300
  abbreviations, 156
  address, 135–136
  attachments, 146–147
  automating, 151
  .com, 136
  described, 134
  domain name, 135
  .edu, 136
  electronic park, 264
  emoticons, 155–156
  Eudora Light, 140–146
  geographic scavenger hunts, 261
  .gov, 136
  headers, 137
  ideas for exchanges, 259–264
  Internet Explorer, 149–150
  lesson plan chain letter, 263–264
  literature swap, 264
  message area, 137
  .mil, 136
  multimedia attachments, 263
  .net, 136
  Netscape Communicator, 147–149
  news stories, 260
  newsletter swap, 261–262
  Olympics related math questions, 260–261
  online services, 138–139
  .org, 136
  poems, 264
  president, letters to, 263
  project ideas using, 259–264
  receiving, 139
  research exchange, 264
  sample activity, 157
  scary-story contest, 262
  sending, 135, 139
  senior citizen interviews, 263
  skateboarding jargon, 261
  standard protocol, 137
  story starters (prompts), 261
  subject line, 137
  surveys, 260
 top-level domain, 135
  troubleshooting, 293
  university network, 139–140
  UNIX network, 139–140
  username, 135
  uses, 134
emoticons, 155–156
Empires Past site, D-19
Encyclopedia Britannica Online site, D-10
encyclopedias, 35
Enhanced CU-SeeMe 3.1 (on the CD), 325
ePALS site, D-10
e-purse, 300
ERIC, 300
ethics, Internet, 38–39
Eudora, 300
Eudora Light
  described, 140–141
  reading mail, 144–145
  receiving mail, 144–145

replying to mail, 145
sending mail, 141–143
updating, 141
Eudora Light 3.1.3 (on the CD), 325
Expect the Best From a Girl site, D-14
external modems, 53

• F •

Fair Use Doctrine, 121
False Pass Java Web Cam Classroom cam, 217
FamilyCam, 217
FAQ files, 179, 300
favorites, 300
Fermi National Accelerator Laboratory, 278
Fetch, 300
file exchange, 16
File Mine, 202
File Transfer Protocol. *See* FTP (File Transfer Protocol)
filtering software, 117–120
filters, 35
  objectionable material, 38
financial considerations, 58–60
Finger, 300
firewalls, 54, 300
FireWire port, 207
Fireworks2 (on the CD), 325
.firm extension, 67
First Aid 2000 (on the CD), 326
flaming, 154–155, 301
frames, 103
FrameServer, 208
Franklin Institute Science Museum site, D-15
free Internet access, 58
freeware, 200
F-Secure Antivirus (on the CD), 326
FTP (File Transfer Protocol), 97, 198–204, 301
  Archie, 202
  compression formats, 204

computer viruses, 203
installing programs, 202
sessions, 199–201
steps for, 199–201
uncompressing files, 202
uses, 198

• G •

gateway, 301
geek, 301
genealogical searches, 107
Geometry site, D-13
German-English Dictionary site, D-12
GhostCam, 217
GIF, 301
Global Learning and Observations to Benefit the Environment, 279
Global Online Learning Adventures site, D-15
Gopher, 301
.gov extension, 67
GrammarNow site, D-12
grants, 59
graphics
  disabling, 85
  saving files, 83
Greatest Places site, D-19
guidelines for Internet use, 33–35

• H •

hacker, 301
harassment, 37
hard drive, 46, 48
Headbone Zone, 279
HGopher, 301
higher level learning goals, 240–241
High-Performance Computing Act of 1991, 13
home page, 30, 124, 126–129, 301
host, 301

HotDog Professional 5 Webmaster Suite (on the CD), 326
How Far Is It? site, D-18
How Things Fly site, D-18
How to Offer a Course Over the Internet site, D-21
HTML For Dummies (Tittel and James), 126
HTML (HyperText Markup Language), 65, 220, 301
HTTP (HyperText Transfer Protocol), 65, 302
HTTPS, 302
hyperlinks, 65
Hypermedia, 65
hypertext, 302

• *1* •

I Can Do That! site, D-15
ICQ, 193, 302
inappropriate content, 37
Incredible Art Department site, D-6
indexed message listings, 166
Indiana University School of Music site, D-6
Infection Detection Protection site, D-11
.info extension, 67
information storage, 221
information superhighway, 302
installing
  CD, 320–322
  FTP (File Transfer Protocol), 202
  Netscape Navigator, 93
instant communication, 275
instant messages, 184, 193–194
Institute for Learning Technologies site, D-21
.int extension, 67
internal modems, 53
Internet, 302
  access, 15
  acceptable use policy (AUP), 40–41
  benefits, 29
  blind communication, 24–25
  challenges, 222–225
  classrooms and, 15

collaborative learning, 23
communication, 24
communication and, 10
as community, 25–26
copyright, 120–122
creative outlet, 25
credibility of sites, 251–253
defined, 9–10
education and, 11–12
emerging tools, 225–229
etiquette on. *See* Netiquette
files, finding, 201–202
filtering, 119–120
gender issues, 223
higher level learning goals, 240–241
history of, 10–13
human contact, 223
information access gap, 224
information storage, 221
interactiveness, 224
navigation, 225
new issues/challenges, 221
opportunities provided by, 22
phone lines, 222
pornography, 223
publishing, 25
real-world examples of integrated knowledge, 23
reasons to use, 22–27
staff development, 239
students' roles, 240–241
targeting information, 24
teachers' roles, 241
telementoring, 23–24
textbooks, replacing, 14–15
troubleshooting, 289–291
URLs, 222
uses of, 16–17
vast amounts of information, 26
Internet addresses, 67
Internet Coach (on the CD), 326
Internet connections, 46, 209–210, 307–318
  cost issues, 308–309
  deciding on, 313–314
  dial-up connections, 310–313
  direct connections, 308–310

ISP. *See* ISP (Internet Service Provider)
items needed for, 45–46
Internet content, 275
Internet Directory, D-1–D-21
Internet ethics, 38–39
Internet Explorer 5 (on the CD), 327
Internet Explorer (IE), 18, 302
  Address Bar, 77, 81
  default home page, 88–89
  e-mail, 149–150
  Explorer Bar, 77
  Favorites file, 87–88
  Favorites tab, 86–87
  graphics display, disabling, 85
  Intellisense, 81
  Link Bar, 77
  Main Browser Window, 77
  Main Menu Bar, 76
  News Services, 89–90
  off-line viewing of Web pages, 82
  Outlook Express. *See* Outlook Express
  printing files, 82–83
  saving files, 83
  starting, 75–77
  Status Bar, 77
  tips for browsing with, 85–90
  Title Bar, 76
  Toolbar, 77
  updated version, 75, 76
Internet Explorer Toolbar
  AutoFill button, 80
  Back button, 78
  Edit button, 80
  Favorites button, 80
  Forward button, 78
  History button, 80
  Home button, 79
  Images button, 79
  Internet Explorer logo, 81
  Larger button, 80
  Mail button, 80
  Preferences (Mac only) button, 80
  Print button, 79
  Refresh button, 78
  Search button, 79
  Smaller button, 80
  Stop button, 79–80
Internet learning activity. *See*
    cyberjourneys
Internet projects
  analysis and, 237
  citing electronic media, 235
  e-mail, 237
  evaluation and, 237
  feedback, 234
  final project, 234
  goals, 234
  materials, managing, 236–237
  mentors, 234
  planning, 233–235
  preview, 234–235
  resources, 234
  role in, 234
  steps, 234
  student management, 236–237
  students with special needs, 237–239
  time management, 236–237
  time parameters, 234
  virtual field trips. *See* virtual field trips
Internet servers, 13
Internet sign-on kit included on, 56
Internet use contract, 40–41
intranets, 220
IP, 302
IRC (Internet Relay Chat), 184–190, 302
  channels, 184
  clients, 184–185
  commands for, 189–190
  exiting, 189
  IRCLe, 185–187
  joining, 188
  list of, 187
  mIRC, 185
  sample, 188
  setup, 186
  shareware programs, 185–186
IRCLe, 185–187
ISDN lines, 53–54
ISP (Internet Service Provider), 48, 302
  accounts, 316
  America Online. *See* America Online

ISP *(continued)*
  choosing, 314–315
  cost, 316
  customer support, 317
  first use of, 15
  Internet information checklist, 57–58
  locating, 314–318
  monthly fee, 316
  newsgroups, 316
  phone lines, amount of, 315
  questions for, 315–318
  software, 52, 318
  special deals for educators/schools, 317
  THELIST, 314
  users, number of, 315–316
  Web space, 317
  Webcasting, 209–210

• **J** •

Japanese-English Dictionary site, D-13
Java, 184–185, 225–226, 302
JavaScript, 225–226
JPEG, 302
Jughead, 302

• **K** •

K12 newsgroups (education), 169
k12, 302
Kaplan site, D-7
keywords, 18
KidPub site, D-12
Kids Can Make a Difference site, D-19
Kids Connect, 279
Kids' Space site, D-11
Kid's Valley Garden site, D-18
KidsClick site, D-8
KidsHealth.org for Kids site, D-11
KidsPsych site, D-14
KidzGolf site, D-11
killer app, 303
Kinetic City Cyber Club site, D-16
knowledge navigation, 16
Kratts' Creatures site, D-16

• **L** •

Learning Interchange, 278
learning links
  Internet ethics, 39
  NREN proposal, 14
lesson plans, sharing, 266–267
lessons, planning, 233–235
Let's Go: Around the World site, D-19
LFF, 34
Librarian's Guide to Cyberspace For
      Parents and Kids site, D-14
Libraries for the Future (LFF), 34
link, 303
Linux Online site, D-8
LISTSERV, 159–166, 303
live conferencing, 17
LM-NET, 165–166
locating people, 151–153
Locker Room, Sports For Kids site, D-12
lurkers, 303

• **M** •

Macintosh computers
  AutoFill feature, 86
  browsers, 66
  CD, installing, 320–321
  Internet connection, 55, 56
  IRCLe, 185–187
  Page Holder feature, 89
  Sherlock, 111
MacPPP, 56
Macs For Teachers, 48
MacTCP, 56, 303
MAD Scientist Network site, D-16
magazine articles, 35
mailing lists
  announcement, 160
  described, 159–160
  digest, 160
  finding, 160–161
  Library Media Network, 165–166
  moderated, 160
  open, 160

posting to, 163–164
subscribing to, 161–163
types of, 160
unsubscribing, 163–165
maillists. *See* mailing lists
Math Baseball site, D-13
Math Brain Teasers site, D-13
MEGA Mathematics site, D-13
memory, 46
RAM. *See* RAM
troubleshooting, 290–291
message boards, 166
.mil extension, 67
MIME, 303
Mindspring, 56
MindSpring Internet Service (on the CD), 323
Minneapolis Institute of Arts site, D-5
mIRC, 185
mirror site, 303
modems, 52–54, 209, 303
external, 53
internal, 53
network, 53
speed, 53–54
moderated, 303
Moscow and Russian Web Cameras, 217
Mother Goose Pages site, D-12
Mozart's Magical Musical Life site, D-6
MPEG, 303
Mr. Holland's Opus Foundation site, D-6
MSNBC site, D-9
multimedia, 65
Museum of Paleontology site, D-16
Museum of Science and Industry site, D-18
Music Education Online site, D-6
Music Technology Learning Center site, D-6

• N •

NASA Live Mission, 206
NASA Quest, 279
National Aeronautics and Space Administration site, D-16
National Association for the Education of Young Children site, D-10
National Attention Deficit Disorder Association site, D-20
National Federation of the Blind site, D-20
National Museum of African Art site, D-6
National Research and Education Network (NREN), 13–14
National Science Foundation, 12
.nato extension, 67
.net extension, 67
Net Nanny, 119
Netcenter's People Directory, 152
NetDay, 60–62
Netiquette, 153–155
appropriateness, 155
capital letters, 155
electronic signature, 153–154
flaming, 154–155
security, 154
Netscape Communicator, 18, 91, 303
Back button, 95
browser window, 94
downloading, 92
e-mail, 147–149
Forward button, 95
Home button, 95
Images button, 95
installing, 93
My Netscape button, 95
Navigation toolbar, 94–96
Print button, 96
Reload button, 95
Search button, 95
Security button, 96
Stop button, 96
tips for, 101–102
Netscape Communicator 4.5 (on the CD), 327
Netscape Navigator, 303
Back button, 95
bookmark lists, 102
bookmarks, 100–101
component bar, 97
customizing, 98–99

Netscape Navigator *(continued)*
  Forward button, 95
  Home button, 95
  Images button, 95
  installing, 93
  Internet Keywords feature, 104
  My Netscape button, 95
  NetWatch feature, 104–105
  Preferences, 98–99
  Print button, 96
  printing Web pages, 103–104
  Reload button, 95
  Search button, 95
  Security button, 96
  Smart Browsing, 104–105
  status bar, 97–98
  Stop button, 96
  visiting URLs, 96–97
  What's Related button, 110
  What's Related feature, 104
'Netting, 303
NetWatch, 104–105
network, 303
network modems, 53
New York Times Learning Network site,
  D-9
newbie, 304
news server, 168
newsgroup servers, 170–171
newsgroups, 17, 304
  accessing, 171
  alt (alternative), 169, 179–181
  AOL, 170
  appropriateness, 179–181
  categories, 169
  comp (computers), 169
  DejaNews Web search engine, 176–177
  described, 167–168
  educators, for, 181
  finding, 168–169
  Internet Explorer, 172–175
  k12 (education), 169
  Netscape Communicator, 170–172
  news (network news/software), 169
  Outlook Express, 172–175
  reading, 170

  reading messages, 175
  rec (recreation), 169
  rules, 177–179
  sci (science), 169
  soc (social), 169
  subscribing, 174–175
  subscribing to, 171–172
  talk (idle chatter), 169
newsreader, 304
newsreader programs, 178
NewsWatcher, 178
Nine Planets site, D-18
node, 304
.nom extension, 67
NREN, 13–14, 304
NSF, 12
NSFNet, 12

• *O* •

O. Orkin Insect Zoo site, D-17
objectionable material, 37–38
Oculus, 208
Office of Special Education & Rehabilitative Services/U.S. Department of
  Education site, D-20
online channels, 183
online chat, 183–195
  AOL, 190–194
  AOL instant messenger (AIM), 193–194
  archiving text, 195
  bad behavior during, 191
  groups, 183
  ICQ, 193
  instant message systems, 193–194
  IRC (Internet Relay Chat), 184–190
  logging text, 195
  one-to-one, 184
  tips for, 195
  types of, 183–184
  video chat, 192
online professional development, 275
online projects, sources for. *See* sources
  for online projects

operating systems, UNIX, 12
.org extension, 67
Outlook Express, 83–84
OwlCam site, D-18

• P •

PACE: Parenting Autistic Children Effectively site, D-20
parallel port, 207
Parent Soup site, D-14
parents, convincing to use Internet in school, 27–30
Parents' Guide to the Internet site, D-14
passwords, 47
PBS MATHLINE site, D-21
PCs For Teachers, 48
PDAs, 272
pdf, 304
PEP Directory of Computer Camps for Kids site, D-9
Pine, 139–140, 304
ping, 304
PKZIP, 304
Plants and Our Environment site, D-18
plug-in, 304
Poetry for the Elementary Classroom site, D-13
Poetry Pals site, D-13
PPP, 304
Princeton Review Online site, D-7
Project Center, 278
projects, Internet. *See* Internet projects
protocol, 304
proxy servers, 54
public domain software, 200
Puppy Cam!, 206, 217

• Q •

QuickTime, 99, 227
QuickTime 3.01 (on the CD), 327
QuickTime VR, 227

• R •

RAM, 46–48
RealAudio, 227
.rec extension, 67
Research-It!, 113
resource credibility, 251–253
responsibility, controversial content, 32
Road to Special Education site, D-20
RWM Vocational School Database site, D-7

• S •

Safe Surfin' site, D-14
SafeKids.Com site, D-14
SafeTeens.Com site, D-14
safety, 36–38
  chat rooms, 37–38
  filtering software, 117–120
  harassment, 37
  newsgroups, 37–38
  supervision, 119
Safety City site, D-11
San Diego Zoo: Animals at Large site, D-17
SchoolHouse Rock site, D-11
schools
  content control, 35
  cost considerations, 34
  guidelines for Internet use, 33–35
  Internet use contract, 40–41
  introduction to Internet, 32–33
Schrock, Kathy, 253
Science Daily site, D-18
Sci4Kids site, D-17
search engines, 71–72, 108
  411, 113
  CNET, 113
  Research-It!, 113
  Shareware, 113
  specialized, 112–113
  Switchboard, 113
  teacher education, 268
  using, 112
  WhoWhere, 112–113

searching, 201–202
  Anarchie, 202
  Archie, 202
  bookmarks, 116
  case sensitivity, 116
  directories, 108
  example, 17–19
  genealogical searches, 107
  inaccurate results, 110
  Internet Explorer, 110–111
  keyword lists, 116
  near term, 116
  Netscape Communicator, 110
  operators, 114–115
  refining, 114–115
  search engines. *See* search engines
  sharing results, 116
  Sherlock, 111
  slow page loading, 116
  tips for, 114–116
security
  computer viruses, 203
  firewalls, 54, 300
  passwords, 47
serial port, 207
servers, 46
  filters, 38
.shar files, 204
shareware, 113, 200, 202, 304
Shareware.com, 202
Sherlock, 111, 153
Sherlock Plug-ins (on the CD), 327–328
.shk files, 204
Shockwave, 226–227, 304
Shockwave (on the CD), 328
.shop extension, 67
Sighted Electronics site, D-20
.sit files, 204
SiteCam 3.0, 208
SiteCam (on the CD), 328
Sites by Kids site, D-9
SLIP, 304
smart appliances, 276
Smart Browsing, 110
smart search engines, 272

snail mail, 138
Society for International Sister Schools,
    280
software
  Internet service providers and, 52
  troubleshooting, 292–293
Software & Information Industry Associa-
    tion (SIIA), 39
Sound Machine 2.7.1 (on the CD), 328
sources for online projects, 277–280
  Connected Classrooms, 278
  Discovery Channel, 280
  Education Services/Staff Development
      Association of Central Kansas, 278
  Fermi National Accelerator Laboratory,
      278
  Global Learning and Observations to
      Benefit the Environment, 279
  Headbone Zone, 279
  Kids Connect, 279
  Learning Interchange, 278
  NASA Quest, 279
  Project Center, 278
  Society for International Sister Schools,
      280
spam, 305
Special Education Resources on the
    Internet site, D-20
special needs, students with, 237–239
specialized search engines, 112–113
Sport! Science site, D-17
Sports Illustrated for Kids site, D-11
staff development, 239
Steve Wozniak's Classroom Camera,
    216–217
student information systems, 274
student-created content, evaluating,
    253–255
students with special needs, 237–239
StuffIt, 305
StuffIt Expander, 305
StuffIt files, 203–204
StuffIt Lite 3.6 (on the CD), 328–329
Super Tutor site, D-10
surfing contest, 267
SurfWatch, 119

Switchboard, 113
system requirements, 319–320

• T •

T-1 lines, 54
T-3 lines, 54
tag, 305
TCP/IP, 11, 305
teacher education, 265–269
  administrators, 267–268
  bookmarks, 268
  e-commerce, 268
  Internet class, 266
  lesson plans, sharing, 266–267
  search engines, 268
  surfing contest, 267
  technology camp, 267
  technology teacher of the month, 266
  Web site creation, 269
teacher preparation, 265–269
teachers, introduction to Internet, 32–33
technology, forefront of, 52
technology camp, 267
technology plan, updating, 249
telecommunications budget, 58–60
telementoring, 239
telephone software, 228
telnet, 305
terminal, 305
Test.com, Inc. site, D-7
Texas Educational Network (TENET) site,
    D-11
textbooks, Internet replacing, 14–15
*The Directory of Electronic Journals,
    Newsletters, and Academic Discussion
    Lists,* 160
THOMAS: Legislative Information on the
    Internet site, D-19
threaded message listings, 166
3-D viewer, 72
Time for Kids site, D-9
Times of London site, D-9
top-level domains, 67
  .arpa extension, 67
  .arts extension, 67

.com extension, 67
.edu extension, 67
e-mail, 135
.firm extension, 67
.gov extension, 67
.info extension, 67
.int extension, 67
.mil extension, 67
.nato extension, 67
.net extension, 67
.nom extension, 67
.org extension, 67
.rec extension, 67
.shop extension, 67
.web extension, 67
Transmission Control Protocol/Internet
    Protocol, 11, 305
trends
  24/7 availability, 275
  communication tool, 275
  convergence, 272
  customization of information, 273
  e-commerce, 274
  instant communication, 275
  Internet content, 275
  online professional development, 275
  PDAs, 272
  smart appliances, 276
  smart search engines, 272
  student information systems, 274
  wireless networking, 272
troubleshooting, 289–295
  browser freezing, 290–291
  can't send message, 293
  CD, 329–330
  custom calling features, 294
  dial tone, 295
  dial-up connections, 294
  hardware, 291–292
  host unknown message, 293
  images, unreadable, 290
  Internet, 289–291
  memory issues, 290–291
  modems, 294–295

troubleshooting *(continued)*
  monitors, 291
  network errors, 289–290
  network problems, 293
  noise, 294–295
  phone lines, 294–295
  screen freezing, 292
  service unavailable message, 293
  sharing phone lines, 295
  software, 292–293
  speed issues, 295
  undeliverable mail, 293
  user unknown message, 293
Trusty's Kids Corner site, D-19
TUCOWS, 202
TurboGopher, 305

• U •

UCARweb Weather site, D-17
Uniform Resource Locator. *See* URLs
United Nations CyberSchoolBus: Elementary Planet site, D-19
United States Department of Education site, D-21
United States Postal Service for Kids site, D-19
UNIX, 12, 305
upload, 305
URL, 305
U.S. Department of the Treasury site, D-13
U.S. Fish & Wildlife Services: Kid's Information Central site, D-18
USB port, 207
Usenet, 305
Uuencode/uudecode, 305

• V •

Veronica, 306
video capture cards, 207
video card, 207
video chat, 192
virtual field trips, 281–285
  archaeological digs, 284
  bridges, famous, 282
  candy manufacturing, 284–285
  historical events, 285
  medical information, 283
  rock star interviews, 282–283
  technology, future of, 285
  tropical islands, 283
  village creation, 282
  Walkabout, 284
Virtual Frog Dissection Kit site, D-18
Virtual Museums site, D-10
Virtual Reality Modeling Language (VRML), 99
Vocabulary University site, D-12
VRML, 72
VT100, 306

• W •

WAIS, 306
Web, 306
Web Accessibility Initiative site, D-20
Web conferencing, 206
.web extension, 67
Web host, 210
Web pages, 210
  creating, 125–129
  creation software, 126
  designing, 125–126
  HTML, 126
  ideas for, 125
  items to include on, 124
  location for posting, 127
  publicizing, 128–129
  publishing, 127–128
  reasons to create, 124
  testing, 128
Web Painter (on the CD), 329
Web Publishing For Teachers, 22, 126
Web sites
  A+ Math, D-13
  Access-Ability, D-20
  ACE, 34
  ACT, D-7
  Algebra Online, D-13
  Algebra.Help, D-13

All-Music Guide, D-5

AltaVista, 152

American Dental Association's Kid Site, D-12

American Directory Assistance, 152

American Veterinary Medical Association Kid's Corner, D-18

Americans Communicating Electronically (ACE), 34

Americans for the Arts, D-6

Apple Computer Education Page, D-8

apprenticeship USA, D-7

ArchNet, D-18

ArtLex, D-5

ArtMuseum.Net, D-5

Arts Education and School Improvement Resources for Local and State Leaders, D-21

ArtsEdge, D-5

ArtsEdNet, D-20

ARTtalk, D-6

Ask Jeeves For Kids, D-10

Association for the Advancement of Arts Education, D-6

Association of Research Libraries, 160

Awesome Library: Current Events, D-9

Basic Punctuation and Mechanics, D-12

Berit's Best Sites For Children, D-10

Best Paper Airplane in the World, D-18

Bigfoot, 152

Bill Nye the Science Guy, D-14

Biography.Com, D-10

Biology4Kids, D-18

Black Belt for Kids, D-12

Bobby, D-19

Bonus.Com the SuperSite For Kids, D-10

Butterflies at The Field Museum, D-18

Center for Disease Control and Prevention, 73

Center for Media Education (CME), 34

Chicago Tribune, D-9

Children's Software Review, D-9

CIA Kid's Secret Zone, D-18

Classroom Connect, 239

CME, 34

CNET, 201

CNET Download.com for PC-Teaching Tools in Education, D-21

CNN, 246

CNN Interactive, D-9

College Board Online, D-7

Community of Science, Inc., D-21

Complete Works of William Shakespeare, D-12

Computer History, D-8

Computers for Learning, D-8

Connected Classrooms, 278

Connecting Students, 262

Cool Science for Curious Kids, D-15

Corporation for Public Broadcasting Education and Technology, D-21

Crayola FamilyPlay, D-5

creating, 269

Creative Writing For Kids, D-12

credibility of, 251–253

Critical Evaluation Surveys, 253

CyberAngels, D-14

CyberPatrol, 120

Cybersitter, 120

Deaf World Web, D-20

Defiance Middle School Computer Center, 206

developing your own, 249–250

DFN, 34

Digital Freedom Network (DFN), 34

Dinosaurs at the National Museum of Natural History, D-15

Discovery Channel, 280

EarthCam - Times Square, NYC, 216

Earthquake Information: United States Geological Survey, D-15

Education Services/Staff Development Association of Central Kansas, 278

Education World, D-8

Educational computing Conference, 29

Educational Testing Service Network, D-7

EdWeb, D-21

E-Education on the WWW, D-21

EFF, 34

Electronic and Information Technology Access Advisory Committee, D-20

Empires Past, D-19

Web sites *(continued)*
  Encyclopedia Britannica Online, D-10
  ePALS, D-10
  evaluating, 251–253
  Evaluation of World Wide Web Sites:
      ERIC, 253
  Expect the Best From a Girl, D-14
  False Pass Java Web Cam Classroom
      cam, 217
  FamilyCam, 217
  Fermi National Accelerator Laboratory,
      278
  File Mine, 202
  Franklin Institute Science Museum, D-15
  Galaxy Network, 59
  Geometry, D-13
  German-English Dictionary, D-12
  GhostCam, 217
  Global Learning and Observations to
      Benefit the Environment, 279
  Global Online Learning Adventures, D-15
  GrammarNow, D-12
  Greatest Places, D-19
  Headbone Zone, 279
  How Far Is It?, D-18
  How Things Fly, D-18
  How to Offer a Course Over the Internet,
      D-21
  I Can Do That!, D-15
  Incredible Art Department, D-6
  Indiana University School of Music, D-6
  Infection Detection Protection, D-11
  Institute for Learning Technologies, D-21
  Internet use contracts, 41
  Japanese-English Dictionary, D-13
  Kaplan, D-7
  KidPub, D-12
  Kids Can Make a Difference, D-19
  Kids Connect, 279
  Kids' Space, D-11
  Kid's Valley Garden, D-18
  KidsClick, D-8
  KidsHealth.org for Kids, D-11

KidsPsych, D-14
KidzGolf, D-11
Kinetic City Cyber Club, D-16
Kratts' Creatures, D-16
Learning Interchange, 278
Let's Go: Around the World, D-19
LFF, 34
Librarian's Guide to Cyberspace For
    Parents and Kids, D-14
Libraries for the Future (LFF), 34
Linux Online, D-8
Locker Room, Sports For Kids, D-12
MAD Scientist Network, D-16
Math Baseball, D-13
Math Brain Teasers, D-13
MEGA Mathematics, D-13
Minneapolis Institute of Arts, D-5
Moscow and Russian Web Cameras, 217
Mother Goose Pages, D-12
Mozart's Magical Musical Life, D-6
Mr. Holland's Opus Foundation, D-6
MSNBC, D-9
Museum of Paleontology, D-16
Museum of Science and Industry, D-18
Music Education Online, D-6
Music Technology Learning Center, D-6
NASA Live Mission, 206
NASA Quest, 279
National Aeronautics and Space Adminis-
    tration, D-16
National Association for the Education of
    Young Children, D-10
National Attention Deficit Disorder
    Association, D-20
National Endowment for the Humanities,
    59
National Federation of the Blind, D-20
National Museum of African Art, D-6
Net Nanny, 119
Netcenter's People Directory, 152
NetDay, 62
New York Times Learning Network, D-9
Nine Planets, D-18

O. Orkin Insect Zoo, D-17
Office of Special Education & Rehabilitative Services/U.S. Department of Education, D-20
OwlCam, D-18
PACE: Parenting Autistic Children Effectively, D-20
Parent Soup, D-14
Parents' Guide to the Internet, D-14
PBS MATHLINE, D-21
PEP Directory of Computer Camps for Kids, D-9
Plants and Our Environment, D-18
Poetry for the Elementary Classroom, D-13
Poetry Pals, D-13
Princeton Review Online, D-7
Project Center, 278
Puppy Cam!, 206, 217
Road to Special Education, D-20
RWM Vocational School Database, D-7
Safe Surfin', D-14
SafeKids.Com, D-14
SafeTeens.Com, D-14
Safety City, D-11
San Diego Zoo: Animals at Large, D-17
SchoolHouse Rock, D-11
Science Daily, D-18
Sci4Kids, D-17
Shareware.com, 202
Sherlock, 153
Sighted Electronics, D-20
Sites by Kids, D-9
Society for International Sister Schools, 280
Software & Information Industry Association (SIIA), 39
Special Education Resources on the Internet, D-20
Sport! Science, D-17
Sports Illustrated for Kids, D-11
S.R.A. Grants Web, 59
Steve Wozniak's Classroom Camera, 217
student-created content, evaluating, 253–255

Super Tutor, D-10
SurfWatch, 119
Test.com, Inc., D-7
Texas Educational Network (TENET), D-11
THOMAS: Legislative Information on the Internet, D-19
Time for Kids, D-9
Times of London, D-9
Trusty's Kids Corner, D-19
TUCOWS, 202
UCARweb Weather, D-17
United Nations CyberSchoolBus: Elementary Planet, D-19
United States Department of Education, D-21
United States Postal Service for Kids, D-19
U.S. Department of the Treasury, D-13
U.S. Dept. of Education: Grants and Contracts, 59
U.S. Fish & Wildlife Services: Kid's Information Central, D-18
Virtual Frog Dissection Kit, D-18
Virtual Museums, D-10
Vocabulary University, D-12
Web Accessibility Initiative, D-20
Web66, D-8, 36
WebElements, D-17
Webworks, D-9
What Teachers Can Do About Learning Disabilities, D-20
White House, 18
White House For Kids, D-19
WhoWhere, 153
WHS ScienceCam!, 217
WWW CyberGuide Ratings for Content Evaluation, 253
Yahoo!, 18
Yahoo! People Search, 153
Young Writers Club, D-13
Youth Sports Network, D-11
ZDNet, D-9

Web66, 36, 124–125, D-8
Webcam, 205, 306
 ADB port, 207
 AV cards, 207
 CamRunner, 208
 connections, 207
 FireWire port, 207
 FrameServer, 208
 HTML code for, 212–216
 JavaScript refresh, 213–215
 live school broadcasts, 218
 META (morphic) refresh, 212–213
 motorized armatures, 207
 Oculus, 208
 options, 207
 parallel port, 207
 refreshing images, 212–215
 remote windows, 215–216
 serial port, 207
 server cams, 207
 setup, 210–212
 SiteCam 3.0, 208
 software, 208–209
 USB port, 207
 video capture cards, 207
 video card, 207
 Web sites, 218
Webcam software, 208–209
WebCam32, 209
Webcasting, 205–218
 bandwidth, 209
 computer, 206–207
 content, 206
 Internet connections, 209–210
 Internet service providers, 209–210
 live school broadcasts, 218
 modems, 209
 real-time delayed pictures, 205
 streaming pictures, 205
 Web host, 210
 Web page, 210
WebElements site, D-17
WebSpace, 72
WebTV, 57, 306
Webworks site, D-9

Wetware, 306
What Teachers Can Do About Learning
  Disabilities site, D-20
White House For Kids site, D-19
WhoWhere, 112–113, 153
WHS ScienceCam!, 217
Windows
 AutoComplete feature, 86
 browsers, 66
 CD, installing, 321–322
 mIRC, 185
Windows 95/98, Internet connection, 55
Windows Media Player, 228
Windows 3.*x*, Internet connection, 55
WinSock, 306
WinZip 7.0 (on the CD), 329
wireless networking, 272
World Wide Web (WWW), 18, 63, 306
 browsers, 65–66
 described, 64
 educational links, 73
 history, 64
 hyperlinks, 65
 Hypermedia, 65
 Hypertext Markup Language (HTML), 65
 HyperText Transfer Protocol (HTTP), 65
 Multimedia, 65
 navigating, 72–73
 URLs, 66–68
WS_FTP LE 4.6 (on the CD), 329
WWW. *See* World Wide Web (WWW)

 • *Y* •

Yahoo!, 18
Yahoo! Pager, 194
Yahoo! People Search, 153
Young Writers Club site, D-13
Youth Sports Network site, D-11

• Z •

.z files, 204
ZDNet site, D-9
.zip files, 203, 204

Notes

From PCs
to Personal Finance,
We Make it Fun and Easy!

**For more information,
or to order, please
call 800.762.2974.**

**www.idgbooks.com
www.dummies.com**

Dummies Books™
Bestsellers on Every Topic!

TECHNOLOGY TITLES

INTERNET

Title	Author	ISBN	Price
America Online® For Dummies®, 5th Edition	John Kaufeld	0-7645-0502-5	$19.99 US/$26.99 CAN
E-Mail For Dummies®, 2nd Edition	John R. Levine, Carol Baroudi, Margaret Levine Young, & Arnold Reinhold	0-7645-0131-3	$24.99 US/$34.99 CAN
Genealogy Online For Dummies®	Matthew L. Helm & April Leah Helm	0-7645-0377-4	$24.99 US/$35.99 CAN
Internet Directory For Dummies®, 2nd Edition	Brad Hill	0-7645-0436-3	$24.99 US/$35.99 CAN
The Internet For Dummies®, 6th Edition	John R. Levine, Carol Baroudi, & Margaret Levine Young	0-7645-0506-8	$19.99 US/$28.99 CAN
Investing Online For Dummies®, 2nd Edition	Kathleen Sindell, Ph.D.	0-7645-0509-2	$24.99 US/$35.99 CAN
World Wide Web Searching For Dummies®, 2nd Edition	Brad Hill	0-7645-0264-6	$24.99 US/$34.99 CAN

OPERATING SYSTEMS

Title	Author	ISBN	Price
DOS For Dummies®, 3rd Edition	Dan Gookin	0-7645-0361-8	$19.99 US/$28.99 CAN
LINUX® For Dummies®, 2nd Edition	John Hall, Craig Witherspoon, & Coletta Witherspoon	0-7645-0421-5	$24.99 US/$35.99 CAN
Mac® OS 8 For Dummies®	Bob LeVitus	0-7645-0271-9	$19.99 US/$26.99 CAN
Small Business Windows® 98 For Dummies®	Stephen Nelson	0-7645-0425-8	$24.99 US/$35.99 CAN
UNIX® For Dummies®, 4th Edition	John R. Levine & Margaret Levine Young	0-7645-0419-3	$19.99 US/$28.99 CAN
Windows® 95 For Dummies®, 2nd Edition	Andy Rathbone	0-7645-0180-1	$19.99 US/$26.99 CAN
Windows® 98 For Dummies®	Andy Rathbone	0-7645-0261-1	$19.99 US/$28.99 CAN

PC/GENERAL COMPUTING

Title	Author	ISBN	Price
Buying a Computer For Dummies®	Dan Gookin	0-7645-0313-8	$19.99 US/$28.99 CAN
Illustrated Computer Dictionary For Dummies®, 3rd Edition	Dan Gookin & Sandra Hardin Gookin	0-7645-0143-7	$19.99 US/$26.99 CAN
Modems For Dummies®, 3rd Edition	Tina Rathbone	0-7645-0069-4	$19.99 US/$26.99 CAN
Small Business Computing For Dummies®	Brian Underdahl	0-7645-0287-5	$24.99 US/$35.99 CAN
Upgrading & Fixing PCs For Dummies®, 4th Edition	Andy Rathbone	0-7645-0418-5	$19.99 US/$28.99CAN

GENERAL INTEREST TITLES

FOOD & BEVERAGE/ENTERTAINING

Title	Author	ISBN	Price
Entertaining For Dummies®	Suzanne Williamson with Linda Smith	0-7645-5027-6	$19.99 US/$26.99 CAN
Gourmet Cooking For Dummies®	Charlie Trotter	0-7645-5029-2	$19.99 US/$26.99 CAN
Grilling For Dummies®	Marie Rama & John Mariani	0-7645-5076-4	$19.99 US/$26.99 CAN
Italian Cooking For Dummies®	Cesare Casella & Jack Bishop	0-7645-5098-5	$19.99 US/$26.99 CAN
Wine For Dummies®, 2nd Edition	Ed McCarthy & Mary Ewing-Mulligan	0-7645-5114-0	$19.99 US/$26.99 CAN

SPORTS

Title	Author	ISBN	Price
Baseball For Dummies®	Joe Morgan with Richard Lally	0-7645-5085-3	$19.99 US/$26.99 CAN
Fly Fishing For Dummies®	Peter Kaminsky	0-7645-5073-X	$19.99 US/$26.99 CAN
Football For Dummies®	Howie Long with John Czarnecki	0-7645-5054-3	$19.99 US/$26.99 CAN
Hockey For Dummies®	John Davidson with John Steinbreder	0-7645-5045-4	$19.99 US/$26.99 CAN
Tennis For Dummies®	Patrick McEnroe with Peter Bodo	0-7645-5087-X	$19.99 US/$26.99 CAN

HOME & GARDEN

Title	Author	ISBN	Price
Decks & Patios For Dummies®	Robert J. Beckstrom & National Gardening Association	0-7645-5075-6	$16.99 US/$24.99 CAN
Flowering Bulbs For Dummies®	Judy Glattstein & National Gardening Association	0-7645-5103-5	$16.99 US/$24.99 CAN
Home Improvement For Dummies®	Gene & Katie Hamilton & the Editors of HouseNet, Inc.	0-7645-5005-5	$19.99 US/$26.99 CAN
Lawn Care For Dummies®	Lance Walheim & National Gardening Association	0-7645-5077-2	$16.99 US/$24.99 CAN

IDG BOOKS WORLDWIDE

For more information, or to order,
call (800)762-2974

BESTSELLING BOOK SERIES

Dummies Books™
Bestsellers on Every Topic!

TECHNOLOGY TITLES

SUITES

Microsoft® Office 2000 For Windows® For Dummies®	Wallace Wang & Roger C. Parker	0-7645-0452-5	$19.99 US/$28.99 CAN
Microsoft® Office 2000 For Windows® For Dummies®, Quick Reference	Doug Lowe & Bjoern Hartsfvang	0-7645-0453-3	$12.99 US/$19.99 CAN
Microsoft® Office 4 For Windows® For Dummies®	Roger C. Parker	1-56884-183-3	$19.95 US/$26.95 CAN
Microsoft® Office 97 For Windows® For Dummies®	Wallace Wang & Roger C. Parker	0-7645-0050-3	$19.99 US/$26.99 CAN
Microsoft® Office 97 For Windows® For Dummies®, Quick Reference	Doug Lowe	0-7645-0062-7	$12.99 US/$17.99 CAN
Microsoft® Office 98 For Macs® For Dummies®	Tom Negrino	0-7645-0229-8	$19.99 US/$28.99 CAN

WORD PROCESSING

Word 2000 For Windows® For Dummies®, Quick Reference	Peter Weverka	0-7645-0449-5	$12.99 US/$19.99 CAN
Corel® WordPerfect® 8 For Windows® For Dummies®	Margaret Levine Young, David Kay, & Jordan Young	0-7645-0186-0	$19.99 US/$26.99 CAN
Word 2000 For Windows® For Dummies®	Dan Gookin	0-7645-0448-7	$19.99 US/$28.99 CAN
Word For Windows® 95 For Dummies®	Dan Gookin	1-56884-932-X	$19.99 US/$26.99 CAN
Word 97 For Windows® For Dummies®	Dan Gookin	0-7645-0052-X	$19.99 US/$26.99 CAN
WordPerfect® 6.1 For Windows® For Dummies®, Quick Reference, 2nd Edition	Margaret Levine Young & David Kay	1-56884-966-4	$9.99 US/$12.99 CAN
WordPerfect® 7 For Windows® 95 For Dummies®	Margaret Levine Young & David Kay	1-56884-949-4	$19.99 US/$26.99 CAN
Word Pro® for Windows® 95 For Dummies®	Jim Meade	1-56884-232-5	$19.99 US/$26.99 CAN

SPREADSHEET/FINANCE/PROJECT MANAGEMENT

Excel For Windows® 95 For Dummies®	Greg Harvey	1-56884-930-3	$19.99 US/$26.99 CAN
Excel 2000 For Windows® For Dummies®	Greg Harvey	0-7645-0446-0	$19.99 US/$28.99 CAN
Excel 2000 For Windows® For Dummies® Quick Reference	John Walkenbach	0-7645-0447-9	$12.99 US/$19.99 CAN
Microsoft® Money 98 For Dummies®	Peter Weverka	0-7645-0295-6	$24.99 US/$34.99 CAN
Microsoft® Money 99 For Dummies®	Peter Weverka	0-7645-0433-9	$19.99 US/$28.99 CAN
Microsoft® Project 98 For Dummies®	Martin Doucette	0-7645-0321-9	$24.99 US/$34.99 CAN
MORE Excel 97 For Windows® For Dummies®	Greg Harvey	0-7645-0138-0	$22.99 US/$32.99 CAN
Quicken® 98 For Windows® For Dummies®	Stephen L. Nelson	0-7645-0243-3	$19.99 US/$26.99 CAN

GENERAL INTEREST TITLES

EDUCATION & TEST PREPARATION

The ACT For Dummies®	Suzee Vlk	1-56884-387-9	$14.99 US/$21.99 CAN
College Financial Aid For Dummies®	Dr. Herm Davis & Joyce Lain Kennedy	0-7645-5049-7	$19.99 US/$26.99 CAN
College Planning For Dummies®, 2nd Edition	Pat Ordovensky	0-7645-5048-9	$19.99 US/$26.99 CAN
Everyday Math For Dummies®	Charles Seiter, Ph.D.	1-56884-248-1	$14.99 US/$22.99 CAN
The GMAT® For Dummies®, 3rd Edition	Suzee Vlk	0-7645-5082-9	$16.99 US/$24.99 CAN
The GRE® For Dummies®, 3rd Edition	Suzee Vlk	0-7645-5083-7	$16.99 US/$24.99 CAN
Politics For Dummies®	Ann DeLaney	1-56884-381-X	$19.99 US/$26.99 CAN
The SAT I For Dummies®, 3rd Edition	Suzee Vlk	0-7645-5044-6	$14.99 US/$21.99 CAN

CAREERS

Cover Letters For Dummies®	Joyce Lain Kennedy	1-56884-395-X	$12.99 US/$17.99 CAN
Cool Careers For Dummies®	Marty Nemko, Paul Edwards, & Sarah Edwards	0-7645-5095-0	$16.99 US/$24.99 CAN
Job Hunting For Dummies®	Max Messmer	1-56884-388-7	$16.99 US/$24.99 CAN
Job Interviews For Dummies®	Joyce Lain Kennedy	1-56884-859-5	$12.99 US/$17.99 CAN
Resumes For Dummies®, 2nd Edition	Joyce Lain Kennedy	0-7645-5113-2	$12.99 US/$17.99 CAN

For more information, or to order, call (800)762-2974

Dummies Books™
Bestsellers on Every Topic!

TECHNOLOGY TITLES

WEB DESIGN & PUBLISHING

Title	Author	ISBN	Price
Creating Web Pages For Dummies®, 4th Edition	Bud Smith & Arthur Bebak	0-7645-0504-1	$24.99 US/$34.99 CAN
FrontPage® 98 For Dummies®	Asha Dornfest	0-7645-0270-0	$24.99 US/$34.99 CAN
HTML 4 For Dummies®	Ed Tittel & Stephen Nelson James	0-7645-0331-6	$29.99 US/$42.99 CAN
Java™ For Dummies®, 2nd Edition	Aaron E. Walsh	0-7645-0140-2	$24.99 US/$34.99 CAN
PageMill™ 2 For Dummies®	Deke McClelland & John San Filippo	0-7645-0028-7	$24.99 US/$34.99 CAN

DESKTOP PUBLISHING GRAPHICS/MULTIMEDIA

Title	Author	ISBN	Price
CorelDRAW™ 8 For Dummies®	Deke McClelland	0-7645-0317-0	$19.99 US/$26.99 CAN
Desktop Publishing and Design For Dummies®	Roger C. Parker	1-56884-234-1	$19.99 US/$26.99 CAN
Digital Photography For Dummies®, 2nd Edition	Julie Adair King	0-7645-0431-2	$19.99 US/$28.99 CAN
Microsoft® Publisher 97 For Dummies®	Barry Sosinsky, Christopher Benz & Jim McCarter	0-7645-0148-8	$19.99 US/$26.99 CAN
Microsoft® Publisher 98 For Dummies®	Jim McCarter	0-7645-0395-2	$19.99 US/$28.99 CAN

MACINTOSH

Title	Author	ISBN	Price
Macs® For Dummies®, 6th Edition	David Pogue	0-7645-0398-7	$19.99 US/$28.99 CAN
Macs® For Teachers™, 3rd Edition	Michelle Robinette	0-7645-0226-3	$24.99 US/$34.99 CAN
The iMac For Dummies	David Pogue	0-7645-0495-9	$19.99 US/$26.99 CAN

GENERAL INTEREST TITLES

BUSINESS & PERSONAL FINANCE

Title	Author	ISBN	Price
Accounting For Dummies®	John A. Tracy, CPA	0-7645-5014-4	$19.99 US/$26.99 CAN
Business Plans For Dummies®	Paul Tiffany, Ph.D. & Steven D. Peterson, Ph.D.	1-56884-868-4	$19.99 US/$26.99 CAN
Consulting For Dummies®	Bob Nelson & Peter Economy	0-7645-5034-9	$19.99 US/$26.99 CAN
Customer Service For Dummies®	Karen Leland & Keith Bailey	1-56884-391-7	$19.99 US/$26.99 CAN
Home Buying For Dummies®	Eric Tyson, MBA & Ray Brown	1-56884-385-2	$16.99 US/$24.99 CAN
House Selling For Dummies®	Eric Tyson, MBA & Ray Brown	0-7645-5038-1	$16.99 US/$24.99 CAN
Investing For Dummies®	Eric Tyson, MBA	1-56884-393-3	$19.99 US/$26.99 CAN
Law For Dummies®	John Ventura	1-56884-860-9	$19.99 US/$26.99 CAN
Managing For Dummies®	Bob Nelson & Peter Economy	1-56884-858-7	$19.99 US/$26.99 CAN
Marketing For Dummies®	Alexander Hiam	1-56884-699-1	$19.99 US/$26.99 CAN
Mutual Funds For Dummies®, 2nd Edition	Eric Tyson, MBA	0-7645-5112-4	$19.99 US/$26.99 CAN
Negotiating For Dummies®	Michael C. Donaldson & Mimi Donaldson	1-56884-867-6	$19.99 US/$26.99 CAN
Personal Finance For Dummies®, 2nd Edition	Eric Tyson, MBA	0-7645-5013-6	$19.99 US/$26.99 CAN
Personal Finance For Dummies® For Canadians	Eric Tyson, MBA & Tony Martin	1-56884-378-X	$18.99 US/$24.99 CAN
Sales Closing For Dummies®	Tom Hopkins	0-7645-5063-2	$14.99 US/$21.99 CAN
Sales Prospecting For Dummies®	Tom Hopkins	0-7645-5066-7	$14.99 US/$21.99 CAN
Selling For Dummies®	Tom Hopkins	1-56884-389-5	$16.99 US/$24.99 CAN
Small Business For Dummies®	Eric Tyson, MBA & Jim Schell	0-7645-5094-2	$19.99 US/$26.99 CAN
Small Business Kit For Dummies®	Richard D. Harroch	0-7645-5093-4	$24.99 US/$34.99 CAN
Successful Presentations For Dummies®	Malcolm Kushner	1-56884-392-5	$16.99 US/$24.99 CAN
Time Management For Dummies®	Jeffrey J. Mayer	1-56884-360-7	$16.99 US/$24.99 CAN

AUTOMOTIVE

Title	Author	ISBN	Price
Auto Repair For Dummies®	Deanna Sclar	0-7645-5089-6	$19.99 US/$26.99 CAN
Buying A Car For Dummies®	Deanna Sclar	0-7645-5091-8	$16.99 US/$24.99 CAN
Car Care For Dummies®: The Glove Compartment Guide	Deanna Sclar	0-7645-5090-X	$9.99 US/$13.99 CAN

IDG
BOOKS
WORLDWIDE®

For more information, or to order,
call (800)762-2974

BESTSELLING
BOOK SERIE

Dummies Books™
Bestsellers on Every Topic!

TECHNOLOGY TITLES

DATABASE

Title	Author	ISBN	Price
Access 2000 For Windows® For Dummies®	John Kaufeld	0-7645-0444-4	$19.99 US/$28.99 CAN
Access 97 For Windows® For Dummies®	John Kaufeld	0-7645-0048-1	$19.99 US/$26.99 CAN
Approach® 97 For Windows® For Dummies®	Deborah S. Ray & Eric J. Ray	0-7645-0001-5	$19.99 US/$26.99 CAN
Crystal Reports 7 For Dummies®	Douglas J. Wolf	0-7645-0548-3	$24.99 US/$34.99 CAN
Data Warehousing For Dummies®	Alan R. Simon	0-7645-0170-4	$24.99 US/$34.99 CAN
FileMaker® Pro 4 For Dummies®	Tom Maremaa	0-7645-0210-7	$19.99 US/$26.99 CAN
Intranet & Web Databases For Dummies®	Paul Litwin	0-7645-0221-2	$29.99 US/$42.99 CAN

NETWORKING

Title	Author	ISBN	Price
Building An Intranet For Dummies®	John Fronckowiak	0-7645-0276-X	$29.99 US/$42.99 CAN
cc: Mail™ For Dummies®	Victor R. Garza	0-7645-0055-4	$19.99 US/$26.99 CAN
Client/Server Computing For Dummies®, 2nd Edition	Doug Lowe	0-7645-0066-X	$24.99 US/$34.99 CAN
Lotus Notes® Release 4 For Dummies®	Stephen Londergan & Pat Freeland	1-56884-934-6	$19.99 US/$26.99 CAN
Networking For Dummies®, 4th Edition	Doug Lowe	0-7645-0498-3	$19.99 US/$28.99 CAN
Upgrading & Fixing Networks For Dummies®	Bill Camarda	0-7645-0347-2	$29.99 US/$42.99 CAN
Windows NT® Networking For Dummies®	Ed Tittel, Mary Madden, & Earl Follis	0-7645-0015-5	$24.99 US/$34.99 CAN

GENERAL INTEREST TITLES

THE ARTS

Title	Author	ISBN	Price
Blues For Dummies®	Lonnie Brooks, Cub Koda, & Wayne Baker Brooks	0-7645-5080-2	$24.99 US/$34.99 CAN
Classical Music For Dummies®	David Pogue & Scott Speck	0-7645-5009-8	$24.99 US/$34.99 CAN
Guitar For Dummies®	Mark Phillips & Jon Chappell of Cherry Lane Music	0-7645-5106-X	$24.99 US/$34.99 CAN
Jazz For Dummies®	Dirk Sutro	0-7645-5081-0	$24.99 US/$34.99 CAN
Opera For Dummies®	David Pogue & Scott Speck	0-7645-5010-1	$24.99 US/$34.99 CAN
Piano For Dummies®	Blake Neely of Cherry Lane Music	0-7645-5105-1	$24.99 US/$34.99 CAN

HEALTH & FITNESS

Title	Author	ISBN	Price
Beauty Secrets For Dummies®	Stephanie Seymour	0-7645-5078-0	$19.99 US/$26.99 CAN
Fitness For Dummies®	Suzanne Schlosberg & Liz Neporent, M.A.	1-56884-866-8	$19.99 US/$26.99 CAN
Nutrition For Dummies®	Carol Ann Rinzler	0-7645-5032-2	$19.99 US/$26.99 CAN
Sex For Dummies®	Dr. Ruth K. Westheimer	1-56884-384-4	$16.99 US/$24.99 CAN
Weight Training For Dummies®	Liz Neporent, M.A. & Suzanne Schlosberg	0-7645-5036-5	$19.99 US/$26.99 CAN

LIFESTYLE/SELF-HELP

Title	Author	ISBN	Price
Dating For Dummies®	Dr. Joy Browne	0-7645-5072-1	$19.99 US/$26.99 CAN
Parenting For Dummies®	Sandra H. Gookin	1-56884-383-6	$16.99 US/$24.99 CAN
Success For Dummies®	Zig Ziglar	0-7645-5061-6	$19.99 US/$26.99 CAN
Weddings For Dummies®	Marcy Blum & Laura Fisher Kaiser	0-7645-5055-1	$19.99 US/$26.99 CAN

For more information, or to order,
call (800)762-2974

IDG Books Worldwide, Inc., End-User License Agreement

READ THIS. You should carefully read these terms and conditions before opening the software packet(s) included with this book ("Book"). This is a license agreement ("Agreement") between you and IDG Books Worldwide, Inc. ("IDGB"). By opening the accompanying software packet(s), you acknowledge that you have read and accept the following terms and conditions. If you do not agree and do not want to be bound by such terms and conditions, promptly return the Book and the unopened software packet(s) to the place you obtained them for a full refund.

1. **License Grant.** IDGB grants to you (either an individual or entity) a nonexclusive license to use one copy of the enclosed software program(s) (collectively, the "Software") solely for your own personal or business purposes on a single computer (whether a standard computer or a workstation component of a multiuser network). The Software is in use on a computer when it is loaded into temporary memory (RAM) or installed into permanent memory (hard disk, CD-ROM, or other storage device). IDGB reserves all rights not expressly granted herein.

2. **Ownership.** IDGB is the owner of all right, title, and interest, including copyright, in and to the compilation of the Software recorded on the disk(s) or CD-ROM ("Software Media"). Copyright to the individual programs recorded on the Software Media is owned by the author or other authorized copyright owner of each program. Ownership of the Software and all proprietary rights relating thereto remain with IDGB and its licensers.

3. **Restrictions on Use and Transfer.**

    (a) You may only (i) make one copy of the Software for backup or archival purposes, or (ii) transfer the Software to a single hard disk, provided that you keep the original for backup or archival purposes. You may not (i) rent or lease the Software, (ii) copy or reproduce the Software through a LAN or other network system or through any computer subscriber system or bulletin-board system, or (iii) modify, adapt, or create derivative works based on the Software.

    (b) You may not reverse engineer, decompile, or disassemble the Software. You may transfer the Software and user documentation on a permanent basis, provided that the transferee agrees to accept the terms and conditions of this Agreement and you retain no copies. If the Software is an update or has been updated, any transfer must include the most recent update and all prior versions.

4. **Restrictions on Use of Individual Programs.** You must follow the individual requirements and restrictions detailed for each individual program in the "About the CD" section of this Book. These limitations are also contained in the individual license agreements recorded on the Software Media. These limitations may include a requirement that after using the program for a specified period of time, the user must pay a registration fee or discontinue use. By opening the Software packet(s), you will be agreeing to abide by the licenses and restrictions for these individual programs that are detailed in the "About the CD" section and on the Software Media. None of the material on this Software Media or listed in this Book may ever be redistributed, in original or modified form, for commercial purposes.

5. **Limited Warranty.**

    (a) IDGB warrants that the Software and Software Media are free from defects in materials and workmanship under normal use for a period of sixty (60) days from the date of purchase of this Book. If IDGB receives notification within the warranty period of defects in materials or workmanship, IDGB will replace the defective Software Media.

    (b) **IDGB AND THE AUTHOR OF THE BOOK DISCLAIM ALL OTHER WARRANTIES, EXPRESS OR IMPLIED, INCLUDING WITHOUT LIMITATION IMPLIED WARRANTIES OF MERCHANTABILITY AND FITNESS FOR A PARTICULAR PURPOSE, WITH RESPECT TO THE SOFTWARE, THE PROGRAMS, THE SOURCE CODE CONTAINED THEREIN, AND/OR THE TECHNIQUES DESCRIBED IN THIS BOOK. IDGB DOES NOT WARRANT THAT THE FUNCTIONS CONTAINED IN THE SOFTWARE WILL MEET YOUR REQUIREMENTS OR THAT THE OPERATION OF THE SOFTWARE WILL BE ERROR FREE.**

    (c) This limited warranty gives you specific legal rights, and you may have other rights that vary from jurisdiction to jurisdiction.

6. **Remedies.**

    (a) IDGB's entire liability and your exclusive remedy for defects in materials and workmanship shall be limited to replacement of the Software Media, which may be returned to IDGB with a copy of your receipt at the following address: Software Media Fulfillment Department, Attn.: *The Internet For Teachers,* 3rd Edition IDG Books Worldwide, Inc., 7260 Shadeland Station, Ste. 100, Indianapolis, IN 46256, or call 800-762-2974. Please allow three to four weeks for delivery. This Limited Warranty is void if failure of the Software Media has resulted from accident, abuse, or misapplication. Any replacement Software Media will be warranted for the remainder of the original warranty period or thirty (30) days, whichever is longer.

    (b) In no event shall IDGB or the author be liable for any damages whatsoever (including without limitation damages for loss of business profits, business interruption, loss of business information, or any other pecuniary loss) arising from the use of or inability to use the Book or the Software, even if IDGB has been advised of the possibility of such damages.

    (c) Because some jurisdictions do not allow the exclusion or limitation of liability for consequential or incidental damages, the above limitation or exclusion may not apply to you.

7. **U.S. Government Restricted Rights.** Use, duplication, or disclosure of the Software by the U.S. Government is subject to restrictions stated in paragraph (c)(1)(ii) of the Rights in Technical Data and Computer Software clause of DFARS 252.227-7013, and in subparagraphs (a) through (d) of the Commercial Computer–Restricted Rights clause at FAR 52.227-19, and in similar clauses in the NASA FAR supplement, when applicable.

8. **General.** This Agreement constitutes the entire understanding of the parties and revokes and supersedes all prior agreements, oral or written, between them and may not be modified or amended except in a writing signed by both parties hereto that specifically refers to this Agreement. This Agreement shall take precedence over any other documents that may be in conflict herewith. If any one or more provisions contained in this Agreement are held by any court or tribunal to be invalid, illegal, or otherwise unenforceable, each and every other provision shall remain in full force and effect.

Installation Instructions

Mac Users: To install the items from the CD to your hard drive, follow these steps.

1. **Insert the CD into your computer's CD-ROM drive.**

2. **Double-click the CD icon to show the CD's contents.**

3. **Double-click the Read Me First icon.**

4. **To install most programs, just drag the program's folder from the CD window and drop it on your hard drive icon.**

Windows users: To install the items from the CD to your hard drive, follow these steps.

1. **Insert the CD into your computer's CD-ROM drive.**

2. **Windows 3.1 or 3.11 users: From Program Manager, choose File⇨Run.**

   Windows 95 users: Click the Start button and click Run.

3. **In the dialog box that appears, type** D:\SETUP.EXE.

   Most of you probably have your CD-ROM drive listed as drive D under My Computer in Windows 95 or the File Manager in Windows 3.1. Type in the proper drive letter if your CD-ROM drive uses a different letter.

4. **Click OK.**

   A license agreement window appears.

5. **Once you click Accept, you'll never be bothered by the License Agreement window again.**

6. **Click OK on the CD Launcher message box.**

7. **The first screen you see is the Category screen.**

8. **To view the items within a category, just click the category's name.**

9. **For more information about a program, click the program's name.**

10. **To install the program, click Continue. If you don't want to install the program, click the Cancel button to return to the previous screen.**

For more information, see Appendix D.